# ASSETS, LIVELIHOODS, AND SOCIAL POLICY

NEW FRONTIERS OF SOCIAL POLICY

# ASSETS, LIVELIHOODS, AND SOCIAL POLICY

Caroline Moser and
Anis A. Dani, Editors

**THE WORLD BANK**
**Washington, DC**

ISBN: 978-0-8213-6995-1
eISBN: 978-0-8213-6996-8
DOI: 10.1596/978-0-8213-6995-1

*Cover photo*: ©Titus Fossgard-Moser/Eye Ubiquitous

*Cover design*: Naylor Design, Washington, D.C.

**Library of Congress Cataloging-in-Publication Data**
Assets, livelihoods, and social policy / Caroline Moser and Anis A. Dani, editors.
  p. cm.
Includes bibliographical references and index.
ISBN 978-0-8213-6995-1—ISBN 978-0-8213-6996-8 (electronic)
1. Saving and investment—Developing countries—Case studies. 2. Structural adjustment (Economic policy)—Developing countries—Case studies. 3. Developing countries—Social policy—Case studies. I. Moser, Caroline O. N. II. Dani, Anis A. (Anis Ahmad)
HC59.72.S3A87 2008
332.609172'4—dc22

2008016693

# NEW FRONTIERS OF SOCIAL POLICY

In many developing countries, the mixed record of state effectiveness, market imperfections, and persistent structural inequities has undermined the effectiveness of social policy. To overcome these constraints, social policy needs to move beyond conventional social service approaches toward development's goals of equitable opportunity and social justice. This series has been created to promote debate among the development community, policy makers, and academia and to broaden understanding of social policy challenges in developing country contexts.

The books in the series are linked to the World Bank's Social Development Strategy. The strategy is aimed at empowering people by transforming institutions to make them more inclusive, responsive, and accountable. This involves the transformation of subjects and beneficiaries into citizens with rights and responsibilities. Themes in this series will include equity and development, assets and livelihoods, and citizenship and rights-based social policy, as well as the social dimensions of infrastructure and climate change.

Other titles in the series:

- *Institutional Pathways to Equity: Addressing Inequality Traps*
- *Inclusive States: Social Policy and Structural Inequalities*

Anis A. Dani
Series Editor
Adviser, Social Policy

# CONTENTS

**BOX**

**FIGURES**

**TABLES**

This series—New Frontiers of Social Policy—aims to promote social development through systematic attention to the underlying social context and the social outcomes of development interventions and public policy. It compels readers to think of social policy in terms of increasing access to productive assets, infrastructure, goods and services; strengthening governance and accountability; enabling the rights and obligations of citizens to promote equitable access to development opportunities; and managing the social dimensions of conflict, natural disasters, and climate change. In doing so, it recognizes the central role of social policy in ensuring that development policies and programs are sustainable.

This book series has been conceived and produced for the broader development community, rather than for social policy specialists alone. This book is particularly, although not exclusively, relevant to those concerned with the one-third of the world's population that still depends on the informal economy for its livelihood. By making the case for an asset-based social policy, it moves well beyond social welfare palliatives for needy households toward public actions that give people the means and opportunities to accumulate assets and have greater control over their livelihoods. To be successful, an asset-based social policy needs to address several challenges—initial inequality, informality, imbalance in asset building opportunity, and inadequate state effectiveness—endemic in many developing countries.

The policy implications derived from these studies fall into three categories relevant to sustainable development:

- Public interventions to increase access to assets—including land, housing, credit, business skills, and community assets—in an affordable, transparent manner
- Investments in local and regional infrastructure and market information to ensure better access to services, affordable energy, and market opportunities to increase the returns on assets that people have

- Policies and rules as resources to transform the value of assets, for example, by ensuring security of tenure, modifying land use regulations, pooling risks to minimize shocks of asset erosion, and improving the investment climate to create new economic opportunities linked directly to poor people's livelihoods.

This book highlights the fact that today's world of growing opportunities requires collaboration between the state and nonstate actors, as well as between domestic and international stakeholders. Development in the 21st century has to face the challenges of a polycentric world that requires partnerships among a wide variety of actors to achieve sustainable development for all.

Katherine Sierra
Vice President
Sustainable Development Network

**Caroline Moser** is a social anthropologist/social policy specialist. She is Professor of urban development and Director of the Global Urban Research Centre at the University of Manchester. Previously she was a Senior Fellow at Brookings Institution, Washington, D.C.; lead specialist, Social Development, Latin America and the Caribbean Region, the World Bank; and a lecturer at the London School of Economics. She has published on urban poverty, household vulnerability, and coping strategies under structural adjustment; human rights; social protection; and gender and development, including *Gender Planning and Development;* and urban violence and insecurity, including *Encounters with Violence in Latin America.* Her current research is on intergenerational asset accumulation and poverty reduction strategies and its implications for international migration and climate change with publications, including *Reducing Global Poverty: The Case for Asset Accumulation.*

**Anis A. Dani** is Adviser, Social Policy, in the Sustainable Development Network at the World Bank. An anthropologist by training, he worked on development research, rural development projects, and the nongovernmental sector in Asia prior to joining the World Bank in 1995. At the World Bank he has engaged in operational work in South Asia, East Asia, and Eastern Europe, conducting social research and managing projects. From 2000 to 2005, he coordinated the Bank's work on social analysis, adapting it into an instrument for ex-ante, poverty, and social impact analysis of policy reforms. His recent publications include *Poverty and Social Impact Analysis of Reforms: Lessons and Examples from Implementation,* co-edited with Aline Coudouel and Stefano Paternostro, World Bank (2006), and *Poverty and Social Impact Analysis of Mining Sector Reform in Romania: A Policy Note* (Social Development Department,

World Bank 2005). His research interests include social policy, social impacts of policy reforms, inequality, community-based natural resources management, and infrastructure services for the poor. He is currently on secondment as Operations Adviser at the World Bank's Quality Assurance Group.

**Mary Amuyunzu-Nyamongo** is executive director of the African Institute for Health and Development (AIHD), Nairobi, Kenya. She has research and program experience in Burkina Faso, Ethiopia, Ghana, Kenya, Malawi, Tanzania, and Uganda, and has published in the areas of health, HIV/AIDS, urban poverty, youth, and gender.

**John K. Anarfi** is associate professor and deputy director of the Institute of Statistical, Social and Economic Research (ISSER), University of Ghana, Legon, Ghana.

**Farooq Azam** is an expert on migration research and migration policy, and has been regional representative for South East Asia at the International Organization of Migration, and director, Overseas Pakistanis Foundation. He is currently country director of a DFID-financed project on health sector reforms in Pakistan and was previously social sector specialist at the World Bank in Pakistan.

**Somsook Boonyabancha** is the director of the Community Organisations Development Institute, Thailand. She is also the founder and secretary-general of the Asian Coalition for Housing Rights.

**Paul Francis** is senior social development specialist in the World Bank's Regional Fragile States, Conflict, and Social Development Unit for Africa. He was senior lecturer in the School of Development Studies, University of East Anglia, United Kingdom, from 1999 to 2003.

**Anthony Hall** is reader in social planning in the Department of Social Policy at the London School of Economics. He spent two years on secondment to the World Bank from 2003 to 2005.

**Sara Jägare** is a project and finance officer in the International Department at the Church of Sweden. She was an intern for ISSER at the University of Ghana after finishing her master's degree in Population and Development at the London School of Economics in 2005.

**Soumya Kapoor** is a consultant with the Poverty Reduction and Economic Management Network of the World Bank. She is also an associate with the Centre for International Development, Harvard University, Cambridge, Massachusetts.

**Arvind Khare** is the director of financial operations and country initiatives for the Rights and Resources Group, secretariat of the Rights and Resources Initiative. He is a former director of the Society for the Promotion of Wasteland Development.

**Augusta Molnar** is the director of the Community and Markets program in the Washington, D.C.-based secretariat of the Rights and Resources Initiative, having moved there from Forest Trends. Previously, she was senior natural resource management specialist at the World Bank, managing community and NRM products in Central America and Mexico.

**Deepa Narayan** is senior adviser in the Poverty Reduction and Economic Management Network of the World Bank and is lead author of *Voices of the Poor*. She is presently leading a global research study on moving out of poverty that explores how people move out of poverty permanently from the perspectives of men and women who have experienced it first hand.

**Vibha Pinglé** is an independent scholar and consultant working on entrepreneurship and is based in Morristown, Vermont, and Cambridge, Massachusetts. She has taught at Brown University, Harvard University, Rutgers University, and Notre Dame University in the United States and the Institute of Development Studies in the United Kingdom.

**Dennis Rodgers** is senior research fellow in the Brooks World Poverty Institute at the University of Manchester and visiting senior fellow in the Crisis States Research Centre at the London School of Economics.

**David Satterthwaite** is a senior fellow at the International Institute for Environment and Development and editor of the international journal, *Environment and Urbanization*. He is also an honorary professor at the University of Hull.

**Andy White** is the coordinator of the Rights and Resources Initiative, a global coalition for strengthening forest tenure and livelihoods.

**Nicola Yeates** is senior lecturer in social policy at the Open University in the United Kingdom. She is also editor of *Global Social Policy* (Sage Publications), an interdisciplinary journal of public policy and social development.

This book was inspired by the desire to explore ways of strengthening the livelihoods, assets, and well-being of the hundreds of millions of people in developing countries increasingly left behind by growth and globalization. The chapters in this book were originally prepared as papers for the conference on "New Frontiers of Social Policy" convened by the World Bank in Arusha, Tanzania, on December 12–15, 2005. The Arusha Conference was organized to examine and address three of the commitments made at the World Summit for Social Development (Copenhagen 1995)—employment, the enabling environment for social development, and social integration—that had received less attention from policy makers and donors and where performance was lagging. This book addresses the first of these commitments.

A particular dilemma was posed by the fact that, to the extent that employment receives any attention from policy makers, their efforts are generally limited to job creation or social protection for workers in the formal sector. Informal sector workers have been ignored to the extent that even their numbers are uncertain. The Commission for Legal Empowerment of the Poor, for instance, estimates that one-third of the economy, involving almost two billion people, operates in the informal sector. Therefore, we decided to use the term *livelihoods* rather than *employment* to ensure that we include those in the informal sector. Finally, after starting to investigate livelihoods in developing countries, we rapidly realized that formal and informal livelihoods are invariably intertwined with the asset-base from which they are derived and to which they contribute. We therefore settled on *assets and livelihoods* as the central theme of this book on social policy.

The Arusha Conference was organized at the request of the Social Development Advisors Network and would not have been feasible but for the inspiration and support of Ian Johnson, Steen Lau Jorgensen,

Per Knutsson, Alexandre Marc, and Timo Voipio. Many others, including Lisa Anderson, Ian Gough, Arjan de Haan, Tony Hall, Tim Kessler, Margaret Levi, Andrew Norton, Jomo Kwame Sundaram, Ashutosh Varshney, and Geof Wood contributed intellectually to the conference.

Preparation of the book itself was a challenge that was made possible by the contributions and revisions by the authors and the patient support provided by Joyce Chinsen and Liane Lohde before and after the conference. Yvonne Byron-Smith, Mary Fisk, and James Pickett painstakingly helped to edit and finalize the draft chapters.

Finally, we would like to acknowledge the generous contributions of the Department for International Development of the U.K., the Swedish International Development Agency, and the governments of Norway and Finland for the Arusha conference; the Irish Trust Fund for supporting the writing and editing; and the Trust Fund for Environmentally and Socially Sustainable Development donors (Norway and Finland) for the production of this book.

Anis A. Dani
Washington, D.C.

Caroline Moser
Manchester, U.K.
March 2008

| | |
|---|---|
| ACHR | Asian Coalition of Housing Rights (Bangkok) |
| ACICAFOC | Indigenous and Campesino Coordinating Association for Central American Community Agroforestry |
| ADP | Asian Development Bank |
| AFSC/CAS | American Friends Service Committee/ Comité Andino de Seviços |
| AIDS | acquired immune deficiency syndrome |
| AMUL | Anand Milk Producers Union Limited |
| APPC | Asia Pacific Philanthropy Consortium |
| APPNA | Association of Pakistani Physicians in North America |
| APPS | Association of Pakistani Physicians and Surgeons of the United Kingdom |
| BGN | Brain Gain Network |
| BOE | Bureau of Emigration and Overseas Employment (Pakistan) |
| BOI | Board of Investment (Pakistan) |
| CAM | Centros de Atencion al Migrante |
| CBS | Central Bureau of Statistics |
| CCI | Centre for Community Initiatives (Tanzania) |
| CCODE | Centre for Community Organization and Development Mchenga Urban Poor Fund (Malawi) |
| CDD | community-driven development |
| CEESP | Commission on Economic Environmental and Social Policy |
| CEPAM | Centro Ecuatoriano para la Promocíon e Accíon de la Mujer |
| CESS | Center for Economic and Social Studies (India) |
| CFE | community forest enterprises |

| | |
|---|---|
| CIB | Chemonics International, BIOFOR (Consortium) (Guatemala) |
| CIFOR | Centre for International Forestry Research |
| CLIFF | Community-Led Infrastructure Finance Facility (India) |
| CODI | Community Organizations Development Institute |
| CONAMU | Consejo Nacional de las Mujeres |
| CPB | Crown Property Bureau (Thailand) |
| CPI | Corruption Perceptions Index |
| DANCED | Danish government |
| DFID | U.K. Department for International Development |
| ECA | Economic Commission for Africa |
| ECOWAS | Economic Community of West African States |
| EU | European Union |
| FDI | foreign direct investment |
| FEPP | Fondo Ecuatoriano Populorium Progressio |
| FLACSO | Facultad Latinoamericana de Ciencias Sociales |
| FLEG | Forest Law and Enforcement Governance |
| FNDI | First Nations Development Institute |
| FSC | Forest Stewardship Council |
| FSEFI | Financial Market Integrity Unit |
| G-7 | Group of Seven |
| GCCBFM | Global Caucus on Community Based Forest Management |
| GCIM | Global Commission on International Migration |
| GDP | gross domestic product |
| GINKS | Ghana Information Network for Knowledge Sharing |
| HIV | human immunodeficiency virus |
| IDS | Institute of Development Studies |
| IIED | Institute for Environment and Development |
| INO | Irish Nurses Organization |
| IOM | International Organization for Migration |
| IT | information technology |
| ITC | International Trade Centre |
| IUCN | International Union for Conservation of Nature |
| LAC | Latin America and the Caribbean |
| LEO | Local Earth Observation |
| MDG | Millennium Development Goals |
| MIDA | Migration for Development in Africa |
| MLA | Member of the State Legislative Assembly |

| | |
|---|---|
| MMSs | Mahila Mandal Samakhyas |
| MOFEMI | Movimento de Familias de Migrantes |
| NADRA | National Database Registration Authority |
| NARC | National Rainbow Coalition |
| NDDB | National Dairy Development Board (India) |
| NGO | nongovernmental organization |
| NHA | National Housing Authority (Thailand) |
| NHS | National Health Service (United Kingdom) |
| NRGS | Non-Resident Ghanaians Secretariat |
| NSDF | National Slum Dwellers Federation (India) |
| NTFP | nontimber forest products |
| NWFP | Nonwood Forest Products |
| ODA | Overseas Development Assistance |
| OEC | Overseas Employment Corporation (Pakistan) |
| OECD | Organisation for Economic Co-operation and Development |
| OPF | Overseas Pakistanis Foundation (Pakistan) |
| OWWA | Overseas Workers Welfare Administration (the Philippines) |
| POEA | Philippines Overseas Employment Administration |
| PRSP | Poverty Reduction Strategy Paper |
| SDI | Slum/Shack Dwellers International (India) |
| SERP | Society for Elimination of Rural Poverty |
| SEWA | Self-employed Women's Association |
| SHG | self-help group |
| Sida | Swedish International Development Cooperation Authority |
| SIPTU | Services, Industrial, and Professional Trade Union |
| SMEs | small and medium enterprises |
| SPARC | Society for the Promotion of Area Resource Centres |
| SSC | Statistical Service Center (United Kingdom) |
| TILCEPA | Thematic Group on Indigenous and Local Communities and Equity in Protected Areas |
| TOKTEN | Transfer of Knowledge Through Expatriate Nationals |
| U.K. | United Kingdom |
| UCDO | Urban Community Development Office (Thailand) |
| UN | United Nations |
| UNCC | United Nations Compensation Commission (Pakistan) |

| | |
|---|---|
| UNCHS (Habitat) | United Nations Centre for Human Settelements |
| UNCTAD | United Nations Conference on Trade and Development |
| UNDP | United Nations Development Programme |
| UNFCCC | United Nations Framework Convention on Climate Change |
| USAID | U.S. Agency for International Development |
| VMSDFI | Vincentian Missionaries Social Development Foundation Inc. (Philippines) |
| WHO | World Health Organization |
| WONCA | World Organization of National Colleges, Academies and Academic Associations of General Practitioners/ Family Physicians |
| WRI | World Resources Institute |
| WTO | World Trade Organization |
| WWF | World Wildlife Foundation |

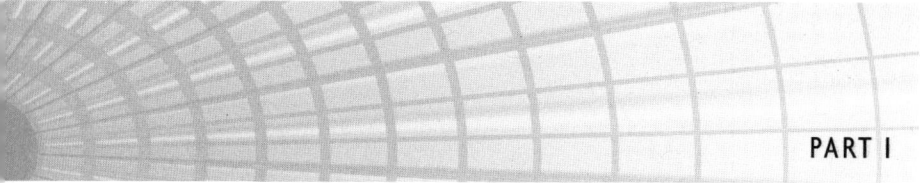

PART I

# THE CONTEXT

# CHAPTER 1

# Asset-Based Social Policy and Public Action in a Polycentric World

*Anis A. Dani and Caroline Moser*

This book explores the ways in which attention to assets can enhance the effectiveness of public policies in achieving social and economic development by increasing the capability of people to strengthen their asset base, obtain higher returns on their assets, and attain more secure livelihoods. An asset-based social policy speaks particularly, although not exclusively, to those struggling to survive in the informal sector as well as those emigrating in search of a more secure future for themselves and their families.

The book's focus on asset-based social policy was triggered initially by concern that support for full employment—one of the key global commitments of the 1995 World Summit for Social Development (WSSD)[1]—had dropped off the agenda in the rush for economic growth. Even the reintroduction of social goals through the Millennium Development Goals (MDGs) in 2000 did not restore the global commitment to full employment.[2] Another immediate challenge to tackling employment was posed by the small size of the formal economy in most developing countries. To ensure that we do not exclude people in the informal sector, we decided to use the term *livelihoods* rather than *employment*. Finally, after initiating an examination of livelihoods in developing countries, we rapidly came to the realization that livelihoods were invariably intertwined with the asset-base from which they are derived and to which they contribute. We therefore settled on *assets and livelihoods* as the central theme of this book on social policy.

## Why Assets and Livelihoods Matter to Social Policy

Despite the impressive gains in overall economic growth by developing countries in recent decades, vast numbers of people continue to be left behind to face structural disadvantages that have proved resistant to conventional social policy. This uneven growth gives rise to social tensions that are fueled by deprivation and perceptions of inequality:

- An estimated 1 billion people live in the poorest countries and are caught in a web of traps (Collier 2007) that prevent them from overcoming poverty.
- More than 900 million people (one-third of urban residents and almost one-sixth of the world's population) are slum dwellers (UN-HABITAT 2003; UN Millennium Project 2005), a number that is expected to grow because of the lag in urban planning, particularly in developing countries.
- An estimated 90 percent of the population in many Sub-Saharan African countries, even in the relatively better-performing ones such as Tanzania, depend on the informal economy (De Soto 2006), placing considerable constraints on the economic activities in which they can engage and from which they can derive benefits.
- At least one-third of the developing world's economy is estimated to be in the informal sector (Commission on Legal Empowerment of the Poor 2008).

In the absence of realistic prospects of formal sector employment, the vast majority of poor people rely on the meager assets with which they are endowed, as well as those they can accumulate through the informal economy. Policy makers in developing countries would be well advised to consider complementary policies rather than to rely exclusively on conventional social policy measures to bring such populations into the formal labor market. Such policies would strengthen the asset base of poor people and expand their opportunities to accumulate and consolidate their assets in a sustainable way and, thereby, to participate as fully entitled citizens in development processes.

Development is a process of change that combines economic growth with improvements in social well-being. The extent to which people participate in, and benefit from, development processes invariably depends not only on their initial asset endowment but also on the extent to which they are able to exercise agency within their available opportunity structure (Alsop, Bertelsen, and Holland 2006, Alsop and Heinsohn 2005, Narayan 2005). Initial inequalities in asset endowment exacerbated by market failures have a debilitating effect on economic growth (Sabates-Wheeler 2008). Poor people are often constrained by unequal power relations (Alsop 2004) and a limited ability to act to further their own interests. This "inequality of agency" plays a central role in perpetuating inequality and poverty (Dani and de Haan 2008; Rao and Walton 2004). Public policy can intervene through policy and institutional reforms and public investments to increase the assets and capabilities of poor people and the opportunities available to facilitate asset accumulation and resilience to external or lifecycle shocks.

## Assets and Power Relations

Assets are the resource endowments and capabilities that people have to sustain their livelihoods and to enhance their welfare. In the development literature, capital assets have generally been understood to include human, social, physical, natural, and financial capital (Bebbington 1999; Moser 1998; Narayan 1997; Sen 1997). This list has been augmented in more recent literature on empowerment (Alsop and Heinsohn 2005; Narayan 2005), which highlights the significance of political and psychological assets in determining people's ability to exercise agency as individuals and social groups. The ability of poor people to exercise agency is essential, because without it power inequities can undermine well-meaning public policy (Alsop 2004). In addition, unequal power relations often reinforce economic and social inequities and perpetuate categories and institutional behaviors that reinforce inequalities (de Haan 2008). This keeps the poor trapped within adverse "terms of recognition" that they themselves often internalize, unless social movements and development opportunities give them the "capacity to aspire" to a better future (Appadurai 2004).

## Asset-Based Social Policy

An asset-based social policy is most relevant for the well-being of households that are compelled to, or prefer to, depend on their own assets for their livelihoods and as buffers against risks. To overcome the constraints of unequal power relations, social policy needs to focus directly on the asset base of poor people.

An asset-based social policy has the potential to expand the opportunity structure for disadvantaged households and to create achievable possibilities for poverty reduction. The purpose of the book,[3] therefore, is to broaden interest in public policies, public investments, and public interventions to enhance the ability of people to access assets, and to accumulate and consolidate them within the structure of opportunities and constraints that they face.

### Underlying Assumptions

The emphasis on public policies, investments, and interventions does not mean that the authors subscribe exclusively to a state-centric view of social policy. On the contrary, the need for a polycentric framework for social and economic development is a central theme. Such a framework enables policy makers to recognize the different interests and claims on assets, and the roles and responsibilities of different social and institutional actors, if such assets are to be accumulated in an equitable and sustainable manner.

The underlying assumption in the book is that people themselves (a) are well placed to utilize their assets and exercise choice in the pursuit of their livelihoods, provided they have access to assets; (b) are equipped with the means and skills to obtain value (or valorize) these assets; and (c) have the information and ability to benefit from transformations in the rules and regulations governing those assets. The fact that policy decisions and public actions can influence each of these dimensions leads us to call this an *asset-based social policy*.

This chapter is organized as follows. Section two summarizes the global commitments on social policy that led to an identification of a gap to which this book on asset-based social policy contributes. Section three discusses four critical challenges faced by current social policy. Section four draws on the case study chapters to justify moving from a state-centric to a polycentric understanding of asset-based social policy. Section five briefly introduces the different chapter themes, followed by the concluding section in which we synthesize the evidence and introduce a pragmatic framework for the diverse policy implications to facilitate dialogue with developing countries and the donor community.

## Global Commitments on Social Policy

Conceptually, the book's focus on assets is inspired by Sen's notion of the role of public policy in enhancing assets and capabilities (1981), or what he now rather famously calls enhancing *freedoms* (1999). Sen's work has had a major impact on the strategies adopted by international development agencies—most notably the United Nations Development Programme (UNDP) and the World Bank, but also most bilateral agencies—that zeroed in on human development as an actionable policy agenda. In this book, we take the position that this interpretation of Sen's notion of assets has been overly restrictive. Public policies and public actions to strengthen peoples' assets and capabilities need to go well beyond attention to human capital assets.

Social policy received a major boost at the WSSD in 1995, which galvanized the attention of the world and succeeded in reaching consensus among state parties, international donors, and civil society organizations on a set of global commitments for social development.[4] The Copenhagen commitments clustered around three main themes: eradication of poverty, full productive employment, and social integration (Wiman, Voipio, and Ylönen 2007). By 2000, however, the WSSD goals had morphed into the revamped global consensus on the MDGs.[5] The evolution from the WSSD commitments to the MDGs and the subsequent agreed set of targets to monitor progress resulted in a remarkable mobilization of global public and private resources to achieve those targets. Backed by a credible theory and immense resources, these agencies have promoted and financed the development of human capital assets at an unprecedented scale. However, what is striking and inexplicable is that two key commitments of the WSSD—full employment and social integration—were discretely excluded from the MDGs, without much debate on the pros and cons of doing so.[6]

The WSSD commitment to support full employment appears to have been sacrificed to the cause of economic growth, with the MDG targets implicitly presumed to be an adequate substitute (Dani 2005; UN Millennium Project 2005). However, there is now growing recognition that without more rigorous attention to employment the MDGs will not be able to eradicate poverty.

In 2006, to rectify the inattention to employment, the Economic and Social Council (ECOSOC) of the United Nations, following-up on the WSSD and the MDGs, decided that the theme for the 2007–08 review and policy cycle by the Commission for Social Development (COSD)[7] would be "promoting full employment and decent work for all." Having let the ball drop during the discussion on the MDGs, the UN's Department for Economic and Social Affairs (UN-DESA) has belatedly promoted employment as a key component of social development (Ocampo and Jomo 2008), arguing that the expansion and improvement of opportunities for employment should be given priority (Wiman, Voipio, and Ylönen 2007). In parallel, employment has become an important topic of policy research at the World Bank, which has introduced a dedicated work program on "employment and shared growth."

At the same time, efforts by development agencies and governments to address the MDGs have focused largely on those in the formal sector or on the economic and social costs of informality. This focus causes concern that even those attempts are likely to miss the 2 billion people living in the informal sector, many of who depend on agrarian livelihoods or are constrained by the insecurities of informal urban settlements. Our interest in developing countries means that our concern focuses on livelihoods, whether arising out of formal employment or informal sector work. As stated, a focus on livelihoods becomes inseparable from the asset base that underpins them.

## Challenges in Developing Country Contexts

Four significant challenges facing most developing countries—inequality, informality, imbalance in asset building, and state effectiveness—can undermine the effectiveness of asset-based social policy.

### Inequality

The effect of economic growth on poverty reduction is substantially influenced by initial inequality and changes in inequality, as found in a recent multicountry study, *Delivering on the Promise of Pro-Poor Growth* (Besley and Cord 2007). In five of the eight countries studied, the poverty reduction effect of growth is offset by rising inequality, indicating that the distributional impact of growth is critical for poverty reduction. This effect is even more pronounced when the data are disaggregated into subnational groupings, because national averages mask significant variations in the regional pattern of growth (Besley and Cord 2007).

The impact of inequality on growth and outcomes, particularly in the context of agricultural assets, is reinforced by another recent study by Sabates-Wheeler (2008). This study investigates the processes and institutions through which inequality is established and reproduced and the impacts that inequality has on production. The findings show that, in addition to market failures, structural inequalities inhibit the ability of different groups to access institutions, which has implications for growth as well as equality. This inhibiting effect of initial inequality is of particular interest to policy makers interested in equity (defined as fairness) of opportunities in agriculture but who are worried about the tradeoff between equity and efficiency outcomes in agricultural growth.

The conclusions relevant to asset-based social policy are as follows:

- Inequalities in asset holdings can lead to forgone agricultural productivity in multiple ways.
- Structural inequalities (gender, ethnicity, and stigma) matter substantially in generating asset inequality.
- Poverty supported by structural inequalities tends to be more persistent unless new forms of public action can be introduced (see Dani and de Haan 2008).

### Informality

The scale of the informal sector remains a second major challenge to an asset-based social policy. Our concern is not with the extralegality of informality but in the limits that this poses for further asset accumulation. A recent study in Tanzania found that although the extralegal economy has assets worth US$29 billion—10 times all foreign direct investment accumulated since independence and 4 times the net financial flows from multilateral institutions in the same period—it is virtually impossible for 90 percent of Tanzanians to enter the legal economy (De Soto 2006). What is true of Tanzania is equally true of much of Sub-Saharan Africa and much of Latin America and South Asia. Informality has its benefits, particularly in the shape of low barriers to entry; however, it also has much greater insecurity and reduced likelihood of entering the path to sustainable asset accumulation.

The root causes and reasons for the growth of informality in Latin America have been analyzed in a fascinating study aptly titled "Informality: Exit and Exclusion" (Perry and others 2007). Here, "exclusion" from state benefits or the modern economy and "exit" decisions by workers and firms opting out of formal institutions explain the causes and consequences of informality in the region. The study concludes that reducing informality levels and overcoming the "culture of informality" will require actions to increase aggregate productivity in the economy, to reform poorly designed regulations and social policies, and to increase the legitimacy of the state by improving the quality and fairness of state institutions and policies.

## *Imbalance in Asset Building*

One obvious way to address inequality is to invest in human capital assets. Over time, accelerated by the MDG focus, such investments are beginning to pay off. Attention to primary education is indeed a prerequisite but real benefits come from high school education, and investment in college education is an important determinant of growth, as shown by a recent study of the contribution of education to growth and inequality in Brazil (Menezes-Filho and Vasconellos 2007). States that invested in both secondary and tertiary education saw the greatest reduction in inequality and the greatest increases in the growth elasticity of poverty (Besley and Cord 2007).

However, the emphasis on primary education in constrained fiscal environments has crowded out public investment for higher education, leading to a decline in human capital at the upper end of the spectrum. The MDG targets need to be supplemented by investments in tertiary education and technical skills, as well as interventions to scale up access to infrastructure and address institutional constraints to create the conditions for increased mobility and shared growth (Narayan and Petesch 2007; Paci and Serneels 2007).

While investments in human capital assets are critically important, they are not sufficient for poor people to compete and benefit as individuals within a market economy. For example, Sri Lanka has the highest human development indicators in South Asia, yet it lags behind other countries of the region in economic development and continues to suffer from ethnic conflict that undermines the potential of a highly literate society. Even in the fastest growing economies such as China and India, the number of rural poor people left behind by the rapid growth of industrial and service sectors is staggering. Human capital investments provide the biggest dividends in a secure environment when parallel investments are made in physical, natural, financial, and social assets to create opportunities for people to utilize their human skills and capabilities.

Poor households can participate in growth through three main channels: employment, transfers from public and private sources, and returns on investment (Besley and Cord 2007). Their study of pro-poor growth indicates that for both agricultural and nonagricultural growth to be pro-poor, public policies need to focus on building assets and creating institutional conditions to allow poor people to increase returns on their assets.

*State Effectiveness*[8]

The extent to which efforts to build human capital have been successful relates directly to the capacity of public institutions to effectively deliver services. Recognizing that the most needy countries were the ones where state institutions were least effective in delivering public services, the World Bank dedicated its flagship report—*World Development Report 2004: Making Services Work for the Poor*—to analyzing the effects of this conundrum and developing strategies to overcome this.

In much of the developing world, most public investments in human capital have been limited to basic health care and schooling, and the ability of poor people to utilize those human assets to improve their well-being remains constrained by their access to livelihood assets and the productivity levels of the meager assets that they are able to access. Poor people in both rural and urban areas are affected by relatively weak public services, especially for water, sanitation, energy, and communication. Given weak administrative outreach, these people often are more vulnerable to insecurities arising out of state fragility, including crime, violence, and the absence of rule of law.

Many developing countries are well endowed with natural resources. At times, these resources, instead of providing the people of these countries with a development dividend, have fueled conflict (Collier 2007). High-value natural resources can certainly be an asset under conditions of good governance as in Norway. However, the experiences with conflict diamonds in Africa (Smillie, Gberie, and Hazleton 2000) and the ongoing conflicts in the oil and gas industry in the Niger delta and the Andes (Bebbington 2007; Ross 2008) provide evidence that these natural assets can be a curse when the benefits are not widely shared.

This book takes the position that social policy needs to confront the more intractable challenges of productive assets that go beyond human capital if poor people are to realize the benefits of these investments. Unlike health and education, whose benefits are universally recognized, livelihood-related assets are often constrained by inequality in asset ownership and competition between those who claim ownership and those who claim rights. Arguably, the political economy of asset ownership and institutional capture may have had a bearing on the *de facto* boundaries currently delimiting social policy. We argue that the impact of social policy will be much more profound if the livelihood-related assets of poor people—land, natural resources, slum dwellings, financial assets—are addressed, and the risks posed by institutional performance and state fragility are explicitly identified and risk management measures put in place as a precondition for effective social policy.

## Assets and Livelihoods in a Polycentric World

One of the key arguments of this book is that in today's world social policy has to be polycentric, that is, it needs to be responsive both to national needs and transnational processes. Second, the assets with which it deals require a holistic approach, but they also involve multiple spheres of interest whose competing claims may need to be reconciled. Third, social policy has to be polycentric in the range of actors and agents who need to be mobilized for it to be effective. These three dimensions of polycentric social policy have been deduced from the case studies in this book although they are not necessarily described in these terms within each chapter.

### Transnational Scope of Social Policy

The chapters on migration provide the most obvious link between national economies and transnational livelihood strategies. Migrants clearly vote with their feet when they depart, largely due to lack of opportunity in their home communities or due to the attractions elsewhere. In Albert Hirschman's terms, the "exit"[9] of migrants is an expression of lack of confidence—in this case, in the opportunity structure offered by the national economy and polity. Invariably, the incentive to migrate arises from the hope of a better future elsewhere driven by complex sociological processes that inform or determine migration practice; in this dynamic, the impact of globalization is of paramount importance.

Several issues are particularly pertinent from an asset-based social policy perspective. First, migration is no longer a static, unidirectional movement but a phenomenon giving rise to new notions of flexible citizenship (Ong 1999) in a transnational world. Concepts of migration circuits from specific *barrios* to specific cities and global ethnoscapes (Appadurai 1996) informed by fundamental technological changes as well as cheap travel mean that migrant households have multilocational status and opportunities and transnational asset-building strategies. This transnationalism has important institutional implications. International migration takes social policy beyond the national level to a transnational level; the traditional premise that social policy relates to people living in a fixed location within a national boundary is no longer valid. Consequently, Yeates calls for transnational action to deal with some of the consequences of international migration of care workers.

Similarly, the chapters on informal settlements and economic empowerment describe local processes that are strongly linked to national and transnational networks, social movements, and markets. The housing federations described by Satterthwaite gained traction as the Mumbai-based coalition became part of the National Slum Dweller's Federation and then catalyzed a global network of community-based housing activists, the Slum/Shackdwellers International. Similarly, the slum upgrading process in Thailand described by Boonyabancha helped create the Asian Coalition for Housing Rights and then went on to become part of the global network of housing federations. Being part of wider national and international networks led to more recognition and some degree of protection from local vested interests. It also helped governments and housing activists learn from the global experience of participatory slum upgrading. Molnar, White, and Khare's chapter on community forestry highlights the linkages between local processes and global partnership networks that are able to mobilize resources and use information effectively to link local benefits to global public goods. Narayan and Kapoor's chapter on creating wealth for the poor illustrates the significance of linking local processes to broader markets to achieve more sustainable asset accumulation.

### Multiple Spheres of Interest in Assets

In the treatment of assets, we continuously ask ourselves who owns these assets, who uses them, and who else has claims on them. In the formal sector, it is assumed that property rights and claims are discrete, exclusive, and alienable. In contrast, the case studies presented in this book describe interactions among different interests that can give rise to multiple claims on assets—sometimes complementing, sometimes competing with each other. In this era of globalization where asset accumulation and asset transfers are not constrained by national boundaries, social policy can play a more active role in providing incentives to encourage investment of individual assets in local or national public goods.

For analytical purposes, we group these interests into three concentric spheres: the inner sphere is constituted by individual households, the second sphere by community interests (including those of social networks and those at the level of local government units), and the third sphere by nationwide interests. Several of the case studies in this book (Anarfi, Azam,

Jagare, Khare, Molnar, White, Yeates) highlight the tension among these three spheres—on the ownership, use-rights, claims, and responsibilities for assets—as individual assets, community assets, and assets as public goods of value to the nation or beyond. Individual and household strategies to acquire, accumulate, and consolidate assets depend on the value individuals place on these three competing spheres of interest—a value conditioned by the responsiveness of state policies to the interests of those individuals and their communities. Social policy involves significant public investment; allowing individuals to internalize all the benefits of these transfers with the possibility of opting out entirely can lead to significant losses to the national economy (Yeates) and the broader social good of the very people that such policies are designed to serve. This concern is expressed in the concept of the "brain drain" from developing countries. Recent shifts in migration policies within sending countries have sought to reverse the trend in two ways: tapping into migrant remittances by encouraging philanthropy among the diaspora to improve the well-being of sending communities and converting the drain into a "brain gain" by leveraging the skills, knowledge, and experience gained by migrants abroad (Anarfi and Azam). Being mindful of these multiple levels of interest can help inform the design of more inclusive social policy.

Table 1.1 gives the reader a summary of the case study chapters and draws attention to the multiple spheres of interest in the assets discussed within those chapters. With the exception of chapter 6, all of the chapters illustrate the interconnectedness between household and community interests; half of them also deal with assets that affect, or are affected by, national interests.

### Who Actually Delivers Social Policy?

Social policy needs to be polycentric not just in terms of its objects—the transnational scope of social policy and the multiple spheres of interest that need to be addressed—but also in the range of actors and agents who need to be mobilized for it to be effective. Social and economic policies and institutions in the 21st century are influenced by supranational organizations and agencies as much as by interest groups within developing countries. The state is one actor, albeit a very important actor; an effective state is one that creates an enabling environment to mobilize and manage other centers of power and resources and to organize the provision of public services. While much has been written in recent years about creating the right investment climate to promote the private sector and encourage

**Table 1.1. The Assets and Livelihoods Nexus**

| Author/focus | Assets | Sphere of interest in assets |
|---|---|---|
| **Hall, chapter 3**<br>Ecuador: social and economic impacts of international migration | Financial: minimum threshold for migration; returns in the form of remittances<br>Human: higher propensity for educated to migrate, but migrants' skills underutilized<br>Social: poor rural households rely on networks for migration; migrants reinvest in community goods (church, school) | Household: direct benefits from remittances; negative effects of split families<br>Community: investments in community assets; indirect economic benefits of consumption by migrant households<br>National: macroeconomic effects of remittances on poverty |
| **Anarf and Jagare, chapter 4**<br>Côte d'Ivoire and Ghana: return migration in West Africa | Financial: remittances, investments, donations<br>Human: acquired through studies and experience abroad; valued more among Ghanaians than Ivorians<br>Social: new social networks and professional contacts of migrants augment hometown networks | Household: direct benefits primarily from consumption and some business investment<br>Community: donations to community facilities (e.g., hospitals, electrification); increased local economic activity<br>National: brain drain; but benefits from assets acquired by diaspora |
| **Azam, chapter 5**<br>Pakistan and Philippines: policies to manage risks of, and opportunities for, migration | Financial: major constraint for migration; government loans for migration<br>Human: education and skills facilitate migration; diaspora skills benefit country of origin (TOKTEN)<br>Social: community networks help emigration; philanthropy for NGOs by emigrants increasing | Household: direct effects of remittances<br>Community/society: significant investments by migrants, particularly in social sector facilities in Pakistan<br>National: migration risk management seen as public policy need; remittances seen as a national benefit |
| **Yeates, chapter 6**<br>Global: international migration of nurses | Financial: survival and asset accumulation strategies of migrants' family<br>Human: affects where potential migrants can go; further skill acquisition can enhance asset accumulation; but deskilling of migrants through downgraded work also occurs | Household: migration as a family asset-accumulation strategy; families of migrants benefit from remittances<br>National: unlike nannies, migration of health workers amounts to depletion of a major collective asset and health deficit in source countries |

(continued)

**Table 1.1. The Assets and Livelihoods Nexus** *(continued)*

| Author/focus | Assets | Sphere of interest in assets |
|---|---|---|
| **Satterthwaite, chapter 7**<br>India and South Africa: influence of federations of slum dwellers on urban policies | Physical: housing is the single most important asset of the urban poor, providing shelter, identity, services, and security<br>Financial: savings groups pool resources for credit and income generation and are "glue" of collective action<br>Social: federations are able to lobby, design, and implement initiatives | Household: housing and livelihoods<br>Community: savings groups create resource pools for credit and investment; federations mediate with government for members' right to live and work; federations also provide services (surveys, credit, community toilets, community construction) |
| **Boonyabancha, chapter 8**<br>Thailand: integrating the poor in urban upgrading | Physical: land, housing<br>Financial: savings pools and government loans increased access to capital<br>Social: capability of savings groups enhanced by partnership with government agencies<br>Political: enhanced capability to negotiate with public authorities | Household: access to land, credit, and basic services enables linkage between house upgrading and sustainable urban livelihoods<br>Community: savings groups leverage funds for land purchase, housing, and income generation; urban upgrading through cooperative ownership of land or communal lease |
| **Francis and Amuyunzu-Nyamongo, chapter 9**<br>Kenya: causes and effects of economic decline and state failure in Kenya in the 1980s–90s | Physical: livelihoods severely constrained by scarcity and inequity in land access<br>Human: failing public services limit alternatives<br>Social: CBOs provide support for rural livelihoods and services; undermined by crime, violence, and insecurity<br>Psychological: resentment against limited and insecure livelihood opportunities; control of assets by elders and feminization of livelihoods manifested in intrahousehold violence | Household: family as economic unit breaking up because of erosion of traditional livelihoods and gender roles<br>Community: support from CBOs important for livelihoods and social services; social capital undermined by rising crime and violence<br>National: dysfunctional public services and corruption prevents emergence of institutional opportunities and adds to social dislocation |
| **Rodgers, chapter 10**<br>Nicaragua: social policy implications of youth gangs in weak states | Social: where the state is deficient or absent, youth gangs can be socially constructive | Community: for local communities, youth gangs can provide protection, substituting for the "coercive guarantee" of the state; the use of violence to protect gang boundaries can breed insecurity |

16

| Chapter | Assets / capital | Levels |
|---|---|---|
| **Molnar, White, and Khare, chapter 11**<br>Global: promoting asset-based livelihoods and forest conservation | Ontological: when the opportunity structure is dysfunctional, the capability to be and act allows human, financial, or social capital to be accumulated and managed<br><br>Natural: despite global demand for forest products, community ownership (or administration) of forest areas is increasing<br><br>Social: indigenous rights and forest rights for communities create assets for rural livelihoods and conservation; community management of forest resources builds on and strengthens social cohesion | Household: in the absence of state-administered security, those wanting to opt out have little option<br><br>Community: globally, 370 million hectares are being conserved by various forms of community management; community forest enterprises tend to have greater interest in social investments and sustainability of forest resources<br><br>National: need to balance demand for forest resources with livelihoods of local communities<br><br>Global: rising interest in climate change is likely to increase the public good value of forest |
| **Pinglé, chapter 12**<br>Africa: women micro-entrepreneurs and sustainable livelihoods | Financial: facilitated access to credit by poor women<br><br>Human: business skills<br><br>Social: local community obligations can constrain poor women; integration into wider networks enhances opportunities for asset accumulation by women entrepreneurs | Household: family demands can inhibit individual entrepreneurship<br><br>Community: the pressure to conform with social norms and obligations tends to make it easier for single women or those without liabilities to become successful entrepreneurs |
| **Narayan and Kapoor, chapter 13**<br>India: conditions for economic empowerment of the poor | Individual: including material, human, social, political, and psychological assets, seen as interconnected<br><br>Collective: including voice, organization, representation, and identity; intermediation by an external (public or private) program enables economic empowerment of the poor | Individual/household: sustained stream of economic and social benefits to participants<br><br>Community: collective agency helps to sustain interest of the poor in collective organization; support to aggregate market needs allows the poor to reach economies of scale<br><br>National: linking the poor to markets while preventing asset erosion (e.g., from health shocks) is a cost-effective way of addressing poverty |

foreign direct investment, several chapters in this book (Boonyabancha, Hall, Khare, Molnar, Narayan, Sattherthwaite, White) focus on the other end of the spectrum—how social policy can create an enabling environment to allow individuals and social groups to exercise agency to best use the assets over which they have more control.

Viewed from this perspective, the role of nonstate actors becomes a dual one: service providers supplement the outreach of public institutions, and intermediaries help poor people escape inequality traps by exercising agency as individuals or groups. The polycentric nature of social and nonstate institutional actors is illustrated by table 1.2, which includes the main actors and agents referred to in the different chapters of this book. For brevity, these have been collapsed under the four themes—migration, informal settlements, weak states, and economic empowerment—that are the focus of the book.

## Structure of the Book

This book examines the potential contribution of an asset-based social policy to a number of new cutting-edge development issues. Chapter 2 introduces a framework for an asset-based social policy aimed at creating opportunities for poor people rather than simply designing policies to protect them from market forces. This is one pillar of the new social policy agenda and is designed to complement parallel work on formal labor markets. The chapter begins by describing the evolution of social development and social policy in developing countries and draws on the institutional history of development agencies where many of these ideas originated. The chapter then compares and contrasts salient characteristics of the Sustainable Livelihoods and Asset-Building frameworks that offer two complementary approaches to poverty reduction. These two approaches provide the analytical and operational background for the formulation of a specific asset-based social policy framework consisting of the nexus of assets-institutions-opportunities surrounding and influencing the livelihood strategies of people. The actual strategies by which people accumulate assets are affected by the institutions (laws, norms, and regulatory frameworks) and opportunities arising from the political and economic context (see chapter 2). Public interventions to strengthen strategies for asset accumulation tend to focus either on strengthening institutions or opportunities.

**Table 1.2. Range of Agents Relevant to Assets and Livelihoods**

| Focus | Key agents influencing outcomes |
|---|---|
| **Migration** (chapters 3–6) | Regional and international organizations: ECOWAS, IOM, UNDP |
| | Governments: regulate and facilitate migration; establish policies and institutions to manage migration risks; lobby for migrant rights and counselor services in receiving countries; regulate and facilitate flows of financial and human capital; formulate development strategies that affect their own territory and that of others |
| | Private sector: facilitate remittances; also facilitate migration (e.g., Banco Solidario); recruiting agents and financial intermediaries influence migration outcomes |
| | Households: social assets most significant source of finance and information for out-migration; maintain transnational links and reinvest in community facilities and local economies, in addition to education of family members; determine the extent to which the benefits of remittances are shared with the community |
| | Civil society: Catholic Church and NGOs most active in welfare of migrant households |
| | Trade unions: union membership can result in better working conditions for migrants |
| **Upgrading urban slums** (chapters 7–8) | Governments: establish national programs for upgrading housing, environmental conditions, and tenure security (e.g., UCDO, CODI); receptive national governments can encourage scaling up of federation-led slum upgrading; partnership with local government critical to success |
| | Local government: UCDO and CODI facilitate partnerships with LGUs and service providers |
| | Civil Society: includes national and local federations, as well as an international network; networks of urban poor come together for citywide upgrading; networks are able to negotiate with local politicians to finance infrastructure in new settlements |
| | NGOs: while some local and international NGOs see federations as rivals, others have played a key role in their success |
| **Weak states** (chapters 9–10) | Government: ensure security and address endemic crime and violence; improve governance and accountability of public services; implement public investments and institutional support to diversify local livelihoods; reform agricultural markets |
| | Civil society organizations: church groups and NGOs have greater likelihood of reaching out to youth gangs and local communities |
| | Community-based organizations: complement support for livelihoods and services with mobilization against domestic violence; explore ways of integrating males into livelihood diversification strategies |

*(continued)*

**Table 1.2. Range of Agents Relevant to Assets and Livelihoods** (continued)

| Focus | Key agents influencing outcomes |
|---|---|
| **Economic empowerment** (chapters 11–13) | International networks: lobby for market reforms to benefit local producers |
| | Governments: reform investment climate and forest regulations to strengthen economic opportunities for the poor; ensure access to social protection and health care to prevent asset depletion; support organizations and federations of the poor |
| | Private sector: provide business skills; forest certification benefits local communities; help the poor scale up and benefit from market information and market opportunities |
| | Civil society organizations: support child care and health care for women entrepreneurs |
| | Community organizations: CFEs have more local investments and interest in longer-term equity |
| | Federations of the poor: help achieve economies of scale as well as collective agency to gain political influence over public resources and bargaining power over the private sector |

In developing an asset accumulation framework, Moser distinguishes between first- and second-generation asset accumulation policies. First-generation policy provides the social and economic infrastructure for human, physical, and financial assets but does not ensure asset accumulation. Second-generation policy consists of public actions that enable the consolidation of accumulated assets and prevent their erosion. Indeed, many developing countries suffer from various degrees of weak administrative capacity, weak enforcement of rule of law, crime and violence, political instability, and absence of adequate disaster management systems. Any one of these can inhibit asset accumulation. The need for a second-generation policy aimed at creating conditions of good governance—citizen rights and security and accountability of institutions—is therefore paramount. While some of the case studies in this book draw attention to these issues, these ideas are developed in greater detail in parallel volumes of this series (see, for example, Dani and de Haan 2008).

The case studies examine the potential contribution of an asset-based social policy to four development issues. These include the asset-building opportunities and the role of policies and institutions in addressing international migration, the largely ignored asset accumulation potential of informal settlements, the constraints on asset building because of pervasive insecurity in weak states, and the comparative advantages of state and nonstate actors in promoting programs of economic empowerment. These case studies, as well as other similar studies (see Moser 2007), show the ways in which asset building can provide the entry point for a new social policy agenda—namely an asset-based social policy.

## Migration as a Livelihood and Asset Accumulation Strategy

The dramatically growing phenomenon of international migration has received considerable attention in development discourse. While the phenomenon is sometimes seen as a threat by citizens of receiving countries due to the supposed impact on local employment and cultural dissonance, it also fills key market niches—such as unskilled labor and care workers, as well as skilled workers, actively sought by industrialized countries.

Migration also involves a tension between costs and risks, which can range from insecure to exploitative terms of employment or, in extreme cases, even physical exploitation of migrants. More often than not, migrants are compelled to accept low-paying jobs or employment that does not reward them for the human capital skills acquired in their country of origin. Thus, the expected benefits of migration may not accrue for a while, if at all.

Nonetheless, in the short run, migrants are often perceived by countries of origin as escapees who have deserted their country for personal gain. This perception results in a lag between migration trends and public policies that address migration in both origin and receiving countries. Our concern in the four chapters dealing with international migration is primarily with migration policies in countries of origin, although the migration of global care workers draws attention to the need for transnational policies.

Economic research has highlighted the instrumental role that remittances increasingly play in a country's macroeconomic development as well as in microlevel poverty reduction (Adams and Page 2005); further work has focused on the human capital implications of brain drain or gain (Ozden and Schiff 2005). Behind the economic measurements of remittances are complex sociological processes that determine migration practice—processes that are profoundly affected by globalization.

Although migration initially appears to be an exit strategy, people who leave may later return or contribute to building local assets through networks of opportunities and the transfer of knowledge. Here the increasing feminization of migration means that gender and household social capital are important determinants of remittance choices (Hall, chapter 3; Moser 2007). The costs in human capital suffered by the country need to be balanced against the benefits accrued through migration (Hall, chapter 3; Yeates, chapter 6). In the totality of transfers, financial remittances are only one of a number of different transfers, each of which can have important impacts on asset accumulation in both home and host country. Orozco (2007), for instance, has categorized these as remittances in cash or kind, economic investments, donations for collective benefit, and goods and services. This categorization assists in clarifying the asset-building opportunities associated with international migration.

In chapter 3, Hall shows that, for Ecuadorian migrants from three of the country's main cities, more than half of transfers are used for household consumption expenditures, nearly a quarter are used for human capital associated with children's education, and only around 3 percent are used for housing or financial capital investments. At the same time, remittance objectives are not simply economic but also relate to enhanced social prestige and status. Transnational social capital bridges the geographic gap and maintains communication.[10] Complex transfer systems are based on social networks particularly and are associated with hometown or village associations (Orozco and Lepointe 2004).

The significance of social assets and networks is also illustrated by Anarfi in chapter 4, where he examines the phenomenon of the return of West African transnational migrants. He finds that, while emigration might initially have been used as a livelihood strategy, return migration also has the potential to enhance well-being. In addition to financial capital, human and social capital transferred by transnational migrants has the potential for substantial development impacts with implications for communities of origin and the broader development process. Given the multiple benefits of return migration—whether permanent or temporary or cyclical—Anarfi makes the case for policies that provide attractive options for returnees. He cites examples to encourage return migration and affect the returnee's contribution to the development process; to introduce dual citizenship to migrants; and to allow members to gain residence, employment, and other rights in other countries.

In chapter 5, Azam examines the different ways in which migration policy in Pakistan and the Philippines can strengthen the asset accumulation of migrants and help them manage migration risks. Both countries view migration as a net gain to the national economy and have introduced migration management systems that include both policies and programs for managing migration risks, as well as facilitating asset consolidation and development. Despite such policies, trafficking for sexual exploitation, bonded labor, and domestic servitude continues, with many being lured by false promises of employment. To address such issues, governments have introduced a range of interventions that include lowering migration costs, enhancing migration benefits, and supporting interventions to make use of the human capital of return migrants.

The social, cultural, and political construction of diasporas also has critical implications for investments in productive social capital. However, the roles of the diasporas are not always benign because they can provide a safe haven for dissidents who mobilize and channel resources for social movements ranging from political opposition to extreme cases of terrorism. On the other hand, an increasing number of countries such as Pakistan are providing special benefits and tax breaks to emigrants to encourage them to maintain ties with their country and communities of origin. Ultimately, the role played by the diasporas depends heavily on the institutional space allowed to express their voice in a legitimate manner.

In chapter 6, Yeates describes the international division of reproductive labor in which the social relations of care are mediated by the manner in which transnational processes intersect with internal social policies. She uses the concept of "global care chains" to describe a "series of personal links between people across the globe based on the paid or unpaid work of caring" (Hochschild 2000: 131). Such chains also lead to the internationalization of asset-building strategies that create transnational families.[11] The example of the global chain of international trade in nursing illustrates how governments, such as the Philippines, have developed specific policies to produce "nurses for export." Such chains present policy challenges relating to labor legislation and social protection issues, but also broader social policy concerns relating to ethical codes of conduct on migration. Because the interconnectedness of migration effects between sending and receiving countries goes far beyond a single transaction, public policy also needs to be globally interconnected.

### Housing as an Asset in Informal Settlements

Traditionally, housing and human settlements have not been seen as components of a social policy agenda, but rather as the policy and institutional domain of urban development, land, and infrastructure. In addition, shifts within urban development policy itself in the past three decades have reflected a reduction in prioritization on human settlements. Their importance as part of basic needs strategies of the 1970s–80s (although even then often limited to site and services and upgrading) shifted with the urban management policies of the 1980s–90s. These focused on land markets and urban finance and, most recently, on issues of municipal governance and the privatization of basic services.

To date, most development agencies have quite correctly prioritized rural poverty. In doing so, however, they have paid scant attention to urban issues in their portfolio despite research showing that housing is often the most important productive asset of the urban poor (Moser 2007; Rakodi 1999). Recently, both the MDGs relating to the urban environment, as well as the dramatic urbanization growth rates associated with globalization, have led to a new resurgence of interest in human settlements. However, as Satterthwaite argues in chapter 7, once again the danger is that a technocratic approach dominated by infrastructure concerns may be adopted. Governments and international financial institutions

(IFIs) financing physical infrastructure or urban housing schemes prefer implementation by contractors and often overlook the capabilities, interests, and aspirations of poor people themselves.

In his eloquent description of the role of pro-poor housing activists among the 6 million slum-dwellers who live in Mumbai as "citizens without a city," Appadurai (2004: 72) elaborates on the deeper process of social transformation that occurs when poor people are able to exercise voice through collective agency. The squatters and civil society alliance in Mumbai enabled the urban poor to organize themselves and reach consensus among the poor, and between them and the more powerful to create savings pools and to improve housing and municipal services. The very process of engagement in the membership-based housing federations[12] strengthened the voice of slum-dwellers to challenge adverse terms of recognition and gain the "capacity to aspire" (Appadurai 2004: 67) to a better future.

While development agencies have largely ignored many of the human settlement concerns of the urban poor, increasing numbers of empowered slum/shack dwellers organizations have been simultaneously addressing housing and livelihood needs. As described in chapter 7, national housing federations are already well established in 12 countries, are emerging, or are in an incipient state in many more. Community savings groups, mostly managed by women, are the foundations of those federations. The groups develop their own housing solutions; learn from, teach, and support each other; and use their solutions as precedents to offer government partnerships for scaling up. In some countries, the groups' programs reach tens of thousands of people, in others hundreds of thousands. While their immediate priority is to change the practices of local governments, these local partnerships may also influence policy and practice at provincial and national levels. With programs to integrate physical, land tenure, economic, and social activities through flexible financial support, upgrading has been reconceived as a powerful basic safety net for the poorest and a support to decentralization and "good" local governance.

In chapter 8, Boonyabancha describes how urban community organizations in Thailand are renegotiating their relationship with the state so that communities become accepted as legitimate parts of the city and have more space and freedom to develop their own responses. The scaling up of slum and squatter settlement upgrading has led to community-driven integrated social development at the city level. An ambitious national slum and squatter upgrading program is the Baan Mankong Program, which was launched by the government in 2003 with a budget of US$270 million.

Approximately 25 percent of the investment is being implemented through the Community Organizations Development Institute (CODI). The program, rooted in 13 years of experience in government-community organization partnership, is unusual in terms of its scale and structure. It has support from urban poor groups' community organizations formed to develop their own comprehensive upgrading and land development programs. However, to scale up and reach communities in 200 urban centers requires a diversity of different initiatives that need to be integrated within a citywide program.

These examples illustrate how federations of urban poor and homeless people are driving changes in the policies of local and national governments for housing, land, and basic services. This social policy innovation is fueled by grassroots organizations in which communities themselves use housing not simply as a need but as a strategy to change state-civil society relationships;[13] the implications extend far beyond housing to urban development and community empowerment issues. Given the policy influence of local innovation and precedent, federations can be effective partners for development agencies if appropriate channels can be established to support their work.

### Erosion of Livelihoods and Assets in Weak States

Poor people face particular constraints in accumulating assets in weak states undergoing the degradation or collapse of many formal institutions, as discussed by Francis and Amuyunzu-Nyamongo in chapter 9. Such countries suffer not only from corruption and political conflict, but also from high levels of violence, fear, and insecurity linked to a breakdown of the rule of law. Not surprisingly, the lack of administrative capacity often gives rise to alternative informal governance systems that can quickly degenerate into protection rackets, drug trafficking, or other forms of illicit activity. Growing recognition of the constraints that state fragility imposes on human security, economic growth, and development makes this a high priority (Migdal 1988) and a cutting-edge issue for social policy.

The multiple outcomes of violence have been analyzed in terms of their direct and indirect effects on each of the five capital assets (Moser and McIlwaine 2004, 2006) and are particularly exaggerated in the case of unstable or weak states. Costs include the drain on financial capital–savings and loss in earnings from resources allocated to reduce or control the phenomenon—as well as on human capital that are the consequence of much gender-based violence. In analyzing the underlying causes of livelihood insecurity, Francis and Amuyunzu-Nyamongo describe the "demasculation" associated with the erosion of the rural economy in Kenya and the related inability of men to meet their established gender roles that has increased gender-based violence, as well as intergenerational conflict.

Violence erodes social capital in terms of reducing trust and cooperation within communities. Informal community-level organizations, for instance, are often affected by insecurity and personal safety, which influence the nature of cohesion among members. When women fear leaving home, the functioning of informal organizations can be fundamentally affected (Moser 2006). However, violence can also reconstitute social capital in different ways. In chapter 10, in his analysis of Managua, Nicaragua, Rodgers describes the manner in which under certain conditions of state fragility urban youth gangs can be seen as socially constructive rather than destructive. He argues that in contexts such as these, gangs are often forms of "social sovereignty" that provide localized systems of "meta-political" order, allowing for the accumulation of physical and financial assets in areas where the state is predominantly absent. Such an analysis suggests that instead of thinking about gangs as "perverse livelihood strategies," it is perhaps more accurate to consider the fact that they tend to emerge in "perverse contexts." Thus, it is the context rather than the gangs that constitute the principal problem from a developmental perspective. That these gangs morph out of their socially constructive role and adopt more violent and destructive behaviors over time also appears to be a consequence of the broader structural context—the penetration of the *barrio* by the drug trade and the continued absence of state sovereignty whereby the possibilities of collective social life in Nicaragua are increasingly perceived to be shrinking.

### Asset-Based Livelihoods Strategies and Economic Empowerment

The previous three sections have discussed the contribution of an asset-based approach to a number of new cutting-edge development issues. In each case, the interaction between asset building and wider opportunities or constraints is mediated by institutions. As indicated by Rodgers, Satterthwaite, and Boonyabancha, asset accumulation and poverty reduction is not achieved by the state alone. Nonstate actors play key roles in different contexts. This is relevant to well-established development sectors where an asset-based approach assists in identifying the role that institutions within state, civil society, and community organizations play in generating livelihoods and well-being.

One such sector is forestry where current debate relates to the future of forests. As Molnar, White, and Khare argue in chapter 11, one vision maintains that the sector has the potential to sustain and improve rural livelihoods while conserving forests and their values. A countervailing vision, however, sees forests as substantially depopulated landscapes under protection for environmental and recreational use. This assumes rural economies will be based on alternative livelihoods with some commercial agroforestry and small islands of intensive, industrial activity in the natural, and largely public, forests. The authors argue that without appropriate policy and regulatory reform and supporting actions, much of the forest-based opportunity for the 1.1 billion people dependent upon forests will be lost. The establishment of a set of civil society partner institutions and donors to create an institutional framework, the Rights and Resources Initiative, and its coordinating mechanism, Rights and Resources Institute, are identified as essential to ensure a fundamental shift in vision and in resource allocation by governments, the private sector, social actors, and international development partners.

A second established sector is microenterprise, undoubtedly one of the most important strategies across the world to support poor women and their families, as well as to build assets. Microenterprise is especially valued for its double impact—social, in terms of empowerment outcomes, and financial, in terms of stabilization of financial flows and purchasing power (Lombard 2006). However, the former cannot be sustained without the latter. Although a large number of women start microenterprises, left to themselves only a small number successfully survive or expand their enterprises. In chapter 12, Pinglé considers factors for success and failure using data from Egypt, Nigeria, and South Africa to show that social capital generated via membership in *local* community associations has no noticeable positive impact on microenterprise sustainability. In contrast, women microentrepreneurs at the periphery of their communities have greater space for autonomous action, integrate into *extra-local* intercommunity networks, and are more likely to develop sustainable microenterprises. Consequently, states and nongovernmental organizations can assist women microentrepreneurs by integrating small communities into wider networks and by enhancing individual autonomy of women via the provision of child care support and emergency and regular medical care.

In chapter 13, Narayan and Kapoor present an integrated conceptual framework for economic empowerment that is an appropriate end to the book. The economic empowerment framework focuses on a broad range of assets that interact to create or erode poor people's wealth and, such as Moser's asset accumulation framework, uses the concepts of agency, opportunity structure, and their interactions to explain economic empowerment of poor people. Narayan and Kapoor's elaboration of the term opportunity structure, introduced earlier by Alsop and Heinsohn (2005), complements and resembles the assets-institutions-opportunities framework Moser presents. The conceptual framework for economic empowerment of poor people rests on two basic propositions:

- Poor people as active agents are most motivated to move out of poverty and have a range of assets and capabilities that need to be built on and protected.
- Poor people operate as producers, consumers, suppliers, or citizens in a wider context of institutions and available opportunities.

In Moser's formulation, the agency of the poor is encapsulated or subsumed within the concept of livelihood strategies.

Citing a well-known finding from the *Voices of the Poor* study that health shocks are the most common cause of households descent into poverty,[14] Narayan and Kapoor propose an integrated approach of economic and social policies. Such an approach needs to create opportunities for poor women and men as producers, while simultaneously protecting their portfolio of assets, including their own health and social, natural, physical, and financial assets. In order to draw policy lessons to support market liberalization from below, the chapter applies this framework to four large-scale programs in India that have built poor people's assets by facilitating their access to markets, while strengthening and protecting their asset base. Their review highlights two approaches that can help to scale up poor people's participation in markets on fairer terms. The first would improve the investment climate to create new economic opportunities linked directly to poor people's livelihoods. The second would invest in poor people's organizations to help to protect their limited assets as consumers and serve as vehicles to aggregate their supply and demand as producers, which can alter their bargaining power in markets. These insights resonate with the two previous chapters on economic empowerment, as well as more broadly with the findings of several of the chapters on migration and housing.

## The Way Forward for Asset-Based Social Policy

We conclude our analysis of the case studies by deductively distinguishing among three manifestations of social policy that can affect asset-based livelihoods (see figure 1.1):

- Public interventions that increase access to assets (*asset accession*)
- Public investments that increase the returns from assets (*asset valorization*)
- Public policies that transform the status and value of assets (*asset transformation*)

These three provide more precise categories than Moser's asset accumulation distinction among acquisition, sustained consolidation, and erosion of assets. These three types of public action lead to very different consequences for livelihoods, depending on the nature of the assets and whose interests are being served by their valorization or transformation. Differentiating among these three types of public policy and their distributional consequences will enhance their policy effectiveness.

To be successful, an asset-based social policy needs to speak to the challenges—inequality, informality, and imbalance in asset building and state effectiveness—described earlier. Initial inequalities in the distribution

**Figure 1.1. Manifestations of Asset-Based Social Policy**

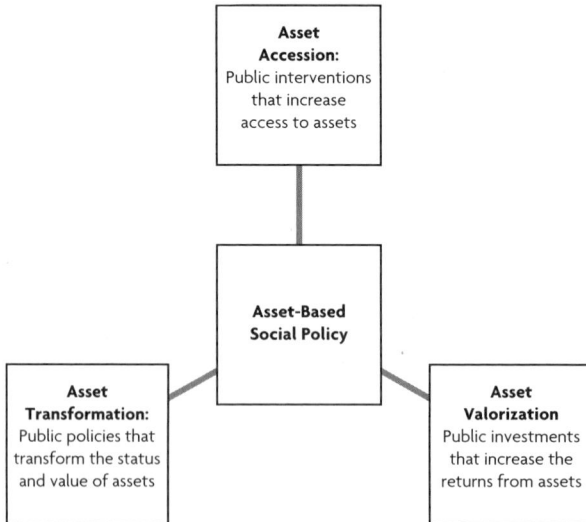

of, and access to, assets, as well as in power relations, voice, and access to public goods and services, are likely to influence social policy outcomes. Given the size of the informal sector, neither social policy nor investment climate reforms in developing countries can afford to limit their focus to the formal sector. The excessive attention to human capital assets needs to be balanced with a more integrated approach to asset building, particularly for those unlikely to be candidates for white-collar jobs; the investments in human capital needs to go beyond the MDGs to secondary education if they are to have real impact on livelihoods. Finally, state effectiveness matters; rather than taking for granted that economic reforms, social policy, and public accountability measures will be implemented by the public sector, in a polycentric world we need to design policies that can benefit from institutional alternatives, tailoring responsibility to capacity.

At a minimum, policy interventions will need to increase asset accession and create an investment climate that confronts institutional impediments and expands opportunities. In addition, the likely distributional effects of asset valorization investments and asset transformation policies and programs need to be examined to determine whether measures are likely to be pro-poor and lead to shared, inclusive growth.

Table 1.3 summarizes how asset-based policies address the specifics of different contexts presented in this book. In each case, public policies are classified according to their relevance for asset accession, valorization, or transformation. Structuring policies in this way allows policy makers to distinguish between actions with relatively modest investments that increase asset accession and those that require substantial investments if assets are to be valorized. Such investments are essential if the latent development potential of the poor's capabilities is to be unleashed.

### Asset Accession

The underlying question for asset accession is "What can be done to strengthen the asset base of the poor?" Once migration is accepted as a mutually beneficial livelihood strategy, key measures include lowering costs, facilitating loans, and regulating recruitment processes. Other public policies that cut across different contexts involve ensuring tenure security, recognizing individual and collective rights to assets (including those that are gender-based), settling claims protecting rights of disadvantaged groups, improving the investment climate to create new economic opportunities linked to poor people's livelihoods, and minimizing asset erosion while strengthening resilience against shocks to assets of the poor.

**Table 1.3. Asset-Based Social Policy—Implications of the Case Study Chapters**

| Focus | Asset accession | Asset valorization | Asset transformation |
|---|---|---|---|
| **Migration** (chapters 3–6) | • Address transaction costs of emigration.<br>• Provide social protection to needy households of migrants.<br>• Give regulatory oversight of recruiting agents.<br>• Provide government loans for migration.<br>• Have gender-based policies and cultural norms determine who can emigrate.<br>• Consider health training, language skills, and historical ties that affect migration. | • Lower transaction costs for remittances.<br>• Match funds for community investments.<br>• Facilitate investment of finance accumulated abroad.<br>• Tap human capital of diaspora (e.g. TOKTEN, MIDA).<br>• Arrange risk insurance.<br>• Ensure access to legal assistance.<br>• Facilitate fund flows.<br>• Influence visa and recruitment policies in host countries by demonstrating quality of human skills and qualifications.<br>• Consider tradeoff between remittance benefits vs. asset stripping and health deficit. | • Lobby host countries for immigrant rights.<br>• Award political rights to migrants (e.g., voting) in country of origin.<br>• Allow dual citizenship to encourage migration reflows.<br>• Ease travel restrictions in sub-region (e.g., ECOWAS protocols on migration).<br>• Show that Pakistan Origin Card allows visa-free travel and investment privileges.<br>• Validate healthworker qualifications.<br>• Agree on bilateral codes (e.g., South Africa and Zimbabwe, Lesotho and Ghana) shift cost of education and training to recruiting body. |
| **Upgrading urban slums** (chapters 7–8) | • Right to residence from local government provides legal identity and entitlement to basic services.<br>• Government financing for community-based savings groups at affordable rates.<br>• Per-family subsidy for infrastructure upgrading. | • Investment in urban services improves returns.<br>• Infrastructure in new settlements lacking roads increases asset value. | • Federations help urban poor renegotiate terms with service providers and the state.<br>• Tenure security enables slum dwellers to leverage housing assets into incomes and induces further asset accumulation.<br>• Collective asset ownership prevents displacement of urban poor. |

| | | |
|---|---|---|
| **Weak states**<br>(chapters 9–10) | • Address inequities in land tenure system.<br>• Add programs to increase land access as needed.<br>• Make public service improvements that will also rebuild credibility and social trust.<br>• In the absence of state sovereignty, have youth gangs provide the institutional means to accumulate physical and financial assets. | • Dysfunctional state-managed agricultural markets have undermined livelihoods; invest in rural infrastructure instead of regulating markets.<br>• An enabling opportunity structure and investments in legitimate livelihoods and security can nurture asset accumulation. | • Security against crime and violence would benefit rural livelihoods.<br>• Co-registration of titles will address gender inequity in land tenure.<br>• Propensity for violence and temptations of the drug trade can rapidly transform benign into perverse social capital. |
| **Economic empowerment**<br>(chapters 11–13) | • Microfinance institutions will target poor women.<br>• Investments in social assets—organizations and federations of the poor—will generate sustained income streams that have high payoff.<br>• Intermediation helps market access, scaling up, and demand responsiveness. | • Support for building local institutions and skills improves conservation outcomes.<br>• Enabling forest policies and public goods infrastructure will benefit forest communities.<br>• Support for child care and health care benefits women entrepreneurs.<br>• Research is needed on the value chain of poor people's economic activities.<br>• Public investments in infrastructure, market information, and information technology will help. | • Add more secure forest tenure and legal use rights that can mobilize community resources for conservation.<br>• Remove constraints in the opportunity structure—information, governance, inclusive and fair processes.<br>• Reform investment climate by amending regulations that constrain economic activities of the poor. |

*Asset Valorization*

The key question in relation to asset valorization is "What public investments can increase the value or return on assets of the poor and other priority groups?" Valorization investments cited in the studies include investments in human capital, public goods infrastructure, local infrastructure and services, business skills, and organizations of poor people to help them achieve economies of scale and security against crime and violence. This list reveals that the scope of social policy needs to be expanded to include the *social dimensions of infrastructure,* thus encouraging larger public investments in expanding public goods infrastructure and services to benefit those regions and economic activities linked directly to poor people's livelihoods. This implies that *social inclusion is an integral part of the appraisal criteria for infrastructure planning and design* to assess the likely effect of infrastructure investments on livelihoods of the poor and other disadvantaged groups.

Similarly, public investments to upgrade business skills of poor households who are already engaged in local enterprises would significantly increase their earnings. Supporting the informal sector through *business skills development to facilitate asset accumulation especially among the poor and other disadvantaged groups* can help build credibility and trust and, with the right incentives, eventually result in the integration of these enterprises into the formal economy.

The studies in this book point to the multidimensional benefits from organizations of the poor. To date, institutional capacity building efforts by multilateral and bilateral donor agencies have privileged the public sector with almost no investment supporting organizations and federations of poor people. Although the public sector needs capacity strengthening, in today's polycentric world this must be complemented by parallel *investments in building capacity of poor people and civil society's organizations engaged in slum upgrading, economic empowerment, or other development processes.*

*Asset Transformation*

The final question relevant to asset transformation is "What public policies can be transformational?" Such policies achieve great success when policy makers have the foresight and determination to overcome political economy constraints. Significant examples of asset transformation are found in each of the subsets of case studies included in this book.

- On migration, the main examples include *actions to facilitate rather than stigmatize or penalize migration.* In Hirschman's language, actions to value the "voice" of migrants, such as by restoring their political rights to encourage their "loyalty" (1970), as well as policies to reintegrate the international diaspora with their countries of origin by relaxing visa restrictions and by encouraging dual citizenship and investment by migrants.
- On urban slums, *recognition of the role of housing federations as mediating organizations for the rights of the urban poor* offers a vehicle with the potential of transforming urban renewal. The evidence both from slum upgrading and economic empowerment cases indicate that enhancing *tenure security* and clarifying and *legitimizing individual rights and collective assets* in informal settlements also have significant transformational value. As illustrated in the book, collective rights minimize the risk of displacement, thereby transforming insecure assets into more valuable ones.
- In weak states, however, there are no quick fixes. The first task is to *restore basic security and rule of law,* which needs to be accompanied by the rapid introduction of measures to transform and valorize their assets to create legitimate livelihoods. Difficult as this task may be, in Kenya for example, this approach would need to include urgent measures to tackle the land question and remove perceived inequities in access to land.
- On economic empowerment, asset transformation consists first and foremost of *removing the legal and institutional regulatory barriers that affect economic activities of the poor.*

In conclusion, it is important to acknowledge that although the state remains an important player, it is not the only provider, nor is it the sole determinant of an asset-based social policy. On the one hand, states need to negotiate policies, policy objectives, and investments with supranational entities, including international and regional organizations, private and donor financing organizations, multinational corporations, and other concerned governments. On the other hand, governments need to contend with increasingly vocal, organized, and capable in-country stakeholders. These include subnational governments, the domestic private sector, civil society organizations, community networks, and multiple interest groups defined by various social, economic, or political characteristics. This makes the job of governing more complex and contentious but also forces a better balance between the rights and responsibilities of citizens and the relationship between the state and other significant nonstate actors in a polycentric world. This process can only enhance the asset building and accumulation potential of millions of poor people around the world.

## Notes

1. WSSD was convened in Copenhagen on March 5–12, 1995.
2. It was not until the September 2005 World Summit that the WSSD goal of "full employment and decent work for all" was reinstated (see Ocampo and Jomo 2008).
3. The chapters in this book were originally presented under the theme of "Inequality, Livelihoods, and Social Inclusion," at the conference on "New Frontiers of Social Policy," organized in Arusha, Tanzania, on December 12–15, 2005, by the World Bank, in collaboration with the Department for International Development of the U.K., the Swedish International Development Agency, and the governments of Finland and Norway.
4. The WSSD commitments were as follows: (1) create an economic, political, social, cultural, and legal environment that will enable people to achieve social development; (2) eradicate absolute poverty by a target date to be set by each country; (3) support full employment as a basic policy goal; (4) promote social integration based on the enhancement and protection of all human rights; (5) achieve equality and equity between women and men; (6) attain universal and equitable access to education and primary health care; (7) accelerate the development of Africa and the least developed countries; (8) ensure that structural adjustment programs include social development goals; (9) increase resources allocated to social development; and (10) strengthen cooperation for social development through the UN.
5. The MDG goals are as follows: (1) eradicate extreme poverty and hunger; (2) achieve universal primary education; (3) promote gender equality and empower women; (4) reduce child mortality; (5) improve maternal health; (6) combat HIV/AIDS, malaria, and other diseases; (7) ensure environmental sustainability; and (8) develop a global partnership for development.
6. For a more detailed discussion of this subject, see the Series preface in Dani and de Haan (2008).
7. COSD is a functional commission of ECOSOC of the United Nations. It consists of 46 members elected by ECOSOC. Since the convening of the WSSD in Copenhagen in 1995, the COSD has been the key UN body in charge of the follow-up and implementation of the Copenhagen Declaration and Programme of Action. It meets once a year in New York, usually in February.

   Each year since 1995, the COSD has taken up key social development themes as part of its follow-up to the outcome of the Copenhagen Summit. In resolution 2005/11, the ECOSOC decided that, beginning with its 45th session, the COSD would be organized in a series of two-year action-oriented implementation cycles, which will include a review and a policy segment, and that the COSD would continue to review plans and programs of action pertaining to social groups. In 2006, the ECOSOC decided that the theme for the 2007–08 review and policy cycle will be "promoting full employment and decent work for all."

8. The authors acknowledge Ashraf Ghani with the origins of this term (see Ghani and Lockhart 2008) and are grateful for his many useful insights that have helped shape some of the arguments in this book.

9. This use of "exit" is derived from Albert Hirschman's book, *Exit, Voice, and Loyalty* (1970), which explains exit as the customer's way of punishing firms that are unresponsive to their needs. Successful firms are able to retain the "loyalty" of their constituency or customer base by giving opportunities to "voice" concerns and by demonstrating responsiveness to that voice.

10. Orozco includes "intangible" transfers such as the transfer of knowledge, the support to communities, and other exchanges under the general heading of social capital within the category of goods and services because he considers these to be material manifestations of cultural identity.

11. In his chapter, Hall (2008) discusses the sociopsychological problems associated with changing family structure as well as the impact on vulnerable children.

12. The civil society coalition in Mumbai consists of three partners: (1) SPARC is a nongovernmental organization formed by social work professionals in 1984 to work with problems of urban poverty in Mumbai; (2) the National Slum Dweller's Federation is a grassroots organization established in 1974, which has its historical base in Mumbai; and (3) Mahila Milan is an organization of poor women set up in 1986, with its base in Mumbai and a network throughout India, and is especially focused on women's issues and local savings schemes. The Mumbai-based coalition has been instrumental in creating a global network of community-based housing activists, called the Slum/Shackdwellers International. See Appadurai (2004) and Sattherthwaite (chapter 7) for more details.

13. Also see the case studies of civil society partnerships with local government in Mitlin and Sattherthwaite (2004).

14. Anirudh Krishna's multicountry study of movements in and out of poverty also finds health shocks to be the single most important factor causing households to descend into poverty (2007: 71–72).

## References

Adams, R. H., Jr., and J. Page. 2005. "Do International Migration and Remittances Reduce Poverty in Developing Countries?" *World Development* 33(10): 1645–70.

Alsop, R., ed. 2004. *Power, Rights and Poverty: Concepts and Connections.* Washington, DC: World Bank.

Alsop, R., and N. Heinsohn. 2005. "Measuring Empowerment in Practice: Structuring Analysis and Framing Indicators." Policy Research Working Paper 3510, World Bank, Washington, DC.

Alsop, R., M. Bertelsen, J. Holland. 2006. *Empowerment in Practice: From Analysis to Implementation.* Washington, DC: World Bank.

Appadurai, A. 1996. *Modernity at Large: Cultural Dimensions of Globalization.* Minneapolis: University of Minnesota Press.

———. 2004. "The Capacity to Aspire: Culture and the Terms of Recognition." In *Culture and Public Action*, eds. V. Rao and M. Walton, 59–85. Palo Alto, CA: Stanford University Press.

Bebbington, A. 1999. "Capitals and Capabilities: A Framework for Analyzing Peasant Viability, Rural Livelihoods and Poverty." *World Development* 27: 2021–44.

Bebbington, A. 2007. "Anatomies of Conflict: On the Inside of Social Protests around Extractive Industries, Development and Democracy." Paper presented at the SDV/DEC Seminar Series on Social Science and Policy, World Bank, Washington, DC, April 24. http://web.worldbank.org/WBSITE/EXTERNAL/TOPICS/EXTSOCIALDEVELOPMENT/0,,contentMDK:21309796~pagePK:210058~piPK:210062~theSitePK:244363,00.html

Besley, T., and L. J. Cord, eds. 2007. *Delivering on the Promise of Pro-Poor Growth: Insights and Lessons from Country Experiences.* Washington, DC: World Bank and Palgrave Macmillan.

Collier, P. 2007. *The Bottom Billion: Why the Poorer Countries Are Failing and What Can Be Done about It.* New York: Oxford University Press.

Commission on Legal Empowerment of the Poor (CLEP). 2008. *Making the Law Work for Everyone.* New York: CLEP.

Dani A. 2005. "Policies for Social Development in a Globalizing World: New Frontiers for Social Policy." Discussion Paper for the Technical Consultation on Social Policy, Meeting of the Social Development Advisers Network, Washington, DC, February 14.

Dani, A., and A. de Haan. 2008. "Social Policy in a Development Context: Structural Inequalities and Inclusive Institutions." In *Inclusive States: Social Policy and Structural Inequalities*, eds. A. Dani and A. de Haan, 1–36. Washington, DC: World Bank.

de Haan, A. 2008. "Citizens, Identity, and Public Policy: Affirmative Action in India." In *Inclusive States: Social Policy and Structural Inequalities*, ed. A. Dani and A. de Haan, 225–48. Washington, DC: World Bank.

De Soto, H. 2006. "The Challenge of Connecting Formal and Informal Property Systems: Some Reflections Based on the Case of Tanzania." In *Realizing Property Rights*, eds. H. De Soto and F. Cheneval, 18–67. Berne: Rüffer & Rub.

Ghani, A., and C. Lockhart. 2008. *Fixing Failed States: A Framework for Rebuilding a Fractured World*. New York: Oxford University Press.

Gough, I., and G. Wood. 2004. *Insecurity and Welfare Regimes in Asia, Africa and Latin America*. Cambridge: Cambridge University Press.

Hall, A. 2008. "International Migration and Challenges for Social Policy: The Case of Ecuador." In *Assets, Livelihoods, and Social policy*, eds. C. Moser and A. A. Dani. Washington, DC: World Bank.

Hirschman, A. 1970. *Exit, Voice, and Loyalty*. Cambridge, MA: Harvard University Press.

Hochschild, A. 2000. "Global Care Chains and Emotional Surplus Value." In *On the Edge: Living with Global Capitalism*, eds. W. Hutton and A. Giddens. London: Jonathan Cape.

Krishna, A. 2007. "The Stages of Progress Methodology and Results from Five Countries." In *Reducing Global Poverty: The Case for Asset Accumulation*, ed. C. O. N. Moser, 62–79. Washington, DC: The Brookings Institution.

Lombard, C. 2006. "Micro-Finance and Property Rights." In *Realizing Property Rights*, eds. H. De Soto and F. Cheneval, 238–46. Berne: Rüffer & Rub.

Menezes-Filho, N., and L. Vasconellos. 2007. "Human Capital, Inequality, and Pro-Poor Growth in Brazil." In *Delivering on the Promise of Pro-Poor Growth: Insights and Lessons from Country Experiences*, eds. T. Besley and L. J. Cord, 219–43. Washington, DC: World Bank and Palgrave Macmillan.

Migdal, J. S. 1988. *Strong Societies and Weak States: State-Society Relations and State Capabilities in the Third World*. Princeton, NJ: Princeton University Press.

Mikkelsen, B., T. Freeman, and B. Keller. 2002. *Mainstreaming Gender Equality: Sida's Support for the Promotion of Gender Equality in Partner Countries*. Stockholm: Sida.

Mitlin, D., and D., Satterthwaite, eds. 2004. *Empowering Squatter Citizen: Local Government, Civil Society and Urban Poverty Reduction*. London: Earthscan.

Mkandawire, T., ed. 2004. *Social Policy in a Development Context*. Houndmills, Basingstoke, U.K.: Palgrave Macmillan and UNRISD.

Moser, C. 1998. "The Asset Vulnerability Framework: Reassessing Urban Poverty Reduction Strategies." *World Development* 26(1): 1–19

———. 2007. "Asset-Based Approaches to Poverty Reduction in a Globalized Context: An Introduction to Asset Accumulation Policy and Summary of Workshop Findings." Global Economy and Development Working Paper, The Brookings Institution, Washington, DC.

Moser, C., and C. McIlwaine. 2004. *Encounters with Violence in Latin America: Urban Poor Perceptions from Colombia and Guatemala*. London and New York: Routledge.

———. 2006. "Latin American Urban Violence as a Development Concern: Towards a Framework for Violence Reduction." *World Development* 34 (1): 89–112.

Narayan, D. 1997. "Voices of the Poor: Poverty and Social Capital in Tanzania." Environmentally and Socially Sustainable Development Studies and Monograph Series 20, World Bank, Washington, DC.

———, ed. 2005. *Measuring Empowerment: Cross Disciplinary Perspectives.* Washington, DC: World Bank.

Narayan, D., and P. Petesch, eds. 2007. *Moving Out of Poverty: Cross-Disciplinary Perspectives on Mobility.* Washington, DC: Palgrave Macmillan and the World Bank.

Ocampo, J. A., and Jomo K. S., eds. 2008. *Towards Full and Decent Employment.* London: Zed Books.

Ong, A. 1999. *Flexible Citizenship: The Cultural Logics of Transnationality.* Durham, NC: Duke University Press.

Orozco, M. 2004. "Remittances to Latin America and the Caribbean: Issues and Perspectives on Development." Report commissioned by the Office for the Summit Process Organization of American States, Washington, DC.

———. 2007. "Migrant Foreign Savings and Asset Accumulation." In *Reducing Global Poverty: The Case for Asset Accumulation,* ed. C. O. N. Moser, 225–38. Washington, DC: The Brookings Institution.

Orozco, M., and M. Lepointe. 2004. "Mexican Hometown Associations and Development Opportunities." *Journal of International Affairs,* 57 (2): 31–49.

Ozden, C., and M. Schiff. 2005. *International Migration, Remittances and the Brain Drain.* Washington DC: World Bank and Palgrave Macmillan.

Paci, P., and P. Serneels, eds. 2007. *Employment and Shared Growth: Rethinking the Role of Labor Mobility for Development.* Washington, DC: World Bank.

Perry, G., W. F. Maloney, O. S. Arias, P. Fajnzylber, A. D. Mason, and J. Saavedra-Chanduvi. 2007. *Informality: Exit and Exclusion.* World Bank Latin American and Caribbean Studies. Washington, DC: World Bank.

Rakodi, C. 1999. "A Capital Assets Framework for Analyzing Household Livelihood Strategies: Implication for Policy." *Development Policy Review* 17: 315–42.

Rao, V., and M. Walton, eds. 2004. *Culture and Public Action.* Palo Alto, CA: Stanford University Press.

Rodgers, G., C. Gore, and J. B. Figueiredo, eds. 1995. *Social Exclusion: Rhetoric, Reality and Responses.* Geneva: International Institute for Labour Studies.

Ross, M. 2008. "Mineral Wealth, Conflict, and Equitable Development." In *Institutional Pathways to Equity: Addressing Inequality Traps,* eds. A. J. Bebbington, A. Dani, A. de Haan, and M. Walton, 193–215. Washington, DC: World Bank.

Sabates-Wheeler, R. 2008. "Asset Inequality and Agricultural Growth: How Are Patterns of Asset Inequality Established and Reproduced?" In *Institutional Pathways to Equity: Addressing Inequality Traps,* eds. A. Bebbington, A. Dani, A. de Haan, and M. Walton, 45–72. Washington DC: World Bank.

Sen, A. 1981. *Poverty and Famines: An Essay on Entitlement and Deprivation.* Oxford, U.K.: Clarendon Press.

———. 1997. "Editorial: Human Capital and Human Capability." *World Development* 25 (12): 1959–61.

———. 1999. *Development as Freedom.* Oxford, U.K.: Oxford University Press.

Smillie, I., L. Gberie, and R. Hazleton. 2000. "Getting to the Heart of the Matter: Sierra Leone, Diamonds, and Human Security." Partnerships Africa Canada. http://www.reliefweb.int/library/documents/2001/pac-sie-jan00.pdf.

UN-HABITAT (United Nations Human Settlements Programme). 2003. *The Challenge of Slums: Global Report on Human Settlements 2003.* London: Earthscan.

UN Millenium Project. 2005. *A Home in the City.* Task Force on Improving the Lives of Slum Dwellers. London: Earthscan.

Wiman, R., T. Voipio, and M. Ylönen, eds. 2007. *Comprehensive Social Policies for Development in a Globalizing World.* Helsinki: Ministry of Foreign Affairs, in cooperation with the Ministry of Social Affairs and Health, and STAKES, the National Research and Development Centre for Welfare and Health.

World Bank. 2004. *World Development Report 2004: Making Services Work for the Poor.* Washington, DC: World Bank.

———. 2006. *World Development Report 2006: Equity and Development.* Washington, DC: World Bank.

# CHAPTER 2

# Assets and Livelihoods: A Framework for Asset-Based Social Policy

*Caroline Moser*

Poverty-focused policy has changed significantly in the South over the past two decades. This change is evident in the shift from residual welfare poverty alleviation strategies, commonly associated with safety nets, to social protection poverty reduction policies. In principle, the latter have a far broader mandate, incorporating risk prevention and mitigation strategies, as well as the perennially necessary safety nets. However, despite such advances, social protection in practice still tends to focus on income/consumption "protection" of the poor through the provision of cash transfers and other residual welfare provisions. This raises important questions about complementary social policy focused on creating opportunities for the poor as opposed to providing protection.

The concept of sustainable livelihoods (SL) moves the focus of social policy in this direction. While linked to social protection, it shifts the focus from income and consumption to addressing directly the critical role played by assets and capabilities in improving individual and household social and economic well-being and associated poverty reduction. Yet the emphasis on livelihoods *per se* means that the importance of asset building (AB), and the accumulation and longer-term consolidation of assets, is often overlooked. In addition, both SL and AB have been identified primarily as poverty reduction approaches, rather than as specific components of social policy.

This chapter seeks not only to compare and contrast salient characteristics of SL and AB, but also to identify their potential conceptual and operational contribution to a "new agenda" of social policy. The chapter then introduces an asset-based social policy and associate framework, incorporating an assets-institutions-opportunities nexus. In the context of new development issues associated with globalization, failing states, natural disasters, post-conflict situations, and accelerated urbanization, the chapter concludes by identifying the way in which a second-generation asset-based policy that ensures accumulated assets are sustained and do not get eroded can provide a critical component of a new agenda for social policy. Here, asset accumulation policy is located in the center of mainstream poverty reduction development debates.

In such a review of the comparative robustness of two frameworks, it is important first to contextualize them in terms of associated political and institutional concerns. When it comes to clarifying the future of a social policy agenda within the International Financial Institutions (IFIs), political concerns relate to the political economy of ideas and to the power of institutions as "epistemic communities,"[1] not only to identify new development ideas, but also to discard them (Boas and McNeill 2004; Deacon 2004). In this chapter, this political concern is of particular importance in relation to the concept of SL.

Institutional concerns, by contrast, relate less to the substance of a policy and more to the institutional fit or misfit that determines where within the organizational structure such policy gets implemented. Of particular significance is the need to avoid what might be termed "institutional determinism." This occurs when the organizational structure determines the substantive content of policy, rather than the content guiding the policy's operational location. This issue has special relevance to the World Bank's Social Development Department in terms of the institutional constraints and opportunities that may determine a new agenda for social policy.

## The Changing Objectives and Associated Strategies of Social Development Policy

By way of background, it is useful to start with a brief summary of the shifting agenda of social policy in the South. Given the extensive and comprehensive literature already focusing on this issue,[2] this chapter limits itself to highlighting three salient issues contextually relevant to its particular objectives. These assist in identifying the extent to which SL and AB frameworks have already been introduced into social policy.

## Priority Issues in the Evolution of Social Development and Social Policy in the South

The first priority relates to the change, over the past five decades, in the "social"[3] as a policy agenda in its own right as opposed to an integrated or subsumed component of economic, health, education, infrastructure, or any other policy. Its objectives have changed, as well as its scope of statutory provision, sectors of intervention, and institutional structure. This reflects shifts from supply through demand and finally to rights-driven social policy. A range of social policy approaches can be categorized as ideal types along a continuum from residual welfare through incremental policies and basic needs to compensatory measures and, most recently, agendas relating to social justice, citizenship, and human rights (see annex 2.1).

An important debate underlying these changes concerns two different approaches to social policy—the sectoral and the holistic (Moser 1995). First started in the 1970s, the debate continues to flourish today. The sectoral approach equates social policy with social sector policy and is based on the premise that particular aspects of human activity can be isolated for separate treatment, differentiating areas such as education, health, housing, or personal social services for individual professional application (Marsden 1990). The holistic or unified approach was defined by the United Nations (UN) (1971) as aiming to address wider issues within which sector concerns were rooted. This approach emerged as a reaction by international organizations to the excessively narrow social services emphasis in social policy and consequent neglect of broader social development goals. It defined its remit in terms of both the social structure of society and the political context in which development decisions were made (Hardiman and Midgley 1982). Although the World Bank's Social Development Family was not formed until 1997, the rich history of social development in the organization dates back to the 1970s, with the first appointments of social anthropologists "to improve the effectiveness of development projects" (Davis 2004: 1).

Second, such changes in the South have not taken place in isolation but have mirrored other changes. These include changing social policy agendas in the North—with previously important distinctions between capitalist and socialist economies.[4] They also include changes in macroeconomic development policy in the South. Again, these can be categorized as ideal types ranging from modernization policies of accelerated growth, through basic needs associated with redistribution, to structural adjustment neoliberal reform models, and most recently to policies associated with globalization (see annex 2.1).

Finally, turning to the current context, there is still no clear or unified consensus as to the coverage or objectives of social policy. Most commonly, distinctions are made within social policy as social sector policy using sectors defined as *social*, such as health, education, and nutrition; social policy as (residual) welfare policy; and social policy as social protection policy through risk prevention, mitigation, or coping strategies (see Kabeer 2004).[5] In contrast, social development is understood to comprise the following:

> A set of objectives that include equity and social justice, which subsume additional objectives including social inclusion, sustainable livelihoods, gender equity, and increased voice and participation (Dani 2005: 2).

## Social Policy, Assets, and Livelihoods

The current scope of social policy, as discussed earlier, makes no reference to assets and livelihoods, although livelihood diversification and insurance mechanisms are important components of risk mitigation under social protection (Holtzmann and Jorgensen 2000). Clearly, these are not traditional "social" policy concerns. While new social policy strategies are being developed in specific operational contexts, innovative donor, government, and nongovernmental organization (NGO) agendas are increasingly influencing the components of social policy. Table 2.1 provides one such example from the social policy of the government of Jamaica, developed by the Planning Institute's social policy thematic team

**Table 2.1. Components of the Jamaican Government's Social Policy**

| Component | Key outcome goal |
|---|---|
| Human security | A peaceful and mutually respectful society with increased safety, security, and freedom from fear in the home and public spaces |
| Social integration | An inclusive and nondiscriminatory society that represents group and individual rights, promotes social justice, accepts diversity, and builds trust and communication among groups |
| Governance | More effective, complementary, and transparent government structures to move decisionmaking closer to people |
| Secure and sustainable livelihoods | Widened, higher quality livelihood and employment opportunities for all Jamaicans, with particular reference to those disadvantaged in the labor market |
| Environment | Improved environment for quality of life for Jamaicans living and as yet unborn |
| Education and skills | An education that facilitates lifelong learning and acquisition of social and life skills for all |
| Health and physical well-being | Policies to enhance the broadly defined health status of the population |

*Source:* Planning Institute of Jamaica 2002.

with support from the Department for International Development of the U.K. (DFID). It illustrates the way in which social policy strategies are moving beyond conventional domains to include such issues as human security, the environment, and indeed secure and sustainable livelihoods. In the same way, the *Human Development Report* 2003 from the United Nations Development Programme (UNDP) identifies the importance of governance and institutional issues for countries promoting social policy (UNDP 2003).

## The World Bank and Social Policy

The World Bank does not have a specifically defined social policy as such. Within the institution, three predominant social policy "domains" can be identified: social sectors, social protection, and social development. The fact that each has a distinct location within the organization has served to create artificial conceptual and operational barriers to a holistic social policy.[6] Of the three, social development has struggled hardest to gain legitimacy and a critically important, associated, operational portfolio. After two decades of progress, the recently completed strategy paper "Empowering People by Transforming Institutions: Social Development in World Bank Operations" (World Bank 2005) is a landmark in terms of the integration of a social development agenda into the World Bank. It defines social development as "transforming institutions to empower people .... with three operational principles to guide its approach to social development: inclusion, cohesion, and accountability." Linked to this are three strategic priorities that are summarized as more macro, better projects, and better grounding (World Bank 2005: 9).

The third strategic priority—"better grounding: Improve research, capacity building, and partnerships to solidify the grounding for better operations"—provides the opportunity to identify a new conceptualization of social policy. In his "Concept Note: New Frontiers of Social Policy," Dani defines this in terms of the achievement of "more equitable and socially sustainable development outcomes.... A holistic social policy seeks to promote policies, institutions, and programs that balance a concern for equity and social justice with the concern for economic growth" (Dani 2005: 1).

## The Identification of Livelihoods as a Social Policy Concern

The World Bank takes as the starting point for its redefinition of social policy the 1995 Copenhagen World Summit for Social Development (WSSD) and the gaps identified by the UN Secretary General in the 2005 follow-up report on the Social Summit. These relate to employment (livelihoods), social integration, and the institutional environment for development. The WSSD's somewhat narrow definition of "livelihoods as employment" reflects contexts where state institutions and the provision of welfare are taken for granted and is less appropriate for resource poor situations. Dani's Concept Note recognizes the need to expand this scope of livelihoods as follows:

> Social development [is] the process of increasing the assets and capabilities of individuals to improve their well-being. The focus will be on policies to offset inequalities in asset endowment with equitable opportunities for asset creation and livelihoods, such as through policies to create equitable and affordable access to basic utilities and infrastructure, and to strengthen livelihoods of those operating in the informal sector. The conceptual approach that is being adopted focuses on integrating the sustainable livelihoods (SL) approach within the social policy framework, expanding the SL approach both beyond its micro-level applications to understand primarily rural livelihoods toward one that is conceptualized and supported by policy making and public actions. As livelihood strategies have become increasingly dynamic and diversified, social policy interventions must respond accordingly (Dani 2005: 1).

### Toward an Asset-Based Social Policy

The prioritization of livelihoods as one of three potential future social policy themes presents conceptual, operational, and political challenges. It envisages a rethinking and expansion of the SL approach beyond its current applications toward a focus on assets and capabilities. Furthermore, it excludes other contemporary asset and capability focused frameworks, in particular a range of AB approaches. This chapter, therefore, extends its coverage to review both the SL approach and a range of AB approaches in terms of origins, substantive and operational commonalities and differences, and their potential contribution to future social policy. It highlights limitations of the SL framework compared with advantages of the AB framework, including the potential political implications of adopting a SL framework at the same time as a number of important actors in its "epistemic community" appear to have abandoned it.

In addition, this review underlines the differences between asset-based approaches to poverty reduction and social protection, which is currently the predominant strategy adopted by many agencies that either did not adopt a SL approach or, if they did, have since ceased to use it. Social protection, a refined, updated version of social welfare, is concerned with protecting the poor and vulnerable against negative risks and shocks that erode their assets. In contrast, the objective of asset-based social policy is the provision of positive opportunities for asset accumulation. Such a policy is concerned not only with the first-generation accumulation of assets, such as human capital and physical capital (housing), but also with second-generation measures to ensure that individuals, households, and communities stay out of poverty through the sustained consolidation of their assets.

This distinction between asset vulnerability and the focus of asset-based social policy on asset accumulation challenges the current scope of social protection. While this is currently defined in terms of safety nets, risk prevention, and risk mitigation (Holtzmann and Jorgensen 2000), in practice such a broad agenda has rarely been implemented, with safety nets still the most important priority. Asset-based social policy that focuses clearly on asset accumulation, as opposed to the "welfarist" income protection of the poorest and most vulnerable, is an important development agenda. As long as "institutional determinism" does not act as an impenetrable deterrent, this provides the opportunity for the (re)differentiation between social protection and social policy.

## Sustainable Livelihoods and Asset-Building Frameworks[7]

Sustainable livelihoods and asset-building frameworks share many similarities and, consequently, are often confused or conflated. This section describes the characteristics of each and in so doing defines them as complementary but different approaches to poverty reduction.

### Commonalities in Backgrounds: From Consumption Poverty to Vulnerability, Risks, and Assets[8]

Both SL and AB frameworks share common backgrounds rooted in the poverty alleviation/reduction debates of the 1990s, rather than in those relating to social policy *per se*. This economic policy debate questioned the measurement of poverty;[9] identified its multidimensionality and the relationship among inequality, economic growth, and poverty reduction in the South; redefined the meaning of poverty itself; and finally elaborated new poverty reduction strategies. Heavily influenced by Sen's (1981) work on famines and entitlements, assets, and capabilities, as well as those of Chambers (1992, 1994) and others on risk and vulnerability, an extensive debate made a distinction between poverty as a static concept and vulnerability as a dynamic one. It focused on defining concepts such as assets, vulnerabilities, capabilities, and endowments and on developing policies to address the impacts of livelihood shocks by focusing on the assets and entitlements of the poor.[10] In the World Bank, this policy shift can be summarized aptly by a comparison between the poverty reduction strategies in the 1990 and 2000 World Development Reports (Moser 2001; World Bank 1990, 2000).[11] This path-breaking work resulted in a consensus around a number of concepts, of which the most prominent was the capital assets of the poor, commonly identified in terms of five types: physical, financial, human, social, and natural (see box 2.1).[12]

---

**BOX 2.1**

**Definition of the Most Important Capital Assets**

**Physical capital** (also known as *produced or man-made capital*): Comprises the stock of plant, equipment, infrastructure, and other productive resources owned by individuals, the business sector, or the country itself.

**Financial capital:** The financial resources available to people, such as savings and supplies of credit.

**Human capital:** Includes investments in education, health, and the nutrition of individuals. Labor is a critical asset linked to investments in human capital, health status determines people's capacity to work, and skill and education determine the returns from their labor.

**Social capital:** An intangible asset is defined as the rules, norms, obligations, reciprocity, and trust embedded in social relations, social structures, and societies' institutional arrangements, which enable its members to achieve their individual and community objectives. Social capital is embedded in social institutions at the microinstitutional level—communities and households—as well as referring to the rules and regulations governing formalized institutions in the marketplace, the political system, and civil society.

**Natural capital:** Includes the stocks of environmentally provided assets such as soil, atmosphere, forests, minerals, water, and wetlands. In rural communities, land is a critical productive asset for the poor; in urban areas, land for shelter is also a critical productive asset.

*Sources:* Bebbington 1999; Carney 1998; Moser 1998; Narayan 1997; Portes 1998; Putnam 1993.

However, the same "new poverty" agenda also produced a proliferation of approaches, described as a "bewildering, confusion of competing intellectual frameworks and alternative paradigms using similar words in different ways" (Longhurst 1994: 17). Deconstructing specific analytical and operational meanings of seemingly overlapping frameworks is, therefore, the focus of this chapter.

### Comparative Analysis of SL and AB Frameworks

A comparative analysis of SL and AB frameworks shows that there is no one framework but many variations of each. While they share such common concepts as assets, capabilities, livelihoods, and vulnerabilities, important differences exist in emphasis between frameworks, as well as variations within frameworks. To unravel some of this complexity, it is useful to distinguish between the following: first, analytical frameworks that construct the conceptual approach; second, operational practice that applies the concept in practice; and third, further analytical adaptations that extend the original framework. The following section uses this three-fold distinction to describe SL and AB. Table 2.2 summarizes these and identifies principle issues and associated examples.

*Sustainable livelihoods approach.*[13] Probably the best known analytical framework to incorporate many of the common concepts of assets, capabilities, and entitlements is the sustainable livelihoods approach (SLA). While the original SL concept was mentioned in the World Commission on Environment and Development (1987), the SLA framework was the outcome of an extensive debate on rural development by Carney (1998), Chambers and Conway (1992), Scoones (1998), and others.[14] As the name implies, the overall emphasis is on livelihoods, with the concept defined analytically as comprising the capabilities, assets (including both material and social resources), and activities required for a means of living.[15] Thus, Carney (1998: 1) defines a livelihood as sustainable when it can cope with and recover from stresses and shocks and can maintain or enhance capabilities and assets both at that time and in the future, while at the same time not undermining the natural resource base.

The SLA seeks to gain an accurate understanding of people's assets or capital endowments and how they convert these into positive livelihood outcomes. The approach is founded on a belief that people require a range of assets to achieve positive livelihood outcomes, with no single category of assets on its own sufficient to yield all the many and varied livelihood

**Table 2.2. Summary of SL and AB Frameworks in Terms of Concepts, Practice, and Applications**

| Framework | Details | Examples of authors or institutions | Examples of implementation |
|---|---|---|---|
| **Critical common concepts** | | | |
| Analytical | Assets and capabilities: Sen<br>Vulnerability and risks: Chambers | | |
| **Sustainable livelihoods** | | | |
| Analytical frameworks | Sustainable livelihoods framework | Carney; Chambers and Ellis; Conway; Scoones | Originally developed as heuristic rural development project-level tool to move beyond cash income to consider the other assets associated with sustainable livelihoods of the poor |
| Operational practice | SLA | DFID | 1997 U.K. government's *White Paper on International Development* commitment to support policies and actions to promote SL (to contribute to achieving the Millennium Development Goals) |
| | | WFP | Colombia: Vulnerability mapping to identify livelihood and security vulnerabilities |
| | SL and human rights | CARE | Kosovo participatory livelihood assessment Food Economy Approach in Zimbabwe and Kenya |
| | Livelihood and governance | World Bank | Participatory poverty assessments; poverty social impact analyses |
| | Livelihoods and rights | Moser and Norton | A conceptual framework for applying a rights approach to livelihood security and sustainable development |
| Emerging agendas | SL and institutions | Bennett | Empowerment and social inclusion |
| | SL and institutions | Kabeer | Analytical framework for institutions, access, and outcome |

**Asset building**

| Category | Topic | Source | Description |
|---|---|---|---|
| Analytical frameworks | Risk, vulnerability, and assets | CPG; Moser; Sabates, Wheeler, and Haddad; Siegel | Asset vulnerability framework |
| | Asset-based approach | Adato, Carter, and May; Hoddinott; Sherraden | BASIS CRSP asset-based approaches; Asset-based welfare policy |
| | Asset building | World Bank | Risk and vulnerability assessment |
| Operational practice | Social protection | | |
| | Asset building and community development | Ford Foundation | Asset-building in financial holdings, natural resources, social bonds, and human capital |
| | | Coady International Institute | Asset-Based Community Development "transformative" methodology; Community asset mapping |
| | Asset-based welfare policy | Fossgard-Moser; Morad; USA Corporation for Enterprise Development; U.K. government | Individual Development Accounts; Child Trust Fund |
| Emerging agendas | Assets and institutions | World Bank | Assets and institutions for social development |
| | Assets and empowerment | Narayan | Empowerment: Assets and capabilities, agency and opportunity structure |
| Emerging framework | Assets and power | Alsop, Heinsohn, and Holland | Assets, empowerment, and agency |
| | Asset-based social policy | Moser | First- and second-generation policy with asset-institutions-opportunities nexus |

Source: Author.

outcomes that people seek (DFID 2000: 5). The SLA framework identifies the same five core asset categories mentioned earlier, upon which livelihoods are built (see annex 2.2). These are presented in a pentagon, or five-axis graph, with access by different groups identified as a useful starting point for debate about suitable entry points, how these serve the needs of different social groups, and the likely trade-offs among different assets.

The SLA is intended to force users to think holistically rather than sectorally about the basis of livelihoods. The framework also requires analysis and understanding of other areas. These include the vulnerability context in which assets exist (trends, shocks, and local cultural practices that affect livelihoods), as well as the structures (organizations from government through to the private sector) and processes (police, laws, rules of the game, and incentives) that define people's livelihood options. Structures and processes determine who gains access to which types of assets. Markets and legal restrictions, for instance, have a profound influence on the extent to which one asset can be converted into another type of asset (Carney 1998: 9).

Turning to operational practice, the rapid popularization of the SLA was influenced by DFID's successful packaging of it as an operational model/tool. The aim was to encourage the natural resource management program to move beyond specific issues, such as agricultural crop production, to a more comprehensive understanding of the livelihood-related problems of the rural poor. DFID's SL program contained a number of core principles that underpinned its implementation. These included the following (Ashley and Carney 1999):

- a people-centered approach
- responsive and participatory processes
- sustainability
- work at multiple levels
- partnership
- flexibility to respond to changes in people's situation.

Operational support for SLA was further enhanced by the 1997 U.K. government's "White Paper on International Development," which committed DFID to supporting SL policies and actions as a direct contribution to achieving the International Development Targets as well as the Millennium Development Goals. The framework rapidly gained popularity beyond DFID, with other bilaterals and multilaterals, such as UNDP and Food and Agriculture Organization, as well as international NGOs such as CARE, UN World Food Programme, and Oxfam (see table 2.2).[16] Many

of these agencies established separate units or programs to develop and support the application of the SLA.

Despite the initial operational success of the SLA, its popularity rapidly declined among large donor institutions. DFID disbanded its Sustainable Livelihoods Support Office, while the UNDP, an early institutional champion, abandoned its global SL program in 2000. In contrast, some international NGOs continue to use an adapted version of the SLA framework. For example, CARE uses a household livelihood security framework and has moved toward incorporating a rights-based approach, while Oxfam has linked its SL analysis to a rights-based approach since 1994.

The wide-scale adoption of the SLA has resulted in an extensive evaluation of its utility as a conceptual framework, as well as an operational tool.[17] Its strengths can be summarized as follows.

- First, as a people-centered approach, it changes ways of doing business to include participatory processes and multidisciplinary teams.
- Second, its multisectoral focus means that it provides a framework for addressing the whole range of policy issues relevant to the poor that transcend individual sectors, while including issues of access to financial services, markets, and justice relating to personal security.
- Third, its interdisciplinary approach means that it does not make the implicit assumption that rural people are farmers but instead recognizes multiple income sources.

However, the SLA has also been criticized, with three particularly pertinent limitations.

- First, at the organizational level, the sectoral character of many agencies makes the comprehensive adoption of the SLA complicated because it is difficult to identify the best thematic fit for the livelihood agenda. In practice, SL often reflects the focus of the sector ministry taking the lead, with a multisector approach still considered too complex.
- Second, at the political level, the framework has shortcomings relating to notions of power and governance. Despite the large number of variables in the "PIP box,"[18] it is perceived as not adequately addressing issues of politics, power and voice, and rights and empowerment.[19] Thus, despite its identification of structures and processes, the SLA framework tends to focus more on the technical nature of development.
- Third, and the most serious operational criticism, the framework is limited in terms of micro-macro linkages. While it provides a robust

micro-level tool, this is so context specific that it has difficulty in establishing micro-macro linkages and designing a macro-level national model that can be used in policy dialogue or for the formulation or implementation of national-level strategies to improve livelihoods (Solesbury 2003). In their discussion of the usefulness of SL for macro-level, national policy planning and making, Norton and Foster (2001) conclude that, while SLA can be informative, it is not necessarily the most appropriate approach to better understand macro-level reality. In contrast, Carney (2002) argues that SL can enrich Poverty Reduction Strategy Papers (PRSPs) by understanding livelihood groups and assets, managing cross-cutting issues, and underlining the importance of participation. Ultimately, however, SLA has not added up at the aggregate level, with insufficient evidence to show that its application has led to better programs or development outcomes.

Both DFID and the UNDP used this third limitation to explain their abandonment of the SL framework for designing poverty reduction policy and programs within five years of its introduction.[20] In shifting their priority from project and programmatic level to policy advice and direct budget support, the limitation in upscaling SLA fundamentally reduced its popularity. Is this an example of the power of the donor-driven epistemic community? The trickle-down effect has meant that in the donor world, the SLA has lost credence. But was it originally developed as a policy-level tool? If not, were such criticisms based on unjustified expectations?

Despite such criticisms, SL is still alive and on the agenda for many.[21] Since its initial development, an emerging agenda has further elaborated the concept, principally so as to address the political and institutional constraints in the original framework. One example is a framework developed by Moser and Norton (2001) that applies a rights approach to sustainable livelihoods. This seeks to address better the power dimensions of development processes by showing what a human rights perspective brings to governance and public policy formulation in terms of openness, transparency, equity, and accountability. The framework operates at three levels. At the normative level, the value added by using a human rights approach derives from the global legitimacy that human rights have acquired.[22] The analytical level identifies ways in which multiple structures of authority and control influence how poor people's claims are processed into outcomes. The political process of contesting claims also requires recognition. Finally, at the operational level, potential entry

points can be identified, including PRSPs and Sector Wide Approaches to Poverty.

The continuing popularity of the SL framework is reflected in the way it has been incorporated into recent research to develop social policy frameworks. Bennett, for instance, identifies an empowerment and social inclusion framework that builds on the SL approach "while placing greater emphasis on power relations as these are defined by social identity and economic status and mediated by institutions and organizations" (2003: 2). Another recent framework by Kabeer (2004) grapples with the interrelationship between SL and institutions. Here, the research focuses not on livelihoods *per se* but on the broader institutional configuration of social provisioning and the extent to which it addresses the needs of the poor. The interface between institutions of social policy and the principles of access they embody and the provisioning efforts of the poor are captured by livelihood strategies. As diagram 2.1 shows, this reinforces the notion that such strategies need to be measured against outcomes (Kabeer 2004).

*AB frameworks.* Under the overall title of AB are a number of conceptual approaches that at first glance appear similar to SL, since they are also concerned with assets and capabilities, institutions, and livelihoods. It is the emphasis that differs, and the policy implications associated with this difference. As the name implies, AB frameworks are concerned more specifically with assets[23] and their associated asset accumulation strategies, rather than with livelihood strategies associated more generally with well-being. Here, the greater emphasis on assets is closely linked to the concept of capabilities. Thus, as Bebbington (1999) maintains, assets are not simply resources that people use to build livelihoods: they give them the capability to be and act. As such, assets are identified as the basis of agents' power to act to reproduce, challenge, or change the rules that govern the control, use, and transformation of resources (see Sen 1997). Assets thus create agency. AB frameworks are not as well known as SL, possibly

**Diagram 2.1. Institutions, Access, and Outcomes: An Analytical Framework**

| Initial | Conditions | Institutional | Processes | Development | Outcomes |
|---------|------------|---------------|-----------|-------------|----------|
| Context | Resources | Institutions | Policy regimes | Livelihood strategies | "Social" outcomes |

Source: Kabeer 2004: 3.

because their definitions are less "homogeneous" and, unlike with SL, a one-for-all "blueprint" operational framework has not been developed. Nevertheless, academics and practitioners in both Northern and Southern contexts have focused on different aspects of AB that can be loosely categorized in terms of four areas.

*Vulnerability, risks, and assets.*[24] The "new poverty debate" has provoked an extensive discussion on the relationship between vulnerability,[25] risks, and assets of the poor. For instance, the asset vulnerability framework that I developed highlights the relationship between vulnerability and asset ownership. Vulnerability analysis involves identifying not only risks or threats but also resilience in resisting or recovering from negative effects of a changing environment. The means of resistance are the assets and entitlements that individuals, households, and communities mobilize in facing hardship. Vulnerability is therefore closely linked to asset ownership. The more assets people have, the less vulnerable they are, and the greater the erosion of people's assets, the greater their vulnerability and associated insecurity (Moser 1998: 3). The poor are managers of complex asset portfolios. Different household capital assets contribute to well-being outcomes,[26] with the associated capacity to manage assets cushioning households and limiting the impact of shocks. Some strategies, however, have unanticipated, negative effects, including increasing inequality and conflict within households and increasing levels of violence, crime, fear, and insecurity in local communities (Moser 1996).

Complementary to this, Siegel (2005), in his asset framework, points out that, while the capital assets a household possesses determines its opportunities, the broader "policy and institutional environment," and the associated existence or absence of risks, influences the behavior of households in terms of livelihood strategies. Most recently, researchers working on the chronically poor (those considered most vulnerable and therefore most likely to be multidimensionally deprived) have also used a vulnerability framework (CPRC 2004; Sabates-Wheeler and Haddad 2005).

Turning to operational practice, issues of risk, vulnerability, and asset accumulation are at the core of the social protection framework developed by the World Bank (Holzmann and Jorgensen 2000; World Bank 2000) and others. The social protection framework uses a two-fold typology of risk to distinguish among micro-level idiosyncratic risks that affect individuals or households, meso-level covariant risks affecting groups of households and communities, and macro-level risks affecting regions or nations. The related risk management framework makes an important distinction between reducing and mitigating risk, as well as coping with shocks, with livelihood diversification and insurance being the two key mitigation strategies.

*Asset-based approaches.* Closely associated with risk and vulnerability is a second AB framework, encompassing asset-based approaches (ABAs) that seek to address the causes and dynamics of longer-term persistent structural poverty primarily in rural Africa and Asia.[27] Of particular importance is the BASIS Collaborative Research Program (CRSP), a policy-focused research group of U.S.-based economists with partners in the South.[28] Drawing on longitudinal data, rather than short-term snapshots of income poverty, it identifies "dynamic asset poverty," as well as distinguishing between "deep-rooted persistent structural poverty and chronic, and other forms of poverty that the passage of time will alleviate" (Adato, Carter, and May 2006).

This ABA differentiates between "churning" or stochastic poverty (the regular drops into or rises out of poverty due to short-term shocks) and structural mobility associated with gains or losses of productive assets. It identifies poverty traps and defines a critical minimum asset threshold below which households cannot take advantages of positive changes or recover from negative changes. Unable to accumulate important assets, such households are trapped in permanent poverty (Barrett and Carter 2006; Carter and Barrett 2006).[29]

BASIS CRSP focuses on identifying policies and programs that are effective in reducing poverty over the long term "through some combination of helping households to accumulate assets, providing access to institutions that increase the returns on those assets and minimizing the impact that shocks can have on a family's asset holding. Successful interventions can involve helping poor or vulnerable families add to their assets, achieve higher returns on those they hold and maintain those they hold in the face of shocks" (Hoddinott and others 2005: 1).[30]

BASIS CRSP has focused its operational practice on the dissemination of research results through its Web site, briefing notes, and conferences. In addition, asset-based assessments and evaluations have assisted policy makers working on such issues as building assets for sustainable recovery and food security in Ethiopia (Little 2002), poverty traps and environmental disasters in Ethiopia and Honduras (Carter and others 2005), and property rights and environmental services in Indonesia (Kerr and others

2005). Most recently, asset-based analysis has identified the extent to which safety net programs in South Africa and Mexico have moved beyond consumption needs to address asset accumulation.

ASSET BUILDING. One of the most developed asset approaches is the U.S. asset-building or asset-based policy. Originally termed *asset-based welfare policy* and developed in 1991 by Michael Sherraden (1991) of Washington University in St. Louis, Missouri, it is based on two simple premises: first, that the poor can save and accumulate assets, and second, that assets have positive social, psychological, and civic effects independent of the effects of income (Boshara and Sherraden 2004). In his original work, Sherraden distinguished between assets (identified as the stock of wealth in a household) and income (the flows of resources associated with consumption of goods and services and standard of living). He argued that welfare policy for the poor had been constructed almost exclusively in terms of income, and he proposed that it be based instead on the concepts of savings, investment, and asset accumulation (see Sherraden 1991: box 2.3). In his "persuasive argument" for a policy shift from income to assets, Sherraden (1991: 6–9) argued that income only maintains consumption, but assets change the way people think and interact with the world. With assets, people begin to think in the long term and pursue long-term goals. In other words, while incomes feed people's stomachs, assets change their heads. Sherraden maintained that welfare policy has gone off track in becoming almost exclusively preoccupied with the income protection of the poor; in contrast, it should seek to empower as well as to protect. In particular, policy should take into account the critical role of asset accumulation in economic and social well-being. This will ensure that we no longer implicitly believe that the poor not only have no wealth, but that they can have no wealth.

Sherraden's research in the United States shows that saving and accumulation are shaped by institutions, not merely by individual preference. The poor are not only asset poor but have few institutional structures within which to accumulate assets. For impoverished welfare recipients, asset accumulation is not encouraged, or even permitted; the "asset test" associated with means-tested income transfer programs preventing the accumulation of more than minimal financial assets. By contrast, an extensive range of asset-based policies exist, operating mainly through the tax system, such as home ownership tax benefits, and 401(k)s.[31] Thus, asset-based welfare policy is designed to promote and institutionalize asset accumulation through a progressive (with greater subsidies for the poor), inclusive (asset inequality in the United States is largely racially based),[32] life-long, and flexible approach (Sherraden 1991).

Since 1991, this AB framework has been effectively translated into operational practice through the piloting of a range of programs aimed at broadening asset ownership in the United States and, more recently, the United Kingdom. Best known in the United States is the American Dream Individual Development Account (IDA) Demonstration, with 300 IDA programs throughout the country—supporting 15,000 account holders. These are matched saving accounts with resources to match contributions by low-income families achieved through a blend of public and private funding (Boshara 2005). Linked to this are functions for community organizations providing financial education, setting IDA balance targets, and matching contributions. Withdrawals are typically restricted to the purchase of assets, such as buying a home, pursuing postsecondary education and training, and starting a small business. Recent evaluations provide evidence that participants can successfully save in structured accounts.[33] This has been instrumental in moving forward federal IDA legislation. At the same time, there is no evidence that IDAs raise the net worth (assets minus debts) of savers (Lerman 2005). However, supporters of this approach argue that, even if accumulations are not large, savers start saving early and enjoy the benefits of compounding: "what matters is not the amount, but the existence of accumulation" (Boshara 2005: 1).

Influenced by the experience in the United States, similar initiatives have been launched in the United Kingdom, including the Child Trust Fund, established as a long-term savings and investment account for every child born since September 2002.[34] In the United Kingdom, opinions vary about asset-based welfare. Proponents argue that such policy is a mechanism for curbing rising inequality and improving the life chances of the vulnerable. Critics doubt the effectiveness of AB policy tools, fearing that they could undermine the established welfare state by transferring responsibilities to individuals and households, and argue that wealth redistribution is more efficiently achieved through reforms to inheritance tax (Maxwell 2005).

ALTERNATIVE BOTTOM-UP COMMUNITY ASSET-BUILDING PROGRAMS. A number of operational programs in both the North and South have extended the AB concept beyond individuals and households to incorporate community assets. They have also shifted from a somewhat Northern "top-down" concern, with the problems of "apathy" of an alienated welfare dependent population, to a "bottom-up," demand-driven approach.

Foremost among these is the Ford Foundation's Asset Building and Community Development Program,[35] which is designed to "reduce poverty and injustice." Building on the work of Sherraden, Sen, Putnam, and others, this asset framework assumes that, when low-income people gain control over assets, they gain the independence necessary to resist oppression, to pursue productive livelihoods, and to confront injustice (Ford Foundation 2004). The program proposes that an asset offers a way out of poverty because it is not simply consumed; it is a "stock" that endures and can be used to generate economic, psychological, social, and political benefits that foster resilience and social mobility. The program highlights inequalities in asset distribution across race, ethnicity, and gender, and it supports grantees in building assets that communities can acquire, develop, or transfer across generations. This includes financial holdings, natural resources, social bonds and community relations, and human assets such as marketable skills. Despite the identification of five pathways[36] for building capabilities for "scalability" that enable large numbers of people and institutions to build assets,[37] there are still formidable barriers in getting to scale.

Along with AB programs, participatory methodologies have been developed to operationalize a community, AB approach. For instance, the Coady International Institute in Nova Scotia, Canada, has designed the Asset-Based Community Development (ABCD), a "transformative" methodology to motivate community leaders to identify assets, to link their mobilization for community activities, and to strengthen their capacity to sustain economic and social development over the longer term (Mathie and Cunningham 2003). Morad Associates has designed an asset mapping methodology as a tool to map community assets and begin the process of building assets (Morad 2003). This has been used in participatory community assessments in private sector companies, such as Shell in their operations in Oman, South Africa, and the United States (Fossgard-Moser 2005).

EMERGING AGENDAS. Building on AB approaches, recent research has provided further AB conceptualizations. The World Bank (2005) Social Development Strategy, for example, states, "Development interventions need to build both assets and improve returns to the assets by transforming social and economic institutions" (2005: 2). The 2000 *World Development Report* on poverty (World Bank 2000) noted that empowerment was directly linked to the expansion of assets. Thus, Narayan states, "Empowerment is the expansion of assets and capabilities of poor people to participate in, negotiate with, influence, control and hold accountable institutions that affect their lives" (2005: 5). Finally, recent analytical work by Alsop, Bertelsen, and Holland (2006) that sought to measure empowerment argues that this is primarily influenced by agency[38] and opportunity structure.[39] Here, asset endowments are used as indicators of agency (that is, a person or group's agency is indicated in large part by their asset endowment), with assets extended to include psychological (Appadurai 2004; Nussbaum 2000), informational, organizational, and material assets.

## Asset-Based Social Policy

This section concludes by showing how assets provide an entry point for cutting-edge development issues and how an AB approach provides a useful contribution to a "new agenda" for social policy on both analytical and political grounds.

### Asset-Based Approaches and Asset Accumulation

As discussed, a range of livelihood and asset-related frameworks, using concepts such as assets, institutions, agency, and opportunities, have already been developed, with differences in objectives determining the relative emphasis on such concepts as well as the associated operational frameworks. Table 2.3 provides a brief summary of these. The greatest difference between AB social policy and previous approaches is its direct focus on creating opportunities for asset accumulation. In addition, the objective of a number of current asset-specific approaches is empowerment (Alsop, Bertelsen, and Holland 2006; Bennett 2003; Narayan 2005). AB social policy identifies asset accumulation as a pre-condition for empowerment, particularly economic empowerment. In this sense, empowerment is the outcome, rather than the means, of poverty reduction (see Alsop, Bertelsen, and Holland 2006).

**Table 2.3. Recent Policy Approaches to Poverty Reduction and Associated Objectives**

| Policy approach | Primary objectives |
| --- | --- |
| Sustainable livelihood approach | Sustaining activities required for a means of living |
| Social protection | Provision of protection for the poor and vulnerable against negative risks and shocks that erode their assets |
| Asset-based social policy | Creation of positive opportunities for asset accumulation |

Source: Moser 2007: 91.

Recent policy-focused research in Guayaquil, Ecuador, on long-term asset accumulation, including intergenerational asset transfers, shows how the accumulation potential of assets depends on the interrelationship between a household's original investment asset portfolio, the broader context at both life-cycle and politico-economic level that provides the opportunity structure, and the wider institutional environment (Moser and Felton 2007).[40]

The research project developed an asset index to categorize the range of assets that individuals and households acquire, the processes by which each accumulates or erodes over time, and the relative importance of different assets in terms of intergenerational poverty reduction. Research data from a 26-year panel data set examines the rate at which different types of capital grew and the investment choices households made. Preliminary analysis shows that from 1978 to 1992 housing grew the fastest, then education, then consumption. However, the rates were in reverse order from 1992 to 2004. Once housing is established, parents make trade-offs between their own consumption and their children's education as a strategy for poverty reduction in the long term (see figure 2.1).

## The Components of Asset-Based Social Policy

AB social policy focuses on creating opportunities for long-term asset accumulation. Given this specific objective, its associated framework incorporates an iterative asset-institutions-opportunities nexus (see figure 2.2).

**Figure 2.1. Asset Building Over Time in Guayaquil, Ecuador**

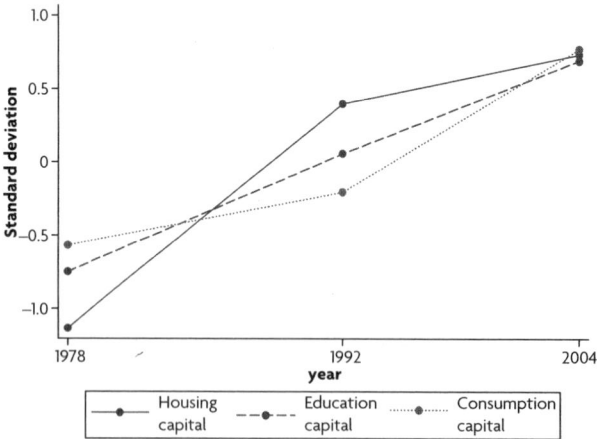

Source: Adapted from Moser and Felton 2007.

**Figure 2.2. Components of Asset-Based Social Policy**

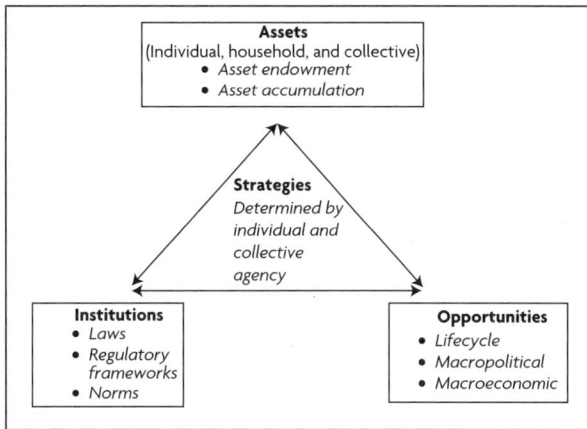

**Assets**
(Individual, household, and collective)
- *Asset endowment*
- *Asset accumulation*

**Strategies**
*Determined by individual and collective agency*

**Institutions**
- *Laws*
- *Regulatory frameworks*
- *Norms*

**Opportunities**
- *Lifecycle*
- *Macropolitical*
- *Macroeconomic*

*Source:* Moser 2007: 94.

The process by which the assets with which individuals and households are endowed and transformed into accumulated assets does not take place in a vacuum. It is closely tied to the wider context in terms of both prevailing institutions and opportunities. In addition, accumulation of one asset often results in the accumulation of others; similarly, insecurity in one can affect other assets. While a detailed description of the interlocking relationships within such a nexus still requires further research and analysis, the basic principles include the following:

- Institutions are the laws, norms, and regulatory frameworks that, in a variety of ways, either block or provide access or positively facilitate asset accumulation.
- Simultaneously, opportunities, namely the formal and informal context within which actors operate, can provide an enabling environment within which asset accumulation occurs. This relates not only to the dynamics of micro-level household lifecycles but also to meso-level and macro-level market opportunities and constraints relating to the broader political and economic context.
- The actual strategy, whether it is termed *livelihood, coping,* or *survival,* can best be identified as the means by which social actors transform endowed assets into accumulated assets. This process is determined by both individual and collective agency. In some contexts, the lack of returns on individual assets and capabilities has resulted in initiatives based on collective agency.

- Entry points to strengthen strategies for asset accumulation are context specific but may be institutional or opportunity-related in focus.

### Distinction between First- and Second-Generation Asset-Based Social Policy[41]

Asset-based social policy is not static but changes over time. Complementing Dani's differentiation among asset accession, valorization, and transformation (chapter 1), a useful distinction can be made between what can be termed *first-* and *second*-generation policy. First-generation asset-based policy provides the social and economic infrastructure essential for assets such as human capital, physical capital (such as housing), and financial capital (durable goods). The common assumption is that these provide the pre-condition for individuals and households to further accumulate on their own and move out of poverty. Thus, current poverty reduction policies still focus almost exclusively on such first-generation strategies, including the provision of water, roads and electricity, housing plots, better health and education, and microfinance. Once these provisions are made, it is assumed that well-being improves and development will occur. However, as important as these are for asset accumulation, the pre-conditions necessary for such accumulation do not necessarily materialize. For instance, when such strategies do not bring the expected development returns and increased human capital (higher education levels and health) and do not result in the expected job opportunities, rising aspirations and growing despair undoubtedly lead to increasing violence, exclusion, and alienation.

Second-generation asset-based policy is designed to strengthen accumulated assets and to ensure their further consolidation and prevent erosion. Given the traditional micro-level focus on assets, this is particularly important in the dramatically globalizing institutional context.

New development opportunities may be accompanied by risks from global warming and natural disasters, corruption, failing states and post-conflict contexts, accelerated urbanization, increasing inequality, and growing violence. In the absence of governance, accountability, and security, returns on assets may not be achieved, and, consequently, the UN Millennium Development Goals (MDGs) may not be met. Second-generation asset-based policy, therefore, needs to make more coherent links between a rapidly changing macro (economic or political) context and the imperative of fulfilling the MDGs through asset accumulation that achieves structural transformations rather than the stochastic changes identified earlier (see Carter and Barrett 2006).

Such strategies need to go beyond issues of welfare and poverty reduction to address concerns relating to citizen rights and security, governance, and the accountability of institutions.[42] A provisional set of recommendations deriving from the Guayaquil research project includes the following:

- strengthening social justice through the judicial system, including a broader range of preventative and punitive interventions
- empowering local communities to access information about legal, economic, and social rights
- identifying appropriate institutional structures for strengthening the financial capital in households that have got out of poverty but are still highly vulnerable
- developing city-level employment strategies to ensure that the gains in human capital are not eroded.

Ultimately, the details of such interventions are context specific. These may include the asset-building, productive opportunities associated with international migration; the monitoring of informal institutions often accountable for asset redistribution in the absence of state governance structures in failing states;[43] and the largely ignored asset accumulation aspects of human settlements that include access to legal frameworks for land titles. The importance of incorporating second-generation asset-based social policy relates to the underlying issues essential for development itself, including the rule of law and citizenship.

## Concluding Comments

This chapter has discussed the comparative contributions to social policy of a body of literature relating to two important poverty reduction frameworks: sustainable livelihoods and asset building. These two approaches provide the analytical and operational background for the formulation of a specific asset-based social policy. It is important to note that at this stage the elaboration of its principles and associated components is very tentative and requires further development on the basis of longitudinal research on asset accumulation. This will confirm whether a framework that identifies an assets-opportunities-institutions nexus provides robust operational entry points to assist poor individuals, households, and communities in achieving long-term asset accumulation, not only to move out of but also to stay out of poverty.

**Annex 2.1. Summary Review of Models of Social Policy in the South, with Some Associated Northern Influences** (in italics)

| Macro-economic model | Social policy model | Primary institutions | Comments |
|---|---|---|---|
| Modernization (1940s–1960s) | Residual Welfare | Weak social welfare government ministries<br>Voluntary organizations with main social welfare burden | Originally introduced by colonial governments<br>Social need through individual effort in the marketplace<br>Government dealt with deviant behavior and when normal structures of supply, family, and market break down |
| *Western Capitalism* | *Institutional* | *Sector ministries* | *Introduced in advanced economies; welfare as an entitlement based on citizenship; comprehensive universal, statutory state provision of medical care, education, housing, and income security* |
| Failure of modernization trickle down (1960s–1970s) | Incremental | Sector ministries | Southern version to replicate institutional model on incremental basis with gradual extension/expansion of existing provision of social services along with increase in budgetary allocation.<br>Assumes budget expansions based on expanding economies: c.f./role of donors; no questioning of relevance of local needs |
| *Western Socialism* | *Structural* | *State provision* | *Welfare defined as the distribution of needs is central social value; satisfaction of needs on basis of equality as main aim of production and distribution; to each according to his need—universal, comprehensive, and free social services of health and education*<br>Goal of many socialist countries in South |

| | | | |
|---|---|---|---|
| Redistribution with Growth (linked to eradication of poverty) | Basic needs | Project level "count-cost-carry" for external provision of goods and services that might/might not alleviate poverty | Needs-based targeted interventions—rather than national policy (except for Sri Lanka)<br>Debate about basic needs as means—conservative anti-poverty program with piecemeal reform within existing international economic order<br>Basic needs as an end—mutually reinforcing set of policies involving structural change |
| Economic Reform and Structural Adjustment (1980s–1990s) | Compensatory safety nets such as social funds | State, private sector, and NGOs<br>Decentralized coverage | Shift from universal comprehensive to targeted compensatory measures to compensate new poor as well as cushion impacts for borderline and chronic poor<br>Concern with efficiency of financing and delivery mechanisms |
| Globalization (1990s–2000s) | Social justice, citizenship, and global human rights as framework for rights-based approach | IFIs—promotion of private welfare systems<br>International pressure for collective interventions | Governments exposed to international trade that then have larger governments and higher social protection expenditures<br>Increased recognition of exclusion on basis of gender, ethnicity, race, and religion<br>Also of holistic social policy that includes integrated livelihoods approach, participatory approaches to identification of needs, human security, and social integration |

**Annex 2.2. Sustainable Livelihood Framework**

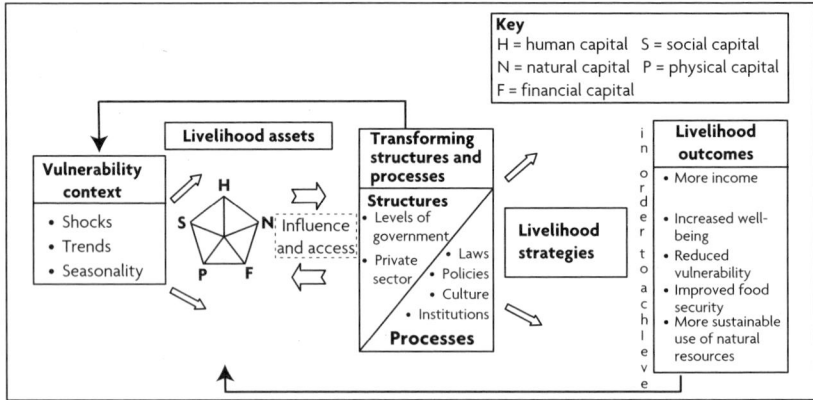

Key
H = human capital   S = social capital
N = natural capital   P = physical capital
F = financial capital

Vulnerability context
- Shocks
- Trends
- Seasonality

Livelihood assets

H S N P F

Influence and access

Transforming structures and processes

Structures
- Levels of government
- Private sector

Processes
- Laws
- Policies
- Culture
- Institutions

Livelihood strategies

in order to achieve

Livelihood outcomes
- More income
- Increased well-being
- Reduced vulnerability
- Improved food security
- More sustainable use of natural resources

*Source:* Ashley and Carney 1999: 5.

## Notes

1. An *epistemic community* is a network of knowledge-based experts or groups with an authoritative claim to policy-relevant knowledge within the domain of their expertise. Members hold a common set of causal beliefs and share notions of validity based on internally defined criteria for evaluation, common policy projects, and shared normative commitments (Haas 1992)

2. One of the earliest reviews of social development policy in the South was undertaken by Hardiman and Midgely (1982). Complementing this during the same period in the North was Mishra's (1981) study of social policy and welfare. More recent reviews that focus on the South include de Haan (2004), Ghai (1997), Kabeer (2004), Moser (1992, 1995), and the IDS (2000). Extensive literature reviews on global social/welfare policy include Deacon (1997) and Gough and Wood (2004).

3. See Kabeer (2004) for a review of the shifting meaning of the *social* in development discourse.

4. Here it is useful to differentiate between those who identify social policy as originating and remaining primarily associated with advanced industrial economies of the North (Kabeer and Cook 2000) and those who emphasize the way social policy has increasingly been formulated as a Southern construct. A timely example from Latin America was the development of social policy as a "social contract" that resulted from highly negative assessments of the social costs of structural adjustment in the 1990s (see Birdsall 2002).

5. Another summary of the scope of social policy provided by Devereux and Cook (2000) includes the entire range from social sectors through social insurance, social protection, and social services to social rights.

6. In a recent review of social policy/social development in the World Bank, Hall identifies three "lines of social policy," with the related activities institutionally located in distinct and sometimes overlapping parts of the organization. Thus, he distinguishes between social welfare services such as education, health, and nutrition located in the Human Development Network; social protection and the construction of targeted safety nets and safeguard policies to protect the weak and vulnerable located in Poverty Reduction and Economic Management, Human Development, and Social Development Vice-Presidency; and social development as a "collection of diverse issues not captured by other sections of the Bank and located in SDV." These include participation and civic engagement, empowerment, community-driven development, conflict prevention, and youth (Hall 2005).

7. Since this chapter was completed in 2006, further analytical and associated operational work has been undertaken on the distinction between asset building as a northern construct and asset accumulation policy as a policy in its own right particularly focused on southern, developing countries. For a detailed elaboration of the case for asset accumulation policy, see Moser (2007).

8. This section draws on Moser (1998).

9. These have been usefully summarized in terms of two "polarized" alternative approaches to poverty (Baulch 1996). First, a "conventional," "objective" approach identified income/consumption as the best proxy for poverty (Ravallion 1992), usually measured through large-scale, random sample household surveys. Second, a "subjective," "participatory" approach rejected the income/consumption approach as a narrow reductionist view, which the technocratic needs of development professionals while failing to understand the complex, diverse, local realities in which the poor live (Chambers 1992, 1994). The "participatory" approach used multiple, subjective indicators of poverty status that emerge out of the poors' reality, which collected through participatory techniques.

10. At the core of this "new poverty" focus is the issue of risk. *Insecurity* is defined as exposure to risk, with vulnerability the resulting outcome in terms of a decline in well-being (World Bank 1990, 2000).

11. In 1990, the World Bank attacked poverty with the so-called two and a half legs of labor-intensive growth and human capital, with safety nets as the poor relation; by 2000, poverty reduction strategy identified the three legs of opportunity, empowerment, and security (World Bank 1990, 2000).

12. Recent researchers have extended this list to include an extensive range of further assets, such as the capacity to aspire (Appadurai 2004) and psychological assets (Alsop, Bertelsen, and Holland 2006). However, the five capital assets identified in box 2.1 as human, social, natural, physical, and financial capital

are firmly grounded in empirical research, which means that they can be quantitatively measured. This characteristic is essential when introducing such concepts to policymakers. This has been well demonstrated by a decade of recent research focusing on the quantification of social capital (see Grootaert and van Bastelaer 2002).

13. This section draws from Moser and Norton (2001).

14. Although originally developed as a rural framework, it was subsequently used as a people-centered approach to reduce poverty in urban contexts (see Rakodi 2002).

15. The *Oxford English Dictionary* shows that the term has been used since the 16th century, with its meaning changing over time from lifetime; manner of life (1581) through income; revenue (1621) and property yielding an income; inheritance (1627) to means of living; and maintenance (1688). It is useful to note the difference between the term as used descriptively and its specific meaning in the SL framework. Along with the changing poverty debate, researchers have themselves shifted in the terminology used to identify the strategies of the poor. This shift is reflected in my own work on urban poverty in Guayaquil, Ecuador. While in the late 1970s I called them "survival" strategies, by the 1990s, I had changed to the term "coping" strategies.

16. For a comparison of the differences in use of livelihood approaches between DFID, CARE, Oxfam, and UNDP, see Carney and others (1999).

17. For further elaboration see Carney (2002); Norton and Foster (2001); Shankland (2000); and Solesbury (2003).

18. PIP is the abbreviation for policies, institutions, and processes, which was given by DFID to the box on "Transforming structures and processes" in the Sustainable Livelihood Framework diagram (see annex 2.2).

19. In fact, DFID itself has since recognized the complexity of the politics of development and has initiated a distinct "Drivers of Change" program that seeks to address many of the issues it was previously assumed a PIP box could encompass (see DFID 2005).

20. For instance, as shown by a recent policy paper, DFID has now shifted its focus from livelihoods to social exclusion (DFID 2005).

21. Certainly those working on rural development continue to find it a useful analytical and operational framework, as demonstrated by a recent *World Development* special issue on livelihoods, forests, and conservation (World Development 2005).

22. A human rights and livelihoods matrix, for instance, identifies from the extensive range of human rights texts those rights that are of particular importance for sustainable livelihoods. The matrix categorizes them according to an expanded typology of capital assets (adding the political domain to the five forms of capital assets listed [see box 2.1]) (Moser and Norton 2001).

23. Originally defined in the *Oxford English Dictionary* as "sufficient estate or effects" (1531) and extended to "all the property a person has that may be liable for his or their debt" (1675).

24. This section draws on Moser (1998). See also Davies (1993), Devereux (1993), and Maxwell and Smith (1992).

25. *Vulnerability* is defined as exposure to hazard or risk and the ability to manage risks stemming from such exposure (Moser 1998; Sabates-Wheeler and Haddad 2005).

26. In this early categorization of assets, I distinguished among labor, human capital, productive assets (which for the urban poor is most frequently housing), household relations, and social capital.

27. For an extensive literature on the construction and measurement of asset indexes, see Adato, Carter, and May (2006); Filmer and Pritchard (1999); and Sahn and Stiefel (2000).

28. BASIS stands for Broadening Access and Strengthening Input Market Systems. The BASIS research program is supported by the United States Agency for International Development and is directed by Michael Carter at the University of Wisconsin–Madison. Linked to it is the Pathways Out of Poverty Program, directed by John Hoddinott at the International Food Policy Research Institute. Anthropological work adopting the same approach has been undertaken by Whitehead (2004).

29. Carter and Barrett (2006) argue that families are unable to educate their children, build up productive assets, and improve economically over time. Poverty traps are most likely to be problematic in areas where markets are thin or weak and families are unable to borrow against future assets to build up their assets.

30. A slightly different variation outlines three steps to combat persistent poverty as follows. First is an increase in the productively of assets, second is facilitating the building and protection of assets required to stay out of poverty, and third is the removal of exclusionary mechanisms that block pathways from poverty for certain segments of the population (BASIS 2004).

31. More than 90 percent goes to households with incomes of more than US$50,000 per year.

32. The ratio of white-to-nonwhite income was 1.5 to 1.0 in 1995 and increasing (Oliver and Shapiro 1990).

33. This was organized by the Corporation for Enterprise Development and the Center for Social Development (Boshara 2005).

34. A further demonstration project in the South has occurred, for instance, in Taiwan (China) where a 200-account Family Development Account Program exists (Boshara and Sherraden 2004).

35. An *asset* is defined as a "stock of financial, human, natural or social resources that can be acquired, developed, improved, and transferred across generations.

It generates flows or consumption, as well as additional stock" (Ford
Foundation 2004: 4).

36. These are identified as developing public policies, fostering communities
of practice, influencing market forces, changing power relationships, and
promoting social learning (Ford Foundation 2004)

37. These include, for instance, creating affordable insurance for low-income
women in India, establishing the Women in Informal Employment Globalizing
and Organizing Network, and strengthening community forest programs.

38. *Agency* is defined as "an actor's ability to make meaningful choices" (Alsop
and Heinsohn 2005: 6).

39. *Opportunity structure* is defined here as the formal and informal contexts within which actors operate. These contexts include laws, regulatory
frameworks, and norms governing people's behavior (Alsop and Heinsohn
2005).

40. These results are drawn from a research project on Intergenerational Asset
Building and Poverty Reduction in Guayaquil, Ecuador, undertaken by the
author. The project is funded by the Ford Foundation in New York.

41. For further elaboration, see Moser (2007)

42. For a recent analysis of the citizenship and the politics of asset distribution, see
Ferguson, Moser, and Norton (2007)

43. See, for instance, research on violence and the erosion of assets (Moser 2004;
Moser and McIlwaine 2004, 2006).

## References

Adato, M., M. Carter, and J. May. 2004. "Sense in Sociability? Social Exclusion
and Persistent Poverty in South Africa." Paper written for BASIS CRSP Workshop, Washington DC, November.
———. 2006. "Exploring Poverty Traps and Social Exclusion in South Africa
Using Qualitative and Quantitative Data." *Journal of Development Studies*
42(2): 226–47.

Alsop, R., M. Bertelsen, and J. Holland. 2006. *Empowerment in Practice: From
Analysis to Implementation.* Washington, DC: World Bank.

Appadurai, A. 1996. *Modernity at Large: Cultural Dimensions of Globalization.*
Minneapolis: University of Minnesota Press.

Appadurai, A. 2004. "The Capacity to Aspire: Culture and the Terms of Recognition." In *Culture and Public Action*, ed. Vijayendra Rao and Michael Walton.
Stanford, CA: Stanford University Press.

Ashley, C., and D. Carney. 1999. *Sustainable Livelihoods: Lessons from Early
Experience.* London: Department of International Development.

Barrett, C., and M. Carter. 2005. "Risk and Asset Management in the Presence of
Poverty Traps: Implications for Growth and Social Protection." In Background

note prepared for World Bank/DFID Project, "Linking Social Protection and Growth: Assessing Empirical Evidence, Developing the Future Agenda," Leuven, Belgium, June 23–24.

BASIS. 2004. "Innovative Development: BASIS CRSP Findings and Policy Recommendations," BASIS Brief No. 27, November, Madison, University of Wisconsin, Department of Agricultural and Applied Economics. Accessible at http://www.basis.wisc.edu.

Baulch, B. 1996. Editorial: "The New Poverty Agency: A Disputed Consensus." *Institute of Development Studies Bulletin* 27: 1–10.

Bebbington, A. 1999. "Capitals and Capabilities: A Framework for Analyzing Peasant Viability, Rural Livelihoods and Poverty." *World Development* 27: 2021–44.

Bennett, L. 2003. "Empowerment and Social Inclusion." Social Development Paper, World Bank, Washington, DC.

Birdsall, N. 2002. "From Social Policy to an Open-Economy Social Contract in Latin America." Working Paper No. 21, Center for Global Development, Washington, DC.

Boas, M., and D. McNeill, eds. 2004. *Global Institutions and Development: Framing the World*. London: Routledge.

Boshara, R. 2005. "Individual Development Accounts: Policies to Build Savings and Assets for the Poor." Policy Brief Welfare Reform and Beyond No. 32. Brookings Institution, Washington, DC.

Boshara, R., and M. Sherraden. 2004. *Status of Asset Building Worldwide*. Briefing document. New America Foundation Asset Building Program, America Foundation, Washington, DC.

Carney, D. 1998. "Implementing the Sustainable Livelihoods Approach." In *Sustainable Rural Livelihoods: What Contribution Can We Make?* ed. D. Carney. London: Department for International Development.

Carney, D., with M. Drinkwater, T. Rusinow, K. Neefjes, S. Wanmali, and N. Singh. 1999. "Livelihood Approaches Compared: A Brief Comparison of the Livelihoods Approaches of the U.K. Department for International Development (DFID), CARE, Oxfam, and the United Nations Development Programme (UNDP)." DFID. Accessible at http://www.livelihoods.org/info/docs/lacv3.pdf.

Carney, D. 2002. *Sustainable Livelihoods Approaches: Progress and Possibilities for Change*. London: Department for International Development.

Carter, M., and C. Barrett. 2006. "The Economics of Poverty-Traps and Persistent Poverty: An Asset-Based Approach." *Journal of Development Studies* 42(2): 178–99.

Carter, M., P. Little, T. Mogues, and W. Negatu. 2005. "The Long-Term Impact of Short-Term Shocks: Poverty Traps and Environmental Disasters in Ethiopia and Honduras." BASIS Brief No. 28, Madison, University of Wisconsin, Department of Agricultural and Applied Economics. Accessible at http://www.basis.wisc.edu.

Chambers, R. 1992. "Poverty and Livelihoods: Whose Reality Counts?" Discussion Paper No. 347, Institute of Development Studies, Brighton, U.K.

———. 1994. "The Origins and Practice of Participatory Rural Appraisal." *World Development* 22: 953–69.

Chambers, R., and G. Conway. 1992. "Sustainable Rural Livelihoods: Practical Concepts for the 21st Century." Discussion Paper No. 296, Institute of Development Studies, Brighton, U.K.

CPRC (Chronic Poverty Research Centre). 2004. *The Chronic Poverty Report 2004–5*. Manchester: University of Manchester, Institute for Development Policy and Management.

Dani, A. 2005. "Concept Note: New Frontiers of Social Policy." Paper prepared for the World Bank Conference, "New Frontiers of Social Policy," Arusha, Tanzania, December.

Davis, G. 2004. "A History of the Social Development Network in the World Bank 1973–2002." Social Development Papers No. 56. World Bank, Washington, DC.

Davies, S. 1993. "Are Coping Strategies a Cop Out?" *Institute of Development Studies Bulletin* 24(4): 60–72.

De Haan, A. 2007. *Reclaiming Social Policy*. New York: Palgrave Macmillan.

Deacon, B. 1997. *Global Social Policy: International Organizations and the Future of Welfare*. London: Sage.

———. 2004. "From Safety Nets Back to Universal Social Provision: Is the Global Tide Turning?" *Global Social Policy* 5(1): 41–62.

Devereux, S. 1993. "Goats before Ploughs: Dilemmas of Household Response Sequencing During Food Shortage." *Institute of Development Studies Bulletin* 24: 52–59.

Devereux, S., and S. Cook. 2000. "Does Social Policy Meet Social Needs?" *Institute of Development Studies Bulletin* 31(4): 63–73.

DFID (Department of International Development). 1997. "Eliminating World Poverty: A Challenge for the 21st Century." White Paper on International Development, Cm 3789. Stationary Office, London.

———. 2000. *Sustainable Livelihoods—Current Thinking and Practice*. London. DFID.

———. 2005. "Reducing Poverty by Tackling Social Exclusion." Policy Paper, DFID, London.

Ferguson, C., C. Moser, and A. Norton. 2007. "Claiming Rights: Citizenship and the Politics of Asset Distribution." In *Reducing Global Poverty: The Case for Asset Accumulation*, ed. C. Moser. Washington, DC: Brookings Press.

Filmer, D., and L. Pritchard. 1999. "The Effect of Household Wealth on Educational Attainment: Evidence from 35 Countries" *Population and Development Review* 25 (1): 85–120.

Ford Foundation. 2004. *Building Assets to Reduce Poverty and Injustice.* New York: Ford Foundation.

———. n.d. *Asset Building for Social Change: Pathways to Large-Scale Impact.* New York: Ford Foundation.

Fossgard-Moser, T. 2005. "Social Performance: Key Lesson from Recent Experiences within Shell." *Journal of Corporate Governance* 5(3): 105–18.

Ghai, D. 1997. "Social Development and Public Policy: Some Lessons from Successful Experience." Discussion Paper No. 89, United Nations Research Institute for Social Development, Geneva.

Gough, I., and G. Wood, eds. 2004. *Insecurity and Welfare Regimes in Asia, Africa, and Latin America.* Cambridge: Cambridge University Press.

Grootaert, C., and T. van Bastelaer, eds. 2002. *Understanding and Measuring Social Capital: A Multidisciplinary Tool for Practitioners.* Washington, DC: World Bank.

Haas, P. 1992. "Introduction: Epistemic Communities and International Policy Co-ordination." *International Organization* 46(1): 377–403.

Hall, A. 2005. "Widening Horizons? Social Development and Social Policy in the World Bank." Paper presented at Economic and Social Research Council seminar on definitions, concepts, and theories. Institute for the Study of the Americas, London, June.

Hardiman, M., and J. Midgley. 1982. *The Social Dimensions of Development: Social Policy and Planning in the Third World.* New York: John Wiley and Sons.

Hoddinott, J., A. Quisumbing, A. de Janvry, and T. Woldehanna. 2005. "Pathways from Poverty: Evaluating Long-Term Strategies to Reduce Poverty." BASIS CRSP Brief No. 30, Madison, University of Wisconsin, Department of Agricultural and Applied Economics. Accessible at http://www.basis.wisc.edu.

Holtzmann, R., and S. Jorgensen. 2000. "Social Risk Management: A New Conceptual Framework for Social Protection and Beyond." Social Protection Discussion Paper No. 0006, World Bank, Washington, DC.

IDS (Institute of Development Studies). 2000. "Social Policy in the South: Revisioning the Agenda." *Institute of Development Studies Bulletin* 31(4).

Kabeer, N. 2001. "Reflections on the Measurement of Women's Empowerment." In Sida Studies No. 3, *Discussing Women's Empowerment: Theory and Practice.* Stockholm, Sweden: Novum Grafiska AB.

Kabeer, N. 2004. "Revisioning 'The Social': Towards a Citizen-Centred Social Policy for the Poor in Poor Countries." Working Paper No. 19, Institute of Development Studies, Brighton, U.K.

Kabeer, N., and S. Cook. 2000. "Editorial Introduction—Revisioning Social Policy in the South: Challenges and Concepts." *Institute of Development Studies Bulletin* 31(4).

Kerr, J., R. Meinzen-Dick, J. Pender, Suyanto, B. Swallow, and M. Van Noordwijk. 2005. "Property Rights, Environmental Service and Poverty in Indonesia."

BASIS Brief No. 29, May, Madison, University of Wisconsin, Department of Agricultural and Applied Economics. Accessible at http://www.basis.wisc.edu.

Lerman, R. 2005. "Are Low-Income Households Accumulating Assets and Avoiding Unhealthy Debt?" Opportunities and Ownership Project No. 1, The Urban Institute, Washington, DC.

Little, P. 2002. "Building Assets for Sustainable Recovery and Food Security" BASIS Brief No. 5, January, Madison, University of Wisconsin, Department of Agricultural and Applied Economics. Accessible at http://www.basis.wisc.edu.

Longhurst, H. 1994. "Conceptual Frameworks for Linking Relief and Development." *Institute of Development Studies Bulletin* 25(4): 21–23.

Marsden, D. 1990. "The Meaning of Social Development." In *Evaluating Social Development Projects, Development Guidelines 5*, ed. D. Marsden and P. Oakley. Oxford: Oxfam

Mathie, A., and G. Cunningham. 2003. "Who Is Driving Development? Reflections on the Transformative Potential of Asset-Based Community Development." Occasional Paper Series No. 5, St. Francis Xavier University, N.C., Canada.

Maxwell, D. 2005. *Challenges for Asset Building in the U.K.* London: Institute for Public Policy Research.

Maxwell, S., and S. Smith. 1992. "Household Food Security: A Conceptual Review." In *Household Food Security: Concepts, Indicators, Measurements*, ed. S. Maxwell and T. Frankenberger. Rome and New York: International Fund for Agricutural Development and UNICEF.

Mishra, R. 1981. *Society and Social Policy: Theories and Practice of Welfare.* London: Macmillan.

Morad, M. 2003. "Mobilizing Community Assets." Washington, DC: One World Economy.

Moser, C. 1992. "From Residual Welfare to Compensatory Measures: The Changing Agenda of Social Policy in Developing Countries." Silver Jubilee Paper No. 6, Institute of Development Studies, Brighton, U.K.

———. 1995. "Urban Social Policy and Poverty Reduction." *Environment and Urbanization* 7(1): 159–72.

———. 1996. "Confronting Crisis: A Comparative Study of Household Responses to Poverty and Vulnerability in Four Poor Urban Communities." Environmentally Sustainable Development Studies and Monograph Series No. 8, World Bank, Washington, DC.

———. 1998. "The Asset Vulnerability Framework: Reassessing Urban Poverty Reduction Strategies." *World Development* 26(1): 1–19.

———. 2001. "Insecurity and Social Protection: Has the World Bank Got It Right?" *Journal of International Development* 13: 361–68.

———. 2004. "'Urban Violence and Insecurity: An Introductory Roadmap' Editor's introduction." *Environment and Urbanization* 16(2): 3–16.

———. 2005. "The Development Implications of Daily Violence in Indio Guayas, Guayaquil." Respondent's Comments, International Workshop on Youth Violence in Latin America, London School of Economics, May 18.

———. 2007. "Asset Accumulation Policy and Poverty Reduction." In *Reducing Global Poverty: The Case for Asset Accumulation*, ed. C. Moser. Washington, DC: Brookings Press.

Moser, C., and A. Felton. 2007. "Intergenerational Asset Accumulation and Poverty Reduction in Guayaquil Ecuador (1978–2004)." In R*educing Global Poverty: The Case for Asset Accumulation*, ed. C. Moser. Washington, DC: Brookings Press.

Moser, C., and C. McIlwaine. 2004. *Encounters with Violence in Latin America: Urban Poor Perceptions from Colombia and Guatemala.* London and New York: Routledge.

———. 2006 "Latin American Urban Violence as a Development Concern: Towards a Framework for Violence Reduction." *World Development* 34(1): 89–112

Moser, C., and A. Norton. 2001. *To Claim Our Right: Livelihood Security, Human Rights and Sustainable Development.* London: Overseas Development Institute.

Narayan, D. 1997. "Voices of the Poor: Poverty and Social Capital in Tanzania." Environmentally and Socially Sustainable Development Studies and Monograph Series No. 20, World Bank, Washington, DC.

———. 2005. "Conceptual Frameworks and Methodological Challenges." In *Measuring Empowerment: Cross-Disciplinary Perspectives,* ed. D. Narayan. Washington, DC: World Bank.

Norton, A., and M. Foster. 2001. "The Potential of Using Sustainable Livelihoods Approaches in Poverty Reduction Strategy Papers." DFID Discussion Paper, Overseas Development Institute, London.

Nussbaum, M. 2000. *Women and Human Development: The Capabilities Approach.* Cambridge: Cambridge University Press.

Oliver, M., and T. Shapiro. 1990. "Wealth of a Nation: A Reassessment of Asset Inequality in America Shows at Least One Third of Households Are Asset Poor." *American Journal of Economics and Sociology* 49: 129–51.

Planning Institute of Jamaica. 2002. *Jamaica 2015: A Framework and Action Plan for Improving Effectiveness, Collaboration and Accountability in the Delivery of Social Policy.* Kingston, Jamaica: Planning Institute of Jamaica.

Portes, A. 1998. "Social Capital: Its Origins and Applications in Modern Sociology." *American Review of Sociology* 24(1): 1–24.

Putnam, R. 1993. *Making Democracy Work: Civic Traditions in Modern Italy.* Princeton, NJ: Princeton University Press.

Rakodi, C. 1999. "A Capital Assets Framework for Analyzing Household Livelihood Strategies: Implication for Policy." *Development Policy Review* 17: 315–42.

———. ed. 2002. *Urban Livelihoods: A People-Centered Approach to Reducing Poverty*. London: Earthscan.

Ravallion, M. 1992. "Poverty Comparison: A Guide to Concepts and Methods." Living Standards Measurement Study Working Paper 88, World Bank, Washington, DC.

Sabates-Wheeler, R., and L. Haddad. 2005. *Reconciling Different Concepts of Risk and Vulnerability: A Review of Donor Documents*. Sussex: Institute of Development Studies.

Sahn, D., and D. Stiefel. 2000. "Assets as a Measurement of Household Welfare in Developing Countries." Working Paper 00-11, Centre for Social Development, Washington University, Washington.

Scoones, I. 1998. "Sustainable Rural Livelihoods: A Framework for Analysis." Working Paper No. 72, Brighton, Institute of Development Studies, U.K.

Sen, A. 1981. *Poverty and Famines: An Essay on Entitlement and Deprivation*. Oxford: Clarendon Press.

———. 1997. Editorial: "Human Capital and Human Capability." *World Development* 25(12).

———. 1999. *Development as Freedom*. Oxford: Oxford University Press.

Shankland, A. 2000. "Analyzing Policy for Sustainable Livelihoods." Research Report No. 49, Institute of Development Studies, Brighton, U.K.

Sherraden, M. 1991. *Assets and the Poor: A New American Welfare Policy*. Armonk, New York: M. E. Sharpe.

Siegel, P. 2005. "Using an Asset-Based Approach to Identify Drivers of Sustainable Rural Growth and Poverty Reduction in Central America: A Conceptual Framework." Environmentally and Socially Sustainable Development Policy Research Working Paper 3475, World Bank, Washington, DC.

Solesbury, W. 2003. "Sustainable Livelihoods: A Case Study of the Evolution of DFID Policy." Overseas Development Institute Working Paper No. 217, Overseas Development Institute, London.

UNDP (United Nations Development Programme). 2003. *Human Development Report*. New York: United Nations.

United Nations. 1971. *1970 Report on the World Social Situation*. New York: United Nations.

Whitehead, A. 2004. "Persistent Poverty in Upper East Ghana." BASIS Brief No. 26, November, Madison, University of Wisconsin, Department of Agricultural and Applied Economics. Accessible at http://www.basis.wisc.edu.

World Bank. 1990. *World Development Report 1990: Poverty*. New York: Oxford University Press.

———. 2000. *World Development Report 2000/01: Attacking Poverty*. Washington, DC: World Bank.

———. 2005. "Empowering People by Transforming Institutions: Social Development in World Bank Operations." Washington, DC: World Bank.

World Development. 2005. *Special Issue on Livelihoods, Forests, and Conservation* 33(7).

World Commission on Environment and Development (Bruntland Commission). 1987. *Our Common Future: Report of the Commission on Environment and Development.* Oxford: Oxford University Press.

PART II

# MIGRATION AS A LIVELIHOOD AND
# ASSET ACCUMULATION STRATEGY

# CHAPTER 3

# International Migration and Challenges for Social Policy: The Case of Ecuador

*Anthony Hall*

International migration has become an increasingly important component of people's livelihood strategies in the developing world.[1] According to the United Nations (UN), there are currently about 200 million international migrants, some two-thirds of whom have sought employment in industrialized countries (GCIM 2005). Nearly 20 million migrants are nationals of Latin America and the Caribbean (LAC). Of these, 7 million reside legally in the United States; three million in the LAC region; and 10 million elsewhere, including Australia, Canada, Europe, and Japan (IOM 2005). Migration has climbed to the top of the global policy agenda due to its sheer scale, as well as to a convergence of interests between North and South. Growing numbers of people from poorer countries view overseas migration as their only hope of securing a higher standard of living. Overall, workers' remittances are now the largest source of overseas income after direct foreign investment. Industrial countries themselves are increasingly dependent on immigrants as their indigenous populations age and domestic labor supplies diminish, especially for less desirable, manual occupations. Furthermore, security concerns following 9/11 have highlighted immigration controls in the United States and Europe.

Yet for all its current economic and political weight, migration has not been granted commensurate space on the social policy agenda. Through a case study of Ecuador, this chapter will first trace the evolution of international migration and look at the major economic and social impacts on migrants and their families back home. Second, it will examine the role and impacts of international migration in three key areas relevant to social policy: livelihood support, social welfare/protection, and asset building. Third, it will consider the mediating institutional responses in Ecuador to this growing phenomenon on the part of government, civil society, and the private sector and then explore the implications for addressing key social policy issues in the three key areas mentioned.

## International Migration from Ecuador

Emigration from Ecuador to the United States and República Bolivariana de Venezuela dates back to the 1940s and 1950s but has risen sharply since the economic crisis of the late 1990s, giving rise to a wave of "new emigration" (Jokisch and Pribilsky 2002). By 2004, as many as two million Ecuadorans (15 percent of the total population) were working overseas. Some 550,000 workers or one-fifth of the labor force have left the country since 1999 (CEPLAES 2005; IOM 2005). Emigration peaked in 2000 but dropped due to controls introduced by the European Union (EU), and especially by Spain, following 9/11 (see figure 3.1). Harsh economic conditions since the 1990s have been instrumental in driving people overseas as a direct response to growing poverty and the lack of economic opportunities at home, reflected in substantially increased rates of open urban unemployment and underemployment. For the first time, middle-income urban groups found themselves in conditions of relative poverty not previously experienced as their monetary incomes fell. Political instability, public mismanagement and frequent crises have compounded this situation. If dealing with poor governance is a fact of daily life to be endured for many, others choose quite literally to vote with their feet.

**Figure 3.1. Net Migration from Ecuador, 1990–2004**

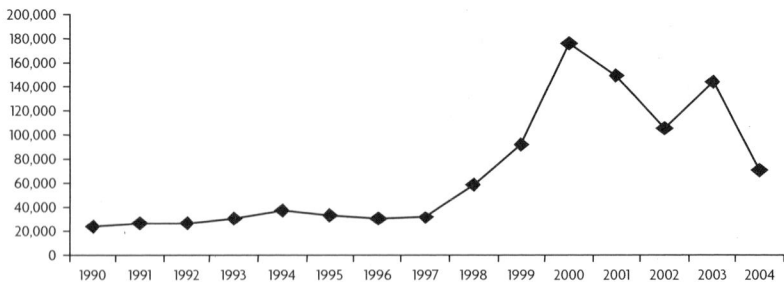

Source: CEPLAES 2005, 25.

## Changing Migration Patterns

There have been significant changes in the pattern of emigration from Ecuador during the new wave. The first relates to countries of destination. From the 1950s until the mid-1990s, most migrants were *mestizo* men from southern Ecuador moving to the United States and the República Bolivariana de Venezuela. Later, urban males and indigenous peoples played a much greater role, while there was a general process of feminization of emigration. Initially emigration was predominantly to the United States but since the 1990s destinations have become more diversified, with Europe as the main goal. It is estimated that 45 percent of Ecuadoran migrants now immigrate to Spain, 32 percent to the United States, and 9 percent to Italy, with smaller proportions finding their way to France and Germany. Fueled by the demand for unskilled and semiskilled domestic and agricultural labor, the number of Ecuadoran migrants arriving in Spain rose from 10,300 in 1997 to 125,000 by 2000 (Jokisch and Pribilsky 2002).

Second, migration is now more ubiquitous in Ecuador, having spread to all regions of the country; the *sierra* (accounting for 58 percent of the total), the coast (38 percent), and Amazonia (4 percent). Overall, three-quarters of migrants are urban in origin, from medium and large centers, divided equally among men and women. However, in the highlands, male migration is more significant (17 percent of the total) compared with females (11 percent). The social landscape of the *sierra* is thus increasingly female as men leave the countryside. As the longest-standing urban center of migration, 82 percent of migrants from Cuenca still immigrate to the United States, building upon prior traditions and contacts. However, those from Quito and Guayaquil (44 and 59 percent respectively), who make up the majority of more recent migrants, prefer Spain.

A third change concerns the growing participation of women. Rather than joining their husbands later as has been customary, women are increasingly traveling alone as independent workers to become the main breadwinner for the family, often leaving their partners and children back home. Thus, in common with some other countries, migration from Ecuador is becoming feminized. This trend coincides with the shift of migration to the EU, and especially to Spain. Women are drawn to Spain by the advantages of a common culture, language, and religion, as well as by cheaper and less risky travel. Furthermore, there are greater employment opportunities for women as carers of the young, sick, and elderly, or as domestic servants. Migrants are also getting younger. According to the 2001 census, some 57 percent of emigrants from Ecuador are between

18–30 years old, while 9 percent are young children and teenagers. This reflects the increasing permanence of the migratory process as sons and daughters join their parents, especially in Spain, the destination for three-quarters of emigrants under 14 years of age (CEPLAES 2005).

Migration from Ecuador is characterized by diversity but is socially selective (see figure 3.2). The poorest generally cannot afford to emigrate and are the least likely to leave the country. One study found that 60 percent of migrants could be classed as non-poor (Herrera, Carrillo, and Torres 2004). Those with a certain financial capital can more easily pay the costs of travel or offer collateral to formal and informal providers of credit. Traditions of social solidarity and ethnicity in the *sierra* provide the support necessary for poorer citizens to emigrate. In contrast, migrants from the coast and Amazonia tend to be from wealthier strata. Urban middle-income groups—those worst affected by the economic crisis—have constituted the bulk of emigrants from Ecuador. Among this group, women tend to predominate, while men make up the majority of poorer migrants. Indigenous people, who comprise around 15 percent of Ecuador's population, are underrepresented among migrants (at 6 percent). As with the

**Figure 3.2. Migrants from Ecuador, by Socioeconomic Status, 2001**

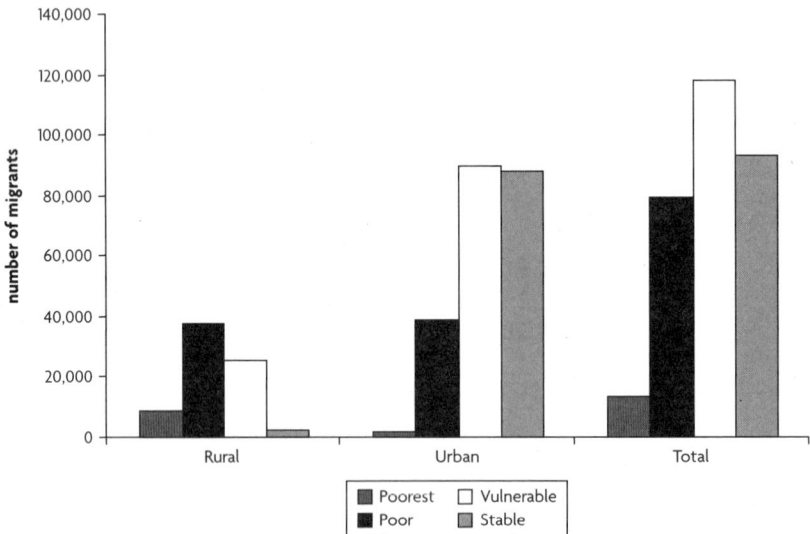

*Source:* CEPLAES 2005, 31.

non-indigenous population, it is the wealthier, urban-based Amerindians who tend to migrate to make a living.[2]

Emigrants generally, and especially women, are not just wealthier but also better educated than the average Ecuadorian. Some 40 percent of female emigrants have completed secondary education while 15 percent have tertiary level instruction, compared with 35 percent and 10 percent respectively for males. This increase in the proportion of better educated migrants from Ecuador parallels global trends since the 1990s. In South America, while just 12 percent of the working population is classified as skilled, more than 40 percent of migrants fall into this category (Özden and Schiff 2006). Although sometimes criticized as a "brain drain" that robs developing countries of their best qualified workers, it is also in part a solution to the age-old problem of educated unemployment. Yet while such labor mobility may allow qualified workers to apply their professional skills overseas, it also testifies to migrants' over-qualification for much of the employment taken up in the countries of destination. For example, half of Ecuadorans employed in the Spanish province of Murcia as rural laborers were originally technical and professional staff or university students.

## *"Irregular" Emigration*

Emigration is an expensive and often dangerous undertaking. Illegal or "irregular" migration has seen a sharp rise and is now common in the wake of greater controls. Migration to the United States by land and sea through Mexico and Central America can take three months and cost up to US$15,000 per person (or the equivalent of three times the average annual Ecuadorian salary). People-trafficking (*coyoterismo*) is big business in Ecuador and is known to be sustained by murky commercial and political interest groups. It is estimated that people-trafficking in Ecuador is worth US$60 million a year to the *coyoteros* alone (*El Comercio*, September 19, 2005). This figure rises to more than US$235 million a year if profits enjoyed by usurious moneylenders (*chulqueros*) are included (Jokisch and Pribilsky 2002).

Furthermore, although no doubt considered a worthwhile investment by those desperate to leave the country, emigration carries with it high risks and other potentially heavy transaction costs. Migrants frequently have to mortgage their houses to raise the necessary capital to pay for their trips. Families left behind often suffer threats of violence if delays in repayment arise. Travel conditions are highly precarious, with cases of sexual abuse against women and children not uncommon. Many harrowing tales of human suffering by migrants en route to a new life have been documented.[3] Networks of *coyoteros, chulqueros,* and travel agencies have sprung up and expanded their activities all over the country to facilitate this process.[4] Although meeting a market demand, the net result of this illegal activity has been a substantial increase in the financial costs, personal risks, and human sacrifice involved in migrating overseas. However, there is no official policy in Ecuador to monitor or control such operations.

## Remittances

In 2005, developing countries received US$167 billion in remittances from overseas workers (World Bank 2006). For Latin America, such transfers have increased spectacularly since the 1990s financial crisis, amounting to US$55 billion in 2005 compared with just US$5 billion in 1990 (Maimbo and Ratha 2005; IDS 2006). This is now equivalent to the whole of foreign direct investment and far exceeds the volume of overseas development assistance to the region. In 2001, at the peak of the emigration curve, remittances were the major source of foreign currency, outstripping even oil and other exports. It is estimated that remittances now account for at least a quarter of the personal income of recipients across Latin America (Terry 2005). In Ecuador itself, remittances have risen from US$201 million (1 percent of GDP) in 1993 to US$1.74 billion (around 9 percent of GDP) in 2004 (see figure 3.3). Inclusion of unofficial transfers would probably double this figure. Ecuador is presently the largest recipient of overseas remittances in the Andean region (Solimano 2005).

The largest sources of remittances are Spain, the United States, and Italy, respectively. Principal recipient areas are the coast (49 percent), highlands (46 percent), and Amazonia (6 percent). The higher volume of payments to the coast—although it has fewer emigrants than the highlands—probably reflects the fact that they are more recent and migrants need to send back relatively larger quantities to repay debts incurred to finance their trips and provide support for their families during the early stages of the migration process. Conversely, the longer-term highland or *serrano* migrants gradually send fewer remittances as time passes.

More than two-thirds of remittances to Ecuador are channeled through some 200 specialized financial institutions such as banks, couriers, and travel agencies.[5] About 80 percent of migrants use courier services and only

**Figure 3.3. Remittances from Ecuadorian Migrants, 1993–2004**

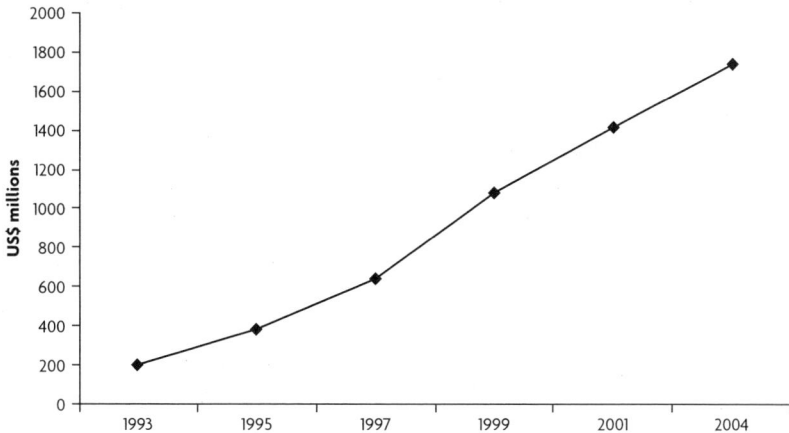

*Sources:* CEPLAES 2005; López-Córdova and Olmedo 2006.

9 percent use banks (FLACSO 2004). It is estimated that about 20 percent of transfers are made through informal mechanisms. Although the cost of transferring money has fallen substantially since 2000, the lowest commission now stands at around 6 percent, with courier companies charging the highest fees but providing greater ease of access for both senders and recipients.

## Social Policy Dimensions: Livelihoods, Protection, and Assets

In Ecuador, where 15 percent of the population now works overseas, international migration has clearly become a critical element in people's lives. Based on the framework set out by Moser (2006), the social policy dimensions of international migration can be disaggregated into three major spheres:

- strengthening livelihoods and the formation of immediate coping strategies
- providing welfare support and social protection to help mitigate the heavy transaction costs of migration
- over the longer term, enhancing, diversifying, and consolidating the asset base of migrants and their families to sustain livelihoods.

*Livelihoods Support*

In the short term, remittances provide an income flow that facilitates the satisfaction of basic family needs, enhancing the quality of daily life and levels of material consumption (for example, through the purchase of food, clothing, and health care). To the extent that such income flows are significant and sustainable, they help reduce risk and uncertainty for migrants' families by offering a cushion against the vicissitudes of an unstable economy and lack of domestic employment opportunities. If experience elsewhere is any indication, there may well have been a net reduction in poverty in Ecuador as a result of remittance multiplier effects in the economy. Based on a comparative study of 71 countries, it was found that a 10 percent increase in the share of remittances in a country's GDP can produce a 2.1 percent decrease in poverty among those living on less than US$1 per day (Adams and Page 2005). However, while livelihood security may be strengthened in the short to medium term, long-term dependence on remittances could decelerate the process of finding lasting domestic solutions to economic and political upheaval if overseas migration serves as a continuous safety valve for social tensions and the government shirks its responsibilities.

It is estimated that some 14 percent of Ecuador's adult population receives remittance payments (Suro 2005). Surveys carried out in the three major cities of Cuenca, Guayaquil, and Quito, showed that approximately half of all migrants send regular payments home about eight times a year. They average US$175 per month, a significant contribution to typical local monthly family incomes of around US$500 (FLACSO 2004; Herrera, Carrillo, and Torres 2004). Monthly payments per family were found to be higher (more than US$300) in Cuenca where migration has a longer history, and lower (under US$100) in Quito and Guayaquil.

Yet the distribution of remittances is highly uneven. Those receiving remittances are mainly siblings and parents (54 percent), followed by children and partners (27 percent). No less than half of all migrants' families and more than a quarter of all partners received no payments at all. These figures reveal an unusually high level of what could be called *remittance exclusion*. This has major implications for providing counseling and welfare support to children, spouses, and other family members whose economic vulnerability is increased through the departure of one or both parents.

In common with other Latin American countries, about 90 percent of remittances in Ecuador are spent on meeting basic family needs (FLACSO

2004; Suro 2005). Around 62 percent of such transfers cover everyday household expenses such as food, clothing, medicine, and consumer goods. A significant 21 percent finances the education of children left behind, illustrating parents' concern over their personal development and representing an important investment in human capital. A further 11 percent is destined for debt repayment and 3 percent for land purchases and construction. Savings and financial investment account for just 3 percent of this expenditure. Not surprisingly, urban males are more likely to invest in land or business enterprises than to save money in banks. Rural women spend the bulk of remittances on more fundamental items such as food and clothing.

## Welfare and Social Protection

Although remittances provide regular income supplements and livelihood support to many households, international migration often involves high transaction costs that social policy makers need to address. Problems range from unduly heavy financial expense and personal burdens associated with illegal immigration and people-trafficking, to the psychological impacts and trauma suffered by the children of absentee parents and the extra burden of care placed upon the extended family. Such responsibilities may be welcomed by the extended family, but in some cases it can generate additional costs and conflicts. The growing need for educational and counseling services tailored specifically to the needs of would-be migrants and their families left behind has created a new potential social policy agenda in Ecuador, currently being addressed by civil society rather than government.

In the process of strengthening capitals (financial, human, social) to develop coping strategies, diversify, and sustain livelihoods, there are many outcomes. As we have seen, remittance exclusion affects a large proportion of migrants' families left behind in Ecuador. For those who do receive regular payments, the immediate economic benefits are considerable, even if their distribution is often unequal. However, other consequences are social and psychological in nature. Migration produces profound changes in family structure and relationships that require adaptation on the part of migrants as well as the reorganization of families left behind. The "transnational family" is an increasingly common feature of Ecuadorian society, with its own specific sociopsychological issues.

Growing emigration of young couples has split households and created the "hollow family" syndrome in Ecuador. Increasingly, as mothers and fathers emigrate to seek work, their children are left behind in the care of grandparents and other relatives. Thus, the extended family—composed of more than two generations and/or wider family members beyond parents and children—has become an increasingly important source of support. Some 52 percent of migrant families are now extended, compared with the national figure of 46 percent. This reflects the greater role of grandparents and other relatives in caring for the younger offspring of absent parents. Nearly one-quarter of families in Ecuador with migrant members are incomplete; that is, without the father and/or the mother, compared with the national figure of 10 percent. Strains are also placed upon couples by prolonged separation, frequently leading to marriage breakdown.

In recent years, there has been an increase in the emigration of educated women from Ecuador to Europe, especially from the coastal region around Guayaquil. This has been facilitated by lower travel costs,[6] faster and more secure travel conditions, and greater ease of entry (at least until recently) compared with the United States. This new wave has been in response to the crisis of care in industrial countries and the consequent demand for domestic servants, as well as care providers for sick, young, and elderly persons. To a much lesser extent, migration has supplied the sex worker market. Around two-thirds of female Ecuadorian migrants leave children behind—normally one or two (48 percent) but also up to three or four (15 percent).

Female migration produces several distinctive social effects. On the positive side, women are more likely than men to ensure financial stability by regularly sending home cash and remaining in touch with the family in Ecuador. For wives and mothers left behind, migration can lead to greater control over decision making with regard to the expenditure of remittances. However, this advance may be tempered by continuing controls imposed from a distance by the spouse and extended family, resulting in minimal empowerment in practice (Herrera 2004). Children's loss of maternal contact frequently produces emotional instability and other psychological pressures that can lead to further problems of poor performance at school and juvenile delinquency. One research study of migrants' children in Cuenca found that, "absence of the mother and/or father causes depression, loneliness, low self-esteem, rebellion, or aggressiveness" (Carrillo 2003: 3).

Male migration can be even more problematic for the nuclear family. Although three-quarters of male migrants have at least one child at home, remittances tend to be sent to their parents rather than their wives or offspring. In a patriarchal society in which multipaternity is common, this is seen as a family survival strategy for the male. However, children may fail to benefit from their fathers' remittances if they do not live with their paternal grandparents. Research suggests that Ecuadorian males are thus failing in their duty toward their children, yet no official child protection policies address this issue.

Notwithstanding such problems, researchers have cautioned against assuming that migration automatically leads to "social dysfunction" and negative consequences (Herrera, Carrillo, and Torres 2004: 20). For example, evidence from El Salvador, Mexico, and other countries suggests that children from households in receipt of remittances often benefit from increased school enrolment and completion rates (IDS 2006). However, it is also noted that overdependence on remittances from overseas can lead to a perverse "culture of dependency" in home communities, as youngsters see an incentive to remain unemployed while they await their own migration opportunity (Maimbo and Ratha 2005).

The burden imposed on extended family members who assume the parental mantle may exacerbate these problems. In extreme cases, children taken in by either the extended family or by others may be exploited as quasi-servants, subjected to psychological and even sexual abuse. Problems of mutual comprehension and values, not to mention conflict over control of remittances, further complicate these intergenerational relationships. Older children often have to take on the role of substitute mother or father, looking after younger brothers and sisters. They must frequently abandon their studies to perform these roles, generating conflicts with absent parents (Carrillo 2003). Furthermore, especially in a male-dominated society such as Ecuador, strains are generated when men lose their role as breadwinners in this fashion, leading to low self-esteem, alcoholism, and even desertion of the family.

Remittances may help compensate for parental absence. Purchase of clothes, electronic goods, motorcycles, and other items for their children and relatives can make up for parents' absence while improving the beneficiaries' quality of life. Such "conspicuous consumption" is criticized in some quarters—especially by the church—for allegedly undermining moral standards, encouraging delinquent behavior, and creating false expectations.[7] Notwithstanding the obvious economic benefits for local commerce, however, many argue that these consumer goods are important for children as a symbolic representation of their parents' presence in their lives and as underlining the continuation of family ties. A similar goal is served by remittance-funded ceremonies such as Holy Communion, the symbolic 15th birthday party for girls, and high school graduation (Herrera 2004).

Yet surveyed children of migrants often express ambivalent feelings. They usually recognize the hardships suffered by their parents to provide them with a better life and the problems associated with working in distant lands, but they remain hopeful that they too will eventually be able to migrate to build their own livelihoods, acquire social status, and demonstrate their personal achievements. They appreciate the economic benefits—although they are more limited than generally perceived—but realize that these often come at a high social and emotional price (Carrillo 2003).

## Asset Building

There has been a strong emphasis in recent international migration literature on the potential for using remittances to promote more "productive" development activities, in addition to providing incomes and immediate livelihood support for households (for example, Maimbo and Ratha 2005; Terry and Wilson 2005; Özden and Schiff 2006; and López-Córdova and Olmedo 2006). Longer-term investment in capital assets can help strengthen economic and social infrastructure that allows individuals and households to move out of poverty. In principle, this could involve channeling investments into multiple assets: for example, into human capital (education, training, and capacity building), physical assets (water, electricity, consumer durables, urban or rural production) and financial capital (savings, housing, and land as stores of value). The prospect of migration may lead people to invest in domestic education and human capital formation in view of the anticipated economic return through remittances (Özden and Schiff 2006). Furthermore, there is scope for international migrants to acquire political capital as they obtain absentee voting rights and build up influential lobbies to influence domestic policy.

Perhaps because the bulk of Ecuadorian emigration is of relatively recent origin, there is a less well developed tradition of systematically investing remittances into economic and social development. In contrast, Mexico, for example, has a much longer history of migration to the United States. Home Town Associations regularly channel funds into asset-building local infrastructure and productive investments back home (IDS 2006; Özden and Schiff 2006). In the case of Mexico, this is encouraged by the government through a system of matching funding.[8] Growing evidence from around the world suggests that there is potential to harness remittances for longer-term asset building, capital accumulation, and macroeconomic development, although this issue has been neglected in policy making

(López-Córdova and Olmedo 2006; Özden and Schiff 2006). However, it is also important that policymakers and practitioners keep a realistic perspective on this issue and not exaggerate the importance of such "productive" potential, basing such judgments more on wishful thinking than on hard evidence (Hall 2007).

Frequently, the primary objective of remittances is not to serve a strictly economic purpose but as a sign of prestige, to enhance social status, and to reaffirm migrants' identity and community membership. Research in Ecuador has noted how, especially in the southern provinces of Cañar and Loja, migrants have contributed substantially to local festivities, church construction, and equipment for schools and colleges, boosting the personal standing of present and absent community members, regardless of any economic spin-off. The loss of status experienced by migrants as low-paid workers in their destination countries may be counterbalanced through such gifts. The strengthening of links between absent workers and their home communities through donations for local works may serve to enhance a form of "transnational social capital" by helping to bridge the geographical gap and maintain communications.

## Institutional Mediation of Social Policies for Migration

In order for assets to be effectively harnessed in the construction of livelihoods and asset-building strategies, a supportive institutional framework should be in place. A variety of bodies is necessary to meet the diverse needs of migrants at their countries of origin, during their journeys, and at the countries of destination. The absence of such support increases the costs incurred by emigrants, reduces the volume of repatriated economic benefits, and increases the subsequent risks of social hardships and psychological trauma. The roles of government, civil society, and the private sector in Ecuador will be considered.

### Government

Ecuador has no integrated policy for dealing with international migration. Government involvement in this field has centered on juridical matters of national and international law. A bill—the Law to Protect Ecuadorian Migrants and their Families—has been placed before Ecuador's Congress to streamline and integrate a number of initiatives under one umbrella (*Anteproyecto de ley especial para la protección, promoción e el ejercicio de los derechos de las personas migrantes ecuatorianos y sus familiares*) but this has not progressed.[9] Ecuador is a signatory to the International Labour Organization's *International Convention on the Protection of the Rights of All Migrant Workers and Their Families* (1990). However, the country has been less successful in bilateral negotiations. For example, it has no agreements with either the United States or Italy on benefit rights for Ecuadorian emigrants. An agreement was signed with Spain in 2001 on the regulation of migratory flows, reflecting EU concerns over increased levels of immigration. Under this agreement, an Ecuadoran-Spanish Selection Committee was established in 2002 to match qualified emigrants with contracted jobs. By July 2004, some 1,300 Ecuadorans had arrived in Spain under this system, but this was well short of the 30,000 target. According to research findings (Herrera, Carrillo, and Torres 2004), the work of this committee remains relatively unknown among the migrant community and activist civil society organizations and even within government circles.

Despite the slow pace of domestic government action, Ecuadorian emigrants have benefited from other changes in legislation. In 2005 Spain announced a three-month amnesty, offering 700,000 migrants residency permits, plus a further 400,000 permits for their relatives.[10] Ecuadorans accounted for a significant 21 percent of applicants (*The Economist* 2005a). In theory, this will allow the legalization of up to 90 percent of Spain's underground workers, while boosting social security revenues and facilitating better planning of health and education services. However, it is feared that many émigrés will continue in the informal economy as employers seek to minimize costs and extort money from illegal workers in some regions of the country (*Financial Times*, May 9, 2005).

There has been little or no action by the state so far to deal with immediate livelihoods issues such as controlling people-trafficking or reducing remittance costs; providing welfare services to would-be migrants and their families back home, or encouraging long-term investment in asset-building development activities. The initiatives that do exist have been instituted by civil society and the private sector. Since remittances are private flows going directly to migrants' families, the government would need to put in place mechanisms to encourage transfers through official channels in order to tap their investment potential. As noted in the case of Mexico, for example, the economic multiplier effect of remittances in terms of building local assets tends to be strong—compared with other foreign exchange sources—since funds go directly to the grassroots (López-Córdova and Olmedo 2006). Ecuador's capacity to address these development issues is not helped by the fact that governance in the field of international migration is characterized by severe institutional fragmentation, with functions spread among several ministries such as Labor, Government, and External Relations, with little or no coordination.[11]

With some two million adult Ecuadorans working overseas, the issue of voting rights in national elections has been under consideration in Congress. Dual nationality has been allowed since 2003 but, unlike in Brazil, Mexico, and Colombia, Ecuadorans are currently not permitted to vote overseas. Appropriate steps need to be taken through the Supreme Electoral Tribunal. Funding needs to be allocated and a voter registration scheme set up to ensure the participation of Ecuadorians in the electoral process. Acquisition of a direct political voice through the vote could stimulate new transnational links and prove to be a critical influence on Ecuadorian policy, for example, in providing more support to migrants and their families for economic and social development.

### Civil Society

Civil society in Ecuador has been more proactive than the government in addressing the needs of migrants and their families. In particular, several prominent nongovernmental organizations (NGOs) and the Catholic Church have played important roles. Together, these institutions have been trying to improve migration policy and practice in Ecuador, with a view to strengthening and improving the efficacy of emigration as a vehicle for enhancing livelihoods. Civil society has been active in the areas of policy dialogue, providing social protection and promoting local development.

Since 2000, Ecuadorian civil society has been instrumental in making the migration issue a subject of national debate and dialogue—through *mesas de diálogo*—with the government. In a first wave of consultation, following the exit of President Mahuad in 2000, many organizations mobilized in a discussion process that involved indigenous and peasant organizations.[12] These talks culminated in a number of proposals, including the right of Ecuadorans overseas to vote in national elections, the approval of various international instruments such as the 2001 agreement with Spain on regulation of migration flows, and the establishment of a development plan and fund (US$1 million initially) for migrants and their families (sustained by a US$10 million debt swap as well as US$5 million from the national budget). A second round of consultations was started through the Secretariat for Social Dialogue and Planning following the election of President Gutiérrez. In 2003, three major consultations took place in

Cuenca, Guayaquil, and Quito, involving comprehensive participation from many segments of civil society.

In terms of social protection, civil society institutions have been instrumental in supporting the rights of Ecuadorans overseas and back home, while offering support services to migrants and their families (Herrera, Carrillo, and Torres 2004). The National Migration Workshop (*Taller Nacional de Migración*), set up in 2002 at a conference organized by the UN, women's organizations (CONAMU), and an Andean-wide NGO, the American Friends Service Committee/Comité Andino de Servicios (AFSC/CAS), is developing a national network and promotes links among local organizations in Cañar, Cuenca, Guayaquil, and Quito. This network supports the Plan for Migration, Communication, and Development, as well as the draft bill for a Migration Law now being considered by Congress mentioned above.

The Catholic Church has been especially active in providing support to migrants and their families through the *Pastoral de Movilidad Humana*. At the provincial level, advice centers known as *Centros de Atención al Migrante* (CAM), funded by the EU, have been established to offer advice to prospective migrants and provide counseling support to families. In Quito, the municipality plays a major role in the *Casa del Migrante*; in Guayaquil, a women's NGO (CEPAM) is in charge of the center. In Cuenca, the *pastoral social* of the Catholic Church runs training workshops and distributes literature to warn migrants of potential hazards and equip them to cope better once they have reached their destinations. It also provides psychological counseling to members of the extended family, especially to migrants' children, some of whom suffer severe trauma due to their parents' absence.[13]

Civil society has taken the lead in using international migration to stimulate local development in Ecuador. The Ecuador-Spain Plan for Migration, Communication, and Development[14] has launched a program in the high out-migration provinces of Azuay, Cañar, Loja, and Pichincha. The aim of the plan is to generate alternative local development options such as small-scale production and microfinance, facilitate improved communications among migrants, provide legal and psychological advice, ease remittance transfers, and lobby for a debt swap to fund such development activities (Caritas 2002). The work is funded by the Spanish Overseas Development Agency and has involved a dozen Ecuadorian and Spanish institutions in the first phase from 2001 to 2005. A Spanish government loan of US$30 million has financed more than 50,000 small operations averaging US$1,370 each. Microfinance has supported projects in the areas of agricultural production and processing, animal rearing and shoe manufacture. Other valuable local development work has been carried out through the church-linked agency *Fondo Ecuatoriano Populorium Progressio* (FEPP).

Most small enterprises in Ecuador fail in their first year, due largely to poor management. Government and civil society should provide training and technical assistance to improve management capacity, undertake feasibility studies, develop marketing channels, and strengthen cooperatives and other associations of producers. Community-based enterprises, such as those under way in programs such as *Codesarrollo*, PRODEPINE, and PROLOCAL based on the principles of community-driven development (CDD), could be extended to include areas of high out-migration. Lessons learned from these experiences should be systematically integrated into any new ventures. Domestic and particularly overseas markets could be penetrated through production of organic crops, exotic fruits, handicrafts, ceramics, textiles, and flowers, among others. For this, cooperation is required between government and civil society programs—such as the above-mentioned *Plan Migración*—within an integrated national migration policy. There might also be the potential to set up hometown associations to finance public works projects and small enterprises.

Another arm of civil society comprises the migrant community itself and the self-help organizations that provide networks of support among emigrants and their families back home. There is little documented evidence of their work to date, but several are well known. These include, for example, the *Movimento de Familias de Migrantes* (MOFEMI), the *Asociación de Familiares de Migrantes Rumiñahui-9 de Enero*, and the *Asociación de Migrantes Ecuador Llactacaru*. The *Associación Hispano-Ecuatoriana Rumiñahui*, set up in 1997, has carried out key advocacy work in Spain on behalf of migrants and has pressured the Ecuadorian government for improvements in support services. Attempts to coordinate the activities of these various organizations have, however, been thwarted by conflicting goals and interests (Hererra, Carrillo, and Torres 2004).

### The Private Sector

The private sector has been active mainly in providing banking services to facilitate the increasingly large cash flows generated by remittances from overseas. As already noted, the number of courier services has grown rapidly both in Ecuador and destination countries such as Spain. These include branches of big companies such as Western Union and Money Gram (28 percent of remittances), as well as local companies like Delgado Travel (34 percent) and small independent enterprises such as Geomil Express, which has branches on both sides of the Atlantic. Banks account for some 17 percent of remittances.

*Banco Solidario*, for example, saw a good business opportunity in the expanding market for remittance transfers to Ecuador and has managed to reduce cash transfer costs. In the case of *Banco Solidario*, only 2,500 of its 65,000 clients are migrants, accounting for US$4 million in an annual turnover of $90 million yet representing 20 percent of the bank's US$20 million in savings accounts.[15] *Banco Solidario* has played a pioneering role through its *Enlace Ecuador* program involving a network linking Ecuador (116 access points, 21 cooperatives) with Spain (8,750 access points, 7 savings banks). The aim is to provide credit to finance travel, channel overseas funds to microenterprises in Ecuador, and offer a range of bank accounts for savings and investment purposes, including house purchase, travel costs, and consumer goods (*Banco Solidario* 2004).

Although charges for sending cash home have generally fallen, costs continue to be both excessive and regressive. Small transfers involve relatively larger fees, adversely affecting poorer migrants. Efforts should be made to reduce exorbitant charges as this would increase remittance flows and help alleviate poverty in the home country. Experience in the United States–Mexico corridor, where transfer costs have halved since 1999, suggests that a move from informal to innovative formal systems is required (FSEFI 2004). For instance, the use of credit unions for cash transfers offers many advantages, including lower transaction costs and convenience (Grace 2005). In Ecuador, the initiative taken by *Banco Solidario* is a good example of what is possible. Other more traditional institutions such as the *Banco Pichincha* are also now entering the microfinance world (*The Economist* 2005b). Greater government regulation is required in the microfinance sector in Ecuador, which charges higher interest rates and commissions than banks, sometimes at usurious levels.

## Conclusion

Ecuador illustrates well the importance of migration as a component of people's increasingly globalized livelihood strategies in the face of persistent economic hardships and political instability at home. Industrialized countries continue to depend on cheap, unskilled, and semiskilled labor. As long as there remains a mutual interest on the part of sending and receiving countries in perpetuating such international movements of workers, this upward trend is likely to continue, notwithstanding temporary controls imposed for national security and political reasons.

Yet in spite of this interdependence, a notable feature of international migration in the Ecuadorian case, and indeed most others, is the lack of government assistance for citizens seeking employment overseas. These citizens rely instead on institutions of civil society and the private sector. This governmental apathy stems in part from nationalistic sentiments and a certain embarrassment on the part of political leaders when countries cannot provide for the well-being of their own citizens. However, it is perhaps due mainly to the dubious, if convenient, assumption that migration is a largely benign process whose economic benefits far outweigh any possible negative consequences, thereby obviating the need for government intervention.

However, official indifference has recently been broken by, among other factors, a belated recognition of the potential of workers' remittances as a source of development funding. This new mantra should not be allowed to obscure the fact that critical social policy dimensions need to be addressed alongside economic issues. Both domestic and international social policies need to incorporate social concerns far more systematically to provide migrants and their families with a degree of support in their quest for more sustainable livelihoods and enhanced well-being. Government has a lead role to play in developing new initiatives in collaboration and partnership with civil society, the private sector, and migrant communities themselves. Without such policies, the social costs of international migration threaten to detract from or even overshadow its economic advantages.

## Notes

1. *International migrants* refers here to those living outside of their country for more than one year and to temporary migrants, not to asylum seekers or refugees. It is recognized, however, that in practice this distinction is often blurred.
2. Such as the well-known *otavaleños*, for example, who successfully market their handicrafts in the United States and Europe.
3. In one incident, a fishing boat carrying Ecuadorian migrants was allegedly sunk by the United States navy (*Latinnews*, July 14, 2004). One family paid US$8,500 each for an arduous sea voyage to Guatemala and overland trip to Los Angeles and then New York. In the notorious case of the *Eloy Alfaro* fishing boat, 45 Ecuadorians and 43 Peruvians were abandoned off the coast

only to be shipwrecked and their possessions stolen (*El Comercio*, June 12, 2005). Between January 2000 and July 2005, the Ecuadoran navy rescued 7,600 emigrants from 56 fishing boats (*El Comercio, September 19*, 2005).

4. For example, between 1998 and 2003 in the southern province of Loja (population 70,000) no fewer than 71 "travel agencies" opened; in 2001–02, more than 30,000 passports were issued.

5. Examples include *Banco Solidario*, Western Union, Money Gram, Delgado Travel, and private postal services.

6. US$4,000 per person, compared with US$12,000 to US$15,000 or more to the United States.

7. Interviews by the author in Cuenca, April 2004.

8. In the Mexican state of Zacatecas alone, from 1993–2004 remittances of US$165 million, matched by US$483 of government money, funded some 1,500 community projects (IDS 2006).

9. The bill proposes action at various levels: (a) a National Council to coordinate initiatives on migration across Ministries and other bodies, (b) a Technical Secretariat within the Ministry of Foreign Relations with the specific task of producing a national migration plan, (c) reactivation of the "Fund for Support, Savings and Investment" for migrants and their families (*Fundo de Ajuda, Ahorro e Inversión*), (d) reduction of transaction costs of remittances, and (e) review of such issues as transferability of social security rights while overseas.

10. Applicants receive annual renewable residency and work permits if they can prove that they have lived in Spain since August 2004 and had six-month job contracts.

11. Government bodies dealing with migration include the National Office of Migration (Police Inspectorate, Ministry of Government), the National Office for the Defence of Migrants (Public Prosecutor's Office), the Consultative Council on Migration Policy (Ministry of Government) and the Sub-Secretariat for Migrant and Consular Relations (Ministry of Foreign Relations).

12. These include CONAIE, CONFEUNASSC, FENOCIN, FEINE, FENACLE, and FEI.

13. Interviews by the author at the CAM, Cuenca, May 2004.

14. *Plan Migración, Comunicación e Desarrollo Ecuador-España*.

15. Interview with *Banco Solidario*, Quito, May 27, 2004.

## References

Adams, R. H. and J. Page. 2005. "The Impact of International Migration and Remittances on Poverty." In Maimbo, S. M., and D. Ratha, eds., *Remittances, Development Impact, and Future Prospects*. Washington, DC: World Bank, 277–306.

Banco Solidario. 2004. "Mi familia, Mi pais, Mi regreso: Rede de Servicios Financieros a Emigrantes." Information sheet, Banco Solidario, Quito.

Caritas 2002. Propuesta de canje de deuda por inversión social. Working paper, Quito.

Carrillo, M. C. 2003. "Jóvenes e migración en la región sur del Ecuador. Ponencia para la asamblea Nacional de Migración, dimension social." Working paper, FLACSO, Quito.

CEPLAES. 2005. "Migraciones Internacionales: Principales Implicaciones de las Migraciones para el Desarrollo del Ecuador." Working paper, CEPLAES, Quito.

The Economist. 2005a. "Let Them Stay." May 12.

The Economist. 2005b. "The Hidden Wealth of the Poor." May 14.

El Comercio. 2005. "El Coyotaje Rinde USD 60 Milliones Cada Año." September 19.

Financial Times. 2005. "Amnesty Fails to Ease Spanish Worries over Immigration." May 9.

FLACSO (Facultad Latinoamericana de Ciencias Sociales). 2004. "La emigración internacional en Quito, Guayaquil e Cuenca." Working paper, FLACSO, Quito.

FSEFI (Financial Market Integrity Unit). 2004. Lessons from the US-Mexico Remittances Corridor on Shifting from Informal to Formal Transfer System. Working paper, Financial Market Integrity Unit, World Bank, Washington, DC.

GCIM (Global Commission on International Migration). 2005. Migration in an Interconnected World: New Directions for Action. Geneva: Global Commission on International Migration.

Grace, D.C. 2005. "Exploring the Credit Union Experience with Remittances in the Latin American Market." In Remittances, Development Impact, and Future Prospects, ed. S. M. Maimbo and D. Ratha. Washington, DC: World Bank, 159–73.

Hall, A. 2007. "Moving Away from Poverty: Migrant Remittances, Livelihoods and Development." In Moving Out of Poverty: Cross-Disciplinary Perspectives on Mobility, ed. D. Narayan and P. Petesch. Washington, DC: World Bank, 307–32.

Herrera, G. 2004. "Remessas, dinámicas familiares e estatus social: una mirada de la emigración ecuatoriana desde la sociedad de origen." Working paper, FLACSO, Quito.

Herrera, G., M. Carrillo, and C. Torres. 2004. "Migración International e Nacional." Working paper, FLACSO, Quito.

IDS (Institute of Development Studies). 2006. "Sending Money Home. Can Remittances Reduce Poverty? Id21 Insights No. 60, January.

ILO (International Labour Organization). 1990. International Convention on the Protection of the Rights of all Migrant Workers and Members of their Families. A/RES/45/158, 69th Plenary Meeting, United Nations General Assembly, New York, December 18.

IOM (International Organization for Migration). 2005. *World Migration 2005.* Geneva: International Organization for Migration.

Jokisch, B., and J. Pribilsky. 2002. "The Panic to Leave: Economic Crisis and the 'New Emigration' from Ecuador." *International Migration* (40) 4: 75–101.

*Latinnews.* 2004. "Ecuador's Foreign Ministry Has Confirmed One of the Sinkings of Fishing Vessels by the U.S. Navy." July 14.

López-Córdova, E., and A. Olmedo. 2006. "International Remittances and Development: Existing Evidence, Policies, and Recommendations." Working paper, Inter-American Development Bank, Washington, DC.

Maimbo, S. M., and D. Ratha, eds. 2005. *Remittances, Development Impact, and Future Prospects.* Washington, DC: World Bank.

Moser, C. 2006. *Assets, Livelihoods and Social Policy.* Working paper, World Bank, Washington, DC.

Özden, C., and M. Schiff, eds. 2006. *International Migration, Remittances & the Brain Drain.* Washington, DC: World Bank.

Solimano, A. 2005. "Remittances to the Andean Region." In *Beyond Small Change: Making Migrant Remittances Count,* ed. D. Terry and S. Wilson. Washington, DC: Inter-American Development Bank, 245–59.

Suro, R. 2005. "A Survey of Remittance Senders and Receivers". In *Beyond Small Change: Making Migrant Remittances Count,* ed. D. Terry and S. Wilson, 21–40. Washington, DC: Inter-American Development Bank.

Terry, D. 2005. "Remittances as a Development Tool." In *Beyond Small Change: Making Migrant Remittances Count,* ed. D. Terry and S. Wilson, 3–19. Washington, DC: Inter-American Development Bank.

Terry, D. and S. Wilson, eds. 2005. *Beyond Small Change: Making Migrant Remittances Count.* Washington, DC: Inter-American Development Bank.

World Bank, 2006. *Global Economic Prospects 2006: Economic Implications of Remittances and Migration.* Washington, DC: World Bank, Washington, DC.

# CHAPTER 4

# Toward the Sustainable Return of West African Transnational Migrants: What Are the Options?

*John K. Anarfi and Sara Jägare*

Transnational migration from the West African region has become an essential livelihood strategy. The issue of the return of these migrants has earned increased attention as the benefits of such return to the overall development process have become apparent. However, the complex relationship among migration, return, and development calls for further exploration, as the process of globalization requires constant modification of any policies related to mobile populations. This chapter considers the issue in relation to Ghana and Côte d'Ivoire. It explores the sustainability of transnational return migration to the West African subregion and the influence of the corresponding financial, human, and social capital transfers. Return migration is not an end in itself; rather, its impact changes with the expansion and deepening of the globalization process. As further understanding of the process develops, the focus of attention has broadened, from addressing the migrant's presence in his or her place of origin, to including the returnee's social networks and his or her contribution to the development process at origin. The effect of capital transfers on the development process at origin is therefore important in exploring issues of sustainability of return migration.

Although transnational migration might initially have been used as a livelihood strategy, sustainable return of migrants also has the ability to enhance livelihoods. The financial, human, and social capital transferred by transnational migrants have the potential for substantial impact on the development process of countries of origin at various levels of society. Financial capital is mainly transferred to the region through remittances, investments, and donations, with remittances alone constituting a large part of the total economy of countries in the region. Most transnational migrants also accumulate some assets in the form of human capital while abroad, generally by studying or learning new skills. This is demonstrated by the comparable data recently collected in Ghana and Côte d'Ivoire (see Black, Tiemoko, and Waddington 2003). In combination with social capital, transfers such as attendance of social gatherings, support of social networks and professional contacts, and engagement in hometown associations can be beneficial for development purposes.

The benefit of these capital transfers depends on the amount of capital that has been accumulated while the migrant is abroad. Moreover, in order to maximize the potential benefit of capital transfers in a sustainable manner, appropriate policies must be formulated, implemented, and assessed. Policies geared to create opportunities for optimal use of assets accumulated abroad should be prioritized. This chapter discusses policy alternatives in a pro-poor context to facilitate development and alleviate poverty.

## Background

One commonly cited benefit of migration for countries of origin is the return of migrants who have gained additional human, financial, and social capital. It is argued that these benefits vary significantly depending on the level of analysis applied and the critical factors considered, including the volume of return migration, characteristics of migrants, degree and direction of selectivity, types of migration, reasons for return, and situation existing in the countries involved in the migration (Ammassari and Black 2001).

More than a century ago, Raveinstein (1885) observed that every migration stream generates a counterstream, suggesting that return migration is taken for granted with any migration. This might explain the silence on the issue in the literature until the global economic crisis of 1973 (Ammassari and Black 2001). Not unexpectedly, nonnationals became targets of discrimination in many European countries faced with economic crises. Since then, three generations of migration studies have focused on the return. To some extent, the literature follows the historical development of the emergence of nation states in Africa, the insurgency and counterinsurgency characterizing many soon after independence, and the new attempts at strengthening democracy as part of the globalization process.

Lee (1966) argued, rightly, that some migrants return because they have acquired attributes abroad that promise to be advantageous in their place of origin. More skilled hands were needed in the new nation states, with, for example, the people referred to as "been-tos" in Ghana occupying special positions in the society to which they returned.

Historical and cultural linkages reinforced the trend toward second generation migration from emigration areas to immigration areas. Mabogunje (1970) put this in the context of a general migration system involving a mutual relationship between a center (immigrant countries) and a periphery (emigration countries). Uncertainty about the conditions in origin areas meant that emigrants went to great lengths to establish social networks. These then could be exploited either to facilitate return migration or to stabilize remaining after a return to origin.

The third generation of studies on contemporary international migration is still evolving (Ammassari and Black 2001) and is caught up in the globalization milieu. Within this context, areas of origin and of destination are linked together in transnational spaces by migrants who acquire social capital cutting across boundaries (Smith and Guarnizo 1998; ECA 1996). Return migration is no longer seen as the closure of the migration cycle, but as one of many steps within a continued movement (King 2000).

This aspect of the contemporary form of international migration has rendered it one of the thornier issues in international relations, especially since the start of the 1990s. It was a major theme of the Group of Seven (G-7) summit of the major industrialized countries in London in July 1991 (Teitelbaum and Weiner 1995). According to the Economic Commission for Africa (1996), the prominence given to international migration is likely to continue well into this century because migration is a manifestation of a new worldview and a result of a globalization process that is steadily expanding from the economic domain to culture, the arts, and societal value systems.

Rather than focus on the migrant's presence at origin, it has become important to put return migration in a larger context. Thus, the focus is shifting more and more toward the social networks and professional contacts of the returnee. The concept of return and its sustainability gained increased attention from refugee and migration policy makers during the 1990s (Black and Gent 2004). Return is now seen as having implications for communities of origin and the broader development process, rather than for the individual alone. The potential impacts of financial capital on the development of the sending household, local community, and country are recognized but have not hitherto been given much attention in policy making, as developing countries have focused primarily on the transfer of human capital upon return.

Most West African countries experienced a net loss of population between 1995 and 2000 (Black 2004). This was particularly the case in countries such as Ghana and Nigeria. Substantial return has been feasible only recently in many West African countries, as the political and economic climate has changed. This chapter explores the options for sustainable return, the potential effect of asset transfers on the development process in West Africa, and possible policies to facilitate such options.

## Sources of Data

This chapter is based on a survey of West African literature. It focuses particularly on empirical evidence on return migration and the influence of financial, social, and human capital on the sending household, local community, and country of migrants. Of particular importance is a study undertaken in Ghana and Côte d'Ivoire in 2002 (Black, Tiemoko, and Waddington 2003) that considered elite and less-skilled returnees to both countries. These two sending countries were selected because of their different development histories, institutions, and cultures. For historic, linguistic, and other reasons, migrants from Ghana generally migrated to the United Kingdom, while migrants from Côte d'Ivoire tended to go to France. However, an increase of migration from both countries to the United States was evident as well.

The study was conducted in three stages, with the first involving collection of preexisting data. During the second stage, the main survey was carried out using a sample of 302 elite returnees and 302 returnees who were considered less-skilled. The work was done by researchers in each country in collaboration with researchers at the University of Sussex. The survey explored the practice of migration, returnees' involvement in different kinds of capital transfers (and how this capital was used), and the barriers and opportunities for returnees in terms of becoming in the development of their home community. In the third phase, in-depth interviews were conducted with returnees at origin and potential returnees in London and Paris. However, it is worth stressing that the survey is not a representative sample, since the total number of returnees is unknown.

Other sources of empirical evidence used include, but are not limited to Kabki, Mazzucato, and Appiah 2004), a study on the economic impact of Netherlands-based Ghanaian migrants on rural Ashanti, which included open-ended interviews in villages and towns in the Ashanti Region, and Orozco's (2005) data on Ghanaian diasporas, development, and transnational integration.

## Sustainability of Return

The sustainability of return migration is closely linked to reasons for return: Return must be voluntary to be considered sustainable (Black and Gent 2004). However, it is important to distinguish between forced migrants and economic migrants. Most literature is concerned with the sustainable return of refugees. However, some factors discussed in the literature also apply to the return and reintegration of economic migrants.

Before determining whether return is sustainable, it is essential to define *sustainable return*. Sustainability of return will be considered first at the individual and household levels and then at the wider community level.

### Definitions

The most basic and narrow definition, apparently more relevant to the voluntary, economic migrant, reduces sustainable return to the absence of remigration after return to origin (Gent and Black 2005). However, even this definition must allow for some remigration, as every country experiences some level of migration. In particular, when professional migrants return but maintain professional and social networks abroad, they can be considered sustainable returnees although they continue to travel (Black and King 2004). Maintaining social networks and contacts abroad could have a positive effect on the development of the wider community, as is shown in the study on Ghanaian and Ivorian returnees (Ammassari 2004).

An alternative definition considers the socioeconomic factors facing the returnee (Gent and Black 2005). The opportunities available to the returnee are determined in terms of factors including employment, housing, and access to basic services. Gent and Black (2005) suggest that return be considered sustainable if the returnee can survive without any external input, although many returnees, largely those related to conflict, are still dependent on aid and remittance from abroad. A third possible definition focuses on the rights of the returnee, including rights to public and social services, property, and freedom of movement. This suggests that return can be sustainable even if the returnee uses the right to move and remigrate.

To expand the definition of sustainability of returnees to the wider community, sustainability of livelihoods may be considered. As Black and Gent (2004) suggest, the livelihood of a community can be regarded as sustainable if it is not dependent on external input or sensitive to external shocks. This suggests a self-contained society with enough assets accumulated to support itself entirely, which is rarely seen in today's world of links and networks across borders. A definition of sustainable return in today's globally interlinked society must consider what Black and King (2004) refer to as *transnationalism*, where the ability to return and remigrate is emphasized. Even if the return of a transnational is only temporary, it can strengthen the links between the emigrant and the home community in a way that can promote development. Transnationalism thus could be considered a form of return in itself, while stable permanent return becomes less relevant (Black and King 2004).

This lack of relevance is evident in the West African context. According to a recent study by Black, Tiemoko, and Waddington (2003), a majority of returnees to Ghana and Côte d'Ivoire described their return as permanent. About two-thirds of all less-skilled returnees in Ghana reported their return as permanent, but more than half of them also claimed that they planned to reemigrate. The elite, however, showed little interest in reemigrating. In Côte d'Ivoire, the most important factor for reemigration was the opportunity to work and develop a business abroad. In Ghana, conversely, more returnees had claimed they had no choice but to return. About half of this group was planning to reemigrate, although they initially described their return as permanent.

According to Black and Gent (2004), migrants often wish to return home, particularly if the initial migration was forced. However, if the migrant has lived abroad for a long period of time, the receiving area might eventually be considered home. This is particularly true if the migrant faces barriers to return to origin, such as reduced economic opportunities, complicated relationships with nonmigrants, and frustration over the business climate and corruption (Gent and Black 2005). If the returnee maintains social and economic networks abroad and has the ability to remigrate temporarily, some of these barriers could be partly overcome. The economic opportunities that might not be available at origin could be accessed through transnational networks across borders.

In short, although many factors influence the sustainability of return, the most important are voluntariness of return and the environment at origin (Gent and Black 2005). If return is not voluntary, the returnee is more likely to remigrate and his or her return is less likely to reduce poverty. Return is also more likely to be sustainable if social and economic opportunities and political freedom exist in the environment of origin. Policies can affect these important factors by encouraging voluntary return and positively influencing the economic and social environment.

## Characteristics of Return Migrants

Demographic characteristics of returnees, including gender, age and marital status, are important when analyzing transnational return. According to Black, Tiemoko, and Waddington (2003) the basic migration experience does not differ greatly between men and women, in the case of Ghana and Côte d'Ivoire. Men and women spend similar amounts of time abroad and are equally likely to work and join associations while away. However, there are some differences (Black, Tiemoko, and Waddington 2003). Ghanaian women are more likely than their male counterparts to migrate to the United Kingdom, while the destinations of Ghanaian males tend to be more diversified. Women are slightly less likely to send remittances home and are much less likely to attend school when abroad.

Transnational migration seems mainly to involve the younger population. According to the 1984 census, about 60 percent of emigrants from Ghana were between 15 and 34 years old (Adeku 1995). However, the age at first emigration has declined over time, particularly among the elite, whose members are often characterized by eagerness to obtain higher education abroad (Ammassari 2004).

Upon return, more than half of the migrants participating in the survey of migrants in Ghana and Côte d'Ivoire were aged between 30 and 49. This suggests that a majority of returnees are still economically active and may influence development. The age of return tends to differ according to gender and level of skill. Less-skilled returnees are generally older than their elite counterparts, particularly if they are female. Reporting on the same data, Anarfi, Kwankye, and Ahiadeke (2005) observed that 81 percent of elite migrants returning to Ghana were married or cohabiting at the time. For the less-skilled, this proportion was about 71 percent. However, a larger proportion of females than males tend to be unmarried upon return, regardless of skill level.

## Influence of Transnational Return

The impact of return migration on the country of origin depends on what the returnee accumulates abroad and brings back in terms of financial, social, and human capital. To ensure sustainable livelihood on return, assets accumulated should be able to withstand stress and shocks, and there must be opportunities for their enhancement at the time of return and in the future. This section explores the impact of financial, social, and human capital transfers on various levels of West African societies, with particular reference to financial capital transfers in the form of remittances. However, it should be noted that all three forms of capital are closely interlinked; the accumulation of one asset often leads to accumulation of another.

### Impact of Financial Capital Transfers

The economic link between migrants and their homes can contribute greatly to the development process. Apart from remittances to families at home, these links include the consumption of goods and services and capital investments in the form of property, businesses, and charitable donations to the home community (Orozco 2005).

Globally, remittances from international migrants have a major impact on the economies of developing countries, in terms of development processes as well as the alleviation of poverty. The global flow of remittance to developing countries has reached US$72.3 billion as estimated by the International Monetary Fund, nearly matching development assistance and foreign direct investment (FDI) in the developing world (Black, King, and Litchfield 2003). This excludes remittance transferred through informal channels. According to Sander (2003), remittances had surpassed levels of Overseas Development Assistance (ODA) by 1995, while, in the past decade alone, the flow of remittances has doubled in value and outgrown the rate of migration. Today, remittances are the most stable and fastest growing capital flow to developing countries.

The level of remittance varies among developing regions. The Latin America and the Caribbean countries receive about 30 percent of global remittances sent to developing countries, while Sub-Saharan Africa receives only an estimated 5 percent (Sander 2003). However, figures for Africa may be particularly distorted by underreporting and lack of data. It is also possible that a larger proportion of remittance to Sub-Saharan Africa is transferred through informal channels and so not included in official figures (Black and King 2004). It could be argued that remittance has a larger direct influence on poverty when flowing through informal channels.

Remittances could have a major impact on the economies of poor countries in various ways. According to the Central Bank of Ghana, remittances from transnational migrants to Ghana were estimated at US$1.4 billion at the end of 2003 (Addison 2005). However, this money probably represented only half of the amount sent from Ghanaians abroad; a recent study in Ghana and Côte d'Ivoire suggests that as much as 40 percent of remittances are transferred informally (Black and King 2004).

The volume of remittances affects Ghana's US$20 billion economy, constituting an important source of foreign exchange and a significant share of the country's income. According to Orozco (2005), transnational remittances represent an amount 10 times greater than Ghana's GDP per capita. The distributive nature of remittances gives rural areas and women increased access to needed capital. In Ghana, 40 percent of remittances are dispersed to areas outside of Accra and the Ashanti region (Orozco 2005). Remittances also tend to have important effect on national savings and play a crucial role in macroeconomic stability. Nevertheless, remittances should not automatically be considered net addition to national income, as they are partly countered by outflows to emigrants abroad.

Remittance from diasporas is the most direct and fastest growing form of engagement (Orozco 2005). The formation of a group of transnational migrants within a diaspora fosters a level of engagement with the homeland that affects the home country on various levels. The economic impact of remittance is closely linked to potential development. Compared with other diasporas, such as Latino migrants in the United States or South East Asians in Hong Kong, Japan, or Singapore, West African diasporas tend to send increasing amounts of money over time (Orozco 2005). This is particularly true among the Ghanaian diaspora abroad and the Nigerian diaspora in the United States. It suggests that West African diasporas maintain transnational commitment to a life in two separate homes. Interviews with Ghanaian migrants in the United States support this suggestion, as a majority implies that they are planning to return. Many migrants also build homes in Ghana to bolster their return.

On the household level, remittances have a direct effect on people's livelihoods and result in increased living standards. For many poor households, remittances are a major source of income and function as insurance against external shocks (Waddington n.d.). Some people, often older parents, rely on remittance for everyday survival. However, although remittance can be used as insurance if saved or invested, it can be a rather insecure source of income. Households often fall back into poverty the moment the remittance flow stops (Kabki, Mazzucato, and Appiah 2004). Waddington (n.d.) has noted that migrants remit mainly to ensure the survival of the family, sustain livelihoods at home and improve social status. A recent study showed that more than 80 percent of those who had sent remittance to Ghana and Côte d'Ivoire did so mainly to meet the subsistence needs of their families (Black and King 2004).

Migration of a family member does not automatically result in improved living conditions in the household at home. The volume and frequency of remittance depend on factors including the time spent abroad, the legal status of the migrant, and his or her relationship with the family (Kabki, Mazzucato, and Appiah 2004). According to Tiemoko (2004) the family plays an important role in the migration process. It is one of the three most commonly reported reasons for return to Ghana and Côte d'Ivoire and seems to have a particularly positive influence on the volume of savings and nature of investment by migrants. One third of all returnees, including both the less-skilled and the elite, returned either for family or for work-related reasons (Black, Tiemoko, and Waddington 2003).

In general, Ghanaians spend longer abroad than Ivorians. More than half of all less-skilled Ivorians have spent less than five years abroad, while almost half of all Ghanaian elite migrants have spent more than 15 years away (Black, Tiemoko, and Waddington 2003).

Overall, the transfer of financial capital was greater to Ghana than to Côte d'Ivoire among both less-skilled and elite returnees, although all people surveyed had sent remittance from abroad and returned with savings. About 42 percent of Ghanaians, including both the less-skilled and the elite, sent frequent remittances home. Among Ivorians abroad, only 31 percent of the less-skilled and 11 percent of the elite did so (Black, Tiemoko, and Waddington 2003). Overall, the evidence suggests that the time spent abroad and the relationship with family at home do impact the level of remittance and other financial capital transferred. However, a possible link between remittances sent and the home country's economic situation still remains to be explored.

The influence of remittances depends not only on their volume and frequency, but also on the ways in which they are used. In general, remittances flow from relatively richer to relatively poorer households and from children to parents. An estimated average of about 80 percent of remittance is used for consumption at the individual and household level (Sander 2003). However, the extended community can benefit as well.

An increase in consumption and individual or household investment creates demand-driven development at community level. The local community benefits from the increased demand and from "spillover" effects. Many migrants abroad invest in businesses at home or other development-related activities, or support the family in doing so. This is particularly evident among less-skilled Ghanaian migrants, as 56 percent returned to self-employment, compared with only 32 percent in Côte d'Ivoire (Black, Tiemoko, and Waddington 2003). Most of these returnees also employed other workers in their businesses, which were largely concentrated in the retail and service sectors. Examples of such businesses in Ghana include communication centers, commercial transportation and trade of second-hand goods (Kabki, Mazzucato, and Appia 2004). Some of these businesses have proved to have had a significant influence on the development of the local community through local employment and the provision of essential services.

Transnational migrants contribute directly to programs for the development of the local home community, either individually or through collaboration with other migrants. As shown in Kabki's study (2004), such projects can include the provision of hospital equipment and contributions to the electrification of the hometown. In the end, the success and sustainability of development initiatives funded by migrants depends on the value of the contribution and the assertiveness of the local leaders.

### Impact of Social Capital Transfers

The concept of social capital is hard to define in quantitative terms and therefore difficult to measure (Black, King, and Litchfield 2003). However, it can have a substantial impact on development when migrants return. Attendance and support at social gatherings, maintenance of social networks and professional contacts abroad upon return, and engagement of returnees in hometown associations are a few ways in which social capital can be transferred from returnees.

Often, a significant amount of migrants' and returnees' time, money, and effort is spent on such events as weddings and funerals, gatherings that provide opportunities for advancing status. These events extend social capital between the migrant and the family and community at home. Kabki, Mazzucato, and Appia (2004) note that the nature and importance of funerals in parts of Ghana has shifted in recent years, becoming more of a way to meet people.

The acquisition of social capital abroad through social networks and professional contacts helps in the development of businesses and professional activities back home (Ammassari 2004). The transfer of social capital from abroad, in particular from elite returnees, often brings together two different worlds, as new worldviews are evolved through the migration and globalization process. These transnational concepts transferred from migrants influence not only the professional life of the migrant but also family, relatives, friends, and sometimes whole communities back home. In the notion of "transnational social spaces," the transfer of social capital functions as a bridge between two separate international places. According to Faist (2000), social and symbolic ties are necessary to mobilize financial and human capital. In other words, social capital accumulation is important in facilitating financial and human capital accumulation.

The engagement of returnees in hometown associations also enhance transfers of social capital gained abroad. Many migrants surveyed from Ghana and Côte d'Ivoire had been members of associations abroad, mainly hometown associations, which often play a role in local community development. About 61 percent of elite returnees reported engagement in associations while abroad, compared with 43 percent of the less-skilled (Black, Tiemoko, and Waddington 2003). However, some evidence suggests that less-skilled returnees gained social capital from the association, since in most cases other members had higher qualifications. Other returnees reported setting up community-based organizations, and some were members of philanthropic organizations focused on development activities.

Frequency of contact with family while abroad could strengthen ties between the migrant and the family members, and so increase the importance of social capital transfers. A majority of migrants originating from Ghana and Côte d'Ivoire have regular contact with their family at home (Tiemoko 2004). However, less-skilled migrants are far more likely to be in regular contact with their family at home than are the elite.

Apart from sending remittances, migrants abroad connect with their home country and family through visits, telecommunication, and purchasing of goods from their home country. Orozco (2005) points out that more than half of all Ghanaians abroad visit Ghana once a year or more. This is one of the highest levels of visits among diasporas, matched only by Nigeria. Ghanaians living in the United Kingdom and the United States visit Ghana more frequently than those living in Germany, but visits from Germany tend to last longer. A similar trend is apparent in frequency and length of phone calls from migrants abroad. Orozco adds that nearly all Ghanaians abroad buy Ghanaian-produced goods, mainly spices and seafood. These ties with home facilitate the eventual and successful return of migrants and are key in determining the type and success of investment established by returnees.

## Impact of Human Capital Transfers

Recently, the effect of human capital on the development process has been of serious concern to governments in many developing countries. The main focus has been on the departure (the "brain drain") and possible return of the highly skilled workers. However, the benefits of less-skilled returnees, in terms of knowledge, ideas, work skills, and experience, should also be recognized.

The Black, Tiemoko, and Waddington (2003) study found that almost 70 percent of less-skilled returnees to Ghana and Côte d'Ivoire reported studying abroad. For elite returnees, this number was close to 90 percent (table 4.1). This suggests that, while elite returnees gain more human capital abroad in terms of education, the potential of the less-skilled returnees to contribute to the development of the country of origin upon their return is greater than is generally recognized.

Results for Ghana and Côte d'Ivoire differed notably when it came to the higher level of education attained abroad among the elite. On average, Ivorians went abroad with a higher level of education than did

**Table 4.1. Human Capital Gained by Surveyed Migrants**

| | Less-skilled | | Elite | |
|---|---|---|---|---|
| Human capital gained | Number surveyed | Percentage | Number surveyed | Percentage |
| Studied abroad | 206 | 68 | 265 | 88 |
| Attended higher level of education than at home | 94 | 31 | 239 | 79 |
| Worked abroad | 242 | 80 | 258 | 85 |
| Reported gaining work experience | 184 | 61 | 254 | 84 |

Source: Black, Tiemoko, and Waddington 2003.

Ghanaians. Among Ghanaians the higher level of education attained abroad usually involved a master's degree after finishing undergraduate studies at home. Ivorians tended to leave with a master's degree to obtain a doctorate abroad (Ammassari 2004).

Since 1990, the level of educational attainment of emigrants from both Ghana and Côte d'Ivoire has shifted, from a large proportion of emigrants being less educated, to a large proportion being medium or well educated, with the trend more significant in Ghana. In 1990, about 50 percent of all Ghanaian emigrants had a low level of education when they departed. This proportion had decreased to 25 percent by 2000 (Docquier and Marfouk 2005). The largest increase was apparent among emigrants with a post-secondary education although the proportion of highly educated emigrants also increased substantially. These findings can be used to justify increased focus on limiting the departure of the highly skilled and encouraging them to return. However, the development potential of emigrants with medium-level education upon return should not be underestimated.

The proportion of returnees who reported working abroad was similar across both groups and countries. However, a much larger proportion of the elites claimed to have gained work experience abroad (Black, Tiemoko, and Waddington 2003). Ammassari (2004) points out that human capital transfers from elite returnees have the potential to positively affect the workplace upon return. However, the extent of impact mainly depends on three conditions: Accumulation of some knowledge and experience abroad, usefulness of things learned abroad in the home context, and desire and ability to apply human capital gained abroad. In the case of Ghana and Côte d'Ivoire, all three conditions were evident. Returnees stated that, although they were faced with difficulties upon return, they felt they had made significant contributions to development both in the public and private sector (Ammassari 2004).

The impact of Ghanaian and Ivorian elite returnees on public and private development appears to have shifted over time. Earlier migrants returning during the independence period were faced with public sector opportunities and usually were anxious to take on leadership roles at home. Many considered it a duty to return and contribute to the development of their country of origin (Ammassari 2004). However, more recent returnees have faced greater difficulties upon return and less formal public sector opportunities. The younger elite migrants also have a different concept of life, evolved through economic difficulties and the process of globalization. Therefore, these returnees have had a larger impact on development in the private sphere.

Recent evidence from Ghana shows that migration also has an important impact on human capital formation at home. Migration affects the level of education at home on two different levels (Kabki, Mazzucato, and Appia 2004). The direct financial support through remittance from migrants abroad helps families to send more children to school. Contact with migrants abroad also helps to change attitudes toward education increasing the importance given to children's education.

From the literature reviewed and empirical evidence studied, it is clear that transnational return migration has many positive influences on the sending household and local community in West Africa. However, to fully utilize transnational return as a development tool, appropriate policies have to be developed and applied.

## Pro-poor Policy Alternatives

Migration is viewed as an important livelihood strategy for many poor people across the West African subregion (Black 2004). It is seen as a way for poor people to diversify their sources of income. For migrants who are better off, "pull" factors in the destination area are more likely to affect their choice of migration than "push" factors at origin. A country study of Ghana (Anarfi, Awusabo-Asare, and Nsowah-Nuamah 2000) showed that the very poor are more likely to migrate than the moderately poor and the non-poor. However, upon return to origin, the moderately poor have the greatest ability to alleviate poverty. Although the relationship between migration and poverty may not be clear-cut, the potential of migration to be pro-poor should be addressed in related policies.

To develop pro-poor growth policies, the relationship between economic policies and poverty reduction has been explored (UNDP 2002), with Poverty Reduction Strategy Papers (PRSPs) used to develop national pro-poor policies. Unfortunately, although pro-poor migration policies can maximize the benefits of migration for poor people and reduce the risks involved in the migration process (Black 2004), this aspect has received little attention in PRSPs in most of Sub-Saharan Africa. Nevertheless, the effect of migration on poor peoples' livelihoods has been acknowledged by PRSPs in some West African countries, particularly in Cape Verde, Mali, and Niger (Black 2004).

In many West African countries, policy initiatives in the field of transnational migration have focused on limiting departure of skilled migrants and encouraging those abroad to return. This has been seen as the most effective way to reverse the "brain drain" and mobilize resources of migrants for development in the home country (Ammassari and Black 2001). However, according to Black and Gent (2004), most programs designed to encourage the return of skilled migrants have been ineffective and have had little impact on poverty. For example, a study by Black, Tiemoko, and Waddington (2003) found that only a small group of Ghanaian elite returnees reported benefiting from government programs upon return. People were generally unaware of the existence of pertinent government policies. As a response, more flexible programs developed recently have focused on the positive effects of diasporas abroad. Examples include the UNDP's Transfer of Knowledge Through Expatriate Nationals (TOKTEN) program, and the International Organization for Migration's Migration for Development in Africa (MIDA).

Diasporas abroad engage in a range of economic practices in their home countries. It is important to identify which of these economic practices constitute remittance and which result in investment. Thus, Orozco states (2005: 39) that "although remittances have an impact on poverty, that is, they keep people out of poverty, remittances per se do not get you out of poverty." The relationship between remittance and development is not fully understood and national policies dealing directly with remittances from abroad are largely missing. Orozco (2005) suggests that both structural reforms with regard to inequality and specific policies for integration and financial democratization of sending and receiving households are necessary to maximize the impact of remittance on poverty. The policy agenda must be set to identify certain dynamics. Orozco (2005) suggests establishing a commission on remittance and development. To maximize positive impacts of migrant investments and savings from the diaspora, bank institutions should offer special favorable interest rates or lines of credit for investment (Orozco 2005).

Ghana and Nigeria have extended dual citizenship to migrants living in diasporas abroad in order to facilitate and encourage return. A similar effort within the Economic Community of West African States (ECOWAS) would provide the opportunity for members to gain residence, employment, and other rights in other ECOWAS countries (Black 2004). Recently, West African governments have increased their efforts to strengthen relations with diaspora communities and associations. A Non-Resident Ghanaians Secretariat (NRGS) was established in 2003 to encourage return of migrants to Ghana, and Homecoming Summits have been organized by the government since 2001 (Black 2004).

The context in which return occurs affect the returnee's contribution to the development process. A returnee is unlikely to contribute much unless some form of capital has been accumulated abroad. It must be possible to use the capital accumulated efficiently in the return country. Policy makers need to identify contexts favorable for the investment of resources upon return and to recognize the type of capital that can best contribute to development in specific circumstances (Ammassari and Black 2001). While there has been much effort to encourage the return of human capital, there has been relatively little investigation into how financial capital, in the form of remittance and investment, is transferred upon return.

It is important that policies be adjusted to changing patterns of migration. Return migration is not an end in itself since focus has shifted away from the migrant's presence at origin. Social networks and the migrant's contribution to development at origin have become increasingly important in promoting sustainable return. This is reflected in recent programs such as the Ghana Information Network for Knowledge Sharing (GINKS), which seeks to provide education across borders through newsletters, CD-ROMs, and the Internet (Black 2004).

## Conclusion and Recommendations

This chapter has provided a brief review of the literature on the sustainability of return and the implications of financial, social, and human capital accumulated abroad, with a particular focus on the West African subregion, mainly comparing data from Ghana and Côte d'Ivoire. It has recognized that sustainable return is not an end in itself and is evolving constantly alongside the globalization process. The definition of sustainable return has, therefore, to be continually under revision. In the case of the West African subregion, it is important that a regionwide definition is established for policy purposes.

Financial, social, and human capital have been identified as important development tools to send to households, local communities, and countries of origin. Statistics cited in this chapter point to the enormous amount of financial capital flowing into the region each year in the form of remittances, investments, and donations. If this capital is managed in a sustainable manner, it could lead to substantial economic development.

A majority of West African returnees report having accumulated human capital abroad that could support asset accumulation within the country of origin upon return. This could increase confidence in the ability of the country to generate resources internally and enhance self-sufficiency, and in turn reduce dependence on aid from abroad. The transfer of social capital, in terms of maintaining close contact with family and friends at home and visiting regularly, is important in facilitating the transfer of financial and human capital. However, social capital, in the form of attending social gatherings, supporting social networks and professional contacts, and engaging in hometown associations, is also important in itself for development.

The options available for promoting sustainable return and maximizing development in the West African region are embedded in the policy alternatives discussed above. Essentially, the recommended policies involve making return an easy and attractive option. The creation of sufficient opportunities for optimal use of assets accumulated abroad should be prioritized, alongside the construction of legal frameworks to make these opportunities attractive to returnees. It is crucial to encourage and implement voluntary return programs, particularly in countries marked by recent conflict. Return migration is unlikely to be sustainable unless it is voluntary. However, when the initial migration was for economic reasons, the key task is to influence the economic and social climate at origin to make return an attractive option.

Hitherto, social policies on migration have focused on limiting the emigration of the highly skilled. Instead, policies should be geared to promote return and the transfer of financial, human, and social capital. The creation of close social and financial links with diasporas abroad is important in promoting sustainable return.

It is vital to maximize the benefits of both financial and human capital transfers in order to create an attractive economic climate at origin. A commission focusing on remittance and development should be established to identify the most effective way to channel remittances for development purposes. Moreover, banking institutions should be encouraged to create special favorable interest rates or lines of credit for investment, to maximize the positive impact of migrant investments and savings from the diaspora.

If one is to simplify the process of return migration to the subregion, it is essential that initiatives be taken transnationally. The creation and expansion of institutions and legal frameworks in the subregion include the extension of the ECOWAS protocols. A regionwide citizenship would enhance the ability of members to attain employment anywhere within the region, to sustain livelihoods. Moreover, expansion of dual citizenships to all West Africans abroad will further make return favorable and easy. However, for such policies effectively to promote return, each state must be responsible for the rights of its citizens and for making these rights universal. By emphasizing migration in PRSPs in all West African countries, the benefits of migration and return could be fully maximized. These possible alternatives to sustainable return and development have been highlighted in a pro-poor context, the aim of which is to further extend the understanding of the complex relationship among migration, return, and development within the globalization milieu.

## References

Addison, E. K. Y. 2005. The Macroeconomic Impact of Remittances. In *At home in the world?: International Migration and Development in Contemporary Ghana and West Africa,* ed. Takyiwaa Manuh. Accra: Sub-Saharan Publishers.

Adeku, J. 1995. Ghanaians Outside the Country. In *International Migration in Ghana,* ed. K. A. Twum-Baah. Accra: Ghana Statistical Service.

Ammassari, S. 2004. "From Nation-Building to Entrepreneurship: The Impact of Elite Return Migrants in Côte d'Ivoire and Ghana." In *Population, Place, and Space,* 10 (2): 133–54. Sussex: John Wiley & Sons.

Ammassari, S., and R. Black. 2001. *Harnessing the Potential of Migration and Return to Promote Development: Applying Concepts to West Africa.* Migration Research Series No. 5. Geneva: International Organization for Migration.

Anarfi, J., K. Awusabo-Asare, and N. Nsowah-Nuamah. 2000. "Push and Pull Factors of International Migration." Country Report: Ghana. Eurostat Working Papers 2000/E(10). European Commission, Statistical Office of the European Communities.

Anarfi, J., S. Kwankye, and C. Ahiadeke. 2005. "Migration, Return, and Impact in Ghana: A Comparative Study of Skilled and Unskilled Transnational Migrants." In *At Home in the World?: International Migration and Development in Contemporary Ghana and West Africa,* ed. Takyiwaa Manuh. Accra: Sub-Saharan Publishers.

Black, R., R. King, and J. Litchfield. 2003. *Transnational Migration, Return, and Development in West Africa.* Brighton: Sussex Centre for Migration Research, University of Sussex.

Black, R., R. Tiemoko, and C. Waddington. 2003. *International Migration, Remittances and Poverty: The Case of Ghana and Côte d'Ivoire.* Brighton: Sussex Centre for Migration Research, University of Sussex.

Black, R. 2004. *Migration and Pro-Poor Policy in West Africa.* Brighton: Sussex Centre for Migration Research, University of Sussex.

Black, R., and S. Gent. 2004. "Sustainable Return to the Balkans." Paper presented at a Conference on the Sustainability of 'Voluntary Assisted Return': The Experience of the Balkans,' Tirana, Albania, September 14.

Black, R., and R. King. 2004. Editorial Introduction: "Migration, Return, and Development in West Africa." In *Population, Place, and Space* 10 (2): 75–83.

Docquier, F., and A. Marfouk. 2005. International Migration by Educational Attainment (1990–2000)." In *International Migration, Remittances & the Brain Drain*, ed. M. Schiff, C. Özden. Washington DC: World Bank.

Economic Commission for Africa. 1996. "Causes and Consequences of International Migration in Africa." Monograph. ECA/POP/WP/96/3.

Faist, T. 2000. *The Volume and Dynamics of International Migration and Transnational Social Spaces*. Oxford: Clarendon Press.

Gent, S., and R. Black. 2005. "Defining, Measuring and Influencing Sustainable Return." Briefing Paper No. 3. Brighton: Sussex Centre for Migration Research, University of Sussex.

Kabki, M., V. Mazzucato, and E. Appiah. 2004. "'Wo benane a eye bebree': The Economic Impact of Netherlands-Based Ghanaian Migrants on Rural Ashanti." In *Population, Place, and Space* 10 (2): 85–97.

King, R. 2000. "Generalisations from the History of Return Migration." In *Return Migration, Journey of Hope or Despair?*, ed. B. Ghosh. Geneva: IOM/UN.

Lee, E. S. 1966. "A Theory of Migration." *Demography* 3 (1): 47–57.

Mabogunje, A. L. 1970. "Systems Approach to a Theory of Rural-Urban Migration." *Geographical Analysis* 2: 1–17.

Orozco, M. 2005. Diasporas, Development and Transnational Integration: Ghanaians in the U.S., U.K., and Germany. Washington, D.C.: U.S. Agency for International Development.

Raveinstein, E. G. 1885. "The Laws of Migration." *Journal of the Royal Statistical Society* 48: 167–235.

Sander, C. 2003. *Migrant Remittances to Developing Countries*. London: Department of International Development.

Smith, M. P., and L. E. Guarnizo, eds. 1998. *Transnationalism from Below*. New Brunswick: Transaction Publishers.

Teitelbaum, M., and S. Weiner, eds. 1995. *Threatened Peoples, Threatened Borders*. New York: W. W. Norton.

Tiemoko, R. 2004. "Migration, Return, and Socioeconomic Changes in West Africa: the Role of the Family." In *Population, Place, and Space* 10 (2). Sussex: John Wiley & Sons.

UNDP (United Nations Development Programme). 2002. *UNDP Support for Poverty Reduction Strategies: The PRSP Countries*. New York: United Nations.

Waddington, C., n.d. "Livelihood Outcomes of Migration for Poor People." Development Research Centre on Migration, Globalisation, and Poverty Working Paper. Forthcoming.

# CHAPTER 5

# Public Policies to Support Migrant Workers in Pakistan and the Philippines

*Farooq Azam*

Declining fertility rates in developed countries have prompted growing demand for international migrants as domestic labor forces shrink. More-over, globalization is easing national barriers to flows of money and goods, and pressure is mounting on developed and comparatively developed countries to relax restrictions on migration flows as well. The situation offers unique opportunities to the citizens of developing countries to access the global employment markets and to build sustainable livelihoods by developing and consolidating their asset bases. The role of policy and institutions is pivotal in enabling migrants to pursue this strategy of development and consolidation.

Pakistan and the Philippines are among the leading migrant "sending countries" in Asia, both having more than three decades of experience in managing international migration. This chapter examines the role of migration policy in these countries from the point of view of the migrants' strategy of building sustainable livelihoods by developing and consolidating their asset bases. The overall role of policy in this context is to provide an enabling environment to migrants and their families for achieving their goal over the long term. A successful policy should not only provide opportunities for asset development and consolidation but also help to manage the multiple risks that could undermine the goal's achievement.

The policy analysis is conducted at two levels: effectively managing risks and improving opportunities for asset development. The discussion on policy regimes is preceded by an account of the contextual background of international migration in Pakistan and the Philippines, including migration

trends and characteristics of migrants. The last section consists of recommendations in the light of policy gaps identified earlier in the chapter.

## Migration Scale and Trends

According to official estimates, more than eight million Filipinos were working or living overseas by 2004 and 3.75 million Pakistanis were in the same
situation by 2001. The largest proportion of overseas Filipinos is in the
region of the Americas (44 percent), mainly in the United States, followed
by the Middle East and Asia (each 19 percent), Europe (10 percent), and
Oceania (4 percent). Overseas, Pakistanis are mainly present in the Middle East (45 percent), followed by Europe (29 percent), and the Americas
(23 percent).

The average annual outflow from the Philippines is more than five times
higher than that of Pakistan; the average figures for the two countries
during 2000–04 were 880,336 and 155,922, respectively. The Philippine
government has followed a more proactive strategy than Pakistan when it
comes to securing access to the global employment markets. The Philippines
Overseas Employment Administration (POEA), the government body for
regulating overseas migration, has a dedicated marketing branch for this
purpose, while its Pakistani equivalent, the Bureau of Emigration and
Overseas Employment (BOE), has no such arrangement. As a result, more
diverse regions are available to Filipino migrants than to Pakistani migrants,
as shown by the annual migration outflow data. During the period of
2000–04, the outflow of Filipino "land-based" migrants (excluding seafarers) to the Middle East region ranged from 44 percent to 50 percent; to
the Asian region 38 percent to 45 percent; to the European region around
6 percent; and to the Americas less than 2 percent. By contrast, outflow
from Pakistan during these years was heavily directed toward the Middle
East, at around 97 percent (see tables 5.1 and 5.2).

Another significant difference between the two countries is that women
dominate migration flows from the Philippines while their participation is
insignificant in Pakistan. In the Philippines, the women's share in migration
increased from 50 percent to 70 percent during 1992–2002.[1] Pakistan's
migration data do not provide gender distribution, but the government's
policy of discouraging the migration of women means that it is generally
men who migrate, constituting probably more than 95 percent of registered migrants. Clearly, this policy also has the effect of limiting access to

**Table 5.1. Pakistan: Regional Trends of Migration Outflows from Pakistan, 1995–2004**

| Year | Total outflow* | Outflow registered by BOE | Outflow to Middle East | Share of Middle East (%) | Share of Asia (%) | Share of Europe (%) |
|---|---|---|---|---|---|---|
| 1995 | 122,620 | 117,048 | 116,212 | 99.0 | — | — |
| 1996 | 127,784 | 119,629 | 118,840 | 99.3 | — | — |
| 1997 | 153,929 | 149,029 | 147,885 | 99.2 | — | — |
| 1998 | 104,044 | 100,706 | 100,325 | 99.6 | — | — |
| 1999 | 80,496 | 78,093 | 76,708 | 98.2 | — | — |
| 2000 | 110,136 | 107,733 | 104,463 | 96.9 | 1.3 | 2.0 |
| 2001 | 130,041 | 127,929 | 123,680 | 96.6 | 0.5 | 1.6 |
| 2002 | 149,127 | 147,422 | 144,592 | 98.0 | 0.4 | 0.8 |
| 2003 | 215,443 | 214,039 | 209,427 | 97.8 | 1.2 | 0.6 |
| 2004 | 174,864 | 173,824 | 168,077 | 96.7 | 1.5 | 1.3 |

Source: Bureau of Emigration and Overseas Employment 2005.
Note: *Total outflow data includes migrants registered by both Bureau of Emigration and Overseas Employment (BOE) and Overseas Employment Corporation (OEC). Region-wise distribution of migrants, however, excludes OEC data where this distribution was not available.
— = Figures not available.

**Table 5.2. Philippines: Deployed Overseas Workers by Destination Region, 1998–2004**

| | 1998 | 1999 | 2000 | 2001 | 2002 | 2003 | 2004 |
|---|---|---|---|---|---|---|---|
| Middle East | 279,767 | 287,076 | 283,291 | 297,533 | 306,939 | 285,564 | 352,314 |
| Asia | 307,261 | 299,521 | 292,067 | 285,051 | 292,077 | 255,287 | 266,609 |
| Europe | 26,422 | 30,707 | 39,296 | 43,019 | 45,363 | 37,981 | 55,116 |
| Americas | 9,152 | 9,045 | 7,624 | 10,679 | 11,532 | 11,049 | 11,692 |
| Africa | 5,538 | 4,936 | 4,298 | 4,943 | 6,919 | 8,750 | 8,485 |
| Trust territories | 7,677 | 6,622 | 7,421 | 6,823 | 6,075 | 5,023 | 7,177 |
| Oceania | 2,524 | 2,424 | 2,386 | 2,061 | 1,917 | 1,698 | 3,023 |
| Unspecified | 2 | — | 6,921 | 11,530 | 10,882 | 46,279 | 1 |
| Workers with special exit clearance | — | — | — | 1,009 | 611 | 307 | 169 |
| Deployed seabased | 193,300 | 196,689 | 198,324 | 204,951 | 209,593 | 216,031 | 229,002 |

Source: Philippines Overseas Employment Administration 2005.
Note: — indicates figures not available.

overseas employment opportunities, especially to those jobs where women are preferred.

## Migration Management Models and Migration Channels

Both Pakistan and the Philippines have put elaborate institutional arrangements in place to facilitate international migration as a main policy focus. According to Abella (Abella 1997), migration management models could be categorized as follows:

- laissez-faire, where market forces guide the emigration process exclusively
- regulated, where the market still takes care of the recruitment for overseas employment but follows a set of standards and procedures imposed by the state
- state-managed, where recruitment is carried out under state regulation, by state-managed agencies, and where the government encourages domestic enterprises to seek contracts overseas for which domestic labor could be employed
- state monopoly, where the state has full control of recruitment and there is no private sector participation.

The Philippines has a "regulated" migration management model in that government legislation on migration, the 1995 Migrant Workers and Overseas Filipinos Act, defines standards and procedures to be followed by private recruiting agents for overseas recruitment or by individual migrants proceeding abroad on their own. Pakistan follows a mix of the "regulated" and the "state-managed" models.

Pakistan's Emigration Ordinance 1979 defines standards and procedures to be followed, but the country has a government recruiting agency as well as private recruiting agents.

Recruiting agents are the primary means of arranging overseas employment for migrants from both countries. The next important means are the informal, transnational networks of a migrant's friends and relatives overseas. Both of these are officially recognized, "regular" migration channels. A third channel of "irregular" migration consists of unauthorized stay overseas and human smuggling and trafficking in persons.

The migration management systems introduced by both Pakistan and the Philippines have aimed to regulate the working of recruiting agents.

In Pakistan, the system was introduced by establishing the BOE in 1979. The Philippines established the POEA in 1982, through a presidential order. The chief responsibilities of BOE and POEA include issuing licenses to recruiting agents, monitoring their working, and ensuring the provision of minimum standards in the foreign employment contracts. The agencies determine the rate of various charges, including the commission to be charged by the recruiting agent to the migrant, and charges to be paid by the migrant for the skill test, medical examination, and travel and other documents.

Both countries follow stringent criteria in selecting private recruiting agents and require them to provide substantial security deposits against penalties for any malpractice, including overcharging of migrants. Although these mechanisms have helped to keep the majority of migration flows in regular channels, smuggling of migrants and trafficking of women and children remain significant challenges for the Philippines and Pakistan.

A high incidence of human trafficking from the Philippines was highlighted by a U.S. governmental report on trafficking in persons (U.S. Department of State 2004: 7). The report notes that "Filipino women who are trafficked for sexual exploitation to destinations throughout Asia, the Middle East, Africa, Europe and North America, are often lured abroad with false promises of legitimate employment." The report adds that, although the government introduced an anti-trafficking law in 2003, its implementation remains weak.

The report also indicates that, from Pakistan, "men, women, and children are trafficked to the Middle East to work as bonded laborers or in domestic servitude. Tougher enforcement efforts in Pakistan and the ban on child camel jockeys in the United Arab Emirates are believed to have reduced the numbers of boys trafficked through Pakistan for that purpose" (U.S. Department of State 2004: 4). The report describes human smuggling as a significant issue in Pakistan and adds that officials do not distinguish between trafficked and smuggled persons. The report notes that Pakistan introduced an anti-trafficking law shortly before the report was published, but the law's implementation remains weak.

## Socioeconomic Characteristics of Migrants

Some earlier studies in Pakistan and the Philippines suggest that migrants do not come from the poorest social strata. Two studies of labor migration from Pakistan to the Middle East, conducted in 1986 and 1987, showed that about 70 percent of migrants belonged to lower-middle income and financial asset groups (Azam 1991). Migration required substantial financial investment, with the payment made to the recruiting agent alone amounting to more than 14 months of premigration salary.

However, another study on "migration potential," based on a survey of migrant and nonmigrant households in high and low out-migration districts in Pakistan, showed that, while financial assets (cash savings and house/land ownership) and human assets (education and training) were the main preconditions for migration, a strong asset position (in land ownership) actually served as a disincentive for migration. Households of migrants in the high migration district relied heavily on subsistence farming, dependent on seasonal rains, supplemented by nonfarm employment for their livelihood, whereas households in the low-migration district owned larger agricultural farms and had secure agricultural income. Households of migrants faced the prospect of fluctuating income levels but possessed the financial assets required to meet the cost of migration. Further, the search for nonfarm occupations induced them to acquire an education and learn more skills and to look for employment in other cities. Other factors facilitating migration were access to information regarding overseas employment, recruiting agencies, and migration networks (Azam 1998).

Based on the Philippines' Family Income and Expenditure Surveys, Saith (1997) and Go (2003) concluded that overseas migrants are more likely to be from relatively wealthier urban families than rural poorer families.

Households facing insecure livelihoods are, therefore, likely to opt for international migration as a strategy to build more secure and sustainable livelihoods for their members. A certain threshold of financial and human assets is required for a member of the concerned household to migrate, with the financial cost of migration substantially eroding a household's asset endowment. The household's goal is not only to recover this investment but also to build up the financial and human assets of the household members for the longer-term sustainability of their livelihoods. This involves the ability to manage effectively the risks international migration poses to the migrant and the family members, as well as to take the initiative in terms of using the financial and human capabilities gained from migration to consolidate and further build the household asset base. Seen in this context, one of the roles of governments and other agencies should be to provide an enabling environment and conditions for migrants and their families to meet these objectives.

## Migration Risk Management Policies

From the above perspective, government policy and agency programs could be categorized broadly in terms of (a) risk management and (b) asset consolidation and development. The interface between the two categories is strong; from migrants' point of view, the categories should be complementary. Risk management strategies could stand on their own if the objective were merely the protection of migrants. The following two sections discuss government policies in these areas.

Government policies regarding risk management have focused mostly on controlling the financial cost of migration (with implications for the erosion of the migrant's current financial assets), ensuring minimum standards in overseas employment contracts, providing guidance and legal protection to migrants during employment overseas, social security coverage, and welfare services to help migrants and the families they have left behind to cope with the stresses resulting from migration.

### Lowering Migration Cost

The financial cost of migration usually includes the amounts incurred by migrants in seeking and securing overseas employment, including the commission charged by the recruiting agent or employer, documents' fees, skills testing and/or medical examination charges, the governmental fee and processing charges, and the transport costs from home to the place of work if not provided by the employer. It also includes mandatory charges by the government to provide welfare services and insurance coverage to migrants.

*Recruiting agents.* In practice, it is the commission charged by the recruiting agent that inflates the cost of migration. Studies have shown that recruiting agents charge eight to 10 times more than the officially prescribed charges (Azam 1998). Although recruiting agents are generally blamed for the overcharging, it is also a result of two types of other hidden costs, one relating to the employer and the other to government bureaucracy.

The intense competition among the labor-sending countries has led many employers in the Middle East to reduce or eliminate the commission paid to recruiting agents. In fact, employers tend to pass on some of their own costs and obligations, such as expenditure on their trips to the sending country and the air ticket costs of the migrant, to the recruiting agent. Moreover, both governments have introduced elaborate systems for checking malpractices by recruiting agents, according to which recruiting agents have to perform the following:

- Get the overseas job offer authenticated by the Labor Attaché in the country of employment.
- Get the terms of employment verified by BOE/POEA as meeting the prescribed minimum standards.
- Get the individual migrant's contract verified by BOE/POEA.
- Get the final clearance from immigration authorities for the migrant to leave the country.

According to recruiting agents, they have to make unauthorized payments at most of these points. The unauthorized charges, when added to the authorized charges, cause the financial cost of migration to rise, as all these charges are passed on to the migrant by the recruiting agent.

To check malpractices by recruiting agents, the Philippines has adopted a policy of restricting the number of recruiting agents (1,337 in 2004) and introduced stringent qualifying criteria for the induction of new recruiting agents (POEA 2004). It has also introduced a rigorous system of penalties and incentives. Recruiting agents applying for a license must have a paid-up capital of 2 million pesos (approximately US$37,500).[2] In addition, they are required to deposit 1 million pesos as an escrow deposit and a surety bond of 100,000 pesos as a guarantee against any malpractice and negligence.[3] The incentive system for recruiting agents involves the following:

- speedy processing of clearances for migrants recruited by them
- no verification of migrants' employment contracts where there is no previous history of employment contract violations
- extension of the agent's license for another four years
- regular provision of information about new employment opportunities abroad (Baldoz 2003).

In the Philippines, the Overseas Workers Welfare Administration (OWWA), set up under the Department of Labor, runs a scheme of predeparture and family assistance loans for migrants. The scheme was introduced in recognition of the fact that many Filipinos sell their financial assets to obtain overseas employment and to make arrangements for the security of their family in their absence. The Migrant Workers and Overseas Filipinos Act of 1995 expanded the scheme by establishing a Migrant Workers Loan Guarantee Fund with a "revolving" total of 100 million pesos (more than US$1.84 million).

Pakistan has a system of licensed recruiting agents, with 1,182 currently registered. Agencies are required to provide 300,000 rupees (approximately US$5,000) as a security deposit. The license is issued for five years. There is no incentive policy linked to the performance of recruiting agencies. However, the emigration laws do provide penalties against overcharging migrants and other related offenses.

*Transnational networks.* Compared with migration through recruiting agents, findings suggest that migration through informal transnational networks has much lower costs and higher employment benefits, including salary. A survey conducted in Kuwait, involving migrants from South Asia (including Pakistan), found that half had used the informal networks for finding overseas employment while the rest had come through recruiting agents. Friends and relatives already working in Kuwait arranged jobs for the migrants in two ways: by introducing the migrant to their employer and the latter sending an employment visa directly to him or her, or by purchasing the visa through a local agent or directly from an employer. In the former instance, only 14 percent had to make any payment to the employer, while in the latter case around 63 percent made some payment. Substantial salary differences were also found, with the migrants coming through recruiting agents earning the lowest salary and the migrants directly contacted by employers receiving the highest salary for similar jobs. Satisfaction with the employment conditions was also greater among the migrants using informal networks than among those coming through recruiting agents. The latter complained of employment conditions and benefits inferior to those provided in their employment contracts (Shah 1998).[4]

*Irregular migration.* In both countries, the issue of irregular migration is not addressed in the context of migration policy but is treated as a separate phenomenon requiring punitive actions, thereby ignoring its linkages with higher migration cost and lack of information on overseas employment opportunities.

### Enforcing Minimum Standards

As part of their regulatory functions, both BOE and POEA have prescribed minimum standards for foreign employment. These relate to the following areas:

- salary and overtime payments
- working hours and holidays

- free food and accommodation
- travel to the receiving country
- injury and death insurance.

In practice, experience of enforcement of these standards has been mixed, with the biggest casualties being salaries and overtime payments. Moreover, migrants are offered crowded living conditions and poor quality food. Complaints by migrants regarding contract violation and contract substitution (where a migrant is asked to sign a new contract with inferior terms upon arrival in the receiving country) have persisted over time. Although the minimum standards are not fully enforced, they do at least provide migrants with a basis from which to negotiate (Waddington 2003).

Sending countries have little influence over the policies of receiving countries, where standards of rights could be very different from those in the sending countries; moreover, the standards could vary from one social group to the other within the receiving country. In many Middle Eastern countries, for example, migrant workers in domestic jobs are not covered by the labor laws. Migrant housemaids generally work under stressful conditions, including long working hours, without compensation, and without other benefits such as proper health coverage.

### Social Security Coverage

Migrants working on employment contracts of limited duration are generally not provided with any social security benefits, including pension arrangements. Pension contributions by employers are tied to a minimum service period, rendering most migrant workers ineligible. In the Philippines, the Labor Department and the Social Security institution have joined forces to provide social security protection for seafarers, including benefits such as medical treatment, accident insurance, and pensions.

Employers generally provide coverage against accidental injury and death, but housemaids generally do not receive this benefit; migrants working in small establishments are not likely to receive this coverage either. However, even where migrants have this coverage, they or their dependents have difficulties making the claims due to lack of knowledge about procedures.

To ensure that migrants are protected against the risks, both Pakistan and the Philippines have introduced schemes providing compulsory insurance cover to migrants against disability and death during their foreign employment. This is over and above any such benefits provided by the employer. In those countries with a significant presence of their nationals, Pakistan has posted Community Welfare Attachés, and the Philippines Labor Attaches and Welfare Officers, in the respective embassies. Officials guide workers in following the relevant procedures to launch their claims. Back home, the Overseas Pakistanis Foundation (OPF) and the Philippines Overseas Workers Welfare Administration (OWWA) guide the worker's dependents and relatives in completing the formalities and filing compensation claims. OPF has so far helped more than 3,000 families to obtain death compensation, amounting to nearly one billion rupees (approximately US$16.7 million) (unpublished OPF data).

The largest operation for compensation claims, undertaken by both OPF and OWWA, was for migrants repatriated from Kuwait following the Gulf War of 1990. Both organizations guided the migrants regarding the United Nations Compensation Commission (UNCC) procedures and helped them to file the claims. OPF filed about 44,500 compensation claims and has received and disbursed to date nearly US$311.4 million (OPF 2005). To help migrants win compensation for their lost income and assets, the organization conducted a comprehensive survey of the repatriated workers at the ports of entry and built a database that guided the UNCC in determining the levels of compensation. The database was also the primary means by which Pakistani migrants and their employers were brought together after the war, helping migrants to regain their livelihoods abroad, as employers' records had been destroyed during the war.

## Legal Assistance and Welfare of Migrants

Both Pakistan and the Philippines have introduced numerous measures to provide legal protection to migrants and to promote their welfare and that of their families. Measures include predeparture briefing of migrants, covering the relevant laws of the receiving country, and procedures for the resolution of disputes with employers through labor attachés posted in their missions abroad. The Migrant Workers and Overseas Filipinos Act of 1995 provides for the establishment of a Legal Assistance Fund of 100 million pesos (more than US$1.84 million) to provide legal services to migrant workers and overseas Filipinos in distress. The act requires the establishment of a resource center at the embassy to provide welfare assistance to migrants, including medical and hospitalization services, and other gender-sensitive services to women. The center also helps undocumented workers to achieve legal status or be repatriated.

The OPF was established in 1979 under the Ministry of Labor, Manpower, and Overseas Pakistanis, to improve the welfare of Pakistani migrants and their families. The Philippines' OWWA was established in 1980, under the Department of Labor. OPF is financed by mandatory contributions from migrants. OWWA demands mandatory contributions from employers through recruiting agents, which in practice are paid by the migrant. Thus both institutions are the main interlocutors for migrants and their families in their dealings with various agencies and organizations. They have also introduced schemes for microenterprise development, housing, education, and health for migrants and their families, and they guide return migrants on business investment opportunities.

## Asset Development Policies for Migrants

Although both governments have introduced more and more policies to help migrants in accumulating and consolidating their assets, much still remains to be done in this area. Initiatives to date include facilitating the flow of funds for migrants and providing guidance and services for the productive investment of their financial and human resources.

### Remittances and Fund Flow Policies

Since 2000, migrants' cash remittances have been steadily increasing for both Pakistan and the Philippines. The total remittances by Pakistani migrants through official channels stood at US$3,826.16 million in the financial year 2003/04 (table 5.3). Migrants' remittances in the Philippines' were US$8,550.37 million in 2004 (table 5.4). The events of September 11, 2001, triggered a ninefold jump in the remittances from the United States

**Table 5.3. Pakistan: Migrant Workers Remittances by Region, 1997/98–2003/04**

|  | 1997/98 | 1998/99 | 1999/2000 | 2000/01 | 2001/02 | 2002/03 | 2003/04 |
|---|---|---|---|---|---|---|---|
| Total | 1,237.68 | 875.55 | 913.49 | 1,021.59 | 2,340.79 | 4,190.73 | 3,826.16 |
| North America | 170.43 | 85.41 | 83.82 | 139.71 | 799.5 | 1,252.71 | 1,247.99 |
| United States* | 166.29 | 81.95 | 79.96 | 134.81 | 778.98 | 1,237.52 | 1,225.09 |
| Europe | 122.61 | 90.78 | 89.34 | 96.33 | 171.92 | 309.59 | 390.65 |
| Middle East | 843.41 | 640.86 | 681.96 | 693.22 | 1,070.12 | 1,892.65 | 1,614.31 |
| Other | 101.23 | 58.5 | 58.37 | 92.33 | 299.25 | 735.78 | 573.21 |

Source: Government of Pakistan 2005.
Note: *Figures for the United States are also included in figures for North America.

**Table 5.4. Philippines: Migrant Workers Remittances by Region, 1997/98–2003/04**

|  | 1998 | 1999 | 2000 | 2001 | 2002 | 2003 | 2004 |
|---|---|---|---|---|---|---|---|
| Total | 7,367.99 | 6,794.55 | 6,050.45 | 6,031.27 | 6,886.16 | 7,578.46 | 8,550.37 |
| North America | 6,443.59 | 4,929.67 | 4,000.02 | 3,300.33 | 3,537.77 | 4,370.71 | 5,023.80 |
| United States* | 6,403.22 | 4,868.88 | 3,944.64 | 3,202.23 | 3,443.55 | 4,299.85 | 4,904.30 |
| Oceania | 17.06 | 87.34 | 21.36 | 21.19 | 34.79 | 44.47 | 42.6 |
| Europe | 329.32 | 457.67 | 534.68 | 406.19 | 889.09 | 1,040.56 | 1,286.13 |
| Middle East | 60.68 | 263 | 594.2 | 711.92 | 1,242.81 | 1,166.38 | 1,232.07 |
| Africa | 0.6 | 1.9 | 4.45 | 3.6 | 3.96 | 11.37 | 3.44 |
| Asia | 401.42 | 645.57 | 831.78 | 1,049.55 | 1,116.34 | 894.31 | 918.33 |
| Other | 115.33 | 409.4 | 63.97 | 538.49 | 61.4 | 50.66 | 44 |

Source: Philippines Overseas Employment Administration 2005.
Note: *Figures for the United States are also included in figures for North America.

to Pakistan in the financial year 2002/03, probably due to feelings of insecurity among some migrant groups. This trend has strong implications for the availability of investment options in Pakistan.

The governments of both countries have followed a policy of encouraging migrants to send their remittances through formal banking channels rather than informal fund transfer mechanisms. Related policies have focused on improving the convenience, flexibility, and profitability of the transactions, which are key to inducing migrants to remit through official channels (Amjad 1989). In Pakistan, this was done by expanding the banking network within the country and in some countries of employment. The foreign exchange regime was liberalized and migrants were allowed to maintain accounts in foreign currency as well as in Pakistan rupees. To encourage investments from migrants settled overseas, Pakistan allowed the free flow and outflow of foreign currency in any amount. To ensure profitability, the government discontinued the official exchange rate policy and floated the rupee, thus eliminating the gap between official and open market exchange rates. Use of official channels was also promoted by improving the safety of transactions and by eliminating the elements of uncertainty and fraud feared by migrants when using informal mechanisms.[5]

In the Philippines, liberalization of government policy has led to private sector companies offering services for delivering remittances to the households within 24 hours (Go 1994).

*Policies for Productive Investments of Savings*

According to studies in Pakistan and the Philippines, initial investments by migrants tend to focus on improving the housing conditions and health and education status of their families (Azam 1991; Tan and Canlas 1989). In later cycles, the focus shifts toward financial assets, particularly real estate and small businesses. The studies show, however, that migrants generally find business investments quite challenging, requiring business guidance and additional funds such as bank loans to make them competitive and profitable.

The process of informing and guiding migrants regarding the investment opportunities in the country, and assisting them in completion of formalities for establishing business enterprises, has been carried out rather unsystematically by OWWA in the Philippines and OPF in Pakistan. In addition, the numerous and complicated formalities involved in establishing a business remain a strong concern.

The Migrant Workers and Overseas Filipinos Act of 1995 provides for the establishment of a Replacement and Monitoring Center for reintegration of returning migrant workers and offers guidance regarding investment opportunities. The Department of Labor and Employment, OWWF, and POEA have all been charged with formulating a program for the returning workers' livelihood and entrepreneurial development and the productive investment of their savings.

In Pakistan, OPF established an industrial division, with responsibility for guiding migrants settled overseas, as well as returning migrants, toward productive business investments, including joint ventures with the private and public sectors in Pakistan. The division has not been able to perform in the desired manner, despite a great need for its services. The OPF, however, has published a "Guide for Investment" for migrants, which provides information on government procedures, as well as the names and addresses of the relevant departments and organizations. Given the potential for investments by migrants, OPF needs to institute a much more organized and comprehensive program.

To facilitate travel and investment by the migrants of Pakistani origin settled abroad and without Pakistani nationality, the government has introduced the Pakistan Origin Card. The holder of the card does not require a visa to enter Pakistan and can stay in the country indefinitely, has the right to open bank accounts in Pakistan and foreign currencies, and can undertake property and business transactions (NADRA 2005).

### Transfer and Use of Human Assets

Migrants learn new skills during employment abroad, at least in certain occupations. This facilitates the transfer of new technologies to their homeland and leads to better, more cost-effective ways of working. A study conducted in Pakistan involving return migrants and their domestic employers found that migrants who had worked abroad as mechanics, welders, and machinery operators had learned the use of advanced tools, instruments, and machinery, and new ways to organize their work. In terms of job performance, their employers rated them much higher than those workers without overseas employment experience (Azam 1988).[6] A similar survey conducted in the Philippines was inconclusive regarding the degree to which the skill acquisition took place during overseas employment, but indicated that migrants received extensive on-the-job training during their time overseas (Carino 1988).

In Pakistan, the UNDP is supporting the Transfer of Knowledge Through Expatriate Nationals (TOKTEN) program, implemented by the government's National Talent Pool in the Ministry of Labor. The program is designed to facilitate the transfer of technical expertise by Pakistani professionals working abroad to institutions and projects in Pakistan in need of such expertise. The expatriate professionals work in Pakistan for a limited period as consultants. Since its introduction in 1980, the program has supported about 35 consultants per annum.

In the Philippines, the Replacement and Monitoring Center is also charged with developing a program for the transfer of technical skills and expertise gained by returning migrant workers during employment abroad. The center works in conjunction with the private sector and is responsible for developing and maintaining a computer database of the skills profiles of returning workers, which can be used by the private sector and government departments to meet skills needs.

### Social Assets: Transnational Networks

Earlier in this chapter the role of transnational networks in facilitating and reducing the cost and maximizing the benefits of migration for employment was highlighted. The networks exist in various forms: community networks are frequently organized on ethnic lines, ensuring a strong social relationship between corresponding communities in the origin and destination countries. According to Ballard (1987), based on his research on Pakistani migrants in the United Kingdom, one of the ways the networks are strengthened is by arranging marriages across communities where the spouse typically ends up in the destination country. There is a dynamic relationship across boundaries between the two communities, evidenced by constant movement of people and resources in both directions (Ballard 1987).

Other transnational networks are organized on the basis of professional lines and/or social causes. Many of these networks work for and with the migrants and their accompanying families in destination countries, as well as with communities and organizations in the origin country. The Islamabad-based Pakistan Center for Philanthropy, supported by the Aga Khan Foundation, has involved the Pakistani diaspora organizations interested in philanthropy work, especially in community-based projects in education and health sectors. To facilitate communication between them and interested organizations in Pakistan, the Pakistan government's Board of Investment provides a list of Pakistani diaspora associations in North America on its Web site (BOI 2006).

The Asia Pacific Philanthropy Consortium (APPC), an Internet-based network established by a group of professionals at Manila University, Philippines, provides information on the Asian diaspora philanthropy organizations and activities (APPC 2004). One of the goals of its Web site is to facilitate networking between the Filipino and other selected Asian countries' diaspora in North America with NGOs involved in philanthropic and development work in origin countries. Another internet-based Brain Gain Network facilitates contacts between Filipino information technology (IT) professionals abroad and the IT industry in the Philippines. Its objective is to make available the expertise gained abroad for technological innovations in the local industry. The group has developed a database of Filipino professionals working abroad for the benefit of the local industry (BGN 2006).

In addition to serving as a dependable conduit for international migration, these networks facilitate the development of community assets in the origin country. The Association of Pakistani Physicians of North America (APPNA) and some other associations of professionals abroad contribute funds for development activities, mainly in health and education sectors in rural areas. Fund distribution is carried out by the National Commission for Human Development, a government-sponsored organization. APPNA has also provided expertise and resources for the establishment of a cytogenetic laboratory for diagnosis of leukemia in children at the National Institute of Child Health, Karachi (APPNA 2006). In addition, the Association of Pakistani Physicians and Surgeons of the United Kingdom plans to establish a facility in Pakistan for improving the skills and expertise of young medical professionals, using their own expertise developed abroad (APPS 2006).

Similar support by the Filipino diaspora to NGOs in the Philippines has been documented. In 2003, the diaspora's financial contributions to NGOs through official channels alone was an estimated US$218 million. Other forms of assistance included technological support and provision of equipment to medical centers and hospitals (Opiniano 2004).

To date, state policy has not been able to come to grips with the concepts of "transnational communities" and transnational networks of migrants for asset development and brain gain activities. In fact, as noted by the Asian Development Bank, in the absence of a proper state policy in most developing countries many professional associations have started their own initiatives of building networks involving diaspora and the home country associations for skills and knowledge transfer (Asian Development Bank 2005).

### Model Human and Financial Asset-Building Initiative by Migrants

The following account offers an indication of the potential for productive utilization, by migrants, of their accumulated human and financial assets. A group of five doctors of Pakistani origin working and living in the United States conceived the idea of providing a state-of-the-art treatment facility in Pakistan and training younger doctors and medical students in the country in the use of related modern technology. They mustered support from other doctors and health care professionals of Pakistani origin in the United States. After a process of feasibility preparation and other formalities, the acquisition of more than 11 acres of land in Islamabad in 1987, and the planning and designing of the project by a hospital development company in Princeton, New Jersey, the Shifa International Hospital was incorporated in 1987 as a private limited company, with more than 450 contributing members. In 1987, it was converted into a public limited company listed on the stock exchange.

The hospital, opened in June 1993 with only eight consultants with seven specialties, now has more than 70 highly qualified consultants, covering most specialties. It has 150 beds with quality care and outdoor patient facilities in 35 different specializations. It has seven operating rooms, 50 bedded intensive care units, 37 specialist clinics, and a physiotherapy center, and offers most modern biomedical technology, especially in the field of diagnostic imaging. It also has an open heart surgery and renal transplantation program. The medical team involves a number of expatriate physicians, surgeons, and other health professionals who spend a fixed period of the year working at the hospital. Young local doctors and medical professionals work with them, receiving on-the-job training.

In 1993, the group also established the not-for-profit organization Shifa Foundation to subsidize the treatment of poor patients. Importantly, work was started in 1998 to establish the Shifa College of Medicine in modern clinical methods and technology; the project reportedly is progressing as planned. Planning has also begun on an educational program, which will begin with the establishment of 250 primary schools providing quality education to poor students. These initiatives will be funded through contributions from Pakistani migrants settled overseas, as well as local sources.

## Conclusion and Recommendations

The study identifies a considerable number of areas where research and new policy measures can contribute to the integration of migration into the development planning processes of Pakistan and the Philippines.

International migration for employment presents a unique opportunity for migrants and their families to improve their livelihoods on a long-term basis by building and consolidating their human and financial assets. Both Pakistan and the Philippines have introduced policies and comprehensive systems intended to protect migrants from the shocks and risks that the multifaceted phenomenon of migration involves for them and their families. However, policies to assist migrants to build their asset bases need to be further strengthened, thereby enabling migrants and their families to achieve their goal of ensuring sustainable livelihoods.

Further research is needed to determine the asset thresholds required for migration, that is, the social groups that benefit from migration and those that do not but have the potential to do so were migration costs lowered. The rules and procedures need to be as simple as possible so that migrants can deal with them comfortably. Such a measure would also help to minimize the unauthorized payments associated with official processing and so to reduce the cost of migration.

The role of migration networks and diasporas needs to be further investigated and supported, given that this mode of migration has proven to entail lower costs. Migration policy should focus on minimizing the risks associated with migration that could erode the financial assets of migrants. Further, the nexus between a high cost of migration and irregular migration, including human smuggling and trafficking in persons, needs to be better elucidated and addressed through more integrated policies.

Providing full information to migrants regarding rules and procedures, as well as opportunities and risks, is the first step toward empowering them and minimizing their vulnerability. The Philippines' experience in this area could be instructive. Enforcing minimum standards in contracts and ensuring migrants' rights under the law cannot be achieved without supporting action by receiving countries. Multilateral agencies can play a role in establishing a dialogue between sending and receiving countries. In the meantime, sending countries need to provide support services to migrants in the countries of employment to mitigate the effects of their rights' violations. The establishment by the Philippines of resource centers in its embassies to provide a package of relevant services is a good example to follow.

Given the substantial participation of women in migration and the increased household responsibility of women in left-behind families, migration policies and strategies need to be gender sensitive. Here again, further studies are needed to determine the vulnerability of women in various occupations abroad and of those in left behind families, in order to develop suitable policy interventions and provide appropriate support services.

Making use of the improved human assets resulting from migration is a challenge. Systems are needed to identify those areas requiring high grade expertise and skills, as well as related opportunities, and to disseminate this information to the migrants, including returning migrants and diasporas. The role of transnational networks in knowledge and technology transfer needs to be better understood and policy evolved to fully utilize the potential.

Bringing remittances into the formal banking channels helps to avert the risks of fraud associated with informal mechanisms of transactions, which deprive migrants of their hard-earned savings. Pakistan's example of improving the accessibility of formal channels by providing various incentives and introducing flexible mechanisms for funds transfer should be studied for possible adoption.

A more proactive policy is needed to harness the investment potential of the diaspora. Pakistan's policy of promoting the ties of migrants settled overseas with their country of origin through schemes such as the Pakistan Origin Card, and the permitting of dual nationality where accepted by the host country, has strengthened transnational networks. However, the investment advisory services for migrants need to be better organized and mechanisms for regular dissemination of information regarding investment and loan opportunities need to be established.

In addition, the role of organizations charged with providing welfare services to migrants and being run on migrants' own contributions needs to focus more on priorities identified by migrants themselves. This would require the involvement of migrant representatives in policies relating to both OWWA and OPF.

Finally, an effective mechanism for monitoring policy implementation needs to be established in sending countries, and a regular system of monitoring migration trends through research and surveys needs to be established. Currently, the biggest gaps are in monitoring return migration and remittances through informal channels, the working and living conditions of migrants in countries of employment, and the pattern of use and investment of remittances and savings by migrants and their households.

## Notes

1. Women's share in various occupational categories increased from 75 percent to 85 percent in the "Professional and Technical Workers" category and from 82 percent to 90 percent in the "Service Workers" category. The most marked increase was in the traditionally male-dominated category of "Production Workers," where the share of women grew from 5 percent to 29 percent (POEA 2005).
2. Initially, an interim license for one year is issued, and the recruiting agent is required to export at least 100 workers to an employer who has never been accredited by POEA to prove their competitiveness.
3. There is an additional requirement of US$20,000 for the escrow account when the export of entertainers (mostly females) is involved. For agents recruiting domestic workers (mostly females) an additional bond of US$2,000 per worker is required. Any claims resulting from the violation of employment agreements are paid out of the escrow account, which the agent is required to replenish. The maximum penalty is cancellation of the agent's license.
4. This is backed up by outflow data for Pakistan, according to which 46 percent of migrants in 2004 went abroad on a "direct visa," the category used for migrants securing overseas employment using their own contacts. The share of this category in the total outflows increased by 31 percent in the period 1977–2004, without any visible effort on the part of the government (BOE 2005).
5. Some other incentives provided by Pakistan include exemptions in customs duties on some personal goods imported by migrants and free issuance and renewal of their passports (OPF 2005).

6. In addition to knowing modern techniques, they performed more accurately and faster and thus cut costs. They adopted proper security measures during work and avoided accidents.

## References

Abella, M. 1997. *Sending Workers Abroad*. Geneva: ILO.
Amjad, R. 1989. "Economic Impact of Migration to the Middle East on the Major Asian Labor Sending Countries: An Overview." In *To the Gulf and Back*, ed. R. Amjad, 1–27. New Delhi: International Labour Organization.
APPC (Asia Pacific Philanthropy Consortium). 2004. *APPC Post*, 18. http://www.asianphilanthropy.org.
Asian Development Bank. 2005. "Brain Drain Versus Brain Gain: The Study of Remittances in Southeast Asia and Promoting Knowledge Exchange Through Diasporas." Paper presented at the Fourth Coordination Meeting on International Migration, Population Division, Department of Economic and Social Affairs, New York, October 26–27. United Nations Secretariat. http://www.un.org.
APPNA (Association of Pakistani Physicians in North America). 2006. *Cyto-genetic Lab Project in Karachi, Pakistan*. http://www.appna.org.
Association of Pakistani Physicians and Surgeons of the United Kingdom. 2006. *APPS UK Newsletter*. http://www.appsuk.org.
Azam, F. 1998. "International Migration Dynamics in High and Low Migration Districts of Pakistan." In *Emigration Dynamics in Developing Countries*, ed. R. Appleyard, 147–75. AldershotAshgate.
Azam, F. 1995. "Emigration Dynamics in Pakistan." *International Migration* 33 (3:4): 729–65.
———. 1991. "Labor Migration from Pakistan: Trends, Impacts, and Implications." *Regional Development Dialogue* 12 (3): 53–71.
———. 1988. *Monitoring Skill Acquisition, Loss, and Utilization: The Pakistan Pilot Survey*. Bangkok: International Labour Organization.
Baldoz, R. 2003. "Managing the Philippines Overseas Employment Program: Key Policy Issues and Responses." Paper presented at the Regional Conference on Migration, Development, and Pro-Poor Policy Choices in Asia. Dhaka: 22–24 June 2003: Asia, June 22–24, 2003. Dhaka: Department For International Development (DFID).
Ballard, R. 1987. "The Political Economy of Migration: Pakistan, Britain, and the Middle East." In *Migrants, Workers, and the Social Order*, ed. J. Eades, 18–41. London: Tavistock.
BOI (Board of Investment). 2006. *Pakistani Associations in USA*. http://www.pakboi.gov.pk.
BGN (Brain Gain Network). 2006. *About BGN*. http://www.bgn.org.

Bureau of Emigration and Overseas Employment. 2005. "International Migration Statistics." Unpublished data. Islamabad.

Carino, B. 1988. "Monitoring Skill Acquisition, Loss, and Utilization: The Pakistan Pilot Survey." Bangkok: International Labour Organization.

Go, S. 2003. "Recent Trends in International Migration and Policies: Philippines. 5–6." Paper presented at the Workshop on International Migration and Labor Markets in Asia, February 6–7. Tokyo: The Japan Institute of Labor.

Go, S. 1994. "Labor Migration from the Philippines to Asian Countries." In *Regional Development Impacts of Labor Migration in Asia*, eds. W. Gooneratne, P. Martin, and H. Sasanami. Nagoya: United Nations Center for Regional Development.

Government of Pakistan. 2005. "Statistical Appendix." In *Pakistan Economic Survey 2004–05*. Islamabad: Finance Division, 84–85.

NADRA (National Database Registration Authority). 2005. "Overseas Pakistani Cards." http://www.nadra.gov.pk.

Opiniano, J. M. 2004. "Biggest Donors to RP." In *APPC Post*, 18: 5–6. http://www.asianphilanthropy.org.

POEA (Philippines Overseas Employment Administration). 2004. *Annual Report 2003*. Manila: POEA.

———. 2005. *Overseas Employment Statistics*. http://www.poea.gov.ph.

Saith, A. 1997. *Emigration Pressure and Structural Change: Case Study of the Philippines*. Geneva: International Labour Organization.

Shah, N. 1998. "The Role of Social Networks among South Asian Male Migrants to Kuwait." In *Emigration Dynamics in Developing Countries*, ed. R. Appleyard, 147–75. U.K.: Aldershot, Ashgate.

Tan, E., and D. Canlas. 1989. "Migrants' Savings, Remittances, and Labor Supply Behavior: The Philippines Case." In *To the Gulf and Back*, ed. R. Amjad, 223–54. New Delhi: International Labour Orgainzation.

United States Department of State. 2004. *Trafficking in Persons Report 2004*. Washington, DC. http://www.state.gov.

Waddington, C. 2003. "International Migration Policies in Asia." Paper presented at the Regional Conference on Migration, Development, and Pro-Poor Policy Choices in Asia, June 22–24. Dhaka: Department for International Development.

# CHAPTER 6

# Transnationalism, Social Reproduction, and Social Policy: International Migration of Care Workers

*Nicola Yeates*

This chapter examines the transnational dimensions of asset-based social policy through a focus on the international migration of care workers. It advances three arguments:

- First, the analytical focus of asset-based social policy must extend beyond individuals, households, and communities to include entire countries and the relations among them and international organizations.
- Second, care labor occupies a central position in social policy, including asset-accumulation strategies, because of its importance to social reproduction and commodity production processes.
- Third, international care worker recruitment is a locus of tensions between individuals and nation states and between different nation states—tensions that have only partially been addressed by policies of ethical recruitment, staff retention, and managed migration.

Although the overall focus of this chapter is on migrant care workers, these arguments are illustrated and developed with particular reference to nurses. Nurses constitute a significant, and in many ways an archetypal, class of international migrant care worker, whose migration crystallizes a number of important policy issues pertaining to competing development paradigms, both nationally and internationally. This group provides a distinctive challenge to asset-based social policy that targets only the poorest individuals and social groups because nurses already possess considerable assets that are, moreover, globally tradable.

## Methodological Transnationalism and Social Policy

Methodological transnationalism captures the broad shift in perspective resulting from the recognition of activities and ties cutting across national domains. These transnational processes, whether "from above" or "from below," institutionalized or noninstitutionalized, formal or informal, are said to have become both more extensive and intensive, generating increasing enmeshment of different national domains (Held and others 1999). This is not to deny the continued importance of interactions occurring within countries, only to emphasize that transnational processes are integral (rather than incidental) to contemporary social organization and lived experience (Pries 2001; Vertovec 2003).

A transnational approach to social policy highlights structures, flows, and impacts obscured by methodological nationalism, including the following:

- movements of capital, goods, services, people, and ideas across international borders (for example, international health, education, and social protection markets; international migration networks; and international policy diffusion)
- the extraterritorial reach and impacts of national institutions, policies, and practices (for example, social entitlements for nationals and non-nationals living abroad, social dimensions of trade, aid and development policy, and the global effects of domestic social policy)
- the implicit and explicit social policies of supranational global and world-regional institutions and agencies, and their connection with, and impacts on, domestic social institutions, policies, and practices.

Essential to such accounts are the local, national, and global structures of power and authority that shape social development conditions, processes, and impacts (Yeates and Irving 2005).

In terms of an asset-based social policy, a key implication of methodological transnationalism is its emphasis on the supranational and global dimensions of the assets-opportunity-institutions nexus, as well as on the national (and subnational) dimensions. Moreover, focusing on the geographical spread of asset-accumulation opportunities and strategies, and the institutions governing them, highlights questions of territoriality and the interconnectedness of socioeconomic spaces across national borders. International migration constitutes one of the most obvious examples of a transnational asset-accumulation strategy pursued by individuals and households, especially when it is to pursue employment, education, or training opportunities. Through the migration process, individuals can acquire financial and human capital (qualifications) assets that increase their ability to maintain and consolidate asset accumulation over the long term. Remittances generated from this migration can be used by the migrant's family for education and health care and can also bring wider social and economic benefits to communities in both the source and destination countries.

Source and destination countries' institutional arrangements and regulatory practices governing the migration process, together with those of supranational organizations, are critical to the success of (and rewards derived from) these transnational family strategies. This concentration on the transnational dimensions of asset accumulation extends the existing focus on the asset-accumulation opportunities available to, and strategies pursued by, individuals, households and communities, to include entire nations and countries. In essence, then, individual, household and community-based strategies must be situated in the context of the wider collective resources of a nation state. This focus on nation states derives from the fact that state development strategies have asset-accumulation dimensions and impacts within their own territory as well as abroad, and that these strategies are framed by a country's position within the international hierarchy of states.

## Care Labor, Social Reproduction, and Commodity Production

No discussion of social policy and development is complete without looking at the importance of care labor to the functioning of social and economic systems. Care (or reproductive) labor is essentially that which creates labor power, as opposed to commodities or products. It is typically divided into human (biological, sexual) reproduction; the maintenance of individuals through the life cycle (feeding, clothing, affective work); and the systemic reproduction (education, social bonds, and ties) that enables the social system to be sustained. Care work encompasses an incredibly wide variety of activities, ranging from highly intimate to less intimate ones, offered on a waged and/or nonwaged basis in domestic or institutional settings. Care workers include a range of groups with different skill levels, situated in diverse occupational positions, working in different settings and under different conditions (Yeates 2004a).

Feminist literature has made significant contributions to our understanding of the relationships among care labor, the maintenance of social systems, and economic production. The primary focus has been on unpaid domestic labor, most of which is carried out by women for other family members. Questions such as who provides care, how much of it, to whose benefit, and to whose cost have made important connections between "private" arrangements and wider social (specifically gender) relations, and the mediating role of institutions and public policy therein. It is typically emphasized that, while unpaid, informal care labor constitutes an important social provision and resource, its provision negatively affects care workers' immediate and long-term accumulation of assets by restricting availability for paid work and access to the economic opportunities, rewards, and securities deriving therefrom (Pascall 1997). The role of care labor within commodity production systems is further emphasized in Marxian analyses. Delphy and Leonard (1984), Mies (1986), and Dunaway (2001), for example, identify unpaid household reproductive labor as a basic input into commodity production processes while highlighting the role of social policies and practices in maintaining gendered household relations that underpin the production of surplus and its unequal division.

## Global Reproductive Labor Markets, and Asset Accumulation

There is growing interest in the global and transnational dimensions of care provision. A large number of studies have grappled with globalization processes through an examination of migrant care workers. In particular, these have considered nannies (Anderson 2000; Chang and Ling 2000; Chin 1998; Cock 1984; Gamburd 2000; Heyzer, Lycklama, and Weerakoon 1994; Hondagneu-Sotelo 2001; Lutz 2002; Momsen 1999; Parreñas 2001), although a growing number of studies highlight how this trade is increasing rapidly for a range of domestic and personal care services (ITC 1998; Yeates 2005). Collectively, these studies point to the massive demand for migrant care workers in wealthier countries and the supply of care workers by a range of less wealthy countries. The growth of this international care services market must be put in the context of greater population movement in general and the feminization of international migration in particular (OECD 2002). These are in part a response to the problem of uneven development.

This capitalist dynamism and the migration it entails are intricately linked to the asset-accumulation strategies of individuals, households, communities, and countries. Working abroad may provide the individual migrant with educational and training opportunities and the possibility of earning a higher income than would be available in the home country. The monies remitted home contribute to the economic survival and health and welfare needs of families and communities. International remittances are also a crucial source of foreign currency for many countries of origin and, in some cases, may exceed the value of foreign aid received. In richer countries, social, demographic, and economic trends, together with a shortage of public care services, make it difficult for women to perform social reproductive work alongside full-time participation in the commodity production economy. For those able to afford it, the outsourcing of domestic care labor relieves women from doing this work themselves and allows them to pursue marketized income-generation strategies, while reducing gender and generational conflicts over the division of reproductive labor within the family.

This outsourcing involves migration on both an intracountry basis (rural–urban migration) and an international basis. Outsourcing may be practiced by the employer as well as by the migrant and entails mobilizing labor supply through informal (kin) networks, as well as through the market mechanism. Thus, richer households in richer regions or countries outsource part of their care labor requirements to members of poorer households, drawn from poorer areas within the same country or from a poorer country in the same region (Hochschild 2000; Yeates 2005). Differences in social standing are reproduced through the outsourcing process, since the employment of a domestic worker is a means of reproducing lifestyle and social status (including those of race, ethnicity, and caste) (Anderson 2000). Those at the lower end of the chain may employ a poorer woman drawn from a poorer area within the same country or region, while those at the end of the chain who are too poor to employ a domestic worker rely on unpaid family female labor to care for children left behind. It is important to situate these transfers within gendered divisions of reproductive labor in both the receiving and sending countries. As Parreñas (2001, 2005) notes in the context of the Philippines, fathers of all social classes tended to migrate elsewhere within the country to take up paid work, enabling them to avoid providing the care labor that was provided by the mother before her emigration. At the same time, the increased use of paid social reproductive labor by households in richer countries needs to be situated in the context of unequal sharing of domestic and care labor between men and women.

Through these outsourcing processes, a series of personal links is established between people across the globe based on the paid or unpaid work of caring. That is, a global care chain (Hochschild 2000). However, the chain consists of more than individuals: it establishes an international network of spatially dispersed, connected households and families, creating transnational households and interfamily links through the employment nexus (Yeates 2005). The structure of each chain varies according to the number of links, the sociogeographical spread of the links and the intensity of their connective strength. Through these global chains, an international division of reproductive labor is established. This international division involves a hierarchy of countries, insofar as poorer ones are supplying domestic care workers and richer ones are receiving them, while the extraction of care labor from poorer countries for consumption by richer ones not only constitutes a major drain on the resources of poorer countries but a subsidy by them to the richer ones (Yeates 2005).

Although the main focus of analysis within the globalization of care literature has been on nannies, the experience of migrant care workers extends beyond social care, the social group to which it is provided and the setting in which the migrants work. Nurses are another major group of migrant care workers. They are a skilled and highly regulated group of migrant workers, who provide health care and work in institutionalized settings involving public and private (commercial) agencies. They are a group in whose human capital formation significant investments have been made; they are a major collective asset to a nation state's health care provision and they are essential to a nation's social and economic development prospects more generally.

Like domestic childcare workers, migrant health workers have been a constant source of labor for core countries' care services throughout the 20th century, although this migration appears to have increased with the current phase of globalization. The major flow is from developing to industrial countries: more than 90 percent of nurses who migrate go to Europe, North America, and the high-income countries of the western Pacific, while only about 7 percent go to developing countries (Sarfati 2003). This broad picture has not changed substantially since the World Bank reported on the issue in 1993. While the general flow is from countries on the periphery of the world economy to countries at its core, there are also distinct regional divisions of labor. One significant destination area is the Middle East, specifically the Arabian Gulf states, where the recent development of health services has mainly drawn on nonnational labor forces, particularly migrants from Bangladesh, the Arab Republic of Egypt, India, and the Philippines. South Africa is also a significant destination for nurses migrating from, for example, Swaziland and Zambia, demonstrating that a nearby regional developed country can be as important a destination as the northern developed countries of Europe and North America (Buchan, Kingma, and Lorenzo 2005; Munjanja and others 2005).

Given the magnitude of the international trade in nurses and the significance of this migration to the asset-accumulation strategies of individuals, households, and countries, they are a group through whose experiences a number of questions can be raised. How effective are institutions in facilitating asset-accumulation opportunities and strategies? How appropriate is it to treat a nation's collective assets as an internationally tradable commodity? To what extent should transnational asset-accumulation strategies by individuals, households, and countries be regulated in the wider public interest? The rest of the chapter examines the international migration of nurses, focusing specifically on governance issues and contrasting policy approaches to nurse migration.

Empirical research on this subject is still in its infancy. Some of the gaps in the evidence are beginning to be filled by large international research programs. However, much research on issues relating to gender and family issues, including basic information on marital and family status of migrant nurses, remains to be undertaken. In this light, it is worth repeating the key points raised by the most recent international study of nurse migration:

- First, the absence of accurate data on the flows of international nurses constrains effective monitoring and limits the ability to assess impact.
- Second, inadequate workforce data and planning capacity in source countries renders it difficult to assess how much of a "problem" outflow to other countries is in comparison to the numbers of nurses underemployed or unemployed in the country (Buchan, Kingma, and Lorenzo 2005: 29).

## The Governance of International Nurse Migration

There is general agreement that the reasons behind nurse migration are mainly economic. "Pull" factors include the lure of higher wages, the desire for wider professional experience, better and more specialized training, increased promotional opportunities, a higher standard of living, and increased socioeconomic and personal security. Conversely, "push" factors include low pay; minimal chances of promotion; unemployment and underemployment; low level of development of, and investment in, health services; low status; and threats to personal security. Not all migration decisions are strictly economic, however, and the desire for travel, adventure, a better climate and greater personal autonomy should not be discounted.

In any consideration of migration, however, it is important to distinguish between different development contexts. There is a difference between migrating from a sending country where family members depend on remittances for their economic survival and where state social provision is minimal (or nonexistent), and migrating from a country where such basic socioeconomic security is not an issue. It is also important to appreciate that, while the focus of analysis and policy attention often lies with the individual migrant, migration decisions invariably have a household or familial dimension. Indeed, migration choices must be understood as part of a family's asset-accumulation strategies. As Redfoot and Houser (2005) argue with regard to India and the Philippines, the choice of nursing as a career and the accompanying migration decision is a decidedly family affair:

> ... family networks are most important in financing nursing education—often with the expectation that the family investment will be returned by the remittances sent by migrating nurses. So, family expectations of migration are often built into the decision to send a daughter to nursing school. (2005: 20)

While individual and household decisions are clearly central to understanding nurse migration, the institutional and policy frameworks in which these decisions are taken are also highly significant. Health is a highly regulated sector; international nurse migration occurs within a matrix formed by government, commercial, professional, and labor interests, policies, and practices.

### Government Policy and Agreements

The extent to which nurses pursue an internationalized asset-accumulation strategy through the migration process and their choice of destination country is shaped by a variety of factors. These include the proximity of countries, which partly relates to the ease and cost of travel, the existence of a culturally available set of options and a common language (Buchan,

Parkin, and Sochalski 2003). Migration routes may also be based on historical (colonial, missionary, and training) connections to particular countries. However, government policies and agreements of sending and receiving countries are of particular importance. For example, the Philippines government has followed a policy of producing nurses for export since the 1970s. Its establishment of an administrative infrastructure to facilitate the emigration of Filipino workers has been key to this policy, resulting in more than 85 percent of employed Filipino nurses working outside the Philippines (150,000 nurses in all) (Buchan Parkin, and Sochalski 2003). Although the Philippines is the best known in this regard, Egypt, and to an extent Cuba and India, have also adopted such a policy, while many Caribbean, African, and Asian states are considering similar policies (Buchan, Kingma, and Lorenzo 2005; Jansen 1974; Thomas, Hosein, and Yan 2005). Receiving countries can strongly facilitate nurse migration through targeted policies of recruitment, such as the fast-track visa systems introduced in Ireland. Alternatively, governments may simply allow market forces to operate, intervening only to validate the qualifications of the incoming nurse, such as in the United States.

While several countries stand out in the nurse trade literature as being predominantly nurse exporters (the Philippines) or importers (Saudi Arabia), in practice many countries import and export nurses simultaneously. This is because out-migration of nurses leads to the need for in-migration of nurses to fill resulting vacancies. Australia, Canada, Ireland, and the United Kingdom, for example, are all significant importers and exporters of nurses (Buchan, Kingma, and Lorenzo 2005; Yeates 2004b). Ireland represents an interesting example of this and illustrates the importance of government policy in both source and destination countries more generally. Historically a major exporter of (nursing) care labor worldwide, Ireland has recently emerged as a major importer of nurses. This inward migration has occurred alongside the continued outflow of Irish nurses to other countries, primarily the United Kingdom and Australia but also the Canada, Kenya, New Zealand, South Africa, and the United States, where they have compensated for these countries' nursing shortages resulting from nurse out-migration. Throughout the 1990s, this international migration into Ireland was mainly from other "developed" countries in Australia, Europe, and North America, but since 2000 "developing to developed" country migration has been of growing importance in sourcing nurses for care work in Ireland. By 2002, following a government recruitment policy focused on the Philippines, Ireland had become the third largest importer of Filipino nurses after Saudi Arabia and the United Kingdom (Yeates 2004b), while most recently Ireland has diversified its recruitment within Asia to include India.

International trade agreements currently have a relatively minor impact on the overall flows of nurses. Indeed, despite the European Union's (EU's) policy of free movement for nurses and other health professionals who are EU nationals, there is little sign of increased internal nurse migration within the EU, and such migration is mainly linked to clusters of countries that share the same language (Buchan, Parkin, and Sochalski 2003). Far more significant is the existence or absence of mutual recognition agreements. These agreements explain why, for example, Ghanaian nurses tend to migrate to the United Kingdom, as they are not required to pass an examination, which they would be required to do if they wanted to migrate to the United States (Buchan, Kingma, and Lorenzo 2005). Moreover, the need for certification can impede access to national health labor markets, as in the United States, where registration as a nurse requires that the applicant pass the National Council Licensure Examination. Some observers claim that this licensing process discriminates against foreign nurses in their attempt to gain access to the U.S. market. In 2004, only 58 percent of foreign applicants passed this exam, compared with 85 percent of U.S.-educated nurses (Redfoot and Houser 2005).

### Recruitment Agencies

Although government policy and agreements provide an important institutional framework within which nurse migration occurs, recruitment agencies constitute an important organizational linkage in global care chains and have a significant influence on the experiences of migrants. These agencies mobilize nursing labor and connect nurses to their eventual employers, but they may also coordinate training, testing, certification, immigration, and transportation. These agents may be private companies, specialist subcontractors, hospital associations, or state or semistate bodies, and they often operate in partnership with one another. Thus, state involvement in the recruitment process may be in the form of a commitment to assist visa and nursing licenses applications, relocation and housing, tuition reimbursement, and continuing education opportunities. Recruitment agencies can also work in cooperation with the state and trade unions, in agreeing, for example, salary scales prior to nurses' arrival. Often these agencies recruit informally as well as formally, relying on contacts between existing staff and their home areas when vacancies arise (Walter 2001).

The regulation of recruitment agencies and practices is a major policy concern as well as a significant factor in how risks, costs, and profits are distributed among the different agents (including the workers themselves) across the global care chain. The terms and conditions of the contract among the nurse, the recruitment agency, and the employer, including whether the agency charges nurses a fee, can vary widely (Stout 2002). Payments to recruitment agencies can represent a barrier to entry to nurse labor markets; to overcome it, migrants and their families are often forced to take out loans that pull them into indentured labor. These loans can create major debts for the migrant and family members. Not only can the loan repayment negatively impact on their economic situation; but also it renders it difficult for migrants to leave unsatisfactory employment in the host country until the debt has been repaid.

In recent years, some recruitment practices have caused major concern among agencies combating transnational crime. In many cases, women are recruited with false promises of legitimate jobs with good pay and conditions. When they arrive in the host country, the promises are revealed to be false and they are pressured into sex work. Complaints have also been reported of recruitment agencies misrepresenting the pay and conditions for migrant workers (Redfoot and Houser 2005). The U.K.'s Royal College of Nursing denounced some reported cases as a "modern form of slavery," with the position of some nurses resembling that of trapped domestic and sex workers. Given the increasingly globalized nursing trade, the matter of the extraterritorial reach of state regulation arises. The concern is that the regulatory powers of host countries' governments do not cover overseas recruitment agencies. This effectively leaves migrant nurses who have legitimate grievances about the terms and conditions of their work in a difficult situation since their only option is to pursue the complaints with the recruitment agency based in their country of origin.

### Human Resource Management and Labor Organization

Once nurses arrive in the host country, they can face a variety of work situations. In many cases, these do not make the best use of their skills or can actually result in their de-skilling. Many qualified nurses from overseas are channeled into low-skilled, low-paid menial and noncareer grades in unpopular specialties and positions that are not concomitant with their skills and aspirations (Bach 2003). It is not uncommon for qualified nurses with specialist skills to end up working as care workers in residential nursing care homes abroad or in the hospital laundry service (Browne 2001). This de-skilling obviously has implications for successful accumulation of assets.

Migrant nurses' experiences abroad and the extent to which their strategies are successful are shaped by whether they work in public or private sectors and which type of nursing care institution in which they work. Related to this is the difference between strongly unionized state health sectors, as in countries in the Organisation for Economic Co-operation and Development (OECD), and less unionized or nonunionized state health systems, as in the Gulf States. In OECD countries, at least, state health care tends to be highly unionized. As hospitals are usually large workplaces and are more likely to be unionized, the trade union position on migrant labor is crucial to the recruitment, organization, and integration of health care workforces. Migrant workers entering unionized public hospital systems receive the same pay and conditions as their colleagues and, with their union membership, have some possibility of protection against discriminatory pay and exploitative conduct that workers entering nonunionized systems do not have (Bach 2003). The involvement of trade unions and organized representation of workers marks a major difference compared with the situation of other care workers in individualized, household settings, who are often isolated and powerless when negotiating terms of employment. This difference between public and private sector employment and, relatedly, between hospitals and nursing homes is noted by Bach. "There are frequently differences between the experiences of employment in a nursing care/aged care environment compared to a hospital setting.... It is in private nursing that some of the worst abuses have been documented" (Bach 2003: 19).

More generally, the organization of migrant labor forces has been of growing importance to trade unions in industrialized OECD countries. In some countries, trade union growth is now seen as being dependent on the unions' abilities to organize migrant labor, and major efforts have been made to extend trade union organization to hitherto unorganized economic sectors where migrant labor predominates. One feature of this is the recognition that migrant workers need special services. For this reason, among others, some unions organize their migrant members separately. For example, the Irish Nurses Organisation (INO) has established a separate section to represent the needs of overseas nurses, while the Services, Industrial, and Professional Trade Union (SIPTU), the major Irish workers trade union, has established a separate section to address the needs of migrant workers generally. This form of union organization can bring benefits to nurses extending beyond the usual advantages of collective bargaining over pay and conditions. One such example relates to the 2004 change in legislation that allowed the spouses of overseas nurses to work legally in Ireland, a change that resulted from lobbying by the INO in partnership with a range of other groups (INO 2004). On this point, it is worth emphasizing that, in a highly competitive global nursing market, the facilitation of household internationalization and asset-accumulation strategies by extending social rights—whether giving nurses' partners a permit to work in the host country or providing guaranteed free education for migrant workers' children—is increasingly appreciated by migrant and trade union activists as well as employers as a key factor in the success of international nurse recruitment and retention strategies.

## Policy Approaches to the Management of Nursing Labor

Nurse migration has been of increased concern to policy makers since the beginning of the 1990s, a concern that has grown in tandem with the identification of a global nursing shortage. This shortage arises from shortfalls in nurse training, together with a decline in the numbers of women choosing nursing as a career option, and the fact that significant numbers of nurses are leaving the profession due to poor pay and working conditions (Thomas, Hosein, and Yan 2005). International nurse recruitment has evolved as a significant policy response to national nursing shortages but probing questions have been raised as to the equity as well as efficacy of such a response globally. The major critical response to international nurse recruitment has highlighted its resemblance to a form of asset stripping, whereby valuable skilled and expensively trained labor is transferred from developing countries that can ill-afford to lose such resources to developed countries.

One regulatory response to international nurse migration has been the development of ethical codes of conduct by governments and nurses' representative bodies. These ethical codes attempt to regulate the import of nurses. The development of these codes has resulted from political pressure by developing nations concerned at the loss of valuable health care workers and also by development lobby groups concerned at the effect of this loss on the implementation of international social policy, in particular the Millennium Development Goals, and the ability of African nations to adequately respond to the threat posed by HIV/AIDS. One such response was Nelson Mandela's 1997 call for the United Kingdom to cease recruiting South African nurses. As a result, the U.K. Department of Health issued guidelines to the National Health Service (NHS) employers urging them to stop recruiting from developing countries suffering from nursing shortages. This ethical recruitment policy led to the drawing up of lists of developing countries, agreed through consultations with their health ministries, from which the NHS could recruit.

This code was a precursor for other ethical codes, issued by the Commonwealth, the Irish government, and various professional and labor organizations (Willetts and Martineau 2004). It has, however, many shortcomings: it is limited to state agencies and does not prevent recruitment by the private sector, which still acts as a major route for overseas nurses into the NHS; it only prohibits active recruitment; and its guidance is only advisory rather than mandatory (Deeming 2004; Grondin 2005). Other ethical codes are also problematic. A review by Willetts and Martineau (2004: i) concluded that "support systems, incentives and sanctions, and monitoring systems necessary for effective implementation and sustainability are currently weak or have not been planned."

While importing countries have introduced codes to regulate international recruitment, some exporting countries have responded by attempting to limit nurse migration. One method, bonding (used by South Africa and Zimbabwe), requires nurses to spend a certain number of years working in their national health services in return for the investment of public resources in their education and training; another (introduced by Lesotho and Ghana) requires graduates to repay their training costs, either in cash or through public service (Padarath and others n.d.). Another policy approach is to alter the economics of international nurse recruitment and remove the cost advantage of recruiting nurses from developing countries by forcing the recruiting body to pay the full cost of educating and training nurses to the source country government (WONCA 2002; Mensah, Mackintosh, and Henry 2005).

A further policy response accepts international migration as inevitable, but advocates managing it in the best interests of both sending and receiving countries, while respecting the individual nurse's right to choose his or her place of work and residence (Grondin 2005). Here, partnership arrangements have been suggested that result in a "win–win" situation for all involved. In the context of the Philippines, for example, bilateral agreements on health human resources with importing countries, involving aid for health care development and compensation for each health care professional recruited, have been suggested; also suggested are partnership agreements between hospitals in the Philippines and importing countries, whereby the importing hospitals provide funds to the exporting hospitals to improve training and working conditions (Tan, Sanchez, and Balanon 2005).

A final response to nurse shortages is a national one that emphasizes staff retention and valorization. Not only could this be more effective in the long run, but also it is a policy that can be applied in equal measure by both importing and exporting countries. This approach includes policy measures addressing the underlying reasons for leaving the nursing profession or national workforce, such as improvements in wages, working conditions, and status, as well as improved training and promotional opportunities. Among actual measures are subsidized car and housing ownership schemes (pioneered in Namibia) and continuing and specialized professional training. In importing countries, measures such as flexible and family-friendly working hours, improved wages, better working conditions, and security measures can address some of the reasons why staff members leave the nursing profession. In the Middle East, health authorities in Oman and Saudi Arabia are introducing measures to "nationalize" their workforce and reduce high levels of dependence on migrant health care workers (their nationals constitute a minority of their nursing labor force) by developing and training a local nursing workforce (Sarfati 2003; El-Gilany and Al-Wehady 2001).

## Conclusions

Centering on the issue of nurse migration, this chapter has focused on the intersections between international labor migration and an asset-based approach to social policy. For the individual migrant and his or her family, emigration is a means of increasing individual human capital as well as generating financial capital, a significant part of which is returned to support the survival and accumulation strategies of the migrant's family and the wider community in the source country. Challenging a dominant notion that this international migration associated with the emergence of global care markets confers mainly positive benefits and rewards to the individual migrant, family member, and the source country, this chapter attended to the contradictions of this dynamic. It was argued that asset accumulation through international migration may often lead to de-skilling of the individual migrant, while, at the national level, it resembles a form of asset stripping of a nation's resources that has profound implications for the survival and asset-accumulation strategies of those remaining in the home country. These contradictions not only arise between individual and national development (and accumulation) strategies but also between development strategies of different nations.

Indeed, this international migration must be seen in broader national and international contexts where different national interests and positions lead to different policy concerns and approaches. For the countries of origin, the concern is with the loss of expensively trained and skilled labor to developed countries, losses that their health systems can ill-afford, and whether state social and economic policies should facilitate this labor export. There is a particular concern that this emigration constitutes a de facto subsidy to developed countries' health care systems and reduces exporting countries' ability to realize national and international social policy objectives. For the receiving countries, policy issues relate to the integration of foreign nursing labor into national health systems and labor forces and the countries from which it is justifiable to recruit. There is an urgent need to address these tensions among individual, household, national, and global socioeconomic objectives.

Regarding the analytical framework for an asset-based approach to social policy, the chapter asserted the following:

- First, an asset-based approach to social policy must focus on formal and informal care labor in order to capture the connections and contradictions between the commodity economy and social reproduction.
- Second, such an approach must analyze the global and transnational dimensions of social policy to capture the globalization of health care services and labor markets and highlight the policy issues associated therewith.
- Third, the selection of a highly skilled class of migrants (nurses) extends the present focus of asset-based social policy from the poorest individuals and social groups to those already possessing globally tradable assets, while also emphasizing the contradictions that this international mobility presents to national social and economic development and to effective poverty-reduction strategies.

It is in the context of this final point that the major issues raised by international nurse recruitment come into focus. If one way to examine the distribution of risks, costs, and benefits across the global nursing chain is by putting in to the foreground costs to hospitals, profits to recruitment agencies, and increased pay to migrant nurses in individual cases of nurse migration, another calculation at the national-societal and global levels is not only possible but essential. From this viewpoint, the major benefits accrue to the health system of the host country, while the major costs are borne by the health care system of the country on the other end of the global care chain. These costs include not only the cost of educating and training the nurse involved, but also the health deficit caused by the migration of the nurse and the effect that a depleted health service has on the social and economic development of the country of origin.

It cannot be denied that the remittances sent by individual migrant workers provide some benefits to the country of origin and its individual households, or that there are recent examples of attempts to mobilize these remittances for general social benefit. Indeed, research suggests that migrant workers "make a major contribution to the economies of their home countries, which far surpasses the initial financial investment of educating the nurses" (Buchan, Kingma, and Lorenzo 2005, 16). However, more research is needed before it can confidently be declared that international nurse remittances balance the *total* economic and social loss involved in nurse emigration. It is in this context of the spread of costs and benefits across the global nursing chain at the individual, employer, government, and societal levels that policy proposals calling for more effective governance of international nurse migration must be formulated.

Of course, this raises the question of what the overall aims of policy should be; how the competing interests of state, commercial, professional, labor, and households can be balanced; and whether these interests can be reconciled. This is complicated by the country's position within the global care chain, whether at the lower or upper end. How does one achieve a balance between the conflicting interests and needs involved? How can the asset-accumulation strategies of individual nurses and their families in low-income countries weigh against the need for nursing staff to fill vacancies in middle- and high-income countries? The need for nurses to take care of older people in developed countries has to be weighed against the need for nurses in developing countries to help care for people with HIV/AIDS. This goes to the heart of the problem as to how far international migration should be regulated in the interests of public health, welfare, and social development.

## References

Anderson, B. 2000. "Different Roots in Common Ground: Transnationalism and Migrant Domestic Workers in London." *Journal of Ethnic and Migration Studies* 27 (4): 673–83.

Bach, S. 2003. "International Migration of Health Workers: Labour and Social Issues." Sectoral Activities Programme Working Paper 209. Geneva: International Labour Organization.

Browne, A. 2001. "Abused, Threatened and Trapped—Britain's Foreign 'Slave Nurses.'" *Guardian* May 29. http://society.guardian.co.uk/NHSstaff/story/0,7991,497983,00.html.

Buchan, J., T. Parkin, and J. Sochalski. 2003. International Nurse Mobility: Trends and Policy Implications. Report. London: Royal College of Nursing. http://www.rcn.org.uk/downloads/InternationalNurseMobility–April162003.doc.

Buchan, J., M. Kingma, and F. M. Lorenzo. 2005. "International Migration of Nurses: Trends and Policy Implications." The Global Nursing Review Initiative Issue Paper 5. Geneva: International Council of Nurses.

Chang, K. A., and L. H. M. Ling. 2000. "Globalization and Its Intimate Other: Filipina Domestic Workers in Hong Kong." In *Gender and Global Restructuring: Sightings, Sites and Resistances*, eds. M. H. Marchand and A. S. Ryan. London: Routledge.

Chin, C. 1998. In *Service and Servitude: Foreign Female Domestic Workers and the Malaysian "Modernity" Project*. New York: Columbia University Press.

Cock, J. 1984. *Maids and Madams: A Study in the Politics of Exploitation*. Johannesburg, South Africa: Ravan Press.

Deeming, C. 2004. "Policy Targets and Ethical Tensions: UK Nurse Recruitment," *Social Policy and Administration* 38 (7): 775–92.

Delphy, C., and D. Leonard. 1984. *Close to Home: A Materialist Analysis of Women's Oppression*. Amherst: University of Massachusetts Press.

Dunaway, W. 2001. "The Double Register of History: Situating the Forgotten Woman and her Household in Capitalist Commodity Chains." *Journal of World-Systems Research*, VII (1): 2–29.

El-Gilany, A., and A. Al-Wehady. 2001. "Job Satisfaction and Female Saudi Nurses." *Eastern Mediterranean Health Journal* 7 (1/2): 31–37. http://www.emro.who.int/Publications/EMHJ/701/04.htm.

Gamburd, M. 2000. *The Kitchen Spoon's Handle: Transnationalism and Sri Lanka's Migrant Housemaids*. Ithaca, New York: Cornell University Press.

Grondin, D. 2005. "The Breakdown of Borders–Shaping the Delivery of Long-Term Care." http://www.aarp.org/ltcforum/dgrondin_keynote.html.

Held, D., A. McGrew, D. Goldblatt, and J. Perraton. 1999. *Global Transformations*. Cambridge: Polity Press.

Heyzer, N., G. Lycklama, and N. Weerakoon, eds. 1994. "Trade in Domestic Helpers: Causes, Mechanisms and Consequences of International Migration." Kuala Lumpur: Asian and Pacific Development Centre.

Hochschild, A. 2000. "Global Care Chains and Emotional Surplus Value." In *On The Edge: Living with Global Capitalism*. W. Hutton and A. Giddens, eds. London: Jonathan Cape.

Hondagneu-Sotelo, P. 2001. *Doméstica: Immigrant Workers Cleaning and Caring in the Shadow of Affluence*. Berkeley: University of California Press.

INO (Irish Nurses Organisation). 2004. Annual Report 2004. Dublin: INO.

ITC (International Trade Centre). 1998. Health Services. Geneva: United Nations Conference on Trade and Development/World Trade Organization.

Jansen, M. E. 1974. "Nursing in the Arab East." *Saudi Aramco World* 25(2). http://www.saudiaramcoworld.com/issue/197402/nursing.in.the.arab.east.htm.

Lutz, H. 2002. "At Your Service Madam! The Globalization of Domestic Service." *Feminist Review* 70: 89–103.

Mensah, K., M. Mackintosh, and L. Henry. 2005. *The "Skills Drain" of Health Professionals from the Developing World: A Framework for Policy Formulation*. London: Medact.

Mies, M. 1986. *Patriarchy and Accumulation: Women in the International Division of Labour*. London: Zed Books.

Momsen, J. H., ed. 1999. *Gender, Migration, and Domestic Service*. London: Routledge.

Munjanja, O. Kopolo, S. Kibuka, and D. Dovlo. 2005. "The Nursing Workforce in Sub-Saharan Africa." The Global Nursing Review Initiative." Issue Paper 7. Geneva: International Council of Nurses.

OECD (Organisation for Economic Co-operation and Development). 2002. *Trends in International Migration*. Paris: OECD.

Padarath, A., C. Chamberlain, D. McCoy, A. Ntuli, M. Rowson, and R. Loewenson n.d. "Health Personnel in Southern Africa: Confronting Maldistribution and Brain Drain. Regional Network for Equity in Health in South Africa." Equinet Discussion Paper Number 3. Harare: Equinet.

Parreñas, R. 2001. *Servants of Globalization: Women, Migration, and Domestic Work*. Stanford, CA: Stanford University Press.

Parreñas, R. 2005. *Children of Global Migration: Transnational Families and Gendered Woes*. Stanford, CA: Stanford University Press.

Pascall, G. 1997. *Social Policy: A New Feminist Analysis*. London: Routledge.

Pries, L. 2001. "The Approach of Transnational Social Spaces: Responding to New Configurations of the Social and the Spatial." In *New Transnational Social Spaces: International Migration and Transnational Companies in the Early Twenty-First Century*. Ed. L. Pries. London: Routledge.

Redfoot, D. L., and A. N. Houser. 2005. "We Shall Travel On: Quality of Care, Economic Development, and the International Migration of Long-Term Care Workers." Washington, DC: AARP. http://www.mecf.org/articles/AARP_immigrant.pdf.

Sarfati, H. 2003. "Remuneration of Nurses in Islamic Countries: Economic Factors in a Social Context." In *Women in Nursing in Islamic Societies*. Ed. Nancy H. Bryant. Oxford: Oxford University Press.

Stout, H. J. 2002. "International Recruiting Network: Addressing the Nursing Shortage." *Portland Business Journal*, March 8. www.bizjournals.com/portland/stories/2002/03/11/focus7.html.

Tan, J. Z. G., F. S. Sanchez, and V. L. Balanon. 2005. "The Brain Drain Phenomenon and Its Implications for Health." Paper presented at the University of the Philippines Alumni Council Meeting, June 24. www.up.edu.ph/forum/2005/Jul-Aug05/ brain_drain.htm.

Thomas, C., R. Hosein, and J. Yan. 2005. Assessing the Export of Nursing Services as a Diversification Option for CARICOM Economies. Report. Caribbean Commission of Health and Development, Washington, DC.

Vertovec, S. 2003. "Migration and Other Modes of Transnationalism: Towards Conceptual Cross-Fertilization." *International Migration Review*, 37 (3): 641–65.

Walter, B. 2001. *Outsiders Inside: Whiteness, Place and Irish Women*. Routledge: London.

Willetts, A., and T. Martineau. 2004. "Ethical International Recruitment of Health Professionals: Will Codes of Practice Protect Developing Country Health Systems?" http://www.liv.ac.uk/lstm/research/documents/codesofpracticereport.pdf.

WONCA (World Organization of National Colleges, Academies and Academic Associations of General Practitioners/Family Physicians). 2002. A Code of Practice for the International Recruitment of Health Care Professionals: the Melbourne Manifesto. WONCA. http://www.ruralhealth2002.net/ melbourne_manifesto.pdf.

World Bank. 1993. *World Development Report*. New York: Oxford University Press.

Yeates, N. 2004a. "Global Care Chains: Critical Reflections and Lines of Enquiry." *International Feminist Journal of Politics*, 6 (3): 369–91.

Yeates, N. 2004b. "A Dialogue with 'Global Care Chain' Analysis: Nurse Migration in the Irish Context." *Feminist Review*, 77: 79–95.

Yeates, N. 2005. "Global Care Chains: A Critical Introduction." *Global Migration Perspectives* No. 44. Geneva: Global Commission on International Migration.

Yeates, N., and Z. Irving, eds. 2005. "Transnational Social Policy," *Social Policy and Society,* special theme issue, 4 (4).

# PART III

# HOUSING AS AN ASSET IN

# INFORMAL SETTLEMENTS

# CHAPTER 7

# Building Homes: The Role of Federations of the Urban Poor

*David Satterthwaite*

As described in Caroline Moser's chapter 2, laws, norms, and regulatory frameworks can, in various ways, provide or block access to assets or asset accumulation by low-income groups. This has particular importance in most urban contexts, where government agencies often act to block lower-income groups' access to assets or diminish or destroy much of their asset base through eviction and the closing down or harassment of informal enterprises. In most urban centers in low- and middle-income countries, large sections of the population have no work opportunities within the formal economy and cannot afford to buy, build, or rent homes within the formal housing stock. The result is that many aspects of their lives are illegal—the informal enterprises through which they earn a living, the accommodation in which they live and the land it occupies, and the services on which they rely, such as water, sanitation, health care, and transport. While city or municipal governments have a limited capacity to reduce poverty, they have a large capacity to create or exacerbate poverty through measures that destroy the homes and livelihoods of low-income groups (Amis 1999).

This chapter describes the strategies used by federations formed by the urban poor and homeless (including those living in slums and informal

This chapter draws on discussions with Jockin Arputham (National Slum Dwellers Federation, India) and Rose Molokuane (South African Federation of the Urban Poor) and on the work of many professionals who work with the federations, including Joel Bolnick, Somsook Boonyabancha, Beth Chitekwe, Celine d'Cruz, Sheela Patel, Diana Mitlin, and Jane Weru.

settlements) to acquire services and tenure of housing they occupy or obtain new housing or serviced land on which housing can be built. It also identifies their role in changing the housing and land policies of local and national governments. Such federations are well established in 14 countries and are emerging in a number of others. Their programs, which have reached hundreds of thousands of people, are designed to address some of the challenges outlined above. Using an asset framework, the chapter considers their strategies, actions, and achievements in terms of concrete outcomes, as well as in terms of their changing relationships with government agencies. The chapter also discusses the challenges and limitations facing the federations, especially in relation to government and international agency interventions.

## Asset Accumulation and Housing Policy in Low- and Middle-Income Nations

While low-income groups may accumulate various different kinds of assets, this chapter is primarily concerned with how they obtain better quality legal housing with access to basic services. Where low-income households can obtain their own housing (instead of renting it or squatting) or land on which they can build, and they have confidence they will not be evicted, they often invest in it. Their house serves not only as a shelter but also as a means of building an asset base (Turner 1976). In many instances, it also serves as the base for income-earning activities. Recognizing this development trend, from the early 1970s many governments and some international organizations sought to support this process—through slum and squatter upgrading and serviced site schemes. This was an approach strongly supported by the World Bank from the early 1970s (Cohen 1983).

If successful, such schemes can contribute considerably to poverty reduction, as they provide low-income groups with legal homes, access to services, and official addresses (often a condition for being able to vote and to access government services). For instance, such interventions can improve health, expand low-income households' capital asset base, and improve security within developing urban communities. From the 1970s, there are many examples of successful local initiatives, some examples of successful citywide programs, and a few examples of national programs or agencies that had some success (Hardoy and Satterthwaite 1989; UNCHS (Habitat) 1996; Mitlin and Satterthwaite 2004). However, most government housing interventions have been limited in terms of their scale or effectiveness and received very little support from international agencies (UNCHS (Habitat) 1996, Satterthwaite 2001). Their ineffectiveness is illustrated by the fact that 30 percent to 60 percent of the population of most cities in low- and middle-income countries lives in overcrowded conditions, in poor quality accommodations, mainly in illegal settlements (UN-Habitat 2003a). During the past few decades, most new urban housing in low- and middle-income countries has been built illegally, with the majority of low-income groups living in housing that was developed outside the law (Hardoy and Satterthwaite 1989, UNCHS 1996, UN-Habitat 2003a). Most illegal settlements have little provision for services; by 2000, at least 680 million urban dwellers lacked adequate provision for water and at least 850 million lacked adequate provision for sanitation (UN-Habitat 2003b).

The ineffectiveness of most governments' housing policies, the disinterest in housing issues shown by most international agencies, and rapid urbanization provided the context from which a new kind of urban poor organization emerged—federations of slum/shack/pavement dwellers who actively sought partnerships with local governments.

## The Urban Poor Federations: Some Common Themes

Federations formed by savings groups that are set up and managed by the urban poor have become increasingly common in low- and middle-income nations.

### Origin and Scope

There is a long history of federations formed by urban poor groups that seek political changes and, where political circumstances permit, negotiate resources and government programs that benefit their members. What distinguishes this new set of federations is the active engagement in developing solutions and in offering governments a partnership in implementing these at scale. Also unusual are the opportunities they offer to women for leadership positions and in the multiple interconnections among the many national federations as they learn from and support one other.

The catalyst for this kind of federation was the change in approach by slum dweller federations in India and the growing role of the National Slum Dwellers Federation (NSDF) in the early 1980s.[1] The head of this

Federation, Jockin Arputham, had been a community leader in Janata Colony in Mumbai. The colony had fought hard to avoid demolition by the Indian government; in 1976, Janata Colony was bulldozed, despite a personal assurance to Jockin by the then-Prime Minister Indira Gandhi that this would not happen. Jockin had to leave India; on his return after the fall of the Gandhi government, he developed a nationwide slum dwellers' federation. At the same time, there was agreement within the federation on a change in strategy. The slum leaders recognized the ineffectiveness of lobbying city and state governments for housing and basic services that these governments were incapable of providing. They also recognized a need to develop their own solutions, to demonstrate to government the kinds of housing and basic service programs that worked for slum dwellers, and to show their capacity to work with governments in implementing these at scale.

The change in approach by the NSDF also coincided with the emergence of a federation of savings groups, formed by women pavement dwellers in Mumbai (*Mahila Milan*) and supported by a recently formed, small local nongovernmental organization (NGO) SPARC (SPARC 1990). The NSDF recognized the advantage of an alliance with *Mahila Milan* and SPARC; this three-strong alliance developed the strategy of demonstrating to governments through concrete projects—for instance, for new housing, for enumerations/community mapping, and for public toilets—how to address the needs of members.

Representatives from the NSDF, *Mahila Milan*, and SPARC were invited to South Africa in the early 1990s, because housing activists and community leaders there were considering how the country's first democratically elected government should address housing issues. These three Indian organizations supported the setting up a South African federation (now called the South African Federation of the Urban Poor) which, like them, began concrete projects to demonstrate to government the capacity of their members. During the early 1990s, several other national federations were formed, drawing advice and support from already-established federations in other nations. Most, like the Indian federations, had a small local NGO to support them. In 1996, with seven active national federations and interest from community organizations from many other nations, the federations decided to form their own small umbrella group, Slum/Shack Dwellers International (SDI) to facilitate their interchange with each other, to support emerging federations in other nations (and other urban poor groups interested in their work), and to negotiate more systematically with international agencies (Patel, Burra, and d'Cruz 2001).

Underpinning each of these federations are savings groups formed and managed by their members. The larger federations have hundreds or thousands of such savings groups. Women are particularly attracted to these savings groups because they provide crisis credit quickly and easily. Money accumulated in federation savings accounts can help fund housing improvements or income generation initiatives. Savings groups not only manage savings and credit efficiently; this collective management of money and the trust it builds within each group increases the capacity to work together on housing and other initiatives. These savings groups are therefore the building blocks of what begins as a local process and can develop into citywide and national federations.

Within each of the federations, each household's savings has intrinsic importance, but also has a more important role as the adhesive or foundation for collective organization, action, and negotiation. Federations often comment that their savings groups are as much to collect people as they are to collect money. In most urban contexts, what the poor can save, even over long periods, is never sufficient to allow them to afford market prices for formally constructed homes. This is why the savings are combined with actions to cut the costs of better housing, obtain land on which they can build housing through negotiation, and secure infrastructure development that they help build and maintain.

In effect, the federations are using their need for housing and access to services as the basis for mobilization and action and as the entry point for renegotiating their relationship with the state. The federations' strategies and actions provide opportunities for federation members to acquire and accumulate assets—especially more secure housing, which, once achieved, represents their most valuable asset. This also generally means better provision for their neighborhood with legal infrastructure and services.

The federations are not NGOs but aggregations of savings groups formed by those who live in illegal/informal settlements, tenements, cheap boarding houses, backyard shacks, and on pavements. All strive to ensure that the lowest income groups are included in their organizations. Furthermore, and perhaps unusually for grassroots federations, all recognize that they must work with local governments since any intervention that reduces poverty is limited in scale and scope without local government support. At the same time, the federations know that a working partnership with government has to be based on what they themselves design and develop, not on what governments or other professional bodies design and plan to build for them.

Table 7.1 provides a summary of the different federations, listing their size, affiliation with local NGOs, and the funds they manage that support

## Table 7.1. Details of the Federations, Support NGOs, and Funds

| Country | Federation | Year founded | Number of members | Support NGO/federation-managed funds |
|---|---|---|---|---|
| Brazil | A federation developing, based on five cities | 2004 | 11,000 | *Interaçao* |
| Cambodia | Squatter and Urban Poor Federation | 1994 | Active in 288 slums | Asian Coalition for Housing Rights Urban Poor Development Fund |
| Ghana | Ghana Homeless People's Federation | 2003 | 12,000 | People's Dialogue on Human Settlements |
| India | National Slum Dwellers Federation and *Mahila Milan* | 1974, 1986 | 2 million plus | SPARC (1984) Community-Led Infrastructure Finance Facility (CLIFF) |
| Kenya | *Muungano wa Wanvijiji* | 2000 | c. 25,000 | Pamoja Trust (2000) *Akiba Mashinani* Trust |
| Malawi | Malawi Homeless People's Federation | 2003 | 20,000 | CCODE – Centre for Community Organiza-tion and Development Mchenga Urban Poor Fund |
| Namibia | Shack Dwellers Federation of Namibia | 1992 | 15,000 | Namibian Housing Action Group (1997) Twahangana Fund (for land, services and income gen-eration) with state funds for housing (Build Together Program) |
| Nepal | Nepal Mahila Ekta Samaj and Nepal Mahila Ekata Samaj (women's federa-tion of savings groups) | 1998 | 3,147 | LUMANTI Nepal Urban Poor Fund |
| Philippines | Philippines Homeless People's Federation | 1994 | 50,000 | Vincentian Missionaries Social Development Foundation Inc. (VMSDFI) Urban Poor Development Fund |
| South Africa | South African Federation of the Urban Poor | 1991 | c. 100,000 | Community Organization Resource Centre The *uTshani* Fund (for housing), *Inqolobane* (The Granary) funds for employment/micro enterprise |
| Sri Lanka | Women's Development Bank | 1998 | 31,000 | JANARULAKA Women's Development Bank Federation |
| Tanzania | Tanzania Federation of the Urban Poor | 2004 | 1,700 | Centre for Community Initiatives (CCI) |

(*continued*)

**Table 7.1. Details of the Federations, Support NGOs, and Funds** (*continued*)

| Country | Federation | Year founded | Number of members | Support NGO/federation-managed funds |
|---|---|---|---|---|
| Thailand | Many regional and city-based federations | 1990 | 5 million within thousands of savings groups | CODI – fund set up by the government of Thailand to support the savings groups and their networks |
| Uganda | National Slum Dwellers Federation of Uganda | 2002 | 3,000 | Actogether |
| Zambia | Zambia Homeless People's Federation | 2002 | 14,000 | People's Process on Housing and Poverty, Saliswano (Urban Poor Development Fund) |
| Zimbabwe | The Zimbabwe Homeless People's Federation | 1993 | c. 45,000* | Dialogue on Shelter *Gungano* Fund |

Source: d'Cruz and Satterthwaite 2005, with updated information from http://www.sdinet.org.
Note: *Not surprisingly, activities in Zimbabwe have slowed considerably in the present climate of hostility to the urban poor from national government, although the federation still has partnerships with some local governments.

their work. In addition to the 16 federations listed, there are savings groups with the potential to form federations in many other countries.

In 12 countries, federations have set up their own urban poor funds to help members acquire land, build homes, and develop livelihoods. These funds are also where members' savings are deposited and where external funding from governments and international agencies is managed. These funds allow external support to be used and managed by the federations, rather than having to conform to externally imposed conditions that are often inappropriate. They also provide accountability and transparency for funders. Often, a contribution to the federation fund from a city government signals a change in government attitude and the beginning of a partnership.

The federations generally focus on "housing"—which includes not only better quality homes but also basic services such as water, sanitation, schools, health care services and getting tenure of the land that their home already occupies or access to land on which to build. Federations work to develop a bridge for their members between the informal and the formal. As low-income households manage the transition from informal or illegal homes and neighborhoods to formal, legal neighborhoods—including in many instances the legalization of their neighborhood—they must simultaneously develop the capacity to make regular payments to official service providers. The savings funds help develop household capacity to make regular payments to utility services. Savings also allow for the accumulation of funds for the one-off payments that are often required when moving to a legal home, such as connection charges for water, sewers, and electricity.

Although much of the work of the federations focuses on housing and basic services, what they are doing in effect is negotiating with the state for the right to live, work, and be active citizens in urban centers. In many countries, having a low income, working in the informal economy and living in an informal settlement become the bases for discriminatory policies—of bulldozing, eviction, harassment, and destruction of livelihoods. The 700,000 people whose homes were bulldozed in urban areas of Zimbabwe in mid-2005 (Tibaijuka 2005) might be considered exceptional. But large-scale forced evictions are also taking place in many other countries (du Plessis 2005); these, like the Zimbabwe evictions, are underpinned by politicians and civil servants who blame "the urban poor" or "migrants" for urban problems.

Negotiations for housing and basic services are to realize federation members' right to live and work in urban areas. These negotiations relate as much to location and security as to physical structures. For low-income groups in cities, a good location in relation to income-earning opportunities is often more important for survival than the quality of the accommodation—and this explains why many low-income individuals or households prefer centrally located tenements, cheap boarding houses, homes on pavements, and squatter settlements on sites at risk of natural disaster, over higher quality, more secure housing in less central locations.

The results of such strategies and actions, when successful, reduce their members' vulnerability to a range of stresses. Secure homes reduce the risk of eviction and the destruction of low-income households' assets and the disruptions to their livelihoods that evictions always bring. Better quality homes and services reduce health risks—and reduce time off work from illness or injury and expenditures on health care. Savings groups provide members with emergency credit rapidly. The interchange between savings groups allows them to learn from each other's methods and successes. Their immediate priority is to change the practices of city and municipal governments; in so doing, however, this has often led to changes in local policy and sometimes changes in policy and practice at provincial/state and national levels (d'Cruz and Satterthwaite 2005).

### The Strategies of Federations for Building Assets

All of the federations use similar strategies in helping their members organize and develop partnerships with local governments and seek housing or land on which housing can be built: savings and credit groups, pilot projects, community-driven surveys/maps, and community exchanges (Patel 2004). These serve to strengthen the federations (including supporting a continuous learning cycle among its member groups) and to change the attitudes and approaches of governments and international agencies. The fact that different federations use a similar set of tools is in large part due to the constant interchange of ideas and experiences between the different federations, supported by SDI.

*Pilot projects and precedents.* All the federations encourage their savings groups to trial pilot projects—an upgrading scheme, a new house development, a community toilet—and if they work well, these become much visited and discussed by other groups, many of whom return home and try out similar initiatives. This allows the initial project to be refined and tested in different places. Observing the first set of pilot projects can encourage other urban poor groups to start a savings group or to undertake a project because they see "people like them" designing and implementing such ideas. Pilot projects are widely regarded as ineffective when designed and implemented by external agencies, because they often fail to develop beyond the initial phase. But if they are planned within citywide processes involving urban poor organizations, they are centers of experiment and learning. Those that work well become precedents that can be shown to potential partners from governments and international agencies and act as catalysts for action elsewhere.

For instance, in India during the 1990s the NSDF and *Mahila Milan* demonstrated their capacity to design, build, and manage community toilet blocks in slums where there was insufficient room or funding for household sanitation. Large-scale toilet programs became possible first in Pune and then in Mumbai, when local government staff saw how the federation's toilets worked better than the contractor-built public toilets they had built previously. The federations, with the support of SPARC, have been responsible for about 500 community-designed and managed toilet blocks that serve hundreds of thousands of households in Pune and Mumbai—with comparable toilet programs developing in many other cities (Patel and Mitlin 2004; Burra, Patel, and Kerr 2003). Similar toilet blocks are now being tested by federations in Kenya, South Africa, Sri Lanka, Uganda, and Zimbabwe, drawing on the Indian federations' experience and advice.

*Surveys.* Household enumerations and settlement surveys are another staple strategy of the federations. In slums and informal settlements, reliable, detailed information and maps are needed for planning upgrading, secure tenure, and services. Governments rarely have such an information base. Community-directed household, settlement, and city surveys are important in helping those living in slums and illegal settlements to look at their own situations and consider their priorities, as well as providing government and other external agencies with the maps and the detailed household data needed for successful projects. Community-directed surveys have demonstrated how to produce the data necessary for successful interventions, both by governments and the federations themselves. For example, in Kenya, the federation has mapped all the slums in Nairobi, supported community enumerations in many of them, and demonstrated that it is possible to reach agreement between landlords and tenants in a land regularization and upgrading initiative (Weru 2004). They also recently completed a citywide survey in Kisumu, encompassing all the informal settlements.

*Community exchanges.* Hosting exchange visits is a strategy pursued to support outside groups interested in learning more about the federations, as well as an important means of spreading knowledge about how urban poor groups can act, organize, and negotiate within each federation. These exchanges allow savings groups to federate and create strong personal bonds among communities that, in turn, allow them to work together rather than see each other as competitors for government resources. Although exchange visits are primarily to support community organizations, civil servants and politicians are also invited to take part—and these visits have often shown officials new ways to implement more effective housing, land tenure, and service provision initiatives. It is also easier to negotiate with government officials when they can see for themselves the results of a new house design, a functioning community toilet, or a detailed slum enumeration. When one local government has accepted a change in approach, officials from other local governments can be brought there by their federations to see how it works—both within and among nations. For instance, the city of Windhoek has been much visited by other federations and their local government officials, to see how the change in house plot and infrastructure standards have made legal land sites more affordable to low-income groups (Mitlin and Muller 2004).

*Land readjustment.* In most illegal settlements, some adjustment to existing plot layouts and plot sizes is needed to facilitate better roads and paths and the introduction or improvement of piped water, sewers, and drains.

Negotiating agreement on these adjustments with a settlement's population has often proved difficult for external professionals—but is something that the federations have managed in many instances. As noted above, in Kenya, this has included negotiating agreements with slum landlords to allow tenants to acquire plots too (Weru 2004).

*Vacant land surveys.* When in situ upgrading is not possible, federations must find land for new housing in convenient locations. Government agencies often have suitable land—and many federations have undertaken surveys of vacant land to demonstrate this to the government and to strengthen their capacity to negotiate for land. For instance, in Mumbai, the savings groups formed by women pavement dwellers put pressure on the local government to provide them with land; when the local government claimed that there was no land available, the pavement dwellers organized a survey around the city, cataloguing how much vacant land was available. When they obtained a site, they designed the housing and supervised its construction. This project encourages other organizations of pavement dwellers to negotiate for land and government support for other such schemes.

*Keeping down costs.* All the federations place a strong emphasis on keeping down unit costs for their initiatives. This is to minimize the gap between the cost per household of what is implemented and what their members can afford to pay. Many federations also make loans available to members, recognizing that any sizeable loan imposes financial costs on poor households that they might find difficult to bear. Combining unpaid labor contributions and low unit costs often enables improvements that federation households can afford without the need for loans or subsidies.[2] This implies a different approach from most conventional loan providing agencies, which judge success by how many loans they provide and how much they lend.

If government subsidies are available for new housing developments, the federations' experience shows that these should support community-driven house construction, not contractor-built houses, because this produces larger, better quality houses. The federations also need to be able to influence the choice of location, if these are not being built within the settlements where they already live. In South Africa, a long-established national housing program provides a one-off subsidy to low-income households to obtain housing. The South African Federation of the Urban Poor has built thousands of good quality four-room houses for the same cost that contractors charge for one-room "core units" (Baumann, Bolnick, and Mitlin 2004).

*Selected Histories*

Two specific examples help illustrate the nature of the federations in greater detail. The South African Federation (which named itself *uMfelanda-Wonye* meaning, literally, "We die together") is the oldest federation in Africa. This is a national network of some 1,500 autonomous savings and credit groups whose size ranges from a minimum of 15 to a maximum of more than 500 members (Baumann, Bolnick, and Mitlin 2004). It has an active membership in some 700 informal settlements, 100 backyard shack areas,[3] three hostels, and 150 rural villages. The work of the federation has included the "delivery" of 12,000 housing units; incremental loans for a further 2,000 houses; infrastructure for 2,500 families; land tenure for 12,000 families; hundreds of small business loans; 3 parcels of commercial land, 10 community centers; and several crèches. In 1994, it set up its own housing fund, the *uTshani* Fund, in which savings are deposited and from which loans are made, including bridging finance for housing and infrastructure loans, access to grants through the government's housing subsidy scheme, and access to credit for small business loans.

The federation has set many important precedents by demonstrating what community organizations can accomplish. It has helped to change national housing policy to be more supportive of self-help and community management, and it has developed a partnership with the city government in Durban for an ambitious citywide program, including an upgrading program involving more than 15,000 households. The federation is also working with the Methodist church in South Africa to identify vacant land owned by the church and allocate it to housing projects for homeless families and, in rural areas, to support their livelihoods. This initiative is important not only for the new land it could provide for housing for low-income households, but also for encouraging more action from the government on land redistribution and tenure reform and in setting an example that other churches in South Africa can follow (Bolnick and Van Rensburg 2005). In May 2006, South African Housing Minister, Lindiwe Nonceba Sisulu, publicly endorsed the work of the federation and promised the equivalent of US$40 million of national and provincial government support for its housing programs.[4]

In India, as noted earlier, two federations work together: the NSDF and *Mahila Milan*, supported by the Indian NGO SPARC. They are working in 70 cities. In Mumbai, seven housing projects have been built. The new houses are for a program to resettle families who have been living beside the railway tracks and will also provide secure homes for more than 50,000 slum and pavement dweller households. These are important precedent-setting projects to demonstrate what urban poor organizations can do. Smaller-scale new housing and upgrading programs are under way in many other cities and smaller urban centers to support local learning and set precedents on which larger programs can be built. The NSDF and *Mahila Milan* also have a partnership with the Commissioner of Police in Mumbai in setting up police stations in hundreds of slums. They provide the inhabitants of these slums with a police station in their community and police who they know and who are accountable to them, and are supported by a committee of community volunteers—seven women and three men (Roy, Jockin, and Javed 2004).

## Achievements and Constraints

The rapid growth in the number of national federations has been remarkable, as has the success in several of them in developing large-scale programs with particular city governments and national governments.

### Notable Successes

The federations have achieved more successes in asset accumulation than many other types of grassroots organizations and NGOs. It is useful to examine their methods in these cases as these may have relevance for grassroots organizations in other nations.

At the core of the federations' successes is their capacity to offer governments effective partnerships in addressing housing and related problems. Where government is supportive, this can be done at a considerable scale. The partnerships produce housing that is more secure and of better quality than public programs, often with much lower unit costs. Federation households that get this housing have not only a home but also a valuable asset. The home often serves as a location for income-earning activities. At the same time, the savings groups that are the foundation of each federation are building households' savings, offering their members small short-term emergency loans and developing each group's capacity to manage finance collectively. From this comes their capacity to undertake other tasks.

The federations have been successful at indirectly promoting the development of another, more intangible asset: social capital. These include both the relationships between members of savings groups and the relationships between the different savings groups that make up the federation. They may not be quantifiable in traditional measures of well-being, but the increased possibilities for individuals (especially women) to be involved in community discussions, plans, and activities contributes to the overall collective agency of the community. The federations' savings groups also manage many local issues on a routine basis, such as resident committees, conflict resolvers, facility managers, and emergency support providers. Through the work of the federations, members develop the confidence and capacity to negotiate with government and develop productive working relationships with government officials. One common theme, when women leaders from the federations describe their work, is how their membership of the federation gave them the confidence to work with and negotiate with government.

As a larger, international community, federations have learned and benefited from one another. Most of this teaching and learning takes place during exchange visits between savings groups within a city. However, exchange visits between cities and international exchange visits have also been important for exposing urban poor groups to new possibilities. It is difficult for outsiders to appreciate the importance of these exchanges—and the number of them. For instance, during 2003 there were more than 100 city-to-city exchanges in India and countless exchanges between communities within cities. One of the reasons why the federations set up SDI was to support international exchanges that strengthen existing federations and help new federations develop.

One of the greatest successes of the federations has been their ability to influence the power dynamic between poor communities and the government. Governments, NGOs, and international organizations often view the "poor" as "clients" or "beneficiaries," not as agents whose individual and community processes can, with appropriate support, improve their own lives. The federations have helped to change this, not only with regard to work with official agencies responsible for housing, but also regarding their members' relationships with the police, the staff of schools and health centers, and municipal agencies or private utilities with responsibility for water, sanitation, garbage collection, and electricity. Individual community organizations are unlikely to move governments to change their policies even if they can negotiate some concessions for their own settlement. Federations with hundreds or thousands of community organizations have a greater chance of success. Changes in government policy and practice are usually required for federation programs to "go to scale" (that is, to greatly increase their scale and scope). Rather than each urban poor group having to negotiate with the politicians or civil servants responsible for their district, federations allow negotiations at the city level to address the urban poor's problems of land tenure, infrastructure, housing, and services at the city scale.

The urban poor federations have also developed a strategy to support the scaling up of government activities. The first step is for community organizations and federations to build a citywide information base on conditions in all of the areas with poor quality housing to provide the necessary facts for a citywide program. This strategy has produced citywide changes in Durban, Mumbai, Phnom Penh, and Windhoek and many cities in Thailand. Some federations' programs have national significance. For instance, the upgrading program of the Cambodian federation received the support of the national government (ACHR 2004); in India, the community toilet program prompted the national government to set up a funding facility to encourage comparable programs throughout the country (Burra, Patel, and Kerr 2003). The *Baan Mankong* program in Thailand is perhaps the most ambitious national program—as described in chapter 8.

Support from national or local governments is often as or more important for the federations than international funds because it is proof of a readiness by these governments to develop a partnership with them. So international funds need to avoid replacing this. One important innovation in this regard is the Community-Led Infrastructure Finance Facility established in India to support the work of the National Slum Dwellers Federation–*Mahila Milan*–SPARC alliance, through which two official bilateral agencies (the Department for International Development and Sida) channel funding. The equivalent of US$10 million is available for loans, guarantees, and technical assistance to support a range of projects, and funds can be drawn as needed. This demonstrates how official donor agencies can support community processes in ways that allow more decision making at the grassroots level. This fund can also be used to leverage resources from local and national governments and help federations manage a larger engagement with the state. Comparable finance facilities are being developed in Kenya and the Philippines.

Another funding innovation is the US$4.6 million made available to the federations through the umbrella organization SDI between 2001 and 2007 to support member savings groups acquire land for housing, support learning and set precedents. This was initiated in 2001 by the Sigrid Rausing Trust, which has provided constant support to the federations ever since.

Additional support was received from the U.K. Big Lottery Fund and the Allachy Trust. To date, these funds have supported tens of thousands of low-income households to obtain land for housing or get tenure of the land they occupy (Mitlin 2003; Mitlin and Satterthwaite 2007). Despite the small scale of available funding—typically grants of between US$10,000 and US$40,000—this shows the value of having funding available at short notice to support community-driven innovations that also leverage local resources, and that can set precedents that help encourage local government support. Wherever possible, funding from this source is recovered for reuse locally. In 2007, the Bill and Melinda Gates Foundation committed an additional US$10 million to support the work of the federations.

The federations have avoided some of the repercussions of partisan politics by avoiding any formal alliance with political parties and individual politicians. In the short term, this can be a disadvantage, as politicians steer government support only to community organizations that supported them and prevent support for communities that did not. But the advantage of this is that it protects their autonomy and capacity for independent action. It allows them to negotiate and work with whoever is in power locally or nationally. The federations' politics has been called the politics of patience, meaning negotiation and long-term pressure, with confrontation used only as a last resort (Patel 2004). As noted earlier, any large-scale success depends on support from government. Many civil servants and politicians come to recognize the value of the federations' work and are invited by the federations to speak with them at local and international events.

### Challenges and Limitations

It would be naïve to think that these mass organizations formed by those with the least income and political power can function effectively without problems or opposition. The federations include some of societies' poorest groups who face the worst discrimination. In many countries, they have to work with state structures that are weak, ineffective, and often corrupt. In addition, no movement in which women having central roles can avoid hostility—both within itself and with some external agencies.

One of the key challenges that the federations face is indifference or hostility from potential partners. This includes hostility even from local and international NGOs and academics that have "housing rights for the poor" as their core agenda.[5] Federations face outside criticism for their community-driven approaches that allegedly absolve national or local governments from their responsibilities. However, one of the key features of the federations' work is their demonstration to governments of more effective ways in which the government can act. A related allegation is that the federations increase aid dependence; again, this criticism is unfounded because they do the opposite. They demonstrate solutions that require far less international funding than conventional donor-funded "upgrading" and serviced site interventions.

Despite considerable progress in developing productive relationships with governments, politicians and civil servants still find it difficult to see urban poor organizations as key partners. Many politicians dislike the federations because they will not align with their election campaigns. Even progressive governments committed to democracy and empowerment find it difficult to work with them because politicians see them as too independent from state institutions. City politicians are often reluctant to relinquish the role of patron dispensing projects to their constituency. Traditional community leaders may resent the federations' growing influence. The federations have also found it difficult to maintain momentum over many years when faced with indifference, inertia, or hostility from the state.

The federations might also be regarded as a threat by powerful local interests, especially when the scale of their work increases. Many contractors dislike the federations because they threaten their profitable (and often corrupt) relationships with local governments. Many slums have powerful vested interests that oppose representative community organizations (see, for instance, Weru 2004). In addition, in prosperous and expanding cities, many federation members occupy sites that become attractive to governments or real estate interests which produces conflicts which are not easily resolved.

The federations have also had failures or limited successes. No large-scale movements such as these—formed by people with the least income and influence, and which encourage their member organizations to try out new initiatives—can avoid these. Projects fail, community organizations cease to function, and loan repayment schedules are not maintained, but one of the key roles of the federations is to learn how to cope with these problems and find out how to avoid them in the future. Some federations have also suffered from unrealistic expectations by external donors of their capacity to rapidly succeed at scale. Almost all local initiatives require difficult and often lengthy negotiations with a range of government agencies, many of which delay progress, even when the political commitment to support the federation is there. In addition, the fact that politicians or senior civil servants support a partnership with the federations does not ensure that all the local government staff with which the federation has to deal also do so.

It is difficult for most official bilateral aid agencies and development banks to work with the federations because these agencies' and banks' structures are designed primarily to work with and through national governments. Supporting the work of the federations is often problematic, in part because recipient governments do not want funds directed to them (or more often, national recipient governments do not want this, even when these federations work successfully with local governments). While most official development assistance agencies channel some funding to city and municipal governments and community processes, these represent a very small proportion of total funding flows (Satterthwaite 2001, 2005). However, there is increasing recognition among some international donors of the need for funding channels that go directly to local processes that target poverty alleviation. Some donors recognize that direct funding cannot be managed from their headquarters and requires intermediary institutions within the recipient country. However, it is a big step for any international donor to entrust the funding it manages and for which it has to be accountable to local organizations or local funds.

## Conclusions

Federations formed by slum/shack dwellers and homeless groups who actively seek partnerships with local governments have successfully implemented a range of initiatives in many countries; in some they have influenced the policies and practices of city and national governments. In most of the countries where they are active, the scale of their work and partnerships with local governments is growing. They have also developed a range of tools and methods that support this—including citywide surveys and slum enumerations and mapping and local, national, and international exchanges. They have also set up their own umbrella organization, Slum/ Shack Dwellers International, to support these international exchanges and facilitate their dialogue with international agencies.

These federations have used their members' need for housing or land for housing and services as the basis for mobilization and action among the urban poor and as the entry point for renegotiating their relationship with the state. A change in strategy by these federations that has particular significance is from making demands on governments (based on their members' "right to housing and basic services") to developing their own solutions (which usually have much lower unit costs than government projects), using these as precedents to show governments what they can do and then offering government agencies partnerships for implementing these on a larger scale.

The means to develop this relationship with government centers on the federations' ability to deliver for local government as well as for their own members. For instance, they need to work with service providers to lower the costs of provision and management and work with government agencies to resolve the need for some of their members to vacate land needed for infrastructure while simultaneously representing the needs of those that have to move. Thus, all the federations seek to change the relationship of "the poor" with government and other actors. The "asset" they use to do so is their capacity to organize and to innovate, to demonstrate cheaper, more effective ways by which poverty can be reduced, and to offer partnerships to government to "scale up." This is very much in line with the emphasis of the asset-building framework to create opportunities for poorer groups to engage in poverty reduction.

The federations' strategies and actions, when successful, reduce their members' vulnerability to a range of stresses—from coping with emergencies and with fluctuations in prices and incomes through their savings groups to reducing health risks (and expenditures on health care and medicines) through better quality housing and basic services to reducing the risks of poverty-creating government measures such as eviction. The strategies and actions of the federations are also central to building their members' capacity to act and to change the rules that influence the control and use of resources and the distribution of public services. Thus, the federations increase the poor's collective capability—to design and implement initiatives (including building or improving housing); to negotiate for basic services, land, or land tenure; to accumulate savings; to leverage funding from local governments; and to change antipoor rules and regulations. The federations are the basis of their members' "power to act to reproduce, challenge or change the rules that govern the control, use and transformation of resources" (see Caroline Moser's opening chapter; also see Sen 1999).

## Recommendations

Despite the many successes achieved by the federations, there is much progress still to be made, especially in translating success in particular initiatives into larger-scale citywide and national frameworks. One of the biggest obstacles is the lack of donor support. If official donor agencies want to provide support to the federations, they need to develop funding channels that can support the kinds of initiatives described in this chapter. There are three needs:

- *international funders who understand the requirements of community organizations and federations for nonproject support—for instance, for community exchanges, slum enumerations, and experimentation:* To date, the main international funders for these have not been the official bilateral or multilateral agencies but international NGOs and Trusts.
- *intermediary funds within low- and middle-income countries on which community organizations and federations can draw and which are accountable to them—while also offering safeguards and well-managed accounts for any international donor:* Most of the federations have their own "urban poor" funds into which member savings go and from which loans are made—and these can be capitalized by governments or international donors.
- *United Nations' agencies and official bilateral and multilateral donor agencies to consider how their work within any country can support the work of the federations:* Staff from these agencies may support the federations, yet the agencies themselves may still have policies and structures that marginalize or ignore them.

## Notes

1. The details about the origins of the Indian federations are drawn from interviews with Jockin Arputham in 2004 and 2005 on his work as a community organizer during the 1960s and 1970s and from discussions and material provided by Sheela Patel, the director of SPARC, who was also one of SPARC's founders. (See SPARC 1990 and Patel and Mitlin 2004.)
2. This is also the strategy of the Pakistan NGO Orangi Pilot Project-Research and Training Institute, as it has shown the inhabitants of informal settlements how to manage the installation of infrastructure (especially sewers and drains) while so reducing the unit costs that low-income households can afford the pay for these. (See Hasan 1997 and Hasan 2006.)
3. Households living in backyard shacks are particularly insecure as they have no legal protection from being evicted and are dependent on the goodwill of the household who sublets the back area of their plot to them.

4. This support was publicly announced by Dr. Sisulu at an International Slum Dwellers Conference organized by SDI and the South African government's Department of Housing in Cape Town in May 2006. (See Sisulu 2006.)

5. The reasons for this are not clear. These may stem in part from the challenge the federations provide for these NGOs' or academics' legitimacy to speak "on behalf of the poor." In part, they stem from different opinions regarding the best strategies to change government approaches or different conceptions of what is possible. (See chapters 10 and 11 in Mitlin and Satterthwaite 2004.)

## References

ACHR. 2004. "Negotiating the Right to Stay in the City." *Environment and Urbanization* 16 (1): 9–26.

Amis, P. 1999. "Urban Economic Growth and Poverty Reduction." Urban Governance Partnerships and Poverty Research Working Paper 2, University of Birmingham, United Kingdom.

Baumann, T., J. Bolnick, and D. Mitlin. 2004. "The Age of Cities and Organizations of the Urban Poor: The Work of the South African Homeless People's Federation." In *Empowering Squatter Citizen; Local Government, Civil Society and Urban Poverty Reduction*, eds. D. Mitlin and D. Satterthwaite, 193–215. London: Earthscan Publications.

Bolnick, J., and G. Van Rensburg. 2005. "The Methodist Church's Initiative to Use its Vacant Land to Support Homeless People's Housing and Livelihoods in South Africa." *Environment and Urbanization* 17 (1): 115–22.

Boonyabancha, S. 2005. "Baan Mankong: Going to Scale with 'Slum' and Squatter Upgrading in Thailand." *Environment and Urbanization* 17 (1): 21–46.

Burra, S., S. Patel, and T. Kerr. 2003. "Community-Designed, Built, and Managed Toilet Blocks in Indian Cities." *Environment and Urbanization* 15 (2): 11–32.

Cohen, M. A. 1983. *Learning by Doing: World Bank Lending for Urban Development, 1972–82.* Washington DC: World Bank.

d'Cruz, C., and D. Satterthwaite. 2005. "Building Homes, Changing Official Approaches: The Work of Urban Poor Federations and Their Contributions to Meeting the Millennium Development Goals in Urban Areas." Poverty Reduction in Urban Areas Series Working Paper 16, IIED, London. http://www.iied.org/pubs/pdf/full/9547IIED.pdf.

du Plessis, J. 2005. "The Growing Problem of Forced Evictions and the Crucial Importance of Community-Based, Locally Appropriate Alternatives." *Environment and Urbanization* 17 (1): 123–34.

Hardoy, J. E., and D. Satterthwaite. 1989. *Squatter Citizen: Life in the Urban Third World.* London: Earthscan Publications.

Hasan, A. 1997. *Working with Government: The Story of the Orangi Pilot Project's Collaboration with State Agencies for Replicating its Low Cost Sanitation Programme.* Karachi: City Press.

Hasan, A. 2006. "Orangi Pilot Project: the Expansion of Work Beyond Orangi and the Mapping of Informal Settlements and Infrastructure." *Environment and Urbanization* 18 (2): 451–80.

Mitlin, D. 2003. "A Fund to Secure Land for Shelter; Supporting Strategies of the Organized Poor." *Environment and Urbanization* 15 (1): 181–92.

Mitlin, D., and A. Muller. 2004. "Windhoek, Namibia: Towards Progressive Urban Land Policies in Southern Africa." *International Development Planning Review*, 26 (2): 167–86.

Mitlin, D., and D. Satterthwaite, eds. 2004. *Empowering Squatter Citizen; Local Government, Civil Society, and Urban Poverty Reduction.* London: Earthscan Publications.

Mitlin, D. and D. Satterthwaite. 2007. "Strategies for grassroots control of international aid." *Environment and Urbanization* 19 (2): 483–500.

Patel, S. 2004. "Tools and Methods for Empowerment Developed by Slum Dwellers Federations in India." *Participatory Learning and Action 50*, International Institute for Environment and Development, London.

Patel, S., S. Burra, and C. d'Cruz. 2001. "Shack/Slum Dwellers International (SDI): Foundations to Treetops." *Environment and Urbanization* 13 (2): 45–59.

Patel, S., and D. Mitlin. 2004. "The Work of SPARC, the National Slum Dwellers Federations and Mahila Milan." In *Empowering Squatter Citizen; Local Government, Civil Society and Urban Poverty Reduction*, eds. D. Mitlin, and D. Satterthwaite, 216–41. London: Earthscan Publications.

Roy, A. N., A. Jockin and A. Javed. 2004. "Community Police Stations in Mumbai's Slums." *Environment and Urbanization* 16 (2): 135–38.

Satterthwaite, D. 2001. "Reducing Urban Poverty: Constraints on the Effectiveness of Aid Agencies and Development Banks and Some Suggestions for Change." *Environment and Urbanization* 13 (1): 137–57.

Satterthwaite, D. 2005. "Meeting the MDGs in Urban Areas: The Forgotten Role of Local Organizations." *Journal of International Affairs* 58 (2): 87–112.

Sen, A. 1999. *Development as Freedom.* Oxford: Oxford University Press.

Sisulu, L. 2006. "Partnerships between Government and Slum/Shack Dwellers' Federations." *Environment and Urbanization* 18 (2): 401–6.

SPARC. 1990. "SPARC–Developing New NGO Lines." *Environment and Urbanization* 2 (1): 91–104.

Turner, J. F. C. 1976. "Housing by People–Towards Autonomy in Building Environments." Ideas in Progress, Marion Boyars, London.

Tibaijuka, A. K. 2005. *Report of the Fact-Finding Mission to Zimbabwe to Assess the Scope and Impact of Operation Murambatsvina.* New York: United Nations.

UNCHS (Habitat). 1996. *An Urbanizing World: Global Report on Human Settlements, 1996.* Oxford: Oxford University Press.

UN-Habitat (2003a). *The Challenge of Slums: Global Report on Human Settlements 2003.* London: Earthscan Publications.

UN-Habitat (2003b). *Water and Sanitation in the World's Cities; Local Action for Global Goals.* London: Earthscan Publications.

Weru, J. 2004. "Community Federations and City Upgrading: The Work of Pamoja Trust and Muungano in Kenya." *Environment and Urbanization* 16 (1): 47–62.

# CHAPTER 8

# Upgrading Thailand's Urban Settlements:
# A Community-Driven Process
# of Social Development

*Somsook Boonyabancha*

The poor across the world employ a variety of strategies to improve their well-being by accumulating assets. In the world's slums, however, the poor have virtually no assets on which to build other than their meager, improvised dwellings. For several decades now, governments and international agencies have supported programs to upgrade basic services in urban slums to facilitate asset accumulation. In most of these, community residents are the passive recipients of projects conceived by governments, designed by engineers and implemented by contractors.

This paper provides a detailed case study of a phenomenon, described in chapter 7, whereby large-scale urban poor community organizations themselves design and implement a more comprehensive community upgrading process. This involves not only infrastructure improvements, but also housing, tenure security, and economic and social revival, using a flexible system of financial support. This new approach is being tested in Thailand in the Baan Mankong Program, a nationwide community upgrading program launched by the Thai government in 2003, and being implemented in 200 Thai towns and cities by the Community Organizations Development Institute (CODI). The program targets 300,000 households in 2,000 informal settlements. The program is unusual both for its national scale and for the way it is structured, with support going directly to community organizations of poor people that manage and implement the whole process. This process builds the capacity of poor people to develop collective responses to many of the other problems facing them.

The Baan Mankong Program continues to show that community improvement and housing development by the community itself can act as a powerful tool to rebuild strong social cohesion and collectivity among the urban poor. As such, community upgrading can be a direct and effective strategy for reducing urban poverty, creating assets for urban poor communities, and enabling them to build partnerships with local authority.

Slum upgrading has brought considerable asset improvement directly to former slums and urban poor people. Generally, land occupied by informal communities has little or no value. Slum land is almost never considered a formal asset, nor is the patched-together houses or informal livelihoods of the slum residents counted by the conventional system of calculating assets. However, when a slum upgrading program can grant security of tenure and communities organize themselves into self-managing social units, a variety of assets are created, both for the people who live in the communities and for the city as a whole. Assets are accumulated by securing land tenure and establishing municipal services and more permanent housing, which generate a range of other economic developments. These, in turn, create further financial assets for community members, as well as for neighbors adjacent to the upgraded slums. Slum improvement interventions also generate community social capital by building the capacity of communities to improve their livelihoods, manage finances collectively, establish communal funds, and look after one another's welfare. Once the upgrading activities solidify people's confidence in their own creativity and legitimacy as active citizens, their capacity to negotiate with the government is developed, thereby also endowing them with political assets.

The Baan Mankong Program is rooted in 13 years of government-community partnership experience. To achieve its goal, it has come to recognize the need for all the community-driven upgrading initiatives to unify into networks of urban poor organizations. These larger organizations are better able to work in partnership with local governments and other development actors, to develop jointly a citywide upgrading program, and to promote community development across the city.

## Community Upgrading in Thailand

Policies and programs are urgently needed to ensure that all slum and squatter households achieve the improvements called for by the Millennium Development Goals.[1] These include not only physical targets, but also improvements in social, tenure security, and livelihood aspects of people's lives. Meeting these targets also requires improvements in the managerial systems within urban poor communities and changes in the relationships between slum and squatter communities and their city authorities.

In the past, slum upgrading generally involved the provision, by government agencies, of such minimal physical amenities as drains, walkways, toilets, or a water supply in informal settlements. At a time when many governments were ignoring or evicting slum communities, slum upgrading came as a positive sign. Although it promised no long-term solutions to serious problems of land tenure and lack of affordable urban housing, upgrading signaled a retreat from forced evictions; the minimal improvements it brought represented an indirect form of recognition that these communities were part of the city, which was a breakthrough.

Until 2003, the Thai government's response to housing problems faced by low-income groups had not reached any significant scale. By 2003, the country had some 5,500 urban poor communities, with 8.25 million inhabitants, living in poor quality housing. In the 3,700 communities whose land tenure was insecure, 30 percent of residents were squatters and 70 percent were land renters, with no secure long-term rental contracts. Many of these communities were under threat of eviction, and more than 70 percent of their inhabitants could not afford conventional housing, either through the market or through conventional government housing programs.

Before 1977, the only approach of the Thai government had been to push slums and squatter settlements out of the city. The government's first slum upgrading program, launched by the National Housing Authority (NHA) in 1977, was an important step forward for the country's urban poor communities because it recognized these communities as part of the city. In the 1980s, between 30,000 and 50,000 households were able to access improvements under this program, but this was done without addressing their legal status or the contravention of various bylaws. Standardized and contractor-built drains and walkways were provided, but without full acceptance that the slums were viable urban settlements and a much-needed stock of affordable housing assets for the urban poor.

Since the 1980s, Thailand has experienced a growth in community movements, nongovernmental organization (NGO) and civil society movements, partnerships between government agencies and community-based organizations, and networks formed by the urban poor. In addition to the NHA's upgrading program Thailand has had some other interesting pilot housing and land tenure initiatives for the urban poor, including land-sharing schemes, through which squatters received secure tenure and infrastructure when they negotiated to share the site they had occupied with the landowner (Angel and Boonyabancha 1988). In 1992, the Thai government set up the Urban Community Development Office (UCDO) to support community organizations with loans for new housing, housing improvements, settlement upgrading, and income generation Boonyabancha (2001, 2003). In 2000, UCDO was merged with the Rural Development Fund to form the Community Organizations Development Institute (CODI), which is now implementing Baan Mankong,[2] the national program for upgrading housing, environmental conditions, and tenure security of urban poor communities, which is the primary focus of this chapter.

### From UCDO to CODI

The work of the CODI evolved out of the UCDO. In 1992, the Thai government set up UCDO to address urban poverty, a move prompted by an increasing awareness that Thailand's economic success during the 1980s and early 1990s had brought little benefit to the poorest groups. Indeed, housing conditions for many had deteriorated and urban poor settlements were at ever-greater risk of eviction as land prices and demand for central city sites increased. There was also recognition of the need to develop more participatory models of support using flexible financial development models, and to support projects determined by communities through community-based savings and credit groups. Several earlier projects carried out by communities with local and international NGOs working in Thailand had also shown the potential for the improvement of housing by low-income communities and networks of communities themselves.

UCDO was provided with an initial capital fund of US$30 million, from which it could make loans to organized communities to undertake a variety of activities related to housing, land acquisition, and income generation. It also provided small grants and technical support to community organizations.

From the outset, UCDO sought to bring together different interest groups, with senior government staff, academics, and senior community leaders on its governing board. Initially, loans were available to community-based savings groups for income generation, housing and land acquisition, for example, to allow communities threatened with eviction to purchase existing slum land or land elsewhere, and to develop housing there. Any community could receive any of these loans, provided its members could show that they had the capacity to manage community finance as a group, through community savings groups, and that the loans could be used to respond to the particular needs of each group. In this way, UCDO developed links with a wide range of community organizations and savings groups. The loans were given at interest rates dramatically lower than those charged by informal money lenders (3 percent for housing and 8 percent for income-generation activities) but high enough to sustain the initial UCDO fund and cover the organization's administrative costs.

As the savings groups became larger, stronger, and more numerous, UCDO facilitated links among individual savings groups that led to the formation of community networks at many levels. UCDO also supported communities in a particular city or province in joining together to form networks negotiating as a block with city or provincial authorities, or to working together on shared problems of housing, livelihoods or access to basic services (Boonyabancha 1999, 2005). Gradually, UCDO began to make bulk loans to these community networks, which then made loans on to their member communities. The emergence of large-scale community networks in Thailand brought immense changes to the community-led development processes in general and to UCDO. Increasingly, these networks became the means by which UCDO (and later CODI) funds were made available to low-income groups around the country. These community networks took many different shapes and forms, some based on shared occupations (such as the taxi-drivers' cooperative), others on shared land tenure problems, a shared public landlord, or common pooled savings. Thus networks of communities formed within the same city, along the same canal, or along the same railway line.

Later, UCDO began to link with other government and bilateral agencies to implement several other development programs, also using flexible community network grants to work on development activities. For example, a small grants program was established for community-managed environmental improvement projects, with US$1.3 million from the Danish Cooperation for Environment and Development (DANCED). This funding supported 196 projects benefiting 41,000 families and strengthened the capacity of community organizations to work together and with local government. Another notable achievement was a program designed to help savings groups facing financial crisis maintain their loan repayments after the Asian financial crisis of 1997, with support from the Thai and Japanese governments. A further initiative established welfare funds for communities to use as grants, loans, or partial loans for education or income generation.

For example, the small installments were used by those needing to pay school fees, as well as for persons who were HIV positive, sick, or elderly, all with the support of the World Bank's Social Investment Fund.

The success of the UCDO is self-evident. By the year 2000, 950 community savings groups had been established and supported in 53 of Thailand's 75 provinces; housing loans and technical support had been provided to 47 housing projects involving 6,400 households; and grants for small improvements in infrastructure and living conditions had been provided in 796 communities, benefiting 68,208 families. More than 100 community networks had been set up, and more than B 1 billion (US$25 million) had been provided in loans, with more than half of these loans since repaid in full. In total, informal estimates suggest that some baht 2 billion was generated by all these projects.

Building on the success of the UCDO, CODI was established in 2000 and continued to support the programs set up under UCDO. But, whereas UCDO had been a special project under the National Housing Authority, CODI's legal standing as an independent public organization under the Ministry of Social Development and Human Security provided it with greater possibilities (such as being able to apply directly to the annual government budget), wider linkages, and new possibilities for supporting collaboration between urban and rural groups. The emphasis on supporting community-managed savings and loan groups and community networks remained strong. Moreover, CODI has forged links with 30,000 rural community organizations, as well as urban community organizations in most of Thailand's cities. Like UCDO, CODI has a mixed board that includes representatives from government and from community organizations.

### New Government Programs for Secure Housing

In January 2003, the Thai government announced two new programs that together sought to provide secure housing for one million low-income urban households.

- The *Baan Mankong* ("secure housing") Program channels government funds in the form of infrastructure subsidies and soft housing and land loans directly to urban poor community organizations. These community organizations then plan and carry out improvements to their land, housing, environment, and basic services. This program is managed by CODI.

- The Baan Ua Arthorn ("We care") Program, implemented by the National Housing Authority consists of the design, construction, and sale of ready-to-occupy flats and houses at subsidized rates to lower-income households that can afford the "rent-to-own" payments of US$25 to US$37 per month.

The next section describes the *Baan Mankong* Program in greater detail to illustrate the role of community organizations in upgrading informal settlements. This process of engagement allows those communities to accumulate a range of assets, improving their quality of life and strengthening their social capital and ability to exercise agency to claim their rights.

## *The Baan Mankong Program*

The Baan Mankong Program was set up specifically to support upgrading processes designed and managed by existing low-income communities and networks. They work with local governments, professionals, universities, and NGOs in their city to survey poor communities, then plan an upgrading program to resolve the land and housing problems covering all urban poor communities in that city in three to four years. Once these upgrading plans have been finalized, CODI channels the infrastructure subsidies and housing loans directly to the communities, who do all the work themselves.

Baan Mankong builds on the community-managed programs that CODI and UCDO have been supporting since 1992, all of which operate on the basis of a strong faith in people's capacity to manage their own needs collectively. The upgrading program stipulates no formula for how communities are upgraded, what physical form the housing or infrastructure solutions take, or whether they should be on the same or on alternative sites. All possible, sensible options can be developed after agreement among the community, the landowner, and other development organizations. In those cases where relocation is unavoidable, the communities must agree to the alternative sites, with support from local development agencies; such sites should be as close as possible to the original sites to minimize the economic and social costs of relocation. Power over all these decisions resides with the community, which owns each upgrading project as a collective. Communities also take responsibility as a group for collectively managing loan repayments for housing construction or land purchase.

The Baan Mankong Program has set a target of improving the housing, living conditions, and tenure security of 300,000 poor households in 2,000 poor communities in 200 Thai cities within five years. This accounts for more than half the urban poor communities in Thailand. The program imposes as few conditions as possible in order to give urban poor communities, networks, and stakeholders within each city as much freedom as possible to design their own program. The challenge is to support upgrading in ways that allow urban poor communities to lead the process and to generate local partnerships along the way, so that the whole city contributes to the solution. A key to this elasticity is the ability to use flexible financial management, which in turn allows communities and their local partners as much scope as possible to make decisions locally. This contrasts starkly with the more conventional, vertical, system-led, contractor or supply-driven approaches.

*Methodology*

The first step in establishing the Baan Mankong Program is to identify the relevant stakeholders and explain it. It is imperative to find the correct audience and ensure that the specificities of the finance initiative are conveyed in a comprehensible manner. The second step is to organize community meetings so that stakeholders can start to take ownership of the program. Ultimately, these meetings establish a joint committee to oversee the implementation of the project. This committee includes urban poor community and network leaders, as well as municipal officials, local academics, and NGOs. It helps to build new relationships of cooperation, to integrate urban poor housing into each city's overall development, and to create a joint mechanism to plan and implement housing development. With leadership established, the joint committee convenes a city meeting to communicate with representatives from all urban poor communities and to inform them about the upgrading program and preparation process.

This process starts by gathering information. The committee organizes a survey to collect information on all households, housing security, land ownership, infrastructure problems, community organizations, savings activities, and existing development initiatives. The survey process also provides opportunities for people to meet, learn about each others' problems, and network. The information collected is used to create an improvement plan covering all the informal settlements in the city. Meanwhile, collective community savings and loan groups are established to mobilize resources within the community and to strengthen community groups by building their collective management skills.

With the preparation work complete, pilot projects are selected on the basis of need, a community's willingness to act as a guinea pig, or the learning possibilities a certain community could provide, both for the community itself and for the rest of the city. Once pilot communities have been selected, development plans are drafted for initiation. These projects are often used as "learning centers" for other communities and actors throughout the process.

Once the pilot projects have been completed, and the extent of their success or failure determined, the model can be extended to other communities. Care must be taken to include those squatters and urban poor who are living outside established communities, for example, the home-less or itinerant workers. Gradually, the projects are integrated into a city-wide housing development process. This transition involves coordinating with public and private landowners to provide secure tenure or alterna-tive land for resettlement, integrating community-built infrastructure into larger municipal service grids, and incorporating upgrading into other city development processes. Community networks are built around common land ownership, shared construction, cooperative enterprises, community welfare, or collective maintenance of canals and other natural amenities. It is vital to create economic space and opportunities for the poor through-out the process and to share lessons learned among communities, through exchange visits of community representatives and government staff.

The per-household infrastructure subsidy in the Baan Mankong Pro-gram has a ceiling of B 25,000 (US$625) per family for communities upgrading or reconstructing in situ, and B 65,000 (US$1,625) per family for communities relocating to new land. These per-family infrastructure subsidies are multiplied by the number of households in a community to determine the maximum subsidy available for upgrading the community's infrastructure. These simple subsidy calculations allow community mem-bers collectively to start discussing, planning, and budgeting all the aspects of their comprehensive upgrading projects. Through CODI, the Baan Mankong Program also provides loans on affordable terms to those who need them for purchasing land or building houses. The program also offers each community a grant equal to 5 percent of the total infrastructure sub-sidy to help fund local management costs and support the organizational process and networking.

## How Baan Mankong Differs from Conventional Upgrading

In contrast to conventional approaches, this poverty alleviation program makes urban poor communities and networks the key actors. They con-trol the funding, manage the projects, and implement the improvements.

They also undertake most of the building themselves rather than using contractors, which means most of the funds remain within the community and work as seed capital for the considerable additional investments people make in their own housing and community.

The program is demand-driven by communities rather than supply-driven by government agencies or contractors, since it supports only communities ready to implement their own improvement projects and allows a great variety of responses, each tailored to a community's needs, priorities, and possibilities. Communities decide such issues as how to use their infrastructure subsidy, which land to buy or lease, and what type of housing they like and can afford. The program does not specify any standard physical outputs and provides flexible finance allowing communities and their local partners to plan, implement, and manage the upgrading according to their own needs and priorities. However, an architect is provided to assist the community with housing planning.

The program also distinguishes itself from other interventions by promoting more than simple physical infrastructure upgrades. As communities design and manage their own physical improvements, the process stimulates deeper but less tangible changes in the community's social structures. These changes lead to the development of such social amenities as community development funds, community welfare systems, and subsidized housing. This collective work also strengthens a community's managerial systems, boosts the confidence of its members, and changes their relationships with local government and other development actors in the city.

Integrating people's own upgrading plans for their communities within the city's planning and development strategies helps to trigger acceptance of poor communities as legitimate parts of the city and as valuable partners in the city's larger development process. Secure land tenure terms are negotiated for most communities individually, using a variety of tenure options, such as cooperative land purchase, long-term lease contracts, land swapping, land sharing, or long-term user rights. Most of the tenure negotiations take place locally, with minimal legal procedures and minimal involvement of national bodies. The emphasis, in all cases, is on collective, rather than individual, land tenure.

## Learning from the Pilot Projects

To explore a variety of possible approaches to upgrading, 10 pilot projects were implemented in 2003. Six of these are described next.

## Charoenchai Nimitmai

The first pilot was a program of land purchase and reblocking. The community of Charoenchai Nimitmai consists of 81 households living on a 0.7 hectare site in Bangkok, bound on three sides by railway tracks, an expressway, and a drainage canal. The people had been renting their land from a private landowner for many years. In 1998, under threat of eviction, they negotiated to purchase the land for about a quarter of its market value. After establishing a cooperative, they took a CODI loan to purchase it. To bring down per-family costs, they developed a reblocking plan that accommodated some other families squatting on land nearby. All but 15 houses had to be moved to new locations within the site to make way for new roads. Many families built their homes using materials from their previous houses and have since been upgrading them incrementally. Agreements negotiated by the community with different municipal departments yielded individual electricity and water connections and building permits. A contractor was hired for the infrastructure requiring heavy machinery; the rest of the construction work was handled by the people themselves using paid community labor, reducing development costs by 30 percent. The average cost per household came to US$6,683, including US$500 for infrastructure; US$1,126 for housing; and the remainder for the cost of land. Each household makes land and housing repayments of between US$27 and US$50 a month.

## Bon Kai

The second pilot program was set up in response to damage wreaked by fire. Bon Kai is a long-established squatter community of 566 households on Crown Property Bureau land in central Bangkok. After a fire destroyed 200 houses in 2001, the community used the crisis as an incentive to form a cooperative and to negotiate a renewable 30-year land lease. Bon Kai was the first case in Thailand of a long-term lease contract on public land being made to a community cooperative. (Land leases are usually made out to only single households and are short term, so they do not provide secure tenure.) The reconstruction was planned in three phases so that no one would have to leave the site. To arrange this, three-story row houses are being built in a tight layout with plots of only 24 square meters. The average unit cost (for land, housing, and infrastructure) is US$4,901 and households repay US$22 to US$30 each month. The first phase of the project has been completed and was inaugurated by the prime minister in July 2004.

### Klong Toey Block 7–12

The third pilot involved the full relocation of an entire community. Klong Toey Block 7–12 was another long-established squatter settlement of port workers, daily laborers, and small traders on land belonging to the Port Authority of Thailand. Over the years, the community experienced fires, chemical explosions, and many attempts at eviction. The original 400 families had dwindled to 49, as some took compensation and moved away and others opted to move to NHA flats or to sites in remote resettlement colonies. After 20 years of struggle, the remaining 49 families negotiated a deal allowing them to develop their own new settlement on Port Authority land one kilometer away with a 30-year lease. The new land could accommodate 114 households, so the project includes homes for some renters and some who had already been evicted from the original settlement.

### Ramkhamhaeng

The fourth pilot consisted of several communities joining together to upgrade their dwellings on a large scale. In Bangkok's Ramkhamhaeng area, two early pilot upgrading projects sparked off a larger development process. The first was a squatter settlement of 124 families, occupying 0.8 hectares of Crown Property Bureau (CPB) land. After forming a cooperative, this community negotiated a 30-year lease and worked with architects to develop a new layout plan with two-story row houses. The second project involved 34 families living on a marshy 0.8 hectare site, also under CPB ownership. Initially, they planned to rebuild their houses on the same site but found the costs of filling the land to be too high. Seven other communities in the same locality decided to join these two schemes and, working closely with the CPB, the nine communities are now preparing a master redevelopment plan to provide secure land and housing for more than 1,000 households on 40 hectares of land in several CPB parcels of land in the area. This master plan will create residential areas linked to markets and parks and will involve reblocking in some areas and nearby relocation in others. Everyone will remain in the general area, with long-term leases obtained through community cooperatives.

### Klong Lumnoon

In the fifth pilot, the canal-side community of Klong Lumnoon experimented with land sharing. Klong Lumnoon was formed 20 years ago on what was once an isolated site. By 1997, the area was becoming gentrified, and the landowner decided to evict the people to develop the land commercially. Some households accepted cash compensation and moved away, but 49 families who worked nearby refused to go. After a long and acrimonious struggle, they convinced the landowner to sell them a small portion of the land they had occupied, at below market rates, in exchange for vacating the rest of the land. After registering as a cooperative, the community took a loan from CODI to buy the land, and worked with young architects to develop a tight plan for 49 row houses and space for a community center. The average unit cost at Klong Lumnoon (for housing, infrastructure, and land) is US$7,740 per household.

*Boon Kook*

The sixth pilot consolidated scattered squatters into a single new community on long-term leases. Boon Kook is a new settlement in the northern city of Uttaradit, where 124 households were relocated from a number of small, scattered squatter settlements. To resettle these households (identified by the community network in their citywide survey), the municipality agreed to purchase a 1.6 hectare site and lease it to the cooperative formed by the new residents on a 30-year lease with a nominal annual rent. The community network helped to start daily savings schemes among the inhabitants, while CODI provided housing loans and the NHA provided the infrastructure. The six model houses designed for the project cost between US$750 and US$3,750, with repayments of US$5 to US$23 per month. The plans for the Boon Kook community also include five collective housing units for the elderly, poor, and physically disabled members of the community.

## Supporting Decentralized Action within Cities

Municipal and local authorities in Thailand are still undergoing a transformation, as national decentralization policies take effect with uneven progress. Local government institutions still need considerable understanding and capacity to open up their systems of governance in ways that allow citizens to feel that this is their city and that they are part of its development. In fact, responsibility for many different aspects of urban management can easily be decentralized to communities. These communities can manage many municipal amenities, such as public parks and markets, maintenance of drainage canals, solid waste collection and recycling, and community welfare programs. Opening up more room for people to become involved in such local tasks is the new frontier for urban management.

Community upgrading is proving a powerful way of sparking off this kind of decentralization and an even more powerful one for enabling a city's poorer citizens to play an active part in its development activities.

## Common Techniques to Scale Up the Baan Mankong Upgrading Process

Pilot projects such as those described above are organized in as many cities as possible, to provide visible examples from which all peer groups can learn, generate excitement, and demonstrate that community-driven upgrading can work. These pilots serve as prototypes for upgrading and are much visited by other community organizations and city government officials.[3]

Twelve cities with strong upgrading processes at the initial stage have been designated as learning centers for other towns and cities in their regions. These communities also hold outreach events. When an upgrading process is launched or a project inaugurated, policy makers, government officials, the general public, and people from neighboring cities are invited to observe. These events can turn an individual city's milestone into a mass learning opportunity. To augment these events, exchanges are held among communities, pilot projects, cities and regions, involving community representatives, officials, NGOs, and academics. CODI subcontracts most of the support and coordination work to partners in cities who are ready to work with communities, including NGOs, architects, university professors, and municipal officers.

Citywide upgrading processes are under way in more than 200 cities. The following offers a summary of the experiences some cities have had tackling their upgrading program.

### Uttaradit

In the city of Uttaradit the upgrading process started with a survey that mapped all the slums and small pockets of squatters, identified all the landowners, and established which slums could remain and which needed to relocate. This process linked communities together and initiated the building of a community network, with support from two young architects, a group of monks, and a very active mayor. Looking at the city as a whole, they began by seeking housing solutions for the 1,000 families with the most serious housing problems. They used a range of techniques, including land sharing in one area and reblocking in another, as well as in situ upgrading and relocation. Solutions included the Boon Kook pilot project described above for people who had previously lived in small squatter settlements scattered around the city.

## Bangkok

Some 1,200 informal settlements in Bangkok provide housing for almost a third of Thailand's urban poor. To divide this sprawling megacity into smaller, more manageable parts for the Baan Mankong process, each of Bangkok's 50 districts have organized a process to select and propose at least two pilot projects in the first year. Each district does its own survey, forms its own joint committee with all key actors, and develops its own three-year districtwide upgrading program.

## Ayutthaya

In the historic capital city of Ayutthaya, a world heritage site, the community network surveyed and mapped all the informal settlements. These total 53 and comprised 6,611 households, mostly situated within the historic areas of the city. The community network then organized a seminar with the city authorities to present the survey information. This showed that it would be possible to improve conditions within the settlements, bring in basic services, construct proper houses, and shift the settlements slightly to allow rehabilitation of monuments.

## Achievements to Date

The tables that follow describe the progress of the Baan Mankong upgrading program in the period January 2003 to September 2005. Initiatives are under way in 415 communities in 140 cities, with projects approved involving almost 30,000 households. The total budget approved is US$25.7 million for infrastructure upgrading grants and US$14.4 million for housing and land purchase loans.

Table 8.1 shows the different kinds of projects supported, with more than three-quarters involving upgrading in situ and most relocation, where necessary, is nearby.

Table 8.2 shows the kinds of land tenure achieved by the project. Overall, long-term land tenure security was provided to 10,794 families (83 percent of the total).

About 60 percent of the families who had faced serious problems of eviction and tenure insecurity were made the top priority by joint city

**Table 8.1. Types of Upgrading Project Supported by Baan Mankong (as of September 25, 2005)**

|  | Number of projects | Number of families | Percentage |
|---|---|---|---|
| On the same site (includes in situ upgrading, in situ reblocking or reconstruction, and land sharing) | 269 | 22,151 | 76 |
| Nearby relocation (within 2 km) | 40 | 2,109 | 7 |
| Relocation (farther away than 2 km) | 105 | 4,784 | 16.5 |
| Shelter house for homeless | 1 | 100 | 0.5 |
| Total | 415 | 29,054 | 100 |

**Table 8.2. Kinds of Land Tenure Achieved by the Project**

|  | Number of projects | Number of families | Percentage |
|---|---|---|---|
| Cooperative land ownership | 158 | 9,849 | 34 |
| Long-term lease to community cooperative | 171 | 14,897 | 51 |
| Short-term lease to community cooperative (less than 5 years) | 32 | 2,282 | 8 |
| Permission to use land | 54 | 2,062 | 7 |
| Total | 415 | 29,054 | 100 |

groups taking part in pilot projects. This demonstrates that a citywide process can detect and deal effectively with eviction problems, in collaboration with all the key local actors.

## What Has Been Learned?

Slums are not aberrations, but a normal part of cities. The citywide scale of the upgrading process helps city authorities and other urban actors to regard slums with greater understanding and less fear. They begin to see them as a vital part of the city's economic and social life, with hope for improvement.

Poor communities contain a mix of better-off and poorer people; layabouts and achievers; those who are disabled, unemployed, or elderly; orphans, drug addicts, and people in crisis. In the market system, only those who can afford to pay can access society's benefits. But in a collective, community process, the challenge is to find ways to deal with these unequal conditions, so that everyone's needs are addressed. This is a crucial part of the upgrading process.

Once people start managing finances and planning upgrading collectively, and once they secure land under a communal lease or cooperative ownership, a lot of communal energy can be unleashed, especially in the social sphere. When people are linked together in this way, through this cooperation, they start to develop new ideas on resolving other social and welfare needs, and to put these into practice. The solutions may be different in each community and region, but the same culture of collective synthesis and mutual assistance underlies them all. This strength has always existed of necessity in poor communities, but the upgrading process is consciously helping to revive it.

For example, in several of the Baan Mankong projects, communities have set aside plots within the collectively purchased or leased land to construct special shelters for needy community members. These "central houses" [*baan klang* in Thai] provide shelter for destitute widows, AIDS orphans, handicapped or elderly people, or unemployed community members. These houses are part of an extremely localized welfare system and represent one way that communities are trying to benefit everyone through the upgrading process.

Savings groups are often discussed as a means to get poor communities organized and involved, working, and thinking together. However, in the upgrading process, the most important aspect of savings and credit activities is that they teach communities to manage finance collectively, in terms of both internal assets and outside finance. This helps ensure that the people themselves become key actors in development. This is in contrast to the way in which most development works, whereby someone else holds the purse, and people, for lack of financial management skills, are left holding their hand out.

### How the Program Changes the Quality of People's Assets

Secure land, more permanent quality of housing and basic services are changing the quality of assets people acquire through the upgrading process. Program participants can negotiate lease contracts with state or private landowners and apply for CODI loans for their new land and housing, often using their land as collateral. This enables Thailand's poorest urban citizens to accumulate assets worth between US$2,500 and US$12,500, combining the value of land, house, and infrastructure improvements. Secure land tenure is an essential precondition, which allows this development and opens the door to additional energy, development resources, and investment in these communities, thereby compounding this increase in the real value of people's assets. When land is owned or leased collectively and becomes a communal asset, it is also a way of mitigating the trend of market forces pushing the poor out of upgraded areas.

Financial assets, in turn, build social capital. Upgrading activities strengthen the capacity of individual people and whole communities to improve their livelihoods. They provide a financial basis for communities to develop welfare activities and support their more vulnerable members. As needed, people start savings groups in their settlements as a means of getting people used to pooling their resources and managing both their internal savings and external funds collectively. These collectively saved funds are like a community bank and represent "countable" financial assets belonging to all the people in the community. When they begin upgrading activities, and as they have to repay their land and housing loans in the longer term, the finances have to be managed responsibly, both by individual households and collectively. Because loans are made only to communities, their members are collectively responsible for repayment and for deciding what to do when someone cannot pay. All this builds a group's social cohesion.

When communities go through the process of managing a large and complex housing and infrastructure construction project, people invariably acquire skills and develop greater confidence to take on more complex jobs. The reconstruction of a community calls for all kinds of inputs and different skills. When a community organizes all these skills to upgrade its housing, people complement each other and build something of their own. This is generally a greater contribution than in their previous employment. When people are given space to manage their own upgrading project, it broadens skills, generates confidence, and becomes a very big skill-development exercise. This, in turn, generates human capital. Many people in upgraded communities, who had previously worked as low-paid construction laborers, have subsequently obtained higher-paid skilled jobs or even become small construction contractors themselves. The communal fund can provide community members with financial support for their investments, as well as enhancing income activities.

In many of the upgrading projects, especially those where people have found inexpensive alternative land to buy that is not directly accessed by roads ("blind land" in Thailand), networks have negotiated with local politicians to get roads, sewers, and water lines extended into the new settlement. When the trunk infrastructure extends to such "blind land," it dramatically increases the asset value of that land and of the neighboring plots as well. Poor communities thus become pioneers in bringing development, investment, and human liveliness into neglected areas of the city. Upgrading becomes a way to transform a city's nonasset areas into lively, thriving, developable asset areas. In this transformation, community members are their own agents.

As soon as communities are able to work together as networks with other city development agencies and local authorities, they can negotiate for their rights as well. They can pursue development with stronger financial capacity and more political bargaining power. Enhanced negotiating power will help balance their participation in city development activities, promoting a more equitable process of development overall.

Community organizations in Thailand have succeeded not only in meeting their explicit target of improving the physical infrastructure of local slum settlements, but also in promoting the accumulation of political, social, human and financial capital. The different types of assets build upon and reinforce one another. Property rights bring with them a sense of legitimacy; infrastructure improvements create much-needed capital; and participation by the poor in organizations such as Baan Mankong gives them a sense of self-agency. Combined, these factors build another, perhaps more important asset: social capital. The accumulation of these varied assets allows Thailand's poor to take command of their own futures, at first through the organization, but ultimately through self-reliance.

Thailand's success story provides a model that can and should be scaled up and replicated elsewhere. As David Satterthwaite points out in chapter 7, community-run organizations such as Baan Mankong are emerging throughout the developing world, but not all are necessarily equally successful. By piloting projects and using strategies that have proven successful in Baan Mankong, such as reblocking, government outreach, and land sharing, similar organizations in other countries can facilitate successful asset accumulation and increase prosperity for the urban poor.

## Notes

1. The Millennium Development Goals recognize the need for action in "slums." They demand "significant improvements in the lives of at least 100 million slum dwellers by 2020"—although has subsequently been recognized that

this is a very inadequate target: Reaching 100 million slum dwellers by 2020 implies reaching only a small percentage of those living in "slums."

2. For a more detailed description of Baan Mankong, see CODI 2004.

3. These are also techniques widely used by other organizations and federations of the urban poor. See examples in the special issue of *Environment and Urbanization* on Civil Society in Action—Transforming Opportunities For The Urban Poor 13(2), 2001; also see Sheela Patel (2004).

## References

Angel, Shlomo, and Somsook Boonyabancha. 1988. "Land Sharing as an Alternative to Eviction: the Bangkok Experience." *Third World Planning Review* 10 (2): 107–27.

Boonyabancha, Somsook. 1999. "The Urban Community Environmental Activities Project, Thailand." *Environment and Urbanization* 11 (1): 101–15.

Boonyabancha, Somsook. 2001. "Savings and Loans: Drawing Lessons from Some Experiences in Asia." *Environment and Urbanization* 13 (2): 9–21.

Boonyabancha, Somsook. 2003. "A Decade of Change: From the Urban Community Development Office (UCDO) to the Community Organizations Development Institute (CODI) in Thailand." Poverty Reduction in Urban Areas Working Paper 12, IIED, London. Accessible free of charge at http://www.iied.org/urban/index.html.

Boonyabancha, Somsook. 2005. "Baan Mankong: going to scale with "slum" and squatter upgrading in Thailand." *Environment and Urbanization* 17 (1): 21–46.

CODI. 2004. *CODI Update* 4, June. Accessible from Asian Coalition of Housing Rights (ACHR), Bangkok, e-mail: achr@loxinfo.co.th.

*Environment and Urbanization.* 2001. Special issue on "Civil Society in Action–Transforming Opportunities for The Urban Poor" 13 (2): 9–143.

Patel, Sheela. 2004. "Tools and Methods for Empowerment Developed by Slum Dwellers' Federations in India." *Participatory Learning and Action* 50, IIED, London.

# PART IV

# THE EROSION OF LIVELIHOODS AND
# ASSETS IN WEAK STATES

# CHAPTER 9

# Bitter Harvest: The Social Costs of State Failure in Rural Kenya

*Paul Francis and Mary Amuyunzu-Nyamongo*

After two decades of stagnation and economic decline, the Kenyan economy has shown consistent growth in the last few years, with growth rates rising to 5.7 percent in 2005 and 6.1 percent in 2006. This economic turnaround is reflected in significant reductions in rates of income poverty, especially in urban areas, with rates falling from 52 percent in 1997 to 46 percent in 2005–06 (Gok 2007b, 2007a). Nevertheless, the economic reverses of the 1980s and 1990s have had severe social consequences which persist, and may be more challenging to reverse than the economic.

In its early years of independence, Kenya was the most prosperous country in East Africa, with a per capita gross domestic product (GDP) rising by 38 percent between 1960 and 1980. The two decades that followed to 2000, however, recorded a zero increase in per capita GDP, and at US$360, per capita income in 2003 was lower than in 1990. Poverty rose during the 1990s from 48.8 percent in 1990 to 55.4 percent in 2001 (World Bank 2003). Kenya's social indicators declined in tandem with the economy: infant mortality rose from 63 (per 1,000 births) in 1990 to 78.5 in 2004. Life expectancy fell from 57 to 48 years during the same period, in part due to the HIV/AIDS epidemic. Persistent food shortages are evidenced in the 19 percent of children under age five who are underweight, and almost one in three (31 percent) who are stunted (CBS 2004). These are averages, but much disparity exists in Kenyan society, with exclusion and disadvantage reflecting stratification by class, gender, and region. Kenya's Gini coefficient (for adult expenditure per household equivalent) is 0.38 for rural areas, and 0.42 for urban (GoK 2007a). Recent trends indicate a slight decrease in inequality in rural areas, and increasing inequality in urban. In terms of deciles, the richest 10 percent of rural households control 35.9 percent of expenditure, while the poorest 10 percent control only 1.6 percent (GoK 2007a).

This chapter explores the causes and effects of the economic decline of the 1980s and 1990s and the growing inequality in Kenya, focusing particularly on the recent escalation of violence in rural areas. This violence takes several forms: social (domestic violence), institutional (violence in schools), economic (property crime), and political (thuggery and ethnic clashes).[1] Moser (1996) has argued that communities' ability to cope with economic crisis depends not only on their material well-being but also on their social capital—the trust, networks, and reciprocal arrangements that link people with their communities. Such social capital might be strengthened by economic crisis to a point, but beyond that threshold, networks become overwhelmed and social systems collapse with disastrous consequences. Physical insecurity exacerbates the breakdown of social capital caused by economic crisis, rendering the provision of positive opportunities for asset accumulation impossible (Amuyunzu-Nyamongo and Ezeh 2005; Rakodi 2002). While increases in violence and crime under conditions of economic decline have been documented in urban environments, especially in Latin America (Moser and McIlaine 2005; Buvinic, Morrison, and Shifter, 1999), this chapter illustrates how similar problems have emerged in rural Kenya.[2]

The chapter is based on research undertaken between February and May 2005 in six Kenyan districts, representing six of its seven provinces: Isiolo district (Eastern), Nakuru (Rift Valley), Bungoma (Western), Kisii (Nyanza), Kiambu (Central), and Kwale (Coast). A range of participatory tools were used to gather qualitative data, including in-depth interviews with key informants, focus group discussions, social and institutional mapping, and participant observation. These tools were complemented by quantitative data collected by use of an interviewer-administered questionnaire (710 people) at the household level.

## Factors Eroding Rural Assets and Livelihoods

Two key factors have been responsible for the erosion of livelihoods and assets in rural Kenya: the widespread decline or collapse of institutions and services, and the pressure on natural resources, particularly on access to land.

## Institutional Degradation and Collapse

Kenya has consistently ranked poorly on Transparency International's annual index of perceptions of corruption. A Corruption Perceptions Index (CPI) score of two or less out of a maximum of 10 indicates severe, endemic, or pervasive corruption; and Kenya's rating has hovered around this level since the surveys began in 1996 (Transparency International 1996–2007).

The six government departments out of 34 ranked by the Kenyan public as the most corrupt in the Transparency International surveys, in order, were police, the teachers service commission, local authorities, the judiciary, the ministry of lands, and provincial administration (Transparency International 2002, 2004, 2005, 2006, 2007).

Given Kenya's widespread reliance on the production of agricultural commodities, the unreliability and inefficiency of its agricultural marketing organizations have severely damaged the livelihoods of rural households. In the case of coffee, for example, marketing transaction costs have risen sharply through the mismanagement, politicization, and fragmentation of coffee cooperatives to which farmers are obliged to sell. Kenyan smallholders now receive less than one-half of the auction price of coffee (Karanja and Nyoro 2002). More disturbingly, many pyrethrum growers were stranded by the virtual collapse of marketing activities by the Kenya Pyrethrum Board in 2002, leaving farmers unpaid for several years of production.

Poor rural services, in part, are the result of the structure and functioning of Kenya's local government system, a fragmented organizational structure with limited powers and resources. As a consequence, local government is too weak to manage and coordinate investments and services effectively. While the arrival of the National Rainbow Coalition (NARC) government in late 2002 led to more resources available at constituency level, these resources are not systematically allocated to specific services; in some cases, they can be diverted for use as political patronage.

## Access to Land

Land, from which 90 percent of rural residents (who account for 80 percent of Kenyans) directly derive their livelihoods, is a key asset for rural households (KLA, undated; GoK 2002). However, a combination of demographic pressure, unequal distribution, and a problematic and corrupted tenure system make access to land increasingly scarce and inequitable. While it differs greatly among areas, the ratio of land under crop cultivation to agricultural population in Kenya (a rough proxy for per capita farm size) halved between the 1960s and the 1990s from 0.46 to 0.23 hectares per person. The distribution of available land is extremely inequitable. The Gini coefficient of land per capita in 1997 in agricultural districts was 0.56, with the lowest two quartiles owning 0.08 and 0.17 hectares of land, respectively, indicating a high level of functional landlessness.[3] In many areas, land degradation and erosion exacerbate the problem of access. Women's access to land, already severely limited, is further jeopardized because they may lose all rights to land and property following the death of their husbands (KLA undated).

Land in Kenya has always been a highly politicized resource. From the 1980s, however, fraudulent allocations of public land, including forest reserve, became a central element in the system of political spoils in all parts of the country. The courts are clogged with land disputes, many of which result in violent clashes between rival claimants (Cross 2002). Land ownership is one of the main sources of tension within households. As an assistant chief of police in Bungoma observed:

> Land is becoming scarce, yet there are too many people who depend on it as the main source of income. Many families have fought because of land. Last night, a woman and her children killed a man over land. He had two wives and he was in the process of applying for an Agricultural Finance Cooperative loan. Fearing that she would lose the land, the woman arranged for his murder. Most fights originate from land.

## Livelihood Shifts and Gender Relations

In recent decades, livelihood diversification has been a widely recognized phenomenon in Africa as households have sought to sustain themselves by means of a wider array of economic activities (Ellis 2000). This growth in importance of generating nonfarm income has been described as "de-agrarianisation" (Bryceson 1996). While these processes can be a positive response to new opportunities, they may also reflect a forced shift into more marginal activities as assets become eroded and former livelihood systems become unviable.

Some forms of diversification recorded in our study included shifts to new farm enterprises, off-farm sources of income, and nonfarm activities. The unreliability of marketing arrangements for export crops has led many households to shift to the cultivation of food crops for sale, in spite of the problems of marketing bulky and perishable produce given the poor state of physical infrastructure. Other activities adopted included tree farming or stall-fed cattle. Off-farm, rural households are increasingly turning to

petty trading (for example, of foodstuffs and secondhand clothes), itinerant hawking, *boda boda* (bicycle taxis), brickmaking, bricklaying, and
water selling to generate income. Beer brewing has also become an
important source of income for rural women.

Casual labor, either on the farms of better-off neighbors or in nearby
urban settlements, may be the only source of income for those without
land or capital, although earnings are low, especially for women (typically
K Sh 50–60 (US$0.67–0.80) per day). Out-migration to both rural and urban
areas is another option. Often these movements follow long-established
patterns, drawing on networks of information and contacts established by
earlier waves of migration. The unqualified go into domestic service or join
the urban casual labor force, while those with some education hold out for
better opportunities. While migration brings opportunities and sometimes
remittances, it can have negative impacts on rural households for those left
at home. It reduces the labor available for agriculture and adds to the vulnerability of households headed by women and elderly persons, especially
in light of the collapse of traditional collective and reciprocal labor arrangements in most areas—a situation exacerbated by the impact of HIV/AIDS).

In many communities, collective responses to livelihood erosion were
apparent in the course of the survey. Community-based organizations,
which have a long history in Kenya, include women's groups, welfare
associations, youth groups, communal self-help groups and savings and
credit associations (Wanyama 2003). These groups have come together to
provide support for their members, promoting income generation. Even
relatively poor communities have banded together to supplement the failing services of the state by providing school and dispensary buildings and
produce buying centers, or by recruiting and paying teachers where government staffing is inadequate.

The shifts in livelihood systems imposed on rural Kenyan households
have not been gender neutral. The collapse of established sources of income from cash crops such as coffee, pyrethrum and sugar; the decline of
pastoralism for political, security, and ecological reasons; and the fall in
labor migration have affected men and women differently and resulted in
profound shifts in gender relations. Broadly speaking, the livelihood systems that have been most severely eroded have tended to be dominated
by men. Traditionally, even though production systems were underpinned
by women's productive and domestic labor—as in cash crop production—
male dominance was secured through patriarchal land tenure systems and
customary norms controlling the disposal of cash income. Pastoralism was

also largely a male preserve. Similarly, men have been the main agents in labor migration.

Concurrent with the "demasculation" of the rural economy, new opportunities—such as food crop production, petty trade, informal services, beer brewing, casual labor, domestic service, and the gathering of firewood and other nontimber forest products—have extended traditional female roles.[3] These factors have contributed to the very different ways in which men and women have responded to change. Men, with unreliable markets for traditional produce, crumbling niches for migratory employment, and declining herds for pastoralists, have found themselves unable to live up to established norms of manhood. Their characteristic response has been one of withdrawal. Women, finding themselves responsible for filling a growing gap in household provisioning, have been obliged to support themselves and their children by multiple means: a combination of intensification, diversification, and cooperation. As a result, women have found themselves not only the domestic but the economic core of households, while men have moved to the periphery. This is also reflected in patterns of residence; more than one in three rural Kenyan households is now headed by women (CBS 2004).

Findings from Isiolo district illustrate some of these points. In Manyatta Demo, where the pastoral economy has never recovered from the brutal government counterinsurgency activities of the 1960s and raiding by groups from the east in the 1980s and 1990s, men have relatively few economic activities. Most have no capital or stock, and are obliged to produce and sell charcoal, an activity that is precarious, low return, and illegal. Women, on the other hand, have a much wider set of pursuits: collecting and selling firewood, selling *miraa* (*khat*), milk, eggs, and honey; gathering wild fruits, herbal medicines, and incense; weaving baskets and mats; and making bread. While most of these activities are small scale and low return, they, nevertheless, amount to a portfolio on which their households can survive. Similarly, in Nakuru, pyrethrum production for export has been replaced by the cultivation of food crops for the domestic market, which women are mainly responsible for cultivating. As one woman said: "The children have to eat and attend school."

Alongside the rising demands on women by changing livelihood systems, domestic care has also increased. The burden of caring for the sick (multiplied by HIV/AIDS) falls largely on women and girls, as well as the responsibilities of childcare, cooking, and the collection of water and firewood. The community responsibilities of women have also increased: women's groups are more ubiquitous, active, and effective than men's.

Hence, while livelihood erosion has undermined the social value, identity, and self-esteem of men, for women the ubiquitous triple burden of economic, domestic, and community responsibilities has intensified in all three spheres. However, men's "disempowerment" (Silbershmidt 2005) is not translated into the empowerment of women, since the recognition of the feminization of the rural economy is obscured and muted by patriarchal ideology. Although women are increasingly the generators of household income, men still control immovable and movable property and seek to retain decision-making power over disposal and expenditure. As one Bungoma man explained: "If she [my wife] buys sugar, I have bought it. If she buys a cow, it is mine because she lives in my house and tills my land free of charge." The increasing divergence between patriarchal ideology and the material reality of household provisioning leads to tensions that more and more often overflow into violence.

## Gender Violence

Half of all Kenyan women have experienced violence since they were 15 years of age; one in four in the 12 months prior to being interviewed (3 in 10 married women) experienced violence. Substantial variations exist in these figures regionally, with domestic violence most endemic in the west. Some 73 percent of women had experienced violence in Western province and 60 percent in Nyanza province, compared with the lowest figure of 30 percent in Coast province. Husbands (58 percent) were the main perpetrators of this violence, followed by teachers (26 percent), mothers (24 percent), fathers (15 percent), and brothers (8 percent) (CBS 2004).

Regional variations in domestic violence appear to relate both to cultural norms and to increasing pressure on land and livelihoods. In Bungoma and Kisii, the "disciplining" of wives was described as if it were an elemental component of local culture. A typical view expressed by a Bungoma man was that "a woman must be beaten by the man to instill respect and a sense of discipline."

Such expressions of timeless patriarchy aside, our interviews indicated that, far from being a hangover from a primitive past, domestic violence is in fact increasing in both incidence and severity.[4] Women emphasized the link between domestic violence and the recent rise in alcohol abuse. In many parts of Kenya, traditional norms, while permitting a man to beat his wife, also circumscribed the scope of violence: if he acted without pretext, drew blood, or broke a limb, he would have to answer to, and compensate, his in-laws. However, these limited protections for women have largely broken down due to the fragmentation of extended family ties.

Growing violence against women is also manifested in the escalating incidence of rape in Kenya. Rape often accompanies other crimes; rural women, frequently obliged to fetch water or forest products during the night, are especially vulnerable to sexual assault. Rape is not reported for many reasons, not least because of the limited seriousness with which it is taken by the police, and so official statistics are of little use in establishing trends. However, police statistics show that 2,800 cases of rape were reported in Kenya in 2004, an increase of 500 compared with the previous year and more than five times higher than in 1990 when only 515 cases were reported. Kenya's Coalition on Violence against Women estimates that only 8 percent of women report rape to health officials or the police.

### Intergenerational Conflict

In many rural Kenyan households, tension between the generations is high. Unemployment among young people is such that they often lack the resources to establish their own households and are obliged to remain in the parental home. Youth wishing to farm are often constrained by the limited land available and its control by the older generation. Unemployment, combined with the expectations created by education, breed hopelessness and frustration. For their part, parents complain that their grown-up children do not pull their weight in contributing to household income. Parental disapproval of children's lifestyles and anxiety over their involvement in risky behaviors, such as substance abuse and crime, is another source of tension. Relationships between male youth and their families are particularly fraught. Media reports of violence between parents and children have become increasingly frequent.

The reasons given for intergenerational violence in the communities surveyed are listed in table 9.1.

Land was the leading cause of tension in the densely populated Kiambu (562 persons per km$^2$) and Bungoma (424 pers/km$^2$) districts, as well as in Nakuru (164 pers/km$^2$) where land shortage was compounded by severe inequity of distribution. In many areas, land is not customarily transferred to children until the death of the father. Thus, sons may hold only provisional rights to land for many years and be reluctant to invest in agriculture. Tradition is only one reason for parent's reluctance to apportion land. In the land-short districts, there were complaints of children selling off family land to offset debts or simply squander. Land was much less of an issue for intergenerational conflict in Kwale (60 pers/km$^2$) and pastoral Isiolo (4 pers/km$^2$). Interestingly, in Kisii, the most densely populated of all rural

**Table 9.1. Reasons for Intergenerational Violence (Percentage of Respondents)**

| Cause | Kiambu (n = 78) | Kwale (n = 10) | Isiolo (n = 50) | Kisii (n = 58) | Nakuru (n = 39) | Bungoma (n = 78) |
|---|---|---|---|---|---|---|
| Access to land | 65 | 9 | 4 | 49 | 33 | 33 |
| Alcohol consumption | 53 | 22 | 35 | 52 | 25 | 28 |
| Arranged marriages | 2 | 3 | 27 | 10 | 3 | 1 |
| Inadequate access to livestock | 1 | 4 | 12 | 8 | 15 | 7 |
| Lack of food | 8 | 17 | 32 | 30 | 25 | 11 |
| Lack of school fees | 23 | 17 | 26 | 56 | 12 | 13 |
| Money/finances | 21 | 17 | 26 | 43 | 14 | 8 |
| Parents fighting | 11 | 5 | 10 | 14 | 8 | 2 |

*Source:* World Bank 2007.

districts (758 pers/ km²), the leading cause of contention between children and parents was school fees. The fragmentation of land is now so acute that agriculture is no longer considered a viable livelihood, and education is seen as the only route out of poverty, even if an increasingly precarious one. In Kwale and parts of Isiolo district, tensions between generations were mostly said to be fueled by alcohol.

Violence against children is also institutionalized in schools. As noted above, the perpetrator of the violence for 26 percent of women had been a teacher. According to Human Rights Watch International:

> For most Kenyan children, violence is a regular part of the school experience. Teachers use caning, slapping and whipping to maintain classroom discipline and to punish children for poor academic performance. The infliction of corporal punishment is routine, arbitrary, and often brutal. Bruises and cuts are regular by-products of school punishments, and more severe injuries (broken bones, knocked-out teeth, internal bleeding) are not infrequent. At times, beating by teachers leave children permanently disfigured, disabled, or dead (1999: 2).

## Crime, Violence, and Insecurity in Rural Areas

As a United Nations report notes, crime

> ... impairs the overall development of nations, undermines spiritual and material well-being, compromises human dignity, and creates a climate of fear and violence, which endangers personal security and erodes the quality of life (1980: 193).

The crime rate in Kenya rose by 51 percent between 1994 and 2000. Between 2003 and 2004 alone (the most recent year for which figures are available), crime reported to the police increased by 8.4 percent (GoK 2005). Assault, break-ins, robbery and allied offences, and other forms of theft accounted for 53 percent of the reported cases (GoK 2005). High levels of violence have long been a feature of Nairobi and, to a lesser extent, other urban areas. However, perhaps the most striking finding of our research was the extent to which crime and violence have permeated rural areas. The trend toward rural criminality is a relatively recent phenomenon, traced by most respondents to the past five years. The new wave of rural crime is also associated with unprecedented levels of brutality; robbery increasingly being accompanied by murder; rape; and the wanton destruction of property. Sometimes such acts of violence are not even accompanied by theft, suggesting that they are driven primarily by frustration, anger, and resentment. In Bungoma district just before our fieldwork, a gang had attacked 10 households, gang-raping women and girls, assaulting men, and destroying property, but stealing nothing. As one informant observed: "It was as if they wanted to humiliate their victims."

With changing patterns of rural crime, the weapons too have evolved. In the past, as we were told in Kiambu, thieves used sticks or stones; now they came with guns, making resistance by victims or neighbors futile or fatal. Decades of instability in surrounding countries and Kenya's pastoralist periphery have made small arms cheap and readily available. Increasingly, thieves act with the arrogance born of impunity:

> ... they come during the day and some even give notice of their intended visit, and there is nothing anyone can do (Bungoma informant).

In Ngecha (Kiambu) a woman commented that

> We are producing clever thieves. Young people are educated to university level but they are jobless. They use their knowledge to steal and are so frustrated that they vent their anger on innocent community members.

Instances of petty theft of food from farms and minor items from houses had increased in all districts as poverty intensified, local enforcement systems and sanctions declined in authority, and the effectiveness of formal policing and justice systems deteriorated. In Nakuru, we were told that food might be stolen while still cooking on the fire, or clothes filched while drying. That these instances were said to be seasonal suggested that they were driven by immediate needs during periods of food shortage. In Kiambu and Bungoma, conversely, petty theft was generally blamed on the needs of young men to feed their alcohol and substance abuse habits.

Stealing from the government (for example, removing forest products from reserves or water pipes from government stock) was not considered locally as culpable as stealing from individuals. Indeed, an outcome of the buckling of livelihood systems has been the recourse to activities that are formally illegal, such as forest exploitation; charcoal burning; commercial sex work; and the brewing, distillation, and sale of alcohol. The illegal nature of these activities expose the poor to extortion by police, local government or forestry officials. However, the lack of alternatives did little to reduce their incidence. In Nakuru, men and women set out at dusk with their bicycles, walking 20 or more kilometers into the forest to collect a shipment of charcoal and transport it under cover of darkness to Nakuru town. If caught by officials, it resulted in a fine, a beating, or both.

Commercial sex work was well established in two of the surveyed communities. In Bulla Pesa, a suburb of Isiolo town in which there is a high military presence, prostitution has become the mainstay of the economy. Clients are said to prefer young girls—children as young as eight years old are involved in the trade, and command the highest prices. This is reflected in the nomenclature: girls between ages 8 and 12 years were known as "*nice,*" teenagers as "*coca cola*" ("sweet but not as good as 'nice'"), and girls 20 and over as "*mitumba*" (secondhand). The inducement of children into commercial sex work at such a young age is a reflection of the extreme desperation of many households, as well as the extent to which community norms have broken down. The ravages of HIV/AIDS could be seen in the number of households consisting only of children and the aged. While aware of the risks of unprotected sex, commercial sex workers nevertheless complained that their clients were often unwilling to use condoms. Desperation was echoed in the words of one young woman: "It is better to live now rather than worry about HIV, which will kill you in 10 years' time."

The exchange of sexual favors for food or money is not limited to commercial sex workers. Many women in Sirisia (Bungoma), Karia (Kiambu), and elsewhere, resorted to extramarital relations to meet their household needs. Such statements may, to a degree, reflect deep-rooted fears about moral breakdown, and in particular the control of female sexuality, but they have a basis in reality. One man in Karia (Kiambu) described his own humiliation: "As a jobless husband, you watch and eat the food knowing well that another man paid for it because you have no alternative."

With crime and violence escalating, security and access to justice are growing concerns in rural Kenya. However, the police are widely regarded as so corrupt and ineffective that they are seen to be contributing to the problem of crime, rather than providing a solution. Allegations that police (and retrenched former police officers) assisted, protected, and armed criminals; hired out their uniforms; received stolen goods; and even undertook crimes themselves were so regular as to be commonplace. Even when criminals were arrested, they were said to be released without charge if they had the means to offer a bribe.

The failure of the government to ensure the security of its citizens has led many rural communities to safeguard their lives and property through the formation of vigilante groups. Such groups patrol communities at night, systematically ostracize suspected criminals and, on occasion, destroy their property. Vigilantes can go further. Lynching has become a widely established phenomenon as communities' frustration at the unwillingness or inability of formal institutions to control rural crime grows. Lynching was considered not only a way to purge the community of persistent troublemakers but also to serve as a disincentive to others. It also reflects growing disenchantment with official ineptitude and collusion with criminals, feelings that outweigh the fundamental injustice of mob action and the inability of alleged criminals to defend themselves.

Community policing, and even the excesses of vigilantism, are generally condoned by the authorities. Nevertheless, the organization of bands of youth to protect the community has created its own problems. It is hard to retain young people, who are a mobile group in search of employment, to serve on a voluntary basis. Sometimes, once created, vigilante groups have turned to crime and extortion themselves or have been manipulated into settling grudges or political scores.

The epidemic of crime and violence in rural areas is having an impact on the social composition of rural communities as the better-off are increasingly unwilling to live in, invest in, or sometimes even visit their home communities, or are driven by repeated gang attacks to the comparative safety of nearby towns where clustered residences facilitate joint security arrangements. In Kisii, middle-class migrants living in Nairobi and other cities often avoid staying overnight when visiting their communities of origin, for fear of being robbed or violated.

Crime is also driving retail and other businesses from rural communities by compounding the costs of doing business though direct losses to criminals; the costs of evasive and protective measures; and the material, psychological, and medical costs of violence. A woman storekeeper in Karai (Kiambu) told us that she had twice been robbed in the past year on her way to the bank. She now varied her patterns and means of transport to avoid another incident, but her profits had been decimated and she was on the verge of abandoning her store.

Growing crime and insecurity are both the results of a decline in the social capital of many communities and causal factors in accelerating that breakdown by reinforcing social differentiation and decreasing levels of trust among neighbors. Traditional or informal institutions can often no longer maintain order; nor do the formal institutions of the state command any confidence.

## Substance Abuse and Psychological Anomie

The erosion of livelihood assets and the advancing culture of violence that has accompanied this erosion have produced substantial psychological effects. Development literature has given little attention to the relationship between social structure and subjective states of mind and feeling; yet there are at least two good reasons for doing so. First, one of the main social costs of violence and crime is a psychological one: fear and the sense of personal insecurity. Second, the motivation for violence increasingly goes beyond the economic to the expressive, with brutality representing the acting out of emotional states of resentment and frustration. With this in mind, three indicators of psychological anomie in Kenya merit consideration: alcohol abuse, depression, and suicide.

*Alcohol abuse.* According to the Kenya Medical Research Institute, alcohol abuse affects 70 percent of households in Kenya. In rural areas, drinking is predominantly, although by no means exclusively, a male pursuit Problem drinking is perceived to have become entrenched relatively recently and to be associated in particular with male and youth unemployment. In Nakuru, for example, opinion was quite specific about linking the onset of widespread alcohol abuse to the collapse of the pyrethrum market and the resulting underemployment of men. Locally brewed beer was customarily consumed at festivals and celebrations and was generally the preserve of older men. Today, drinking has become an everyday activity, starting early in the day, and locally distilled spirits have gradually replaced beer. Youth have taken over from elders as the most hardened drinkers. Drinking by both primary and secondary school children is now widely reported by teachers. A recent survey for the National Agency for the Campaign

Against Drug Abuse (NACADA 2004) found that, of a sample of 10- to 24-year-olds, 60 percent of nonstudents and 9 percent of students had used alcohol within the past month. Other common intoxicants used by young people included tobacco, marijuana, khaat, and inhalants such as glue and petrol (of these, only marijuana is illegal).

In most of rural Kenya, women are responsible for the brewing and sale of alcohol, often the most profitable of the limited sources of livelihood open to them. Yet, as the main victims of its consequences (lost household income and domestic violence), women are also most vocal in condemning the epidemic of alcohol abuse. In some areas, women highlighted alcohol abuse as the greatest problem facing them, above infrastructure, land, credit, and services. The tension between women as brewers and as wives surfaces on occasion when women act collectively to dispose of alcohol and isolate brewers in protest at the damage that drinking does to their families.

*Depression.* According to the World Health Organization (2001), depression is the leading cause of disability worldwide in terms of years lost to disability, and the fourth leading contributor to the global burden of disease (and the second in the 15–44 age group).[5] Given the low level of development of mental health services in Kenya, data on the prevalence of depression there are unreliable, but what is available is a cause for concern.[6] Our quantitative survey included several questions on depression and hopelessness; the results indicate that an average of 37 percent of people had depression, varying between 59 percent in Kiambu and 27 percent in Kwale. Poverty and money matters were the main causes of depression, followed by health, unemployment, and domestic violence.

Other sources indicate high rates of depression among young people—with 10 percent of young men and 7 percent of young women reporting being depressed nearly all the time to the point of giving up (Centre for the Study of Adolescence 2003). These rates of depression (especially for males) are significantly high relative to global rates, which are generally higher for females than males.[7]

*Suicide.* Young people in Kenya also have an alarmingly high rate of attempted suicides. Official statistics for actual suicide are unreliable given that cases are rarely reported or even mentioned because of the intense social stigma. However, in a recent survey, 7 percent of males and as many as 10 percent of young Kenyan women reported having attempted suicide at least once (Centre for the Study of Adolescence 2003).[8]

## Conclusions

This chapter has documented several aspects of the rising violence and insecurity that currently characterizes rural Kenya, and traced their origins to the erosion of livelihoods. Population growth and the inequity of the land tenure system have undermined access to key physical assets, while institutional malfunction has debilitated agricultural marketing, health, education, and other services. HIV/AIDS has increased the burden of ill health and dependency in rural households, as well as on service providers through the loss of staff.

Faced with these circumstances, rural households have had to adapt their livelihood strategies by diversifying into new farm enterprises, off-farm, and nonfarm activities. However, limited assets severely restrict their choices, often forcing them into marginal and even illegal activities. These shifts have had a markedly gendered character. The livelihood systems that have been most severely eroded (such as cash crop production, pastoralism, and labor migration) were those dominated by men, while new opportunities often extend what were traditionally female activities. As a result, men find themselves unable to meet their long-established roles in supporting the household, while women's burdens in the economic, domestic, and collective spheres intensify. These shifts in gender roles have had a destabilizing effect on households which, while not empowering women in any real sense, leave men feeling disempowered. The growing tension characterizing relations between men and women has led to a growth in domestic violence. At the same time, the decline in opportunities for youth has strained relations between the generations.

The violent character of rural intrahousehold relations can be seen as a facet of the spread of violence at all social levels—against women, children, political opponents, in disputes over land, in schools, and on the street. The brutal nature of this violence appears to be an expression of extreme anger, frustration, and resentment; a psychological anomie, also exhibited in alcohol and substance abuse. It is clear that the devastating impacts of inequality, corruption, and lack of opportunity are mediated by destructive emotions as much as by rational "economic" coping strategies. The inequalities in the distribution of power and resources that have come to characterize Kenyan society are both the start and the end point of the processes of social dislocation described in this chapter. Inequality, by concentrating power in the hands of the elite, stifles opportunity, facilitates corruption, and creates a climate of despair and desperation among the poorest.

Our account of the origins of violence in the erosion of economic and institutional assets indicates that the consequences of economic policy and mismanagement have been devastating and have reached deeply into the foundations of society itself. The implication is that, without equitable growth and widespread institutional reform, these social tensions are unlikely to be resolved. Taking social justice seriously would most importantly require reforms in rural and urban land tenure to increase equity of access, and in local administration to promote a rational system of decentralization to increase the accountability of local service providers to communities. Human security could be addressed through police reform, community-based policing, and other local-level initiatives. Peace, security, and the associated social capital are not only conditions for holding and building assets, but are themselves community assets that have hitherto been undervalued in policy (Moser 2006). Beyond this, at the societal level, it is clear that current policy approaches to gender and youth are not adequate to the scale of the problems faced. It will be essential to address not only the growing burden of labor and responsibility falling on women, but also the simultaneous "disempowerment" of men and youth.

## Notes

This chapter was completed and presented in December 2005, two years before the elections of December 27, 2007 and the widespread violent crisis that ensued, leaving (at the end of February 2008, when it remained unresolved) over 1,500 dead and 300,000 displaced.

1. The classification of violence as political, institutional, economic, and social follows Moser and McIlwane (2005).
2. FAOSTAT and Kenya Agricultural Monitoring and Policy Analysis 1997 quoted in Jayne and others (2001).
3. We use the term "demasculation" to refer to the process by which the diminishing role of men in rural livelihoods has, in the context of the "feminization" of the rural economy, led to tension with the predominant patriarchal idealogy.
4. Because the 2003 Health and Demographic Survey was the first survey in which gender-based violence in Kenya has been systematically surveyed, there is no statistical evidence on trends in domestic violence in Kenya.
5. If current trends continue, by 2020 depression is set to become the second leading cause of Disability Adjusted Life Years lost for all age groups and both sexes (WHO 2001).
6. Ndetei and Muhangi (1979) found a 20 percent incidence of psychiatric illnesses, especially depression and anxiety, among 140 rural medical walk-in patients in Kenya. Dhadphale, Cooper, and Cartwright-Taylor (1989) found a

prevalence of depressive disorders in 9.2 percent, about a third having moderate to severe depression, among a sample of 881 primary health care patients. Other research in Kenya and elsewhere (Maj and others 1994) has shown a significantly higher rate of depression in symptomatic seropositive individuals than in matched seronegative controls.

7. Globally, it is estimated that the point prevalence of unipolar depressive episodes (that is, those suffering depression at any particular time) is 1.9 percent for men and 3.2 percent for women, and that 5.8 percent of men and 9.5 percent of women will experience a depressive episode in a 12-month period. (Global Burden of Disease surveys 2000, quoted in WHO 2001.)

8. Based on countries for which complete data are available, the global age standardized-suicide rate for 1996 was 15.1 per 100,000. The rates were 24 per 100,000 for males and 6.8 for females. The rate of suicide is almost universally high among men compared with women, by an aggregate ration of 3.5 to 1. Male suicide rates are also rising much more rapidly than female.

## References

Amuyunzu-Nyamongo, M., and A. C. Ezeh. 2005. "A Qualitative Assessment of Support Mechanisms in Informal Settlements of Nairobi, Kenya." *Journal of Poverty* 9 (3): 89–107.

Bryceson, D. F. 1996. "De-agrarianisation and Rural Employment in Sub-Saharan Africa: A Sectoral Perspective." *World Development* 24: 1 (97–111).

Buvinic, M., A. Morrison, and M. Shifter. 1999. "Violence in Latin America and the Caribbean: A Framework for Action." Technical Study, Sustainable Development Department, Inter-American Development Bank, Washington, DC. March.

Central Bureau of Statistics. 2004. *Kenya Demographic and Health Survey, 2003.* Central Bureau of Statistics, Nairobi, July.

Centre for the Study of Adolescence. 2003. *The Situation of Young People in Kenya Survey, 2003.* CSA, Nairobi.

Cross, S. 2002. "A Comparative Study of Land Tenure Reform in Four Countries: Uganda, Tanzania, Malawi and Kenya." LADDER Working Paper No. 31, Overseas Development Group, University of East Anglia, Norwich.

Dhadphale, M., G. Gooper, and L. Cartwright-Taylor. 1989. "Prevalence and Presentation of Depressive Illness in a Primary Health Care Setting in Kenya." *American Journal of Psychiatry* 146: 659–61.

Ellis, F. 2000. *Rural Livelihoods and Diversity in Developing Countries.* Oxford: Oxford University Press.

GoK (Government of Kenya). 2002. *Kenya Population and Housing Census: Analytical Report on Population Dynamics Vol. III.* Nairobi: Central Bureau of Statistics.

————. 2007a. "Basic Report on Well-Being in Kenya: Based on Kenya Integrated Household Budget Survey 2005/06. April 2007." Kenya Bureau of National Statistics, Ministry of Development and Planning, Nairobi.

————. 2007b. "Economic Survey 2007. May 2007." Ministry of Development and Planning, GoK, Nairobi.

Human Rights Watch International. 1999. "Kenya: Spare the Child: Corporal Punishment in Kenyan Schools." Report, 11(6) (A), September. http://www.hrw.org/reports/1999/kenya/index.htm.

Jayne, T. S., T. Yamano, M. Weber, D. Tschirley, R. Benefica, D. Neven, A. Chaot, and B. Zulu. 2001. "Smallholder Income and Land Distribution in Africa: Implications for Poverty Reduction Strategies." MSU International Development Paper No 24. Department of Agricultural Economics, Michigan State University. East Lansing, Michigan.

Karanja, A. M., and J. K. Nyoro. 2002. "Coffee Prices and Regulation and their Impact on Livelihoods of Rural Community in Kenya." Report. Tegemeo Institue of Agricultural Policy and Development, Egerton University, Nairobi.

KLA. 2003. "Land Use in Kenya: The Case for a National Land Use Policy." Report. Nairobi: Kenya Land Alliance.

Maj, M, R. Janssen, F. Starace, M. Zaudig, P. Satz, B. Sughondhabirom, M. Luabeya, R. Riedel, D. Ndetei, H. Calil, E. Bing, M. St. Louis and N. Sartorius. 1994. "WHO Neuropsychiatric AIDS Study, Cross-Sectional Phase I: Study Design and Psychiatric Findings." *Archives of General Psychiatry* 151: 39–49.

Moser, C. 1996. "Confronting Crisis: A Comparative Study of Household Responses to Poverty and Vulnerability in Four Poor Communities." Environmentally Sustainable Development Studies and Monograph Series No. 8. World Bank, Washington DC.

Moser, C., and C. McIlaine. 2005. "Latin American Urban Violence as a Development Concern: Towards a Framework for Violence Reduction." *World Development* 34 (1): 89–112.

Moser, C. 2006. "Assets, Livelihoods, and Social Policy." *Assets and Livelihoods: A Framework for Asset-Based Social Policy.* Washington, DC: World Bank.

NACADA (National Agency for the Campaign Against Drug Abuse). 2004. *"Youth in Peril: Alcohol and Drug Abuse in Kenya."* Report. National Agency for the Campaign Against Drug Abuse, Nairobi, Kenya.

Ndetei, D.M., and J. Muhangi. 1979. "The Prevalence and Clinical Presentation of Psychiatric Illness in a Rural Setting in Kenya." *British Journal of Psychiatry* 135: 269–72.

Rakodi, C. 2002. "A Livelihood Approach–Conceptual Issues and Definitions." In *Urban livelihoods: A People-Centered Approach to Reducing Poverty,* eds. C. Rakodi, and T. Lloyd-Jones. London and Sterling, VA: Earthscan Publications.

Silbershmidt, M. 2005. "Poverty, Male Disempowerment, and Male Sexuality: Rethinking Men and Masculinities in Rural and Urban East Africa." In *African Masculinities: Men in Africa from the Late Nineteenth Century to the Present*, eds. L. Ouzgane and R. Morrell. New York: Palgrave Macmillan.

Transparency International 1996–2005. "The TI Corruption Perceptions Index." http://www.transparency.org/surveys/index.html#cpi.

———. 2002, 2004, 2005, 2006, 2007. The Kenya Bribery Index, 2002, 2004, 2005, 2006, 2007. http://www.transparency.org/surveys/index.html#kubi.

United Nations. 1980. Report of the 6th United Nations Congress on the Prevention of Crime and the Treatment of Offenders A/RES/35/171. http://www.un.org/documents/ga/res/35/ares35.htm.

Wanyama, F. 2003. "Civil Society and the Lopsided Democratization Process: The Unfulfilled Expectations of Community-Based Organizations in Rural Kenya." *East African Journal of Human Rights and Democracy* 1 (1): 43–57.

World Bank. 2003. "Economic Survey." GoK, Nairobi.

———. 2007. Kenya Country Social Analyses. Unpublished report, Environmentally and Socially Sustainable Development, Africa Region, World Bank, Washington, DC.

WHO (World Health Organization). 2001. *The World Health Report 200–Mental Health: New Understanding, New Hope*. Geneva: World Health Organization.

# CHAPTER 10

# Youth Gangs as Ontological Assets

*Dennis Rodgers*

Despite the fact that the last of the civil wars that plagued the region during the 1970s and 1980s was formally brought to an end in 1996, violence has continued to affect Central American societies unabated into the 21st century. Although the region's political conflicts may seem to have been "resolved" through peace accords between armies and insurgents, the everyday lives of much of the region's population—particularly the poor—remain overshadowed by more social and multifaceted forms of violence in the form of crime and delinquency (Pearce 1998). Indeed, crime is now so prevalent in Central America that in many instances levels of violence are comparable to, or in some cases even higher than, the previous decades of war (Moser and Winton 2002). The most emblematic form of brutality that has emerged from these new Central American "savage wars of peace" is undoubtedly youth gang violence. Even if the phenomenon is widespread throughout the whole of Latin America (Rodgers 1999), it is particularly virulent in Central America, where gangs are widely seen as constituting a form of social pathology (Arana 2001; Liebel 2004).

Through a detailed analysis of Nicaraguan youth gangsterism, this chapter argues that such a vision of gangs is based on a fundamental misunderstanding of the phenomenon.[1] It begins by challenging the notion that gangs inherently constitute pathological social forms, underlining the importance of taking structural circumstances into account when evaluating them, particularly in "fragile" state contexts. It then presents a two-part ethnographic case study of the dynamics of a youth gang in a poor neighborhood in Managua, Nicaragua, drawing on longitudinal research carried out between 1996–97 and 2002–03.[2] The first half of the case study highlights how, under conditions of failing state sovereignty, gangs can provide localized frameworks of order which allow individuals and groups in poor urban neighborhoods to coherently formulate sustainable livelihoods, to the extent that in social policy terms, gangs may correspond to what might be termed "political" assets. The second half of the case study focuses on the evolutionary trajectory of gangs, showing how they mutated from a communitarian social form to a more exclusive economic organization. This suggests that gangs constitute highly volatile political assets, an issue that has critical ramifications for the formulation of sustainable social policy.

### Youth Gangs as "Perverse Livelihoods"?

Classic social science conceptions of youth gangs tend to interpret them as dysfunctional social forms, variably the reflection of the social disorganization of poverty and exclusion (Whyte 1943), lower class subculture (Cohen 1955), forms of resistance to blocked opportunities (Cloward and Ohlin 1960), instances of savage capitalism (Sánchez Jankowski 1991), the result of deviant personality traits (Yablonsky 1963) or macho identity creation processes (Bloch and Niederhoffer 1958). Horowitz (1990: 53) has pointed out, however, that these different interpretations are not necessarily contradictory and simply correspond to different dimensions of the gang experience, which constitutes something of a holistic "way of life." In social policy terms, the obvious analogy would be to say that gangs constitute "livelihoods," insofar as they are institutionalized practices that provide gang members with a means of living, generally in difficult and extreme circumstances. Such a characterization is an uncomfortable one, however, because of the intimate association between gangs and violence. Beyond the eminently debatable ethical issues, a livelihood is generally seen to be a sustainable set of activities that maintains or enhances the capabilities and assets of social agents. The more assets they accumulate, and the greater the spread of assets they possess or can access, the less vulnerable they will be (Moser 1998). Violence as a social practice is considered to erode the assets that social agents draw upon to constitute their livelihoods, thereby increasing their vulnerability.

From this perspective, following Rubio (1997), livelihoods based on violence might plausibly be labeled "perverse," with gangs constituting perhaps paradigmatic examples of such "perverse livelihoods." Although this labeling makes a good deal of intuitive sense, numerous instances exist in which violence can constitute a very productive means through which groups and individuals enhance their asset portfolios, for example, by enabling the accumulation of physical or financial capital assets through the dispossession of others, or by enhancing intragroup social capital, most obviously in the form of scapegoating. This raises a critical theoretical issue, which is whether the evaluation of a livelihood as "productive" or "perverse" ought to be based on its means or its outcome. In many ways, this issue largely depends on the wider structural context within which a particular livelihood practice is articulated, and it is a question that in certain contexts significantly shifts the potential focus of analysis.

## Assets, Livelihoods, and Social Protection in "Fragile" States

This shift is particularly obvious in the context of what are variously described as "fragile," "weak," "crisis," or "failed" states (see, for example, Bøås and Jennings 2005; Crisis States Programme 2001; Fukuyama 2004; Rotberg 2004). Whatever the label, the basic premise is straightforward. States are the primary form of social organization in the contemporary world, but some states are clearly less able to organize than others, and are therefore considered "fragile" in implicit contrast to "robust" states. The issue of fragility or robustness is seen to derive principally from a state's ability to establish "a certain order ... over a given territory," and to back up this order with "a centralized coercive guarantee" (O'Donnell 1999: 135). This is important because it has ramifications for the coherent construction of livelihoods by social agents, both in terms of the spread of their assets as well as the maximization and operationalization of these assets, insofar as the state's coercive guarantee allows for predictability in social exchanges. This coercive guarantee extends irregularly across the territory and the functional relations that "fragile" states supposedly regulate, making the viable construction of livelihoods and management of asset portfolios by social agents harder.

In social policy terms, the state's coercive guarantee effectively amounts to a basic form of social protection because it relates to the prevention, management, and overcoming of risks and vulnerabilities that might affect social agents in the accumulation and maximization of their assets and the elaboration of sustainable livelihoods. The importance of this coercive guarantee emerges clearly in relation to much of contemporary Central

America, including in particular Nicaragua. Although the renowned leftist *Sandinista* revolution of the 1980s led to the modernization of Nicaraguan state and society, including a dramatic expansion in the provision of social welfare services, this process underwent a drastic reversal following the electoral defeat of the *Sandinista* regime in 1990. The subsequent structural adjustment program imposed on the country, the high levels of corruption and concomitant political disillusion, the declining levels of international aid, and a profound economic crisis all combined to provoke a steady institutional erosion of the Nicaraguan state, to the extent that Isbester (1996: 455) argues that a veritable process of "state disintegration" has occurred.

This has been starkly reflected in the huge surge in criminal violence that has affected the country during the past 15 years (see Serbin and Ferreyra 2000), which is undoubtedly related to the Nicaraguan state's institutional weakness. Certainly, a 1999 survey on crime found that 43 percent of respondents who had been victims of crime stated that they had not reported the crime to the police because "it was no use" (Cajina 2000: 178). The Nicaraguan police have only limited patrolling capacities in urban areas and are completely absent in 21 percent of the country's 146 municipalities (Cajina 2000). Regionally, they have the lowest number of personnel per capita and per crime, the lowest budget per crime, the lowest budget per police personnel, and the lowest average salaries in Central America (Call 2000). This penury makes the police susceptible to corruption (Grigsby 2003) and limits their technical and material capabilities, as was underlined by the Police Commissioner Franco Montealegre in a media interview in 2001, when he complained that the police were outgunned by criminals (Nicaragua Network 2001).

At the same time, situations of state "fragility" tend to be uneven. States are not necessarily unitary, nor do they exercise the same degree of control over the territories and functional relations they supposedly regulate. O'Donnell (1999) proposes a threefold color-coded spatial representation of the extent to which a state is territorially and functionally present, dividing states into "blue," "green," and "brown" zones. Blue zones have a high degree of state presence in the form of an effective bureaucracy, a functioning legal system, and a clear monopoly over the legitimate use of violence. Green zones are characterized by a high degree of territorial penetration by the state—particularly in the form of its symbolic trappings—but a lesser degree of functional presence. Finally, brown zones are areas where the state is negligibly present and unable to enforce its control.

Although there are blue and green zones in Nicaragua that have been made safe for those living in them—the socioeconomic elite—through a process that effectively amounts to their "disembedding" from the rest of society (Rodgers 2004b), the country is principally made up of brown zones, including most paradigmatically the slums and poor neighborhoods that constitute the overwhelming majority of its urban areas. The Nicaraguan state is incapable—or unwilling (see Rodgers 2006b)—to provide even the most basic form of social protection to those living in brown zones; consequently it is increasingly difficult for this population to accumulate assets and construct sustainable livelihoods in the resulting context of chronic violence and insecurity. This was graphically reflected in an interview with an informant called *Doña* Yolanda, in the poor Managua neighborhood *barrio* Luis Fanor Hernández:[3]

> There's so much delinquency, it's impossible to live.... They'll kill you for a watch.... They'll kill you for a pair of shoes.... They'll kill you for your shirt.... they're everywhere; you've got to watch out.... They could be your neighbor, even your friend, you can never be sure.... You can't go out any more, you can't wear rings, bracelets, nice shoes, anything that makes us look a little better than we really are.... How can we live? It's not possible....

At first glance, youth gangs seem the most prominent contributors to the chronic violence and insecurity that affects contemporary Nicaragua. At its most basic, a gang, or *"pandilla,"* consists of a variably sized group of generally male youths,[4] ranging from 7 to 23 years of age, who engage in illicit and violent behavior—although not all their activities are illicit or violent—and have a particular territorial dynamic. Most notably, gangs are associated with a specific urban neighborhood,[5] although larger neighborhoods often have more than one gang, and not all neighborhoods have one, as a critical demographic mass of youth is clearly needed for a gang to emerge. They furthermore tend not to develop in affluent neighborhoods. Gangs can be traced back to the 1940s in Nicaragua, but they were small scale and innocuous youth aggregations until the early 1990s, when their numbers increased massively and they became significantly more violent (Rodgers 2006a). The 1999 survey on crime cited previously found that gangs were considered the most likely perpetrators of crime in Nicaragua by more than 50 percent of respondents (Cajina 2000).

At the same time, a clear difference exists in the social experience of gang violence depending on one's standpoint. For example, when viewed from a general perspective, gangs seem to anarchically transform large swathes of Nicaraguan cities into quasi-war zones, as they fight each other with weaponry ranging from sticks, stones, and knives to AK-47 automatic rifles, fragmentation grenades, and mortars, yielding dramatic consequences both for gang members and the general population. When considered from a localized perspective, the picture is more nuanced, with gangs emerging as much more socially constructive—albeit variably so—phenomena. This is not as implausible as may initially seem. O'Donnell (1999) contends that, where the state is deficient or absent, alternative forms of social structuration that are functionally equivalent to the state will inevitably emerge to lay down informal rules, allowing for the protection of assets and the construction of livelihoods through sustained asset accumulation and portfolio management. Social life would be impossible otherwise. These alternative forms of social structuration will vary considerably, however. In green zones, for example, state-corrupting forms of power such as "personalism, familism, prebendalism, clientelism" are likely to develop (O'Donnell 1999, 140), while in brown zones, non-state-based "systems of local power which tend to reach extremes of violent, personalistic rule … open to all sorts of violent and arbitrary practices" will emerge (O'Donnell 1999: 138).

Youth gangs are paradigmatic examples of the latter. Obviously they constitute forms of power on a very different scale to the deficient state, but they are analogous insofar as they are both fundamentally about the promotion of order. As Taylor (2002) has underlined, the primary measure of any form of social order is not so much its magnitude, but rather the degree to which it is imbued with "social imaginary." This notion, which refers to the self-understandings that are constitutive of a collective unit, therefore relates to deep institutional structure: "The social imaginary is not a set of ideas; rather it is what enables, through making sense of, the practices of a society" (Taylor 2002: 91). The modern nation state is perhaps the clearest example of an institution imbued with social imaginary (Anderson 1983), but it is something that can also apply to less universal social forms, such as youth gangs, as the following case study of the *barrio* Luis Fanor Hernández gang demonstrates.[6]

## The Barrio Luis Fanor Hernández Gang in 1996–97

In 1996–97, the gang in *barrio* Luis Fanor Hernández was made up of about 100 youths between 7 and 22 years of age,[7] who on a par with other gangs in Managua, engaged in violent activities ranging from petty delinquency to gang warfare. These activities all complied with a cardinal "golden rule," however, which was not to prey on local neighborhood inhabitants. The victims of the local gang were outsiders, and gang members would actively go out of their way to protect local neighborhood inhabitants from outside criminals and gangs, frequently "rescuing" local inhabitants, and often acting as bodyguards for them when they went on errands in surrounding areas. Even what seemed to be the most destructive and harmful form of gang violence—gang warfare—was a socially constructive process when viewed from the local level. For example, gang warfare obeyed certain behavioral rules that played fundamental roles in the construction of the individual gang member's self-identity and contributed to the constitution of the gang as a group by reaffirming the collective unit.

But gang warfare was also about a broader form of social construction that went beyond the gang group or individual and related to the local neighborhood community. The gang members qualified their violence as being primarily motivated by their "love" ("*querer*") for the neighborhood, justifying their fighting other gangs as "acts of love" for their neighborhood. As one gang member called Julio explained:

> You show the neighborhood that you love it by putting yourself in danger for people, by protecting them from other gangs.... You look after the neighborhood; you help them, keep them safe....

This is by no means implausible, as gang warfare was semiritualized, following set patterns. The first battle of a gang war typically involved fighting with stones and bare hands, but each new battle involved an escalation of weaponry: first to sticks and staffs, then knives and broken bottles, then mortars, and eventually to hand guns, AK-47s, and fragmentation grenades. Although the rate of escalation could vary, its sequence never did—that is, *pandillas* did not begin their wars with mortars, guns, or AK-47s.

The ritualized nature of gang warfare could be seen to have been a kind of restraining mechanism. Escalation is a positive constitutive process, in which each stage calls for a greater but definite intensity of action and is always, therefore, under the actors' control. It also provided local neighborhood inhabitants with an "early warning system" of future and increasingly violent conflagrations. As such, gang wars were "scripted performances," which offered the wider neighborhood community a means of circumscribing what Arendt (1969: 5) has described as the "all-pervading unpredictability" of violence. Even if gang wars had negative consequences for the local population, these were indirect insofar as gangs never directly victimized the inhabitants of their own neighborhoods, protecting them instead. The threat to local neighborhood populations stemmed from *other* gangs, with whom the local gang would engage in a prescribed manner, thereby limiting the scope of violence in its own neighborhood and creating a predictable "safe haven" for local inhabitants.

In a wider context of chronic violence and insecurity, this function was very much seen as a positive one, even if it was not always effective, since bystanders were frequently injured and even killed in the cross fire of gang wars. Certainly, local inhabitants recognized it as a positive phenomenon, as an informant called *Don* Sergio confirmed:

> The gang looks after the neighborhood and screws others; it protects us and allows us to feel a little bit safer, to live our lives a little bit more easily.... Gangs are not a good thing, and it's their fault that we have to live with all this insecurity, but that's a general problem about gangs, not of our gang here in the *barrio*. They protect us, help us—without them, things would be much worse for us.

Local neighborhood inhabitants, in other words, distinguished between the gang phenomenon in general and the local manifestation of the gang. While critical of the former, they were usually positive about the latter. This is not to say that they never had anything negative to say about the gang— certainly the parents of gang members frequently worried about their off- spring and would often publicly berate their gang member sons—but there was no fear of the local gang in the neighborhood, and it was seen as the principal source of security.

At the same time, however, the gang was more than just the purveyor of a sense of security. The positive view of the gang also stemmed from the fact that it was the only form of local collective organization that dis- played some sort of encompassing interest for the neighborhood. There were no other pan-*barrio* collective organizations—even households and families were in the process of being eroded (Rodgers 2007)—and con- sequently its violent "care" for the *barrio* stood in sharp contrast with the wider atomization and social breakdown. From this perspective, the gang not only acted to protect the *barrio* and its inhabitants—thereby enabling them to live reasonably predictable lives—but also provided the neighborhood with a concrete medium for the enacting of an otherwise absent form of community.

Neighborhood inhabitants exhibited a strong sense of identification with the local gang and its violent exploits, which provided the prin- cipal anchor point for a notion of community in a context of extreme social fragmentation. This was actualized through a "communal aesthetic pleasure" (Bloch 1996, 216) that developed as a result of the gang's violent activities, as neighborhood inhabitants avidly swapped stories about the gang, exchanged eyewitness accounts, spread rumors, and retold various incidents over and over again. This had the effect of converting the gang and its violence into a symbolic index of community in *barrio* Luis Fanor Hernández, and provided a primary source of what Giddens (1991: 38) has termed "ontological security." As such, the gang became the institutional medium through which practical and symbolic rules and norms for living were laid down locally, allowing for the coherent—albeit limited—formulation of sustainable livelihoods by *barrio* inhabitants and the management of their limited asset portfolios.

Broadly speaking, this "ontological security" corresponds to a form of political authority, but one that is perhaps less "political" in the classic political economy sense of "the distribution and struggle for power in society" (Mair 1962: 11), but rather at the more basic level of "the imposition of a sense of order in the chaos of many people doing many things with many meanings" (Nicholas 1966: 49). This is a conception of the political that relates less to notions of right and wrong, but rather to the way "things fit together" in order to permit notions of right and wrong. In other words, "the ways in which people imagine their social existence, how they fit together with others, how things go on between them and their fellows, the expectations that are normally met, and the deeper normative notions and images that underlie these expectations" (Taylor 2002: 106). This is crucial to social life. As Schmitt (1985 (1933): 19) has pointed out, "every general rule demands a regular, everyday frame of life to which it can be applied and which is submitted to its regulations." This context of regularity, which is fundamental for social agents to be able to exercise their agency and therefore manage their asset portfolios and strategize their livelihoods, is precisely what gangs provided. Local inhabitants in *barrio* Luis Fanor Hernández were able to articulate coherent—although admittedly limited—livelihoods through the sustained management of their meager asset portfolios because the gang provided a measure of stability and predictability that facilitated regularized social exchange and interaction in a wider context of anarchy and breakdown.

The obvious question that such an analysis raises is the extent to which such a form of order is developmentally sustainable, particularly considering the well-established line of thinking that suggests that forms of "social sovereignty" (see Latham 2000) can eventually become forms of "state sovereignty"? This is most famously claimed by Tilly (1985, 2002) who argued that the rise of European states in the Middle Ages was the result of the gradual development of encompassing interests by warlords over the areas they dominated. These warlords, who became increasingly tied to their domains through forms of systematic economic extraction as opposed to one-off plunder, incidentally established the institutional trappings of statehood. They provided their subjects with autonomous rights in order to maximize their own economic interests, because large-scale systematic economic exploitation requires collective coordination, and decentralization is the most effective means to achieve this. Such an analytical framework is attractive because it provides clear policy leads, insofar as attempts could be made to potentially nurture forms of "social sovereignty" and integrate them into deficient state-based social protection structures. As the continuation of the case study demonstrates, however, the *barrio* Luis Fanor Hernández gang's evolutionary trajectory suggests that Nicaraguan gangs are following an almost precisely opposite path to Tilly's idealized movement from warlordism to statehood.

## The Barrio Luis Fanor Hernández Gang in 2002–03

By early 2002, the *barrio* Luis Fanor Hernández gang had transformed radically, such that it could no longer be construed as providing a sense of either "ontological" or even just generic security. The gang was now made up of just 18 youths from 17 to 23 years of age. Although all had belonged to the gang in 1996–97, the gang's practices and attitudes had changed profoundly, in particular the nature of the group's violent and illicit activities. Gang warfare had disappeared, levels of intraneighborhood gang-related violence had increased, local inhabitants now bore the brunt of it, and the gang was intimately connected to a thriving local crack cocaine-based drug economy. The gang members were an intimidating and threatening presence in the neighborhood, no longer imbued with an ethos of "loving" the *barrio*, as one called Roger made clear:

> We couldn't give a fuck about the *barrio* inhabitants anymore.... If they get attacked, if they're robbed, if they have problems, who cares? We don't lift a finger to help them anymore, we just laugh instead; hell, we even applaud those who are robbing them.... Why should we do anything for them? Now we just hang out in the streets, smoke crack, and rob, and nothing else.

The changed behavior patterns can undoubtedly be linked to gang members' crack consumption, insofar as crack is a drug that makes users extremely violent and unpredictable. Although they were by no means the only crack users in the neighborhood, the gang constituted a privileged site of crack consumption and gang members were clearly involved in the overwhelming majority of the drug-related violence affecting the neighborhood. At the same time, their changed behavior patterns and the subsequent rise in insecurity can, to a larger extent, be attributed to the gang's intimate association with the local drugs trade. Gang members were the lowest rung of drug dealing and acted as the local drug economy's security apparatus. Gang members made sure that drug-related transactions in the neighborhood proceeded smoothly, enforcing contracts, roughing up any recalcitrant clients for drug dealers, maiming or killing rivals from other neighborhoods, and guarding drug shipments as they were moved both within and outside the neighborhood.

They also made sure that potential clients could enter the neighborhood without being attacked by either the local population or outsiders. This was one of the reasons why the ritualized gang wars of the past had disappeared, as they would have discouraged or made it difficult for clients to come into the neighborhood. The gang had also instituted a regime of terror at the level of the neighborhood. Gang members strutted about the streets, menacingly displaying guns and machetes and verbally warning *barrio* inhabitants of the potential retribution if they denounced them or others involved in the local drug trade; these threats were frequently backed up these threats with multiple random acts of terrorizing violence. As a gang member called Chucki explained succinctly, the gang's new ethos was essentially: "We give the orders here" ("*nosotros mandamos aquí*"). The changed relationship with the wider neighborhood community was described by *Doña* Yolanda as follows:

> Five years ago, you could trust the gang, but not anymore.... They've become corrupted due to this drug crack.... They threaten and attack people from the *barrio* now, rob them of whatever they have, whoever they are ... They never did that before.... They used to protect us, look out for us, but now they don't care, they only look out for themselves, for their illegal business (*bisnes*).... People are scared, you've got to be careful what you say or what you do, because otherwise they'll attack you.... Even if you say nothing, they might still come and rob you, come into your home, steal a chair, food, some clothes, whatever they can find.... They often do,

you know it's them, but you can't blame them, otherwise they'll come and burn your house down.... It's their way of telling you to be careful....

If you say anything to them, if you do anything, if you denounce them, then they'll come at night and wreak their vengeance.... We live in terror here in the *barrio*, you have to be scared or else you're sure to be sorry.... It's not like it used to be when you were here last time, Dennis, when the gang was made up of kids we could be proud of because of what they did for us and for the *barrio*.... They're like strangers to us now; they just do things for themselves and never for the good of the community like before....

The social order that the gang now upheld was obviously a much more exclusive one than in the past, focused on the regulation of the local drugs trade for the benefit of its members and those associated with the wider drug economy. At the same time, this exclusive social order was still eminently collective in nature, insofar as the regime of terror imposed by the gang generally constrained the ways in which neighborhood inhabitants determined their livelihoods and managed their assets. It was a collective social order that was very different from the one the gang had promulgated in the past, however. While in 1996–97 the gang had constituted a form of order based on a *barrio*-wide "encompassing interest," in 2002–03 it was an order that related to the gang's parochial economic interests and was much closer to being the "perverse livelihood" that such social phenomena are often depicted to be.

Part of the reason for evolution is that the means through which the gang articulated its authority in 2002–03 were very different to those of the gang in 1996–97. These now stemmed from the gang's ability to carry out arbitrary acts of violence that displayed little regularity or consistency, rather than through the imposition of universal norms and rules. A parallel can be made with Schmitt's (1985 [1933]: 5) notion of "sovereign power," which he saw as being "not about the monopoly to coerce or to rule, but ... the monopoly to decide." This was the "purest" form of political authority, an expression of "raw" power that originated in the ability to decide the "state of exception," a condition during which the regular rules and norms by which social agents organize their lives are suspended and those with power can impose their will in an unconstrained and therefore arbitrary manner. This is just what the gang did in 2002–03; they kept the neighborhood in a permanent "state of exception" through its unpredictable and random terrorizing. In doing so, however, the gang reached what Agamben (1998: 32) has called "the point of indistinction between violence and law, crossing the threshold on which violence passes over into law and law passes into violence."

## Conclusion

This chapter has described the dynamics of youth gang violence in contemporary urban Nicaragua through a longitudinal ethnographic case study of a youth gang in the poor Managua neighborhood of *barrio* Luis Fanor Hernández. It has highlighted the way in which gangs can, under certain conditions, be conceived as socially constructive rather than destructive social forms. This is the case, for example, in what O'Donnell (1999: 140) terms the "brown zones" of fragile states such as contemporary Nicaragua. Gangs emerged there during the mid-1990s as localized forms of social structuration that provided relatively safe, stable, and predictable neighborhood environments in which local inhabitants were able to coherently formulate sustainable livelihoods and manage their asset portfolios within a wider structural context of failing state sovereignty. They were forms of "social sovereignty" that functionally substituted for the state in wider circumstances of state disintegration, exclusion, and socioeconomic hardship, and provided positive "enabling environments" for local communities.

From a social policy perspective, this can be formulated in terms of gangs constituting an underlying "ontological" asset that structured the very constitution of asset portfolios upon which livelihoods were constructed. As Bebbington (1999: 5) has remarked, assets "are not simply resources that people use to build livelihoods," but the things that "give them the capability to be and act." This second kind of asset is rarely taken into account in policy formulation, which tends to focus on more immediate tangible assets such as natural, physical, social, financial, or human capital. Yet, it is the prior existence of viable ontological assets that determines how human, financial, or social capital assets can be accumulated and managed. This is precisely what gangs in Nicaragua achieved during the 1990s.

By the early 2000s, gangs had mutated into very different predatory social forms that promoted and protected exclusive socioeconomic orders through the imposition of veritable regimes of terror that were detrimental for the majority of those living under their sway. Their principal raison d'être was no longer the protection of the *barrio* and concomitant facilitation of asset building, but rather the gang members' economic and consumer gain from the local drug trade. Such an evolutionary trajectory would seem to suggest that Nicaraguan gangs tend toward a developmentally negative outcome, in contrast to classic analyses of similar social forms such as Tilly's (2002 [1985]). Some might be tempted to interpret this as an inevitable corollary of the gang's inherently violent nature, but this would fail to recognize the fact that "coercion and force are as much a part of everyday life as markets and economic exchange" (Bates 2001: 50). Instead, the evolutionary path of the gangs has to be placed within a broader structural context, one whereby the possibilities for collective social life in Nicaragua are increasingly shrinking.

As Núñez (1996) has argued, the basis of social life in postrevolutionary Nicaragua has undergone a process of "scaling down" during the past 15 years, along a trajectory that has seen the principal locus of social organization move initially from the nation state to the *barrio*, and then from the *barrio* to the gang. Although gangs can be seen as having constituted relatively productive—albeit limitedly so—ontological assets in Nicaragua during the mid-1990s, emerging as a desperate reaction to the wider circumstances of chronic insecurity and social breakdown, their transformed nature in the 2000s indicates that they were ultimately overwhelmed by an inexorably worsening structural situation and became more parochial and highly perverse in nature. While this points to the nonsustainability of gangs as ontological assets, it also highlights that it is not so much gangs that constitute the principal development problem *per se*, but very much the tragic wider socioeconomic circumstances characteristic of "fragile" states such as Nicaragua, insofar as gangs are, in the final analysis, simply their epiphenomena.

## Notes

1. There exist a range of differences between Nicaraguan youth gangs and their counterparts in other Central American countries, including the fact that they are not an importation of U.S. gang culture and nor are they as violent as the latter—even if they are by no means as innocuous as Nicaraguan government crime statistics suggest (see Rodgers 2004b). At a general level, however, they arguably epitomize dynamics that are relevant to the whole of the Central American region, and indeed to the Latin American context more generally.

2. The first period of fieldwork was carried out between July 1996 and July 1997, as part of a social anthropology Ph.D. (Rodgers 2000). The second period was conducted in February–March 2002 and December 2002–January 2003 as part of the London School of Economics Crisis States Programme. For methodological details see Rodgers (2004a).

3. This is a pseudonym, as are all the names of informants mentioned in this chapter.

4. Female gang members are not completely unknown in Nicaragua but are extremely rare. This gender bias derives partly from the fact that being a gang member involves behavior patterns that revolve around activities that are "very much the essence of machismo's ideal of manhood" (Lancaster 1992: 195), such as taking risks or displaying bravado in the face of danger. Female gang members therefore inherently challenge Nicaraguan machismo's ideal of womanhood, associated with subordination and domestic roles. Indeed, to a certain extent it can be argued that being a gang member is in many ways a heightened expression of machismo. There did not seem to be equivalent female youth organizational forms. This absence can be linked to another facet of machismo, namely the gendered organization of space along the lines of "street = public = male/home = private = female" (Ekern 1987: 55).

5. Pandillas are overwhelmingly an urban phenomenon principally found in Managua, although media reports do signal their presence in other urban centers, including Chinandega, Estelí, Granada, León, and Matagalpa.

6. The case study presented is limited to a single gang in a specific neighborhood, so caution must be exercised in extrapolating about the general nature of Nicaraguan youth gangs. However, anthropological studies have amply shown the validity of drawing on small-scale cases to think about the dynamics of larger social processes. Moreover, many parallels exist between the findings presented here and those of other studies of gangs in Nicaragua such as Rocha (2000, 2005), and Sosa Meléndez and Rocha (2001).

7. This constituted about 15 percent of neighborhood youths within this age bracket.

## References

Agamben, G. 1998. *Homo Sacer: Sovereign Power and Bare Life*. Stanford, CA: Stanford University Press.

Anderson, B. 1983. *Imagined Communities: Reflections on the Origin and Spread of Nationalism*. London: Verso.

Arana, A. 2001. "The New Battle for Central America." *Foreign Affairs* 89 (6): 88–101.

Arendt, H. 1969. *On Violence*. New York: Harcourt Brace & Company.

Bates, R. H. 2001. *Prosperity and Violence: The Political Economy of Development*. New York: W. W. Norton & Co.

Bebbington, A. 1999. *Capitals and Capabilities: A Framework for Analysing Peasant Viability, Rural Livelihoods, and Poverty in the Andes*. London: International Institute for Environment and Development.

Bloch, H. A., and A. Niederhoffer. 1958. *The Gang: A Study in Adolescent Behavior*. New York: Philosophical Library.

Bloch, M. 1996. "La 'Consummation' des Jeunes Hommes Chez les Zafimaniry de Madagascar." In *De la Violence*, ed. Françoise Héritier. Paris: Odile Jacob.

Bøås, M., and K. M. Jennings. 2005. "Insecurity and Development: The Rhetoric of the 'Failed State.'" *European Journal of Development Research* 17 (3): 385–95.

Cajina, R. J. 2000. "Nicaragua: De la Seguridad del Estado a la Inseguridad Ciudadana." In *Gobernabilidad Democrática y Seguridad Ciudadana en Centroamérica: El caso de Nicaragua*, eds. Andrés Serbin and Diego Ferreyra. Managua: Coordinadora Regional de Investigaciones Económicas y Sociales (CRIES).

Call, C. 2000. *"Sustainable Development in Central America: The Challenges of Violence, Injustice and Insecurity."* Central America 2020 Working Paper No. 8. Institut für Iberoamerika-Kunde, Hamburg.

Cloward, R. A., and L. E. Ohlin. 1960. *Delinquency and Opportunity: A Theory of Delinquent Gangs*. New York: Free Press.

Cohen, A. K. 1955. *Delinquent Boys: The Culture of the Gang*. Glencoe: Free Press.

Crisis States Programme. 2001. "Concepts and Research Agenda." London School of Economics Crisis States Programme Working Paper No. 1. Crisis States Research Centre, London. http://www.crisisstates.com/download/wp/wp1.pdf.

Ekern, S. 1987. *Street Power: Culture and Politics in a Nicaraguan Neighbourhood*. Bergen: University of Bergen.

Fukuyama, F. 2004. *State Building: Governance and World Order in the Twenty-First Century*. London: Profile Books.

Giddens, A. 1991. *Modernity and Self-Identity: Self and Society in the Late Modern Age*. Cambridge: Polity.

Grigsby, W. 2003. La Policía en su Laberinto: Trampas, Claves y Pistas. *Envío*, 257. http://www.envio.org.ni/articulo.php?id=1271.

Horowitz, R. 1990. "Sociological Perspectives on Gangs: Conflicting Definitions and Concepts." In *Gangs in America*, eds. C. Ronald Huff. Newbury Park: Sage.

Isbester, K. 1996. "Understanding State Disintegration: The Case of Nicaragua." *The Journal of Social, Political and Economic Studies* 21 (4): 455–76.

Lancaster, R. 1992. *Life Is Hard: Machismo, Danger, and the Intimacy of Power in Nicaragua*. Berkeley: University of California Press.

Latham, R. 2000. "Social Sovereignty." *Theory, Culture & Society* 17 (4): 1–18.

Liebel, M. 2004. "Pandillas Juveniles en Centroamérica o la Difícil Búsqueda de Justicia en una Sociedad Violenta." *Desacatos* 14: 85–104.

Mair, L. 1962. *Primitive Government: A Study of Traditional Political Systems in Eastern Africa*. London: The Scholar Press.

Moser, C. O. N. 1998. "The Assets Vulnerability Framework: Reassessing Urban Poverty Reduction Strategies." *World Development* 26 (1): 1–19.

Moser, C. O. N., and A. Winton. 2002. "Violence in the Central American Region: Towards an Integrated Framework for Violence Reduction." Overseas Development Institute Working Paper No. 171, Overseas Development Institute, London.

Nicaragua Network. 2001. *Nicaragua Network Newsletter* 9 (6), February 5–11. http://www.tulane.edu/~libweb/RESTRICTED/NICANEWS/ 2001/ 2001_0205. txt.

Nicholas, R. W. 1966. "Segmentary Factional Political Systems." In *Political Anthropology*, eds. Marc J. Swartz, Victor W. Turner, and Arthur Tuden. Chicago: Aldine.

Núñez, J. C. 1996. *De la Ciudad al Barrio: Redes y Tejidos Urbanos en Guatemala, El Salvador y Nicaragua*. Ciudad de Guatemala: Universidad Rafael Landívar/ PROFASR.

O'Donnell, G. 1999. *Counterpoints: Selected Essays on Authoritarianism and Democratization*. Notre Dame: University of Notre Dame Press.

Pearce, J. 1998. "From Civil War to 'Civil Society': Has the End of the Cold War Brought Peace to Central America?" *International Affairs* 74 (3): 587–615.

Rocha, J. L. 2000. "Pandillas: Una Cárcel Cultural." *Envío*, 219. http://www.envio. org.ni/articulo/1012.

Rocha, J. L. 2005. "El Traido: Clave de la Continuidad de las Pandillas." *Envío*, 280. http://www.envio.org.ni/articulo/2982.

Rodgers, D. 1999. "Youth Gangs and Violence in Latin America and the Caribbean: A Literature Survey." World Bank Latin America and Caribbean Region Sustainable Development Working Paper No. 4, World Bank, Washington, DC. http://wbln0018.worldbank.org/LAC/LACInfoClient.nsf/0/ 1e051e74b34f8253852567ed0060dde7?OpenDocument.

Rodgers, D. 2000. *"Living in the Shadow of Death: Violence, Pandillas, and Social Disintegration in Contemporary Urban Nicaragua."* University of Cambridge. Ph.D. dissertation.

Rodgers, D. 2004a. "Haciendo del Peligro una Vocación: La Antropología, la Violencia, y los Dilemas de la Observación Participante." *Revista Española de Investigación Criminológica* 2 (1): 1–24.

Rodgers, D. 2004b. "Disembedding the City: Crime, Insecurity, and Spatial Organisation in Managua, Nicaragua." *Environment and Urbanization* 16 (2): 113–24.

Rodgers, D. 2006a. "Living in the Shadow of Death: Gangs, Violence, and Social Order in Urban Nicaragua, 1996–2002." *Journal of Latin American Studies* 38 (2): 267–92.

Rodgers, D. 2006b. "The State as a Gang: Conceptualising the Governmentality of Violence in Contemporary Nicaragua." *Critique of Anthropology* 26 (3): 277–92.

Rodgers, D. 2007. "Each to their Own: Ethnographic Notes on the Economic Organisation of Poor Households in Urban Nicaragua." *Journal of Development Studies* 43 (3): 391–419.

Rotberg, R. 2004. "The Failure and Collapse of Nation States: Breakdown, Prevention, and Repair." In *Why States Fail: Causes and Consequences*, ed. Robert I. Rotberg. Princeton, NJ: Princeton University Press.

Rubio, M. 1997. "Perverse Social Capital–Some Evidence from Colombia." *Journal of Economic Issues* 31 (3): 805–16.

Sánchez Jankowski, M. 1991. *Islands in the Street: Gangs and American Urban Society*. Berkeley: University of California Press.

Schmitt, C. 1985 [1933]. *Political Theology: Four Chapters on the Concept of Sovereignty*. Cambridge, MA: MIT Press.

Serbin, A., and Diego Ferreyra, eds. 2000. *Gobernabilidad Democrática y Seguridad Ciudadana en Centroamérica: El caso de Nicaragua*. Managua: Coordinadora Regional de Investigaciones Económicas y Sociales (CRIES).

J. J. Sosa Meléndez and J. L. Rocha. 2001." Las Pandillas en Nicaragua. In *Maras y Pandillas en Centroamérica*, eds. ERIC, IDESO, IDIES, IUDOP. Managua: Universidad Centroamericana (UCA).

Taylor, C. 2002. "Modern Social Imaginaries." *Public Culture* 14 (1): 91–124.

Tilly, C. 2002 [1985]. "War Making and State Making as Organized Crime." In *Violence: A Reader*, ed. Catherine Besteman. New York: Palgrave Macmillan.

Vilas, C. M. 1992. "Family Affairs: Class, Lineage, and Politics in Contemporary Nicaragua." *Journal of Latin American Studies* 24 (2): 309–41.

Whyte, W. F. 1955 [1943]. *Street Corner Society: The Structure of an Italian Slum*. 2nd ed. Chicago: University of Chicago Press.

Yablonsky, L. 1963. *The Violent Gang*. New York: Macmillan.

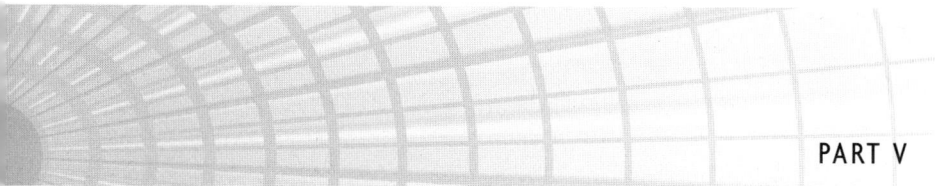

# PART V

# ASSET-BASED LIVELIHOODS STRATEGIES
# AND ECONOMIC EMPOWERMENT

# CHAPTER 11

# Forest Rights and Asset-Based Livelihoods: Catalyzing Rural Economies and Forest Conservation through Policy Reform and Collective Action

*Augusta Molnar, Andy White, and Arvind Khare*

Forests cover about 30 percent of the world's land area. They provide food, wood, medicinal plants, and numerous other goods and services to billions of people worldwide. They harbor a significant portion of the globe's biodiversity and perform a range of environmental services. Yet despite their importance and the substantial efforts that have been made to manage forests in a sustainable manner, this critical share of the global landscape is beset with problems, ranging from persistent poverty to unsustainable use, from illegal exploitation to the loss of cultural and biological diversity.

More than two billion people, a third of the world's population, rely on fuelwood to cook and heat their homes; a similar or greater number use medicinal plants and animals, many harvested from the forests, as their primary source of health care (McNeely and Scherr 2003; Calibre and SCC 2000). Forests are of particular importance to poor women living in rural communities. It is women, more often than men, who search for fuel wood; manage tree gardens around the home; collect, process, and trade nontimber forest products (NTFPs); and search for clean sources of water. The direct overlap between forests and rural poverty in many countries puts forests and forest use at the center of the current national and global debate over poverty reduction, rural development, forest protection and rehabilitation, and sustainable economic growth (WRI and others 2005).

Unfortunately, the contribution that forests could make to rural development, forest conservation, and economic growth has been persistently undermined by conventional approaches to forestry. These often discourage or deny local people's rights to own, use, and trade forest products and services. In many countries, most of the forest estate remains publicly owned and managed, despite legitimate local claims to the forests, extensive occupation by agrarian people, and the limited ability of governments to protect these vast resources.

Furthermore, prevailing models of industrial development and the state subsidies that provide support for forest industries often reinforce this inequity and abuse of local rights. Large-scale industrial forestry makes a relatively small contribution to sustained rural economic growth or sustained government revenues. Private sector commercial concessions in public forests have been hard to control, even after decades of experience with varied regulatory and incentive models. In short, conventional approaches to forestry often perpetuate poverty, reduce biodiversity, and discourage local investment in enterprises that could improve incomes and growth (Scherr, White, and Kaimowitz 2004).

This chapter examines the nature of the ongoing transition in the sector and identifies the challenges and opportunities for promoting asset-based livelihoods that contribute to forest conservation.[1] It analyses the social policy discourse in the environmental and poverty agenda and proposes a new agenda for government, donors, academics, nongovernmental organizations (NGOs), and the private sector that is more consistent with rights and opportunities. The ongoing policy and tenure reforms limit the options of forest people to manage forests as an asset and to provide environmental goods and services from forests that benefit society as a whole.

## Transitions in the Global Forest Sector

Major transitions in the forest sector are under way, creating new opportunities for forest communities, as well as an unfinished agenda for reformers.

### What Has Changed?

Over the past two decades, major changes in the marketplace and in government policies have eliminated historical barriers to community participation in markets to varying degrees. Demand is shifting dramatically, affecting the supply chain. Population growth and the spending power of the middle class in developing countries have led to higher levels of growth in domestic demand than in trade to developed countries. China is the extreme example of rapid demand change—it has moved from being the seventh largest consumer in the world to first in less than a decade, importing more than 100 m$^3$ of timber per year (Xu and others 2004). This has had a serious impact on forest governance in Asia and the Russian Far East, where there is overharvesting of logs and rapid increases in supply of timber and wood products from South East Asia and in softwoods globally (Xu and others 2004). A vibrant manufacturing sector in the Mekong region relies on imported wood supplies, with processing completely disconnected from the main forested areas and forest dwellers of these countries. India is close behind China in its growing wood demand, also relying heavily on imports, mainly from Africa, while its own forest population is underemployed and often living in poverty.

The forest industry has two major components:

• Large-scale industry consumes half of the timber volume but employs fewer people and is focused on plantations and commercial concessions in public lands.
• Small-scale industry constitutes the bulk of employment and is more linked to natural forests and smallholder plantations.

### Large-scale Industry

Processing industries of commodity wood, and pulp and paper face increasing competition and are consolidating rapidly to take advantage of new technologies and contracted timber from industrial-scale plantations outside natural forests. The top 50 companies processed 41 percent of all timber a few years ago; fewer companies will process the same amount in the future (Lebedys 2004). Over the past century, forest plantations have increased from a negligible share to more than 187 million hectares worldwide. Outgrower schemes are creating sources of income for farmers; companies contract for raw material purchase, financing, technical assistance, or inputs. Standardization of container shipping has reduced global transport costs so much that Australian, Brazilian, Chilean, and South African softwood is cheaper (free on board) in Baltimore than local pine from North Carolina (Bull and others 2005). Advanced technologies enable large processors to handle smaller-dimension wood, particularly from plantations, and wood substitutes (Mater 2003).[2]

*Small-Scale Industry*

The other half of the forest industry is based on small- and medium-scale enterprises in the wood and nonwood product sector. Many opportunities exist in furniture manufacture, construction finishing, remodeling, and rattan and bamboo products. Approximately 30 million of the 47 million permanent jobs in the forest industry are found in informal, small enterprises, of which many have less than 20 employees (Poschen and Lovgren 2001). While statistics are generally not complete for tropical countries, specific country surveys and information from other sources confirm that small- and medium-scale enterprises are the main component of forest industry in these countries as well (FAO 2005; WRI and others 2005). Small- and medium-scale enterprises make up 96 percent of all enterprises in Brazil, 20 percent of GDP, and the bulk of Brazilian forest sector operations (May, Goncalves da Vinha, and Mcqueen 2003). They constitute 95 percent of all forestry enterprise activity in India (Bose and Saigal 2004), of which only 150,000 out of 500,000 jobs are in the formal sector (May, Goncalves da Vinha, and Mcqueen 2003).

Locally, greater domestic demand offers local producers a competitive edge to supply nearby markets (Bull and White 2002). Ecosystem service markets and forest certification create new green market options, although until now communities in certified markets have been highly dependent on subsidies from the government or donor initiatives (Molnar, Scherr, and Khare 2004). Forest certification is a positive step for more sophisticated enterprises that learn from the management evaluation process and can demonstrate sustainability to government and society through obtaining an ecolabel. Some local producers benefit from niche markets with exports to Europe or U.S.-certified markets.[3]

*Nonwood Forest Products*

Nonwood forest products (NWFPs) markets are also highly segmented. These markets include thousands of products and millions of people. Natural medicinal products, foodstuffs, condiments, raw material fibers, thatching and bedding, flowers and ornamental plants, animals and animal products, and utensils are increasing in value and scale in domestic and international markets. High-value products from natural forests tend to be overharvested as their international trade expands, compared with the relative sustainability of NWFPs that can now be cultivated (Shanley, Pierce, and Laird 2005). Some bark extracts from tropical hardwoods with high medicinal potential are forecast to disappear completely within one or two decades because of the fierce competition for use of the species as timber, such as *pau d'arco* in the Amazon (Shanley, Pierce, and Laird 2005). Others, such as rattan or bamboo, have flourished because they are less regulated than comparable wood species (Ruiz-Perez and others 2004).

Developing country elites and some developed country markets are increasingly interested in traditional fibers, herbs, medicines, food preparation, wood species for furniture and flooring, and ornaments that are harvested or produced by local people. Niche markets for wood and non-wood products, which are expanding as a result of interest from both domestic and global consumers, tend to require a greater degree of market awareness and organization to produce the quantities and qualities demanded (Campbell, Cunningham, and Belcher 2005).

### Policies and Regulations

Governments are exploring new institutional arrangements for forest management and development. Government-led models (such as industrial concessions in public forests and protected areas with minimal commercial use) and more participatory but locally controlled government and NGO-led models (such as social forestry, private conservation concessions, and buffer zone programs) have given way to market-driven strategies. In parallel, communities have been allocated forest concession areas (such as Petén Guatemala) and conservation concessions to areas of priority biodiversity. Tenure transfer has been incomplete in many instances, with continued restrictions on access and use of forests, or strict regulations (White and Martin 2002). Comanagement models for parks or forests often continue to vest most decision-making authority with government or nongovernmental park officials (Molnar, Scherr, and Khare 2004).

Under most forest arrangements, markets have tended to bypass or harm the poor as a result of various internal and external factors. Externally, politicized rules have facilitated the emergence of monopoly sellers and buyers. Subsidies to industry scale forestry and commercial plantation outside of natural areas have combined with discriminatory market policies to limit community competitiveness, with more than US$20 billion spent on commercial plantation subsidies between 1994 and 1998—eight times the expenditure on conservation (Scherr, White, and Kaimowitz 2004). Regulations have criminalized large segments of the marketplace—including fuel-burning industries, headloading, small-scale sawmilling, non-timber product collection in state forests—or have made compliance burdensome and costly (Contreras-Hermosilla 2004).

Many reforms in favor of communities have been partial, limiting use rights. This is the case in the Amazon region, where indigenous communities can engage in commercial enterprises only with special permits (Sousa and Gomes 2005). Internal factors limiting market participation within communities include inadequate finance and poor information and technology flows. Poor producers lack market links, are unable to exploit economies of scale due to size and organizational gaps, and lack business expertise (Scherr, White, and Kaimowitz 2004).

### Changes in Global Forest Tenure

A significant shift has occurred in global forest tenure, with the doubling of the area under community ownership or administration over the past 15 years. This is an active trend, with every indication that communal tenure will double again over the next 15 years (see figure 11.1).

The recognition of traditional and indigenous peoples' rights or reservation of forest lands for community administration has important implications for the forest policies of forest-rich countries—both developed and developing—and for the nature of their forest conservation and forest economies. It creates an asset for forest producers that can be harnessed for their own development. The challenge for policy makers and governments is to reform outdated regulatory and incentive frameworks to support community management of the forests for income, conservation, and rural livelihood and well-being.

**Figure 11.1. Changes in Community Forest Tenure—Now and in the Next Decade**

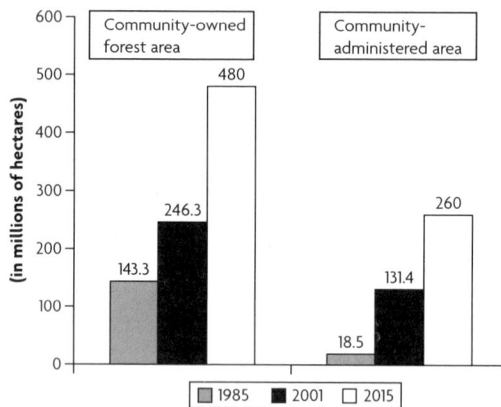

Source: White and Martin 2002.
Note: Community Forest Management totaled 377 million hectares in 2001 and at least 740 million hectares by 2015. Community-administered forests in 2001 were three times the forest area under private sector or industrial ownership.

## Changes in the Patterns of Conservation

There is a growing recognition of the extent of human presence in the most biodiverse regions, both inside and outside of public protected areas. More than one billion people (at least 25 percent of whom are malnourished) who live in the 25 global biodiversity "hot spots" identified by *Conservation International* subsist on less than US$1 dollar per day (McNeely and Scherr 2001). Population growth in the world's last remaining wilderness areas is twice the world average (Cincotta and Engleman 2000). Recognizing this change, the recent Durban Accord endorsed a more mainstream approach to biodiversity that moves beyond protected areas and seeks to address root causes of biodiversity loss and to promote biodiversity at a landscape level (World Parks Congress 2003).

The current system of public protected areas is severely underfunded with declining allocations, and includes only a subset of the world's priority biodiversity and natural habitats (Khare and others 2005). Moreover, current proposals for expanding public protected areas in many developing countries continue to be made without adequate appreciation of their impacts on human rights, or the social, economic, or political costs or alternative choices. Just as expanding public protected areas to any great extent is not an option in most developing countries, effective exclusion of population from many parks is neither viable nor affordable.

Evidence from a range of sources indicates that, in parallel with the transition in community forest tenure, there is a large forested area in which communities invest an important amount in conservation, most outside of public protected areas. Not only are communities important conservation agents; they collectively invest more in forest conservation than governments, the private sector, or the international community. According to recent data from Africa, the Americas, and Asia more than 370 million hectares are being conserved, with varying degrees of effectiveness, in systems in community lands, in public forests where communities practice active management, and in forest-agriculture mosaics.

Figure 11.2 combines the global threat overlay created by First Nations Development Institute (FNDI) and Local Earth Observation (LEO), comparing relationships among forests, tenure, biodiversity, global hot spots, and human presence, with community conservation data from numerous case studies to provide a lower estimate of the scope of community conservation.[4] The data exclude public protected areas but include buffer zones of some reserve sites where communities have legal rights—such as the Maya Biosphere in Guatemala.

**Figure 11.2. Community Conservation Overlay on Biodiversity in Plant and Bird Distributions**

COMMUNITY CONSERVATION OVERLAY ON BIODIVERSITY IN PLANT AND BIRD DISTRIBUTIONS

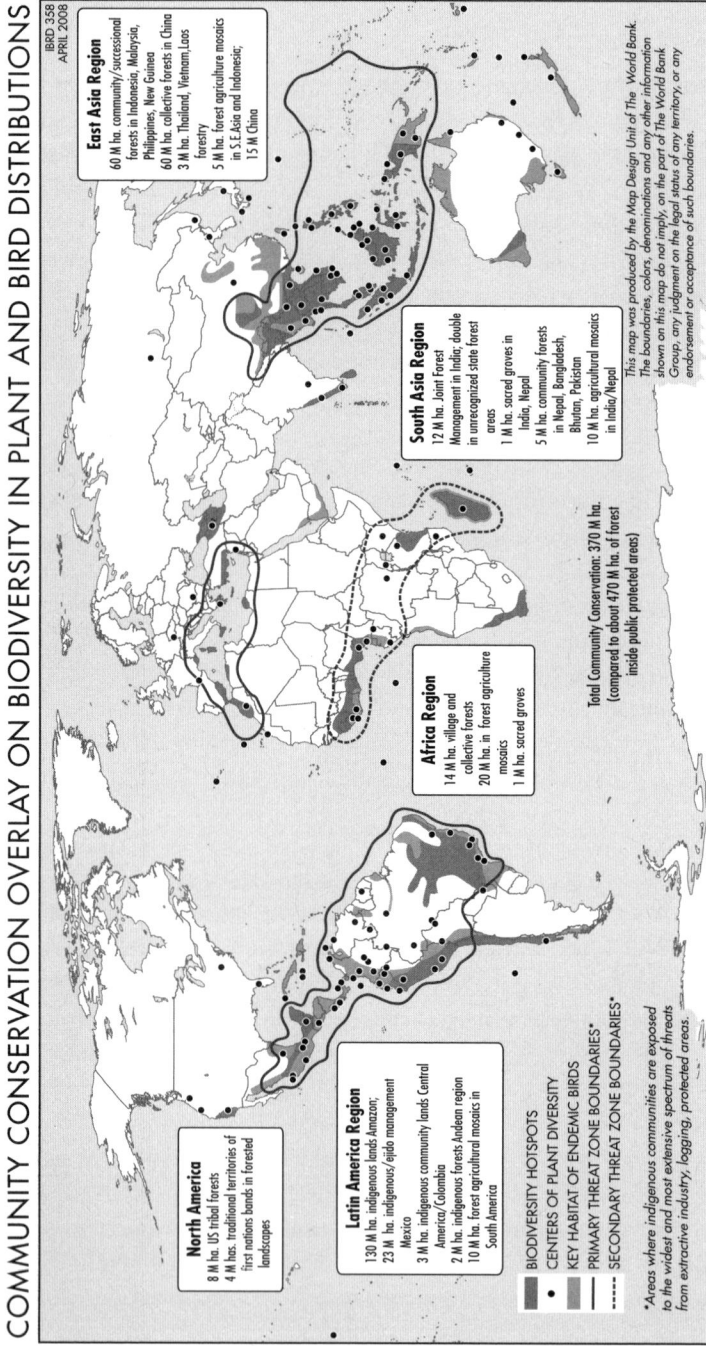

IBRD 358
APRIL 2008

**East Asia Region**
60 M ha. community/successional forests in Indonesia, Malaysia, Philippines, New Guinea
60 M ha. collective forests in China
3 M ha. Thailand, Vietnam, Laos forestry
5 M ha. forest agriculture mosaics in S.E. Asia and Indonesia; 15 M China

**South Asia Region**
12 M ha. Joint Forest Management in India; double in unrecognized state forest areas
1 M ha. sacred groves in India, Nepal
5 M ha. community forests in Nepal, Bangladesh, Bhutan, Pakistan
10 M ha. agricultural mosaics in India/Nepal

**Africa Region**
14 M ha. village and collective forests
20 M ha. in forest agriculture mosaics
1 M ha. sacred groves

Total Community Conservation: 370 M ha. (compared to about 470 M ha. of forest inside public protected areas)

**North America**
8 M ha. US tribal forests
4 M ha. traditional territories of first nations bands in forested landscapes

**Latin America Region**
130 M ha. indigenous lands Amazon;
23 M ha. indigenous/ejido management Mexico
3 M ha. indigenous community lands Central America/Colombia
2 M ha. indigenous forests Andean region
10 M ha. forest agricultural mosaics in South America

BIODIVERSITY HOTSPOTS
CENTERS OF PLANT DIVERSITY
KEY HABITAT OF ENDEMIC BIRDS
PRIMARY THREAT ZONE BOUNDARIES*
SECONDARY THREAT ZONE BOUNDARIES*

*Areas where indigenous communities are exposed to the widest and most extensive spectrum of threats from extractive industry, logging, protected areas.

This map was produced by the Map Design Unit of The World Bank. The boundaries, colors, denominations and any other information shown on this map do not imply, on the part of The World Bank Group, any judgment on the legal status of any territory, or any endorsement or acceptance of such boundaries.

Source: Community conservation data have been compiled by the authors in the global biodiversity map in the Global Threat Overlay map series prepared by the First Nations Development Institute (FNDI) and Local Earth Observation (LEO). FNDI, 2003.

264

Community-conserved forest landscapes identified in the three geographic regions fall into four main categories, based on forest use intensity, cultural relationship, and historic forest use:

- *large, contiguous areas of natural forest that are only lightly used and are legally owned or administered by indigenous and traditional communities in their ancestral territories* (minimum 120 million hectares).
- *forest landscape mosaics that contain large patches of natural habitat interspersed with concentrated land uses, owned or administered by long-settled communities*: Land use activities include natural forest management, agroforestry, agriculture, or grazing in converted lands (minimum 100 million hectares).
- *forest frontier zones where recent settlers are extractivists, agriculturalists, and pastoralists, with or without legal rights over their resources*: Land uses include low-intensity use of the remaining forest and agroforestry or grazing that conserves ecosystem functions (minimum 50 million hectares).
- *intensively-managed landscapes where long-settled communities practice individual and community-based resource management and restoration* but may or may not have legal resource rights (minimum of 100 million hectares).

Community conservation is not a solution for biodiversity conservation any more than public protected areas. It would be wrong to directly compare them or suggest that one is superior Community conservation clearly entails more active land use than public protected areas. What are now public protected areas are often products of past land use by indigenous and other communities.

However, communities offer new institutional models for conservation that should be strengthened (Borrini-Feyerabend and others 2004; Geisler 2002). Some traditional communities in large intact forests (Type 1) require more secure tenure rights and legal use rights, support for building local institutions, and skills for better conservation outcomes. Others require stronger partnerships with their government or private partners where their presence and control of boundaries are under threat from outsiders. Successful community managers in fragmented forest landscapes (Type 2) have developed organizational structures that have competitive advantages that outside models too often seek to change rather than replicate. Communities in newly settled forest areas (Type 3) tend to require clarified and stronger tenure rights and more outside assistance to develop their management structures and seek viable enterprises. Communities that are actively restoring forested landscapes or agriculture-forest mosaics (Type 4) may already have secure tenure rights. Yet policies or regulations often place formidable barriers and create disincentives for these communities to undertake conservation or economic activities.

This opportunity is very relevant in the emerging discussions on the impacts of climate change and the importance of reducing emissions through avoided deforestation. Forest carbon entering atmosphere as a result of clearing or degradation of cover currently contributes 25 percent of the world's carbon emissions. The recent Stern Report produced for Great Britain's government argues that the least costly means of capturing or reducing carbon emissions is through avoided deforestation, and argues that too little attention has been paid to the role of local forest dwellers and low-income producers living near the forests (Stern 2006). Until now, most of the solutions identified for avoiding deforestation have assumed greater command and control or payments for non-use, but not looked at the synergies with community management or local liveihoods (Stern 2006).

## Communities and Markets

### Opportunities for Low-income Producers

In Latin America, where forest policy reforms have favored local forest communities, the new political and tenure agenda has led to the emergence of a large number of diverse and dynamic community forest enterprises (**CFEs**) Bray and Merino 2003; Gretzinger 1998; Bray and others 2003; Barry and others 2003; Chemonics 2003). These enterprises supply timber, wood, and some nonwood products, while providing a wealth of other goods and services to society and the community, including investments in biodiversity. In agricultural frontier regions of Central America, CFEs have developed along similar lines to Mexico, but under different tenure arrangements.

In Bolivia, the response to new, comprehensive, legal frameworks established as part of a sectoral reform in the 1990s has opened lowland forests to management by indigenous communities and agricultural settlers in the tropical Amazon and linked them to remote markets. There, the number of hectares managed by community enterprises has increased from zero in 1999 to 1.1 million in 2003, while smallholder production has increased fivefold (Pacheco 2002, 2004; Contreras-Hermosilla and Vargas

Ríos 2002). In Brazil, new forest legislation recognizes that small-scale producers are the main suppliers of the Amazon Basin's timber and numerous nonwood forest products and gives greater use rights in indigenous reserves. Smallholders and communities in areas in the agrarian and ranching expansion are given more secure forest rights, and protected areas and commercial concessions are demarcated (Smeraldi and Verissimo 1999; Shanley and others 2005).

Accordingly, can low-income producers and communities supply a significant share of market demand in these countries sustainably? At a global level, research analysis by the Centre for International Forestry Research (CIFOR) and Forest Trends has identified a range of market opportunities for poor producers in large and niche markets (Scherr, White, and Kaimowitz 2004):

- commodity and pulp wood from farm forests and outgrower schemes
- high-value timber from communities with secure rights and organization
- nontimber forest products from communities and organized farmers and collectives
- integrated processing by more sophisticated communities and cooperatives
- carbon offsets in regions that can achieve large-scale landscape coverage and water payments in key water catchments
- certified wood where communities have high-quality products.

Community enterprises create a different economy than individual enterprise or private industry. Time scales are longer for resource management, both for generating employment and for conserving forest to support their livelihoods and social and cultural values. CFEs invest more locally, fostering social cohesion, longer-term equity, and social investments. Organizational structures can be more flexible; they are able to switch among different blends of products and self-exploit, that is, not pay themselves the true cost of labor or provide voluntary in-kind inputs and not remunerate themselves when profits come in, when necessary—as well as absorb labor costs during difficult stages of operation or transition. Moreover, they often apply traditional knowledge and innovative approaches and find new ways to boost employment and diversify income strategies.

More important, CFEs can be very profitable. Case study examples from Mexico, Guatemala, India, Mexico, and Nepal show returns of from 10 percent to 50 percent from timber and NWFP activities. Rising prices of hardwoods, other natural forest species, and selected non-wood forest products, and increasing consumption of natural medicinal products, traditional foods, and crafts all favor CFE economies.

### Barriers to Market Access and Participation

As with other small- and medium-sized enterprises (SMEs), market barriers limit the success of CFEs. Internally, they can be constrained by social conflicts, lack of skills, and past deforestation; externally, they can be constrained by limited road and energy infrastructure or credit and finance access. Government reinforces barriers with artificial size allocations or unreasonable permit limits that affect an already small-scale production. In riskier country settings with unstable economies and/or social conflicts, new CFEs lack the reputation with consumers to enter markets.

Above all, regulatory and policy barriers can constrain CFE emergence and growth. While tenure rights have been recognized or expanded in many forest areas, implementation of new legislation can be very slow and allocation rights to access and use forests and forest products unreliable. For example, while 160,000 hectares of The Gambia is officially in community forest, only 14,000 hectares are effectively transferred. In Cameroon, only 40,000 of the more than one million hectares for community management are effectively transferred.

Regulatory frameworks impose slow and costly permit processes, employ unworkable business models, or require nonexistent formal documents—processes that encourage corruption and rent-seeking. Even in Vietnam, where permits are not needed for the harvesting of produce, officials issue fines on overweight transport vehicles carrying legal loads (IIED 2004).

Mandatory management plans can cost several times more than the returns from a community enterprise. Such plans require environmental and technical standards that many public forests fail to meet, and promote exactly the unsustainable practices that standards are supposed to prevent. In short, markets for NTFPs are notoriously restricted.

Taxation structures often make the mistake of imposing taxes at the point of extraction or primary processing, rather than seeking to maximize fiscal revenues from the full economic value chain. Studies of enterprises in Mexico have found that the elimination of stumpage fees has enabled community enterprises to invest more, increase staff numbers, diversify productive activities, boost trade and retail product sales, and fuel improvements and investments in the rural economy. Direct and indirect government subsidies to support plantation programs; tax breaks to larger forest industries, along with preferential provision of infrastructure; and technical and financing support to others in the sector all create unfair competition (Myers 2003).

## Role of Community Associations and Networks in Promoting Reforms

One response to the challenges from community forest managers has been the development of networks and associations, many emerging during the 1990s. As Marcus Colchester and colleagues have summarized (Colchester and others 2003), national forest associations have emerged in the Amazon Basin, India, Indonesia, Nepal, and Thailand. While still at the early stages of development, some associations and networks have begun to form higher-level associations (Colchester and others 2003). Subregional and national groups from different countries have begun to collaborate to take action in the international arena, often with support from international NGOs. In 1991, the Indigenous and Campesino Coordinating Association for Central American Community Agroforestry (ACICAFOC) emerged to press for reforms in favor of coalition communities. The International Alliance of Indigenous and Tribal Peoples of the Tropical Forests was established as a result of coalitions in Amazonia and the Philippines.

The International Network of Forests and Communities was founded in 1998. It currently has 400 members in 54 countries who promote sustainable community forestry. It recently evolved into the Global Caucus on Community Based Forest Management (GCCBFM) (see http://www.gccbfm.org/en/about.php). While most organizations have concentrated their efforts on acquiring and protecting land and forest rights, GCCBFM is more active in lobbying for major reforms in forest markets to benefit local producers.

## Making Markets Work for Communities

### Community Ownership of Environmental Regulatory Processes

One issue policy makers will have to address is the equity of national environmental regulatory frameworks and environmental safeguards. Making investor and donor social responsibility policies socially inclusive and enabling communities and their associations to retain control of these processes, standards, and values will present a substantial challenge.

Two instruments for sustainable forestry illustrate the dilemmas for social actors—the Forest Law and Enforcement Governance (FLEG) initiative for combating illegal logging in the tropics; and forest certification schemes, for which Forest Stewardship Council (FSC) certification has been the standard in tropical forests. Communities have limited leverage in either, because too few organizations attend policy-making events internationally and because their political influence as stakeholders in national processes is limited by existing power relationships and their own capacity.

The FLEG process includes commitments from buyers of tropical hardwoods and wood from temperate and boreal natural forests to purchase legally obtained wood, and from producer countries to establish governance measures against illegal logging. In countries where the rights of local people to forest resources are lacking, and policies and regulations for extraction either are unclear or costly to implement, much of the forest extraction and trade carried out by local people is also defined as illegal, even when these activities have a long history or are key to local livelihoods and incomes. Where FLEG processes are sensitive to these issues, they can lead to positive change. Otherwise, they penalize the poor, while allowing the wealthy to circumvent the rules. Poor legislation can make entire markets illegal—headloading by women in India, wood kiln usage by potters in Mexico, or smallholder forests in the Brazilian Amazon.

In parallel, forest certification is a market-based instrument for measuring sustainability. Until now it has been affordable only for those with high-value timber, exporting to markets that demand certified products, favoring plantations over natural forests, large operations over small, and associations of producers over individual smallholders or communities. As a prize for good management, certification can be a beneficial label for community enterprises and cooperatives. For enterprises that are new or far from the established standards and criteria, certification can become a barrier to entry to international markets and market chains. In some countries, government certification of public forests has resulted in squelching land claims by private citizens on these forests (Cashore, Auld, and Newsom 2005).

There is a danger of concentrating the market demand and market chain for certified forest products to exclude most small-scale and tropical natural forest enterprises in favor of industrial scale natural or plantation forestry or temperate growing regions where forest management is less costly. There is an additional danger of imposing standards on emergent community enterprises without understanding local innovation, losing cultural practices or manipulating fragile institutions and undermining their viability (Markopoulos 1999). The Forest Stewardship Council (FSC) has sought to modify standards and criteria for small-scale operations, as well as for group certification to save costs and tighten procedures. These provide more flexibility to smaller operations but still need flexibility in different social contexts.[5] A third danger emerges from the focus on timber or high-value NTFPs with known management standards; when enterprises generate diversified products and services, including NTFPs or cultural or ecosystem services, developing and conforming to standards becomes too costly (Shanley, Pierce, and Laird 2005). In addition, forest communities increasingly face issues of multiple certifications—organic farming, tourism, timber, ecosystem services—all with additional rules and costs not tailored to local payoffs. In the United States, where most wood produced comes from private, mostly smallholder holdings, less than 5 percent of smallholders are certified or interested in certification because of the problems it brings. In Europe, certification has been highly effective in regions where farmers are already organized as collectives, or where companies take steps to ensure they can meet conditions (Cashore, Auld, and Newsom 2005).

As more institutions such as the World Bank endorse voluntary forest certification as an investment criterion, making it "mandatory" for community enterprises approaching scale or partnering with private industry, the need to get the policy right increases. FLEG and certification can either support or completely undermine those communities with fragile tenure recognition and emergent management strategies.

## Creating Enabling Conditions for Community Enterprises

A historic opportunity has arisen to make dramatic improvements in the incomes and livelihoods of forest producers and communities in developing countries. The next few decades are particularly critical. The forest development and conservation approaches dominant today do not adequately reflect the aspirations of local people, and markets and policies still serve external rather than local interests. Moreover, local, national, and international institutions have artificially segmented forestry into different branches—biodiversity protection, watershed management, and production forestry—each focused on controlling land use rather than inspiring development, and none with the political weight or competence to control forest markets. Although important gains have been made in establishing protected areas, conditions of the forest poor and forests beyond the parks have deteriorated.

As developing countries begin to recognize tenure rights of rural people in forests, decentralize, and modify their regulatory frameworks to include new incentives and controls and institutional responsibility and authority, it is vital that policy makers understand the opportunities and threats that such changes can bring. Transitions in the forest sector, including changes to the rights of indigenous and other communities, and new demands and markets for products and environmental services, undoubtedly present new challenges. Policy makers need to ensure that forest policy reforms benefit low-income producers, strengthen tenure rights, and enable community access to green markets and international forest carbon trading opportunities that yield benefits in social, environmental, and economic terms. Similarly, there needs to be a shift in focus from exclusively protected areas to a judicious blend of approaches. This would not only advance biodiversity conservation and mitigate impacts of climate change but also benefit low-income forest producers.

Historically, however, social policy has not been particularly helpful in advancing these issues. Poor analysis of the overall social, environmental, economic, and political framework within which communities manage their forests has led to criticisms of wooly thinking (Sanderson and Redford 2006). There has been a mixing of first- and third-generation issues, with most communities under threat to defend even their first-generation gains and rights. Communities complain that much of the funds allocated to forests has been spent on fees—to government, to planning, to third-party consultants and specialists, to reporting and monitoring. They rightly look to markets to provide them with more freedom of movement, but where is the support to reach those markets?

## Conclusions and Recommendations

Social policy has a key role to play in helping guide sound forest policy reforms, appropriate to national and regional contexts and market realities—to secure forest tenure and access, reduce the regulatory burden, level the playing field for local producers, invest in essential public goods infrastructure, and involve low-income producers in policy negotiations (Hudson 2005; Kaimowitz 2003, 2004). This requires more strategic understanding of the transition under way, of the lessons learned in successful policy reforms, and of the implications of new environmental instruments and global goals. It also requires supporting participation by the emerging associations and networks of forest communities, not only civil society advocates. For the forest sector, an ambitious agenda is needed, given that 40 percent of the developing world's forests will be community-owned or administered by the year 2015.

Successful models have a long history; for example, most commercial forest enterprises in Latin America have more than 10 years of experience. With overseas development assistance increasingly rare, it is crucial to target resources and interventions strategically, with the largest payoff for indigenous peoples and other forest producers. Environmental "do no harm" or "minimum standards" need to fit the reality of small-scale forests. In the community-conserved areas discussed above, traditional communities in large intact forests (Type 1) require more secure tenure rights and legal use rights, and support for building local institutions and skills (Borrini-Feyerabend and others 2004; Geisler 2002). These and recent settlers (Type 3) require stronger partnerships with their government or private partners where their presence and control of boundaries are under threat from outsiders. Those actively working to restore habitat are prime candidates for prioritized support from conservation and rural land agencies to match their efforts and improve the technical models and inputs.

It is possible to achieve the seemingly irreconcilable goals of alleviating poverty, conserving forests, and encouraging sustained economic growth in forested regions. However, for this to happen, the rights of poor communities to forests and trees, as well as their rights to participate fully in markets and the political processes that regulate forest use must be recognized and strengthened. In fact, people-oriented forestry creates important opportunities to reduce impacts of climate change by avoided deforestation, reduce civil conflicts in the forested regions, and reduce poverty through improved forest-related livelihoods. The Millenium Development Goals—to eradicate extreme poverty and to ensure environmental sustainability, with a target of halving the proportion of people whose income is less than US$1 a day by 2015—will not be met in many developing countries unless forest tenure and rights are significantly reformed (Hudson 2005).

Governments have a key role to play in enabling and establishing rules; this role should be enabling rather than directive. An agenda that can move communities and forest conservation forward would include the following:

- secure tenure rights and resource access; respecting indigenous peoples' rights and development aspirations
- adequate institutional regulatory and policy support and flexibility to strengthen local community institutions

- fair access to markets, including green markets
- finance channeled in a flexible way to complement local initiatives, rather than designing models from outside or governing from above
- engagement of communities in conservation science and as research partners.

Technical assistance and support should be analyzed as an investment, not a "subsidy" for the productive future of community and local enterprises and of sustainable forests. Supporting local community managers and helping the next generation of community leaders to take control of their enterprise and forest management is important for sustained conservation.

## Notes

1. (White and Martin 2002; Scherr, White, and Kaimowitz 2004; Molnar, Scherr, and Khare 2004).
2. The ability to process small dimensions and use substitute materials creates a new challenge for natural forest managers, driving down the price per log and limiting margins for costly forest management, as well as requiring small producers to become more savvy in seeking markets that favor naturally-produced timber.
3. World Wildlife Foundation (WWF) and the Rainforest Alliance have long had programs of support to bring small-scale and large-scale enterprises into certified markets. WWF promotes buyer groups and links them to suppliers, while Rainforest Alliance has been building relationships between certified SMEs and specific industries or retailers for product delivery.
4. Data sources include Cincotta and Engleman 2000; McNeely and Scherr 2002; FNDI and LEO 2003; Barrow, Gichohi, and Infield 2000; Chomitz and others 2004; Borrini-Feyerabend 2002. Other websites, such as the Commission on Economic Environmental and Social Policy (CEESP) and the Thematic Group on Indigenous and Local Communities and Equity in Protected Areas (TILCEPA) in the IUCN knowledge portal assemble a large number of community conservation examples inside protected areas (Borrini-Feyerabend and others 2004).
5. A study in Native American enterprises in the United States, for example, found a strong resistance to spending limited community funds on outside experts to complete certification initiatives, combined with an ideological rejection of the idea that indigenous management choices should be subject to "white" evaluation (Janzen 2002).

# References

Benjamin Cashore, Fred Gale, Errol Meidinger, Deanna Newsom, eds. 2006. *Confronting Sustainability: Forest Certification in Developing and Transitioning Countries*. Yale F&ES Publication Series. New Haven: Yale School of Forestry and Environmental Studies.

Barrow, Edmund, Helen Gichohi, and Mark Infield. 2000. *Evaluating Eden (05)— Rhetoric or Reality? A Review of Community Conservation Policy and Practice in East Africa*. International Institute of Environment and Development. London: Earthscan.

Barry, Deborah, Jeffrey Campbell, James Fahn, Hein Mallee, and Ujjwal Pradhan. 2002. "Achieving Significant Impact at Scale: Reflections on the Challenge for Global Community Forestry." Paper presented at the Rural Livelihoods, Forests and Biodiversity Conference, April 18, Bonn, Germany.

Borrini-Feyerabend, Grazia. 2002. "Indigenous and Local Communities and Protected Areas: Rethinking the Relationship." *Parks* 12 (2): 5–15.

Borrini-Feyerabend, Grazia, Michel Pimbert, M. Taghi Farvar, Ashish Kothari, Yves Renard, eds. 2004. Sharing Power: *Learning-by-Doing in Co-Management of Natural Resources Throughout the World*. Teheran, Iran: International Institute for Environment and Development and World Conservation Union (IUCN/ CEESP/CMWG, Cenesta).

Bose, Sharmistha, and Sushil Saigal. 2004. "Thinking Big about Small-Scale Enterprises." *ITTO Tropical Forest Update* 14 (1).

Bray, David, and P. Klepeis. 2005. "Deforestation, Forest Transitions, and Institutions for Sustainability in Southeastern Mexico, 1900–2000." *Environment and History* 11: 195–223.

Bray, David, P. Negreros, L. Merino-Perez, Juan Manuel Torres Rojo, Gerardo Segura, and H. F. M. Vester. 2003. "Mexico's Community Managed Forests as a Global Model for Sustainable Forestry." *Conservation Biology* 17 (3): 672–77.

Bull, Gary, and Andy White. 2002. "Global Forests in Transition: Challenges and Opportunities for Communities, Commerce and Conservation." Global Perspectives on Indigenous Peoples' Forestry: Linking Communities, Commerce and Conservation: An International Conference Vancouver, British Columbia, Canada June 4–6. http://www.forest-trends.org/resources/meetings. htm#amsterdam2003.

Bull, Gary, Michael Bazett, Olaf Schwab, Sten Nilsson, Stewart Maginnis, and Andy White. 2005. "Subsidies for Industrial Forest Plantations: Impacts and Implications." University of British Columbia, Bazett and Associates, International Institute for Applied Systems Analysis, Forest Trends, World Conservation Union.

Bull, Gary, Mike Bazett, Olaf Schwab, Sten Nilsson, Stewart Maginnis, and Andy White. n.d. "Industrial Forest Plantations Subsidies: Impacts and Implications."

University of British Columbia, Bazett and Associates, International Institute for Applied Systems Analysis, Forest Trends, International Union for the Conservation of Nature. Unpublished article.

Calibre Consultants, and Statistical Service Center. 2000. "Number of Forest-dependent People." In *A Feasibility Study for the UK Department for International Development Forestry Research Programme.* Calibre Consultants and the Statistical Service Center, University of Reading, UK.

Campbell, B., A. Cunningham, and B. Belcher. 2005. "Carving Out a Future: Planning for Woodcarving in the 21st Century." In *Carving out a Future*, eds. A. Cunningham, B. Belcher, and B. Campbell. London: Earthscan.

Cashore, B., G. Auld, and D. Newsom. 2005. *Governing Through Markets: Forest Certification and the Emergence of Non-state Authority.* New Haven, CT: Yale University Press.

Chemonics International, BIOFOR Consortium. 2003. *Community Forest Management in the Maya Biosphere Reserve: Close to Financial Self-Sufficiency?*, ed. C. I. B. Consortium. Guatemala City, Guatemala: USAID/Guatemala.

CIFOR (Center for International Forestry Research). 2005. "Contributing to African Development Through Forests: CIFOR's Strategy for Engagement in Sub-Saharan Africa." Strategy Paper. Bogor, Indonesia: Center for International Forest Research.

Chomitz, Kenneth M. 2004. "Forest Cover and Population Density in Latin America." Research notes, Research Department, World Bank, Washington, DC.

Cincotta, Richard Paul, and Robert Engelman. 2000. *Nature's Place: Human Population and the Future of Biological Diversity.* Washington, DC: Population Action International.

Colchester, M., T. Apte, M. Laforge, A. Mandondo, and N. Pathak. 2003. *Bridging the Gap: Communities, Forests, and International Networks.* Bogor, Indonesia: Center for International Research on Forestry.

Contreras-Hermosilla, Arnoldo, and Maria Teresa Vargas Ríos. 2002. *Social, Environmental and Economic Dimensions of Forest Policy Reform in Bolivia.* Washington, DC: Forest Trends.

FAO (Food and Agriculture Organization of the United Nations). 2005. "Community Based Tree and Forest Enterprises." http://www.fao.org/forestry/site/25491/en.

Geisler, Charles C. 2002. "Endangered Humans." *Foreign Policy* 130 (1): 80–81.

Hudson, J. 2005. "Forestry's Contribution to Poverty Reduction and Trends in Development Assistance." *International Forestry Review* 7 (2): 156–60.

Jansens, Jan-Willem, and Steven Harrington. 2002. "The Place of Third-Party Forest Products Certification in Native American Forestry." In *Forest Certification on Tribal Land*. First Nations Development Institute.

Kahrl, F., W. Horst, and S. Yufang. 2005. *An Overview of the Market Chain for China's Timber Product Imports from Myanmar.* Washington, DC: Forest Trends.

Kaimowitz, D. 2003. "Not by Bread Alone: Forests and Rural Livelihoods in Sub-Saharan Africa." In *Forests in Poverty Reduction Strategies: Capturing the Potential,* ed. T. Oksanen, B. Pajari, and T. Tuomasjukka, eds. European Forest Institute, Joensuu, Finland. EFI Proceedings 47: 45–64. http://www.efi.fi/publications/Proceedings.

———. 2004. "Conventional Wisdom about Sustainable Forest Management and a Pro-Poor Forest Agenda." In *Working Forests in the Neotropics: Conservation through Sustainable Management?,* eds. Daniel J. Zarin, R. R. Janaki, Frances E. Alavalapati, and Marian Putz, 379–87. New York: Columbia University Press.

Khare, Arvind, Andy White, Augusta Molnar, and Sara Scherr. 2005. Forest Finance, Development Cooperation and Future Options. *Review of European Community & International Environmental Law* 14 (3): 247–254.

Lebedys, A. 2004. "Forest Finance: Trends and Current Status of the Contribution of the Forestry Sector to National Economies." Report. Rome: Forest Products and Economics Division of the Food and Agriculture Organization.

Markopoulos, Matthew. 1999. "Community Forestry Enterprise and Certification in Mexico: A Review of Experience with Special Emphasis to the Union of Zapotec and Chinantec Forest Communities." UZACHI, Oaxaca.

Mater, C. 2003. "The U.S. Furniture Industry: Trends in Outsourcing and Emerging Certified Demand." In *From Forest to Furniture: New Green Market Opportunities for China.* Shanghai: Forest Trends.

May, Peter H, Valeria Goncalves da Vinha, and Duncan Macqueen. 2005. *Small and Medium Forest Enterprise in Brazil.* London: Grupo de economia do meio ambiente e desenvolvimento sustentavel Rio de Janeiro, International Institute for Environment and Development.

McNeely, Jeffrey A., and Sara Scherr. 2001. "Common Ground, Common Future— How Ecoagriculture Can Help Feed the World and Save Wild Biodiversity." International Union for Conservation of Nature, Gland, Switzerland.

———. 2003. *Ecoagriculture: Strategies to Feed the World and Conserve Wild Biodiversity.* Washington, DC: Island Press.

Molnar, A., S. Scherr, and A. Khare. 2004. *Who Conserves the World's Forests? Community-Driven Strategies to Protect Forests and Respect Rights.* Washington, DC: Forest Trends.

Myers, N. 2003. "Biodiversity Hotspots Revisited." *Bioscience* 53 (10): 916–17.

Nepstad, D., Schwartzman, S., Bamberger, B., Santilli, M., Ray, D., Schlesinger, P., Lefebvre, P., Alencar, A., Prinz, E., Fiske, G., and Rolla, A. 2006. "Inhibition of Amazon Deforestation and Fire by Parks and Indigenous Lands." *Conservation Biology* 20 (1), 65–73.

Poschen, Peter, and Mattias Lovgren. 2001. *Globalization and Sustainability: The Forestry and Wood Industries on the Move.* Geneva, Switzerland: International Labour Office.

Ruiz-Perez, M., B. Belcher, Maoyi Fu, and Xiaosheng Yang. 2004. "Looking Through the Bamboo Curtain: An Analysis of the Changing Role of Forest and Farm Income in Rural Livelihoods in China." *International Forestry Review* 6 (3–4): 306–16.

Sanderson, Steve, and Kent Redford. 2006. "No Roads, Only Directions." *Conservation and Society* (4) 3: 379–82.

Scherr, S., A. White, and D. Kaimowitz. 2004. *A New Agenda for Forest Conservation and Poverty Reduction: Making Markets for the Ecosytem Services.* Washington, DC: Forest Trends.

Shanley, Patricia, Alan Robert Pierce, and Sarah A. Laird. 2005. *Beyond Timber: Certification of Non-timber Forest Products.* Washington, DC: Forest Trends.

Smeraldi, R. and A. Verissimo. 1999. "Hitting the Target Timber Consumption in the Brazilian Domestic Market and Promotion of Forest Certification." Friends of the Earth Amazonia Programme, São Paulo, Brazil.

Smeraldi, R. 2003. "Expedient plunder? The New Legal Context for Amazonian Logging." *In Growing Exports: The Brazilian Tropical Timber Industry and International Markets*, ed. J. Myers and S. Bass. Small and Medium Enterprises (SME) Series. London, United Kingdom: International Institute for Environment and Development.

Stern, Nicholas. 2007. "The Economics of Climate Change: The Stern Review." London: HM Treasury. http://www.hmtreasury.gov.uk/independent_reviews/ stern_review_economics_climate_change/stern_review_report.cfm.

Sousa, R., and D. Gomes. 2005. *Producao Familiar Rural: Tendencias e Oportunidades de Atividade Madeireira no Acre e Para.* Washington, DC: Forest Trends.

White, A., A. Molnar, and A. Khare. 2004. "Who Owns, Who Conserves and Why It Matters." *ARBORVITAE* 26: 8–11. IUCN/WWF Forest Conservation Newsletter, September. Gland, Switzerland.

White, A., and A. Martin. 2002. *Who Owns the World's Forests? Forest Tenure and Public Forests in Transition.* Washington, DC: Forest Trends.

World Parks Congress. 2003. The Durban Accord. Our Global Commitment for People and Earth's Protected Areas. http://www.iucn.org/wpc2003.

WRI (World Resources Institute), World Bank Group, United National Environment Program, and United Nations Development Program. 2005. *World Resources 2005: The Wealth of the Poor—Managing Ecosystems to Fight Poverty.* Washington, DC: World Resources Institute.

Xu, J., G. Q. Bull, S. Nilsson, A. White, and A.J. Pottinger, eds. 2004. Special issue. "Forestry in China: Policy Consumption in Forestry's Newest Superpower." *International Forestry Review* 6: 237–53.

# CHAPTER 12

# Microenterprise and Sustainable Livelihoods

*Vibha Pinglé*

In situations of entrenched poverty, microenterprises offer individuals a means to support themselves and their families. However, while many people establish microenterprises, only a few succeed in developing their enterprise and generating a sustainable living. To better elucidate the challenges and improve the outcomes, this chapter addresses two key questions:

- What resources and strategies enable some individuals to gain sustainable livelihoods from their microenterprise while others fail?
- What social policies and programs could be developed to assist other people living in poverty to earn sustainable livelihoods and accumulate assets from their microenterprise activity?

In response to the first question, much of the debate has concentrated on the availability of microcredit. That covers the supply side. It does not tell us what kinds of people use microcredit effectively, or the kinds of micro-entrepreneurs who would not consider using microcredit facilities. Consequently, the chapter investigates the demand side of microfinance.

In recent years, the asset building and sustainable livelihoods approaches have been interpreting social policy in innovative ways. The asset-building perspective explores the nexus among assets-institutions-opportunities (Moser 2008) and argues that the process by which asset accumulation occurs is closely related to the institutional and social setting in which it is embedded, as well as the opportunities available to individuals living in that environment. Extending this argument, this chapter explores how women microentrepreneurs enhance their assets and capabilities, the social and institutional circumstances under which they do so, and the kinds of opportunities they find most appealing.

Contrary to conventional wisdom that social capital is significant for entrepreneurial development among poor people, this chapter is based on research indicating that being at the periphery of one's community can be helpful for the development of microenterprises that provide sustainable livelihoods. Associational networks within the community constrain poor women's entrepreneurial abilities by generating pressures to conform.

Based on research on black women microentrepreneurs in South Africa, Muslim women in the Arab Republic of Egypt, and Muslim Hausa-Fulani and Fulani women in Nigeria, this chapter argues that state and nonstate actors can help support women microentrepreneurs to earn sustainable livelihoods and accumulate assets from their entrepreneurial activities by integrating smaller, locally based communities into wider networks that enhance the available opportunities. More important perhaps, the networks inspire them and make them aware of the different ways to generate sustainable livelihoods. Second, states and nongovernmental organizations (NGOs) can assist by adopting policies and programs that promote individual autonomy in the community. Two specific kinds of support are critical for this: childcare support, and convenient emergency and regular medical care. Given this support, women microentrepreneurs are likely to have the autonomy to "exploit" the available opportunities that, in turn, can lead to an increase in their assets.

Here, two notions of community are at play: the internal (the local) and the external (broader social networks linking individuals from various local communities). The former is usually culturally based, is geographically bounded, and can inhibit individual autonomy. The latter, which associated with networks outside the immediate community, can often enhance individual autonomy, especially where it concerns women microentrepreneurs. It is this second notion of community that is critical to the success of women microentrepreneurs.

## Microfinance and Microentrepreneurs

Microfinance institutions emerged because mainstream banks were not meeting the credit and banking needs of economically disadvantaged and vulnerable individuals in developing countries. In addition to providing banking facilities to the poor, many of these institutions are concerned with empowering vulnerable individuals, facilitating developmental activities, and reducing poverty.

Following Robinson (2001), a distinction is proposed between micro finance institutions that adopt the *financial systems approach* and those that adopt the *poverty lending approach*. The former covers limited commercial financial services for economically disadvantaged individuals who are employed or self-employed and the latter involves subsidized financial services (often accompanied by training or other assistance) for economically disadvantaged and marginalized individuals (Kabeer 2005). Poverty lending approaches are particularly concerned not just with offering easy and inexpensive alternatives to high-interest informal moneylenders, but also with providing accessible credit to the poor to be used in entrepreneurial ventures that contribute to sustainable livelihoods and reduce poverty.

How effective are these microfinance institutions at providing banking facilities and credit to the poor and at promoting entrepreneurship and reducing poverty? The available data are not entirely appropriate for answering this question from a comparative perspective. Microfinance institutions have tended to evaluate their performance from the perspective of their sustainability and growth, not in terms of whether their activities contribute toward the accumulation of assets by the population to which they cater, or whether their activity generates sustainable, successful microenterprises (de Aghion and Morduch 2005).

While evaluating the performance of microfinance institutions in terms of their sustainability and, in some cases, profitability is reasonably straightforward, evaluating their impact on poverty reduction, development, and entrepreneurship is more complicated. De Aghion and Morduch (2005) observe that the difficulty of evaluating varying kinds of microfinance programs that service many different types of customers has complicated the evaluation of microfinance programs and the identification of factors that contribute to successful versus unsuccessful programs. Moreover, microfinance programs rarely lend to random economically disadvantaged individuals. Instead, communities, neighborhoods are carefully selected, and potential borrowers are identified based on criterion such as age, education, and social status. This further complicates the analysis of the impact and performance of microfinance programs (de Aghion and Morduch 2005). Many evaluations of impact focus, therefore, only on the "treated" population, ignoring the response of a "control" population. While such evaluations might usefully inform donors of how a microfinance institution might improve its programs, they are not helpful for adequately and rigorously assessing the impact of microcredit on poverty reduction and entrepreneurship.

In a recent article, Kabeer (2005: 4709) attempts to analyze the impact of microfinance on poor women's ability to ameliorate their everyday situation and also focus on their longer-term strategic goals. She concludes that, given the wide variety of microfinance programs offered, it might be more useful to evaluate how specific microfinance organizations in particular contexts have performed than to evaluate microfinance programs in general.

If the impact of microfinance is unclear, so too is who turns to microfinance, in particular, who seeks a loan to develop their microenterprise and who does not. Providing microentrepreneurs access to financial services does not imply that they are using the offered financial services. As a recent World Bank study observes, microentrepreneurs who have access to microfinance might choose to not avail of loans for social or cultural reasons (Beck, Demirguc-Kunt, and Martinez Peria 2005).

Staying with the arguments discussed above, this chapter looks at variations in terms of microfinance usage among women microentrepreneurs and examines the kinds of women microentrepreneurs who consider it appropriate to seek financial assistance for their microenterprise. For this, we study the social, cultural, demographic, and locational attributes of poor women who are able to take advantage of microfinance programs, and examine why they are so equipped. Such an inquiry is intended to lead to the development of policies that are neither caught in anthropological particularities and confusion, nor entrapped in ideological black boxes. More importantly, it will indicate policies that are likely to enable other women microentrepreneurs to succeed.

## The Conceptual Framework

The conceptual framework presented in this chapter builds on the social capital literature and the capabilities approach. Such a framework allows us to think afresh about how the state and nonstate actors (such as NGOs) can contribute toward generating sustainable livelihoods and accumulating assets. It helps us to explicate how individuals interpret the opportunities available to them and how institutions constrain or encourage microentrepreneurs to enhance their assets and capabilities.

## The Social Capital Argument

Social capital literature argues that levels of social capital indicate why economic development occurs in certain communities and not others, and why some entrepreneurs succeed where others fail. According to this argument, entrepreneurs who are embedded in strong social capital networks draw on the high levels of trust to sustain and expand their business, demand better services from the state, and engage in cooperative activities that improve their chances of a better quality of life.

In his classic book on social capital, Putnam (1994) points to the argument made by Piore and Sable (1986) about flexible production in northern Italy. High levels of social capital in northern Italy generate high levels of trust that allow manufacturing firms flexibility in production schedules and processes, such that they are able to outperform their competitors. Does social capital work in a similar manner among the poor women microentrepreneurs?

A review of the available literature offers notoriously unclear evidence. This is partly a function of researchers using varying definitions and indicators for social capital. It is also because of different studies sampling from different categories of poor individuals, and not always recognizing that men and women are likely to use, contribute to, and relate to social capital differently.

Consider, for instance, a study about social capital and its role among agricultural traders in Madagascar. Fafchamps and Minten (2002) argue that traders with greater social capital (that is, strong relationships with suppliers, customers, and other traders) were more successful than those without social capital. They point out that social capital, like other kinds of capital, can be accumulated and has a positive impact on the performance of the trader's business. Their conclusion is based on measuring social capital in terms of the number of relatives in agricultural trade, the number of traders known, the number of people who can help, and the number of suppliers and customers known personally. The Fafchamps and Minten study focuses on male traders—their average respondent was married, had three children, and was in his thirties. It is not clear whether the argument would also apply to women traders and entrepreneurs, and whether it operates in a similar manner across cultural contexts.

A widely cited article, by Narayan and Pritchett (1997), on social capital and household income that defines social capital as the quality and quantity of associational life observes that social capital contributes to household income. Narayan and Pritchett also point out that, in their study, households with more social capital also enjoyed better public services, had adopted more advanced agricultural practices, and used credit for further improving it.

Several important issues, however, remain in need of clarification:

- Did all households and individuals in the village benefit to the same extent, and if they did not, why?
- Did all households and individuals draw on the village social capital? If they did not, why?
- Did all the households and individuals involved in the study put the social capital to which they had access to use in line with developmental goals?

We need to examine variations in the utilization of social capital to explore the impact of social capital on the performance of women microentrepreneurs. This involves specifying the relationship between the social and the individual/household characteristics. Instead of examining associational contexts and their impacts in the aggregate, we need to study how different individuals engage with these associational contexts.

The social capital perspective assumes that the trust and cooperative sensibilities generated by social capital motivate individuals to improve their lives economically, financially, and socially—improvements considered necessary by the development community. We should also consider how social capital motivates individuals to act in ways that undermine the development agenda by enhancing restrictions on women's autonomy, and strengthening cultural values and practices that do not particularly contribute to entrepreneurialism.

For development to be sustainable, it needs to be meaningful and desired by the vulnerable who will benefit, and socially sustainable in a highly multicultural and globalized world. This requires individuals to balance the demand for cultural recognition and respect with that for the enhancement of economic development. Whether and how associational membership makes individual lives meaningful, and how these relate to the development agenda is uncertain. Individual responses need not always be in line with the development agenda. Social capital may best be understood as an organizational device that promotes cooperative and collaborative behavior from any ideological, political, or development perspective. It says nothing about the direction of the cooperative behavior. Being able to cooperate is not the same as desiring economic development.

## The Capability Approach

The development community's attempt to specify trajectories of development has increasingly drawn upon the capability approach proposed by Amartya Sen (1995). According to this approach, development ought to consist of enhancing people's capabilities. If the activities individuals actually engage in are termed *functionings*, then the activities that they might engage in, given their skills, abilities, and opportunities, reflect their *capabilities*. The aim of development is to enlarge or enhance the set of capabilities a person can possess.

This aim is complicated by the fact that local contexts and cultural beliefs and practices influence an individual's desired capability set, and this desired capability set is not always identical to the capability set the development community considers worthwhile. This divergence, important for this chapter, begins to conceptually indicate why credit opportunities that might be useful, or social capital that might prove to be critical for entrepreneurial success, are not always drawn upon (see figure 12.1).

**Figure 12.1. Functionings, Capabilities, Desired Capabilities, and Policy-Defined Desired Capabilities**

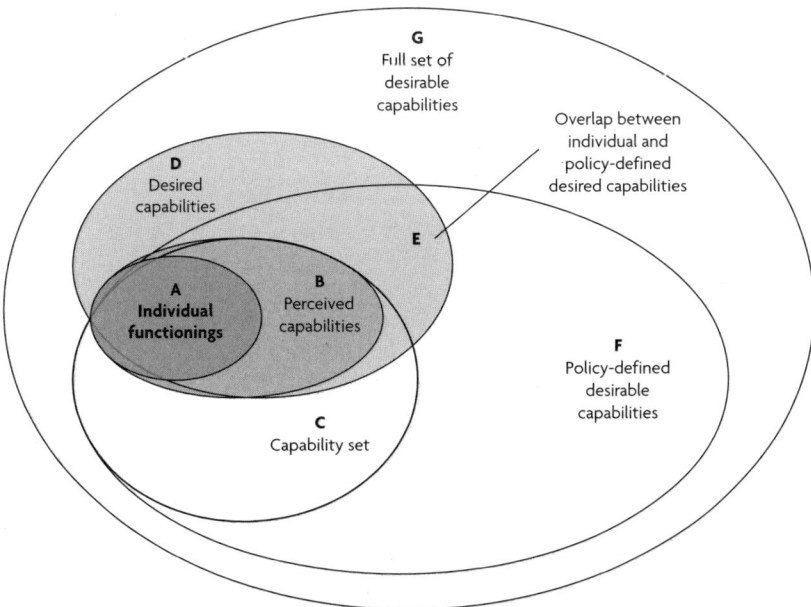

*Source:* Adapted from diagram in paper presented by Pinglé and Houtzager 2003.

The capability set that can be provided to individuals via state programs and policies or NGO intervention needs to be meaningful and desirable to the individuals if it is to contribute toward enhancing their freedoms and enlarging their existing choices or capability set. Teaching a devout woman in Saudi Arabia to drive, and altering the law so she is allowed to drive, is not likely to enhance her freedom in a meaningful way if driving is not part of her desired capability set. If development programs and policies are to enhance the desired capabilities of individuals, we need ways of determining these desired capabilities and factoring them into the design and implementation of the developmental activities.

### Identities and Microenterprise Development

Why some individuals choose not to avail of microfinance opportunities, for example, is partly a function of their identities. Sen (2005: 335) suggests that that, within limits, identities appear to shape the choices an individual makes. This would suggest that the reasons why some individuals choose not to draw upon some resources to succeed economically might be a function of how they see themselves.

Exploring the relationship between identity and development, Appadurai (2004) argues that it is critical to understand an individual's capacity to aspire. He observes that though economically disadvantaged individuals do indeed wish, want, plan, or aspire to improve their socioeconomic condition, poverty diminishes their ability and inclination to aspire. This, unfortunately, impacts their ability to escape poverty.

In principle, the simplest way to discover how identities influence the performance and development of microenterprises would be to conduct surveys investigating what capabilities people desire. Surveys can help us to understand what people aspire to. However, the responses are likely to be influenced by immediate concerns and needs of the respondents, not by a reflection on the overall life people would desire to have and the capabilities they would need to acquire to realize it. An alternative method of discovering people's desired capabilities might be to enquire about the kind of life they would like to have or how they would like to define their identity in the future. Answers to the following questions would provide better insight: "What do they consider a full life?" "What gives them dignity?" "What are the rights and obligations vis-à-vis others?"[1]

In an attempt to find answers to these three questions, informal interviews were conducted with women microentrepreneurs in the Arab Republic of Egypt, Nigeria, and South Africa.[2] In particular, the history of their microenterprise, their relationship to their community, and their aspirations were discussed, and the responses from the three countries were compared.

## Basic Patterns of Social Capital and Microentrepreneurial Performance

Research results show that what enables some microenterprises to generate sustainable livelihoods is less dependent on the type of microenterprise, or on the state's microenterprise policies, or on the availability of capital, as is often believed; success or failure is more dependent on the individual's involvement in associational networks in their community. The greater the number of associational memberships, the less likelihood there was of entrepreneurial success. Membership of one or two groups had minimal negative impact on the performance of microenterprises; but membership of three or four groups significantly decreased the likelihood of the micro-enterprise becoming successful. Microcredit programs, and the self-help groups supported by them, certainly facilitated creation of microbusinesses but did not contribute to the development of these microbusinesses.

Successful microenterprises in the sample were connected to networks outside their community through NGOs, state agencies, or economic associations. These connections informed them of growth possibilities, inspired and motivated them, and provided technical assistance. It is important to add that the NGOs covered in the study were those seeking to promote local developmental initiatives; they were not interested in setting up cooperatives. In other words, the NGOs were concerned with enhancing the capabilities of the women microentrepreneurs, while allowing them the autonomy to engage in entrepreneurial activities regarded as appropriate by the women themselves.

Further, data gathered indicated the reasons why individuals choose to participate in some networks as opposed to others. Such data analysis is critical to identify and fine-tune the social policies that seek to create an enabling environment for individuals to escape poverty. Poor women join associations in their community for social support—whether in the event of medical or family emergencies or for childcare and childrearing support.

*South Africa.* According to the interviews conducted, trust generated within community organizations does not contribute to economic activities and relations. On the contrary, according to the interviewees, the trust generated puts pressure on the women to conform rather than to act in an innovative or entrepreneurial manner. Those involved in fewer associations internally were more successful as microentrepreneurs than those involved in a greater number of internal associations.

The women who developed their microenterprises into successful and sustainable businesses that enabled them to accumulate assets tended to be single, lived at the margins of their communities (in that they had fewer associational ties within their community), and had children older than 10 years of age. Moreover, they were linked to support systems such as NGO networks outside their community. This was true of both urban and rural women.

In the case of both rural and urban women microentrepreneurs in South Africa, relations with their local community were defined by a strong belief in equal dignity. What appeared to dignify them was their ability to gain the respect of their community and also be good mothers. Being a good member of one's community or gaining its respect was considerably more complicated for women heavily involved in local political and social associations. They faced greater pressures than women at the margins of the community who had to meet fewer expectations. Leading a life at the margins meant that the woman was not involved in local political and social organizations or that she attended the meetings but did not participate in the proceedings). In rural areas, it also meant that the woman was unrelated or unconnected to the chief and his family.

Thus, the success of women microentrepreneurs related (a) negatively to how involved they were in their local communities, and (b) positively to their connections to networks and associations outside their community. These NGO networks provided the women microentrepreneurs with information, financial assistance, and/or managerial help. More important, the NGO networks in South Africa had "inspired" many of the women microentrepreneurs to develop their businesses and to regard growth as a possibility.

*The Arab Republic of Egypt.* Egyptian microbusinesswomen operate in a very different cultural setting than those in South Africa because of the dominant role of Islam in the cultural landscape. Nevertheless, the outcomes are more or less the same, even though in the Arab Republic of Egypt, unlike in South Africa, both rural and urban women microentrepreneurs are required to fulfill the obligations of being good Muslim women. Egyptian women microentrepreneurs define their full life as one that enables them to follow the principles of Islam in their daily life—pray at the specified times, visit Mecca at least once in their life, and engage in the activities of their local mosque. They understand their obligations to others in their community and family in accordance with the tenets of Islam.

Three conclusions may be drawn about the factors contributing to, or not contributing to, the success of Egyptian microbusinesswomen. First, in the Arab Republic of Egypt, as in South Africa, membership of local community organizations does not appear to increase a woman micro-entrepreneur's ability to make her business successful. This was true among women living in Cairo, as well as those living in a rural area in Upper Egypt around Minya. While all women in the sample were involved with their local mosque, very few successful microentrepreneurs were members of local community associations. Nearly all of the stagnant and survivalist[3] microentrepreneurs were heavily engaged in extended family networks and activities.

Second, as in South Africa, women who developed their microenterprises into successful, sustainable businesses that enabled them to accumulate assets were single, lived at the margins of their community, and were linked to supportive organizations and networks outside of their community. In interviews, married women suggested that they regarded their role as wives and mothers as more important than their role as microentrepreneurs. Consequently, acquiring the skills to be a successful microbusinesswoman was valued less than acquiring skills that would help in being a better Muslim wife.

In contrast, single women (whether widowed, divorced, or abandoned) had more time to focus on their microbusiness and their ability to succeed was limited only by the economic opportunities available to them. Furthermore, expanding their business allowed them to fulfill their obligations as Muslims, such as making charitable contributions, more easily. Consequently, they had fewer constraints and had the incentive to define an evaluative space that was different from that defined by married microbusinesswomen.

Third, as in South Africa, successful women microentrepreneurs in the Arab Republic of Egypt tended to have teenage or older children. Women noted that whether single or married, having young children meant that they were compelled to join social associations such as self-help groups, rotating credit societies, or women's social groups not primarily to access the credit, but to develop ties with women outside their immediate families who could assist them with childrearing. For the same reason, they were also compelled to maintain strong ties with their extended families.

*Nigeria.* Like the Arab Republic of Egypt, the communities in northern Nigeria lived in a landscape defined by Islam. However, pre-Islamic African traditions and cultural idioms also determined their ways of being and acting. Negotiating the boundaries between the two was not always straightforward and appeared to have had implications for how women microentrepreneurs viewed their activities and regarded themselves. Though the cultural impulses among Muslim communities in northern Nigeria differed in many ways from those among blacks in South Africa or Muslims in the Arab Republic of Egypt, the patterns of entrepreneurial behavior among microentrepreneurs were remarkably similar.

Hausa-Fulani (Muslim) women microentrepreneurs were much more likely to engage in nontraditional businesses than Fulani women microentrepreneurs. However, the former appeared to be more constricted than Fulani Muslim women by religious beliefs and edicts that they perceived as politically driven, frequently including extreme positions and in some aspects contrary to local customs and traditions. In contrast, the Egyptian Muslim microentrepreneurs viewed religion and culture as interwoven. This discouraged poor Hausa-Fulani (Muslim) women from being entrepreneurial. The Fulani women microentrepreneurs interviewed were seemingly able to negotiate the relationship between culture and religion more easily and were more willing to take entrepreneurial risks within their cultural boundaries. Nonetheless, these cultural boundaries circumscribed a very limited space for autonomous action by women. As a result, both groups of Muslim women (Hausa-Fulani and Fulani) faced cultural incentives and constraints—albeit different—that discouraged the success of microenterprises.

Of the 50 microentrepreneurs of both ethnic groups interviewed, only six might be considered successful, 13 stagnant, and the majority, 31, may be categorized only as survivalist. The paucity of successful microenterprises, compared with those identified in South Africa and even the Arab Republic of Egypt, is more likely a reflection of the state of economy in northern Nigeria and the overall opportunities for entrepreneurial development available. Despite this variation, it is interesting to note that single women, women with older children, and women linked to networks outside their communities fared best.

## Broader Implications

In the various communities studied, social pressures to conform (placed by the community on microbusinesswomen) and the absence of connections to external networks appear to undermine the ability of women micro-entrepreneurs to generate sustainable livelihoods from their business.

### Community and Conformity

In all three countries, microbusinesswomen, who were among the poor and very poor in their community, observed that it was difficult to see themselves as businesswomen, because of community pressure to conform to the local cultural ideal of a "good woman."

They saw their entrepreneurial activities as part of their daily household activities, were not comfortable regarding themselves as businesswomen, and certainly not comfortable being viewed by others as businesswomen. All felt compelled to "fit in" with their community and viewed "standing out from the crowd" as difficult because it led to family pressure. Women at the margins of their community were less likely to face the pressure to conform than were women well integrated into the social fabric of the community.

Women microentrepreneurs in the Arab Republic of Egypt, northern Nigeria, and South Africa, in both urban and rural areas, commented that they tried to stay under the social radar to maintain their autonomy. Those who did so were more successful as entrepreneurs. "I mind my own business" and "I keep to myself" were frequent refrains. While all women microentrepreneurs commented on the social pressure to conform to the ideal of a "good woman," married women and women with young children (especially those under the age of 10) faced greater pressure to conform.

*Single women.* Not surprisingly, then, across the sample, single women were much more likely to be successful than married women as microentrepreneurs for several reasons. First, they faced fewer pressures to conform, and those with children over 10 years of age were also less involved in familial networks and claimed they had more autonomy when it came to taking business decisions. Second, because they were more willing to define themselves as businesswomen, they felt comfortable seeking assistance from microfinance institutions and state agencies concerned with supporting microenterprises.

Consider the experience of the 36 South African women (28 of whom were single) who came together to establish a corn mill in a rural community in South Africa a few years ago. They took risks and were clearly entrepreneurial. Their mill was a great success, prompting the women to start other entrepreneurial ventures in the village—a childcare center, a sewing school, and a vegetable farm. During the interviews the women emphatically defined themselves as businesswomen. They sought technical advice as and when needed, and some women from the group had enrolled in an accounting course.

Even in the Arab Republic of Egypt and northern Nigeria, where Islamic restrictions on women's movements and participation in activities outside the home might suggest that single women would be worse off than married women, single women fared better at running a microenterprise. Rashida, who ran a successful embroidery/sewing microenterprise in Cairo, explained that as a widow she only had to satisfy the demands placed on her by her religion and religious leaders and her microenterprise. As a married woman, she would have to satisfy the demands of her husband and his family as well. Rashida's house was as precarious as the rest of the dwellings in Cairo's Mansheit Nasser neighborhood, yet she and her microenterprise were anything but precarious. She stitched and embroidered clothes worn by belly dancers. She sold these clothes to shops in the markets of old Cairo—shops frequented by foreign tourists. Rashida's neighbor, Heba, stood in sharp contrast. Heba started her sewing business because her husband's salary was insufficient to support their family. However, her business was not successful. Her familial obligations and ties with her in-laws compelled her to cater to their needs and demands, and this, she observed, had limited her opportunities for growth.

Also illustrative is Salamatu's experience in Nigeria. Salamatu supported her five teenage children with the income from her *fura* (cooked millet cakes) business. Salamatu's business was very popular with local residents, both in her village and the neighboring town. She said that she saved up money after her divorce to launch her *fura* business and was careful about how she conducted it. She remarked that she would like to apply for a loan to expand her business so as to be able to compete with the larger *fura* businesses.

Women owning and running a bakery in the Eastern Cape in South Africa also observed that, since many of them were single (or single by default as their husbands were migrant workers in Johannesburg, Port Elizabeth, and elsewhere) they were able to devote a considerable amount of time to the bakery business—something they would not have been able to do had their husbands been around.

Single women viewed themselves as businesswomen to a greater extent than married women. They regarded themselves as the heads of their households, the primary breadwinners, and argued that so long as they had the tacit approval of their community they were fine. Married women appeared to face the pressure to conform to community norms to a greater extent than single women. In the Arab Republic of Egypt, northern Nigeria, and to a lesser extent in South Africa, poor married women had a harder time getting the tacit approval of their community for defining themselves as businesswomen. This did not mean that they were not allowed to work to support the household income; it did mean that they were not encouraged to be highly successful at it and to view themselves as businesswomen.

*Women with young children.* One factor that compelled both married and single women to immerse themselves in community networks was having to raise young children. Women with young children drew on familial and community networks for support with childcare and childrearing. While clearly a benefit, these networks also constrained women from becoming successful microentrepreneurs, unfortunately undermining the woman's ability to run business in ways that promoted entrepreneurialism and innovation.

As a group of young women microentrepreneurs in Soweto observed, their self-help group helped them negotiate the daily drama involved in raising children and managing households. They needed friends they could trust and call on in times of medical emergencies, and the group acted as a useful support network. Forming a self-help group had helped cement these ties and strengthen their social capital. Unfortunately, they also observed that these ties dissuaded them from individually aspiring to more than what the others in the group aspired to. Doing so, led others to believe they were being looked down upon and they consequently withdrew their support.

*External connections.* A significant number of successful microentrepreneurs were linked to networks and associations outside their community. NGOs that promote microbusinesses by assisting them with daily operations in the initial phase were widespread in South Africa. Such NGOs were hardly found in northern Nigeria, even though such programs existed in Nigeria. In the Arab Republic of Egypt, national NGOs had a greater presence in this field than international NGOs.

Connections with networks and associations outside their community allowed women microentrepreneurs to gain valuable operational assistance, technical skills, and in some cases financial assistance. Moreover, the links ensured that the women gained insights into how they might develop their businesses. More important, the links and assistance allowed the women to establish businesses that were more likely to provide sustainable livelihoods. It should be noted that none of the NGOs had established cooperatives. How cooperatives compare with NGOs providing entrepreneurial support is a question this study did not consider.

## Policy Recommendations

This chapter has attempted to avoid what is seemingly inevitable: the anthropological-sociological trap of concluding that local contexts are so different and their impacts are so strong that broad conclusions and patterns cannot be identified. Rather, it has attempted to explore local variations and provide comparative inferences that could inform social policies aimed at encouraging microentrepreneurs to earn sustainable livelihoods.

According to the study, it would be reasonable to conclude that, in situations of dire poverty, microenterprises help provide entrepreneurs with incomes. Whether these businesses can also provide sustainable livelihoods depends on whether the women are in a position to develop and nurture their businesses; and whether their desired capabilities are appropriate for succeeding as an entrepreneur.

Three issues emerge:

- Caring for young children precludes women from developing their microenterprise; it takes time and encourages women to join associations and networks that might provide them with emergency family assistance and childcare support. Unfortunately, these networks also put pressure on women to conform to the others in the group and discourage risk taking and entrepreneurship. This suggests that providing childcare facilities in urban areas, and possibly creating such programs in public schools in both urban and rural areas, might be beneficial.
- Poor women turn to civil society associations and networks for assistance at times of medical emergencies. Ensuring that emergency medical assistance and regular medical care are available would certainly help them become less dependent on social networks that discourage entrepreneurial activity.
- NGOs can help broaden the horizons of women at the margins of society NGOs and networks located outside the community play a very significant role in motivating and supporting women microentrepreneurs. Encouraging such activity is critical to enabling greater numbers of poor women to enhance their existing capabilities and explore what capabilities it would be desirable to possess.

One area this chapter did not explore through interviews was the relationship between education and microentrepreneurial performance. While it was clear from the responses that none of the women interviewed for this study had a college education, the women were not asked about their level of education.[4] Further study is necessary to understand the role of education in successful outcomes: whether women who had completed high school were better entrepreneurs than those with little or no education. Education might well be a critical factor not only for empowering women, broadening their horizons, and generating different aspirations, but also for enabling them to be better entrepreneurs.

These policy suggestions imply that, rather than offering women facilities for livelihood activities that they do not find particularly meaningful, it would be better to work toward self-empowerment, enhancing their capabilities and offering them greater possibilities to provide for themselves and their families.

Perhaps it is time for a shift away from policies that "target" specific groups of women with the aim of "moving" them in one direction or the other, and seriously revisit ideas about targeted antipoverty programs and policies and the relationships among identities, culture, and development. As the Arusha Statement observes: "[T]argeting public resources at the poor alone is not always the most effective way of empowering and building their capabilities."[5]

## Notes

1. Taylor (1989) discusses these three questions relating to identities.
2. The data used for this chapter were gathered in an ethnographic manner between the years 1997 and 2003. The basic methodological strategy was developed during the South African stage of the fieldwork and used to conduct research in the Arab Republic of Egypt, and then northern Nigeria. The women microentrepreneurs interviewed were identified in the following way. First, specific communities for study in all three countries were identified in both rural and urban areas. Second, various civil society associations were identified—social clubs, religious societies, trade associations, cooperatives, burial societies, rotating credit societies (or *stokvels* as they are known in South Africa, or *gamayyiat* in the Arab Republic of Egypt), political associations, and ethnic-based associations in rural and urban areas. The aim was to include as broad a range of organizations as possible. The staff and/or heads of these associations were then interviewed. They were asked to describe the association, its history, and its membership. A list of members

in each association who are microentrepreneurs was then compiled and each person on the list was interviewed.

A second list of microentrepreneurs in each community under focus was compiled with the help of community members and researchers familiar with the area. From these lists, a sample of microentrepreneurs and civil society organization members were selected for interviews. In South Africa, an additional database was compiled of all the entrepreneurs who had been awarded the entrepreneur of the month prize by the *Sowetan* newspaper from 1989 to 1999. More than 50 percent of these entrepreneurs were contacted.

Some 150 women from seven of South Africa's nine provinces were interviewed. Interviews were conducted with microentrepreneurs located in rural and urban areas and former townships, and mining "hostels." In most cases, the interviews were conducted in the homes or the workplace of the microentrepreneurs.

The data in the Arab Republic of Egypt were gathered through interviews with rural and urban microbusinesswomen in Cairo, Minya, and rural areas in Upper Egypt. A total of 50 interviews were conducted. In Nigeria, interviews were conducted with 50 microentrepreneurs in the Jigawa, Kano, and Katsina provinces. The interviews lasted more than an hour on average. Follow-up interviews took place as required. The names of the interviewees quoted in the chapter have been changed to protect their privacy.

3. (a) A "successful" microenterprise had grown considerably since its establishment. Such a microentrepreneur clearly demonstrated entrepreneurialism and creativity. (b) A "stagnant" microenterprise was one that continued to operate but was not particularly creative or entrepreneurial. (c) A "survivalist" microenterprise had not grown in any demonstrable way and barely provided a basic income for the entrepreneur.

4. It would have been crass to ask the women about their educational levels and would have put the interview process on an uneven plane; consequently, the women may not have been forthcoming about other critical aspects of their lives and microenterprises deemed more pertinent to this study.

5. The Arusha Statement is the joint statement agreed to, and issued, at the conference on "New Frontiers of Social Policy" in December 2005. See http://web.worldbank.org/WBSITE/EXTERNAL/TOPICS/EXTSOCIAL DEVELOPMENT/0,,contentMDK:20761071~pagePK:210058~piPK:2100 62~theSitePK:244363,00.html.

## References

Appadurai, A. 2004. "The Capacity to Aspire: Culture and the Terms of Recognition." In *Culture and Public Action*, eds. V. Rao and M. Walton. Stanford, CA: Stanford University Press.

Beck, T., A. Demirguc-Kunt, and M. S. Martinez Peria. 2005. "Reaching Out: Access to and Use of Banking Services Across Countries." Working Paper 3754, World Bank, Washington, DC.

de Aghion, B. A., and J. Morduch. 2005. *The Economics of Microfinance*. Cambridge, MA: MIT Press.

Fafchamps M., and B. Minten. 2002. "Social Capital and the Firm: Evidence from Agricultural Traders in Madagascar." In *The Role of Social Capital in Development*, eds. C. Grootaert and T. van Bastelaer. Cambridge, UK: Cambridge University Press.

Kabeer, N. 2005. "Is Microfinance a 'Magic Bullet' for Women's Empowerment? Analysis of Findings from South Asia." In *Economic and Political Weekly*, October 29: 4709–18.

Moser, C. 2008. "Assets and Livelihoods: A Framework for Asset-Based Social Policy." In *Assets, Livelihoods, and Social Policy*, eds. A. A. Dani and C. Moser. Washington, DC: World Bank.

Narayan, D., and L. Pritchett. 1997. "Cents and Sociability: Household Income and Social Capital in Tanzania." Policy Research Working Paper 1796, World Bank, Washington, DC.

Pinglé, V., and P. Houtzager. 2003. "Capabilities and Cultural Contexts." Paper presented at the Capabilities Conference, September 7–9, Pavia, Italy.

Piore, M., and C. Sable. 1986. *The Second Industrial Divide: Possibilities for Prosperity*. Cambridge: Basic Books.

Putnam, R., R. Leonardi, and R. Y. Nanetti. 1994. *Making Democracy Work: Civic Traditions in Modern Italy*. Princeton, NJ: Princeton University Press.

Robinson, M. 2001. *The Microfinance Revolution: Sustainable Finance for the Poor*. Washington, DC: World Bank.

Sen, A. K. 2005. *The Argumentative Indian: Writings on Indian History, Culture, and Identity*. New York: Farrar, Straus, & Giroux.

Sen, A. K. 1997. "Economics, Business Principles, and Moral Sentiments." *Business Ethics Quarterly* 7 (3): 5–15.

Sen, A. K. 1995. *Inequality Reexamined*. Cambridge, MA: Harvard University Press.

Sen, A. K. 1992. "The Political Economy of Targeting." Paper presented at World Bank Conference on "Public Expenditures and the Poor: Incidence and Targeting," Washington, DC.

Taylor, C. 1989. *Sources of the Self: The Making of the Modern Identity*. Cambridge, MA: Harvard University Press.

World Bank. 2006. "Arusha Statement." Statement of the World Bank conference on New Frontiers of Social Policy: Development in a Globalizing World, December 12–15, Arusha, Tanzania. http://web.worldbank.org/WBSITE/EXTERNAL/TOPICS/EXTSOCIALDEVELOPMENT/0,,contentMDK:20761071~pagePK:210058~piPK:210062~theSitePK:244363,00.html.

# CHAPTER 13

# Beyond Sectoral Traps: Creating Wealth for the Poor

*Deepa Narayan and Soumya Kapoor*

Poor people live in an unequal world, wherein the wealth from economic growth is unequally shared. Proportionate gain is of little help to the bottom poor. Inequality in power, opportunity, agency, organization, and human development perpetuates unequal incomes or widens income disparities even alongside economic growth. Poor women and men need to participate in much larger numbers and on fairer terms to make shared growth a reality.

Based on the analysis of worldwide experiences, this chapter presents an integrated conceptual framework for economic empowerment, focusing on a broad range of assets that interact to create or erode poor people's wealth. It then applies this framework to four large-scale programs in India that have built poor people's assets by facilitating their access to markets, while strengthening and protecting their asset base. Finally, it draws policy lessons to support market liberalization from below.[1]

## Sectoral Traps

In the past decade, a variety of policies and program approaches have been developed to reduce poverty. The policies address one aspect or another of poor people's lives, rather than the interrelatedness of the different dimensions of their lives determining their decisions on consumption versus investment. Living at low levels of consumption and saving, poor people have little surplus to withstand shocks. Thus, assets are exchanged for survival, and small loans are used for consumption, food, health care, marriage, and death ceremonies. Even when this finding is well known, it has not influenced the design of policies and programs, because agencies dealing with finance are different from those dealing with health care, education, and infrastructure.

Poverty traps are perpetuated by sectoral traps and the mind-sets that underlie them. Thus, economic growth is considered to be the purview of economic policy, while the livelihoods of the poor remain isolated under social policy. However, creating wealth for the poor requires an integrated approach—one that creates opportunities for poor women and men as producers, while simultaneously protecting their portfolio of assets, including their own health and social, natural, physical, and financial assets. The Voices of the Poor study, conducted in 60 countries, reported health shocks as the single most frequent reason cited by poor people for falling into poverty despite their productive activities (Narayan and others 2000b; Narayan and Petesch 2002). Therefore, a focus on asset building alone will not lead to wealth creation for the poor if heavy expenses on health care drain out all accumulated resources, pushing people backwards again. Similarly, singular attention to risk management will ignore strategies that can provide better returns for the poor's labor as producers, so they can build a range of assets that can be capitalized to help them move out of poverty.

### Conceptual Framework

The conceptual framework for economic empowerment of poor people rests on two basic propositions.[2] The first is that poor people themselves are active agents, the most important resource and the most motivated to move out of poverty. They have a range of assets and capabilities that need to be built on and protected. The challenge is to tap into these capabilities and their energy, motivation and talent (Narayan and others 2000a, 2000b; Narayan and Petesch 2002; World Bank 2000). The second is that poor people do not operate as producers, consumers, suppliers, or citizens in a vacuum. They do so in a wider context of institutions and available opportunities. Unequal power relations and the underlying social and political processes are beyond the control of poor people, even though the processes have a major impact on their interactions with markets, the state, and civil society.

The framework uses the concepts of agency, opportunity structure, and their interactions to explain economic empowerment of poor people. There are four building blocks, as shown in figure 13.1:

- institutional climate
- social and political structures
- poor people's individual assets and capabilities
- poor people's collective assets and capabilities.

The first two building blocks constitute the opportunity structure that poor people face, while the second two make up their capacity to exercise agency to create wealth. The opportunity structure of a society is defined by the broad institutional, social, and political context of formal and informal

**Figure 13.1. Overview of the Conceptual Framework**

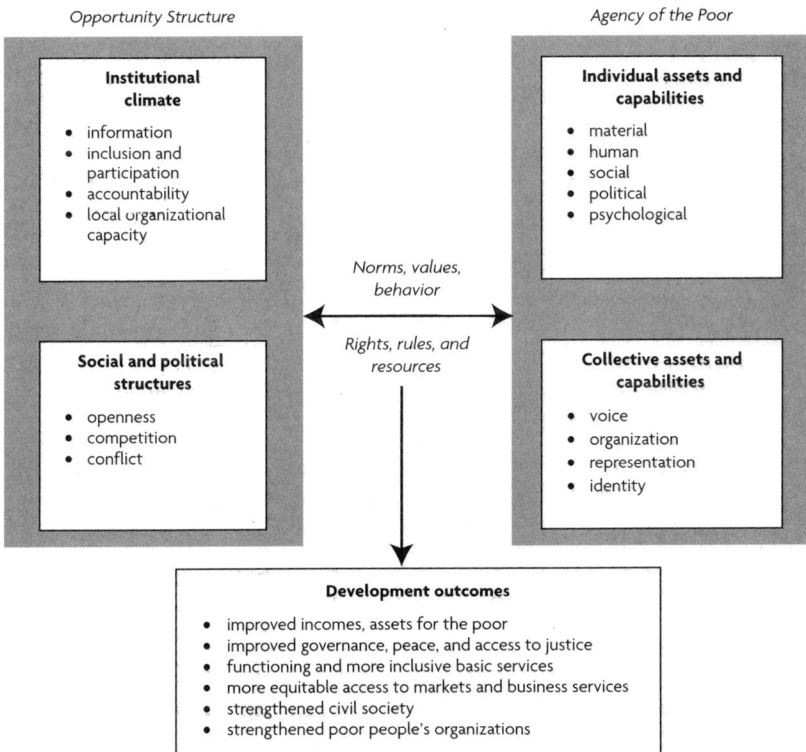

Source: Narayan 2005.

rules within which actors pursue their interests. Agency is defined by the capacity of actors to take purposeful action, a function of both individual and collective assets and capabilities.[3]

## Poor People's Agency

Poor people have limited ability to act to further their own interests. This "inequality of agency" plays a central role in perpetuating inequality and poverty (Rao and Walton 2004). Embedded in a culture of inequality, poor people need to build a range of assets and capabilities to influence, negotiate, control, and hold accountable other actors in order to increase their own well-being. Faced with inequality as well as higher vulnerability to shocks, direct interventions to protect these limited assets become even more crucial.

For those most marginalized, their collective agency in organization, representation, voice, and identity is critical in overcoming the social discrimination that leads to economic, social, and political exclusion, and inequality. Without this collective capacity to negotiate, control, and bargain, individual assets and capabilities remain unused or underused. Groups of poor men and women also offer their members a security mechanism against shocks, for example, a self-help group of poor, marginalized women might extend financial help to a member affected by a health shock. The importance of collective agency for building and protecting the assets of socially excluded individuals has been largely overlooked.

Assets include material, human, social, and political assets that enable people to withstand shocks and expand their horizon of choices. These assets interact with each other to create or erode poor people's wealth. Capabilities, conversely, are inherent in people and enable them to use their assets in different ways to increase their well-being. However, the fact that two people with similar assets and capabilities exhibit different propensities to act on their own behalf implies that psychological dimensions of individual agency are also important. Self-confidence and a sense of self-efficacy are important precursors to action (Bandura 1998). Finally, capacity to aspire is crucial to different and better futures (Appadurai 2004). Generating this capacity to envision a different future becomes, therefore, an important part of policy interventions and solidarity movements.

## The Opportunity Structure

Investment in and protection of poor people's individual and collective assets and capabilities will not bring about change without a corresponding transformation of the institutional climate and/or social and political structures within which poor people pursue their interests.

The institutional climate creates incentives for action or inaction. Key formal institutions include the laws, rules, regulations, and implementation processes upheld by states, markets, civil society, and international agencies. Informal institutions include norms of social solidarity, superiority, social exclusion, helplessness, and corruption that can subvert formal rules. Because the rules, regulations, and actions of the state are so important in affecting the conditions in which poor people and other actors make decisions, empowerment efforts often focus on changing the unequal power relationship between the state and poor people. The same analysis can be applied to the relationship between poor people and private businesses or civil society organizations. Although there is no single model for bringing about such reforms, experience shows that four key elements are almost always present when such efforts are successful: access to information; inclusion/participation; accountability; and the enabling environment for local organizational capacity.

Opportunities for the poor depend also on the nature of social and political structures, that is, the extent to which they are open or closed, inclusive or exclusionary, cooperative or conflictual. When social divisions are deep and systemic, opportunities and access to services are determined less by individual characteristics than by a culture of inequality that discriminates against entire social groups. Political and social structures are generally more difficult to change than the institutional climate.

## Four Large-Scale Programs

Reaching the poorest of the poor in India is a challenge. Change is extremely difficult when discrimination is the norm, and the perception of a life of poverty as just is embedded in social and economic institutions. Consider *dalit* women, who are considered untouchable. They live on the fringes of society and are illiterate. They eke out a living on seasonal wage labor, are frequently beaten by their husbands, and often see their children end up as bonded labor. Changing their lives is an extreme challenge. Seeing them as entrepreneurs and as potential business partners is fantasy.

This section focuses on four large-scale programs in India. They show that unlocking poor people's potential reduces poverty, enables them to contribute directly to achieving shared economic growth, and is profitable.

### Andhra Pradesh Self-Help Groups

In the state of Andhra Pradesh, self-help groups (SHGs) have spread from small beginnings in 1996, when poor illiterate women were organized into groups of 10 to 15 to start their own savings and then link to banks. Now they extend throughout the state, transforming women's lives. The SHG model addresses the multitude of social and economic problems facing women, including livelihood support, food insecurity, and health and links women to existing government programs. Originally called *Velugu* (meaning *light*) and recently renamed *Indira Kranti Patham*, the government program has organized 7.8 million poor women into 617,472 self-help groups—almost half the self-help groups in the country. The groups already mobilize US$250 million in savings every year, receiving US$475 million from banks[4] (CESS 2005).

### Self-Employed Women's Association (SEWA): A Union of Poor Women Workers

In India, 93 percent of the total workforce does not have the benefit of a labor union. This includes agricultural workers in the informal economy (Unni 2002). After a protracted struggle with government regulations, Ela Bhatt, a lawyer in the state of Gujarat, established the first trade union for women workers in the informal economy in 1972. Members included poor women who were street vendors, daily wage laborers, home workers, such as those doing embroidery or raising vegetables in backyards, salt workers, gum collectors, and those involved in many other trades.

Today, SEWA is the largest trade union in the world of poor women in the informal economy. It has over 700,000 members working in more than 70 trades in seven states across India. It fights to build assets for its members by seeking fairer wages and benefits, and training them in livelihoods such as embroidery and salt farming. Its cooperatives include banks as well as collectives that support women's agricultural and handicraft products. SEWA Bank provides an integrated set of services to its 257,000 women account holders, who deposited US$14.4 million in the year 2003. In addition, SEWA protects the limited assets and capabilities of its members by operating health care centers, childcare crèches, and insurance programs for its members (SEWA Annual Report 2003).

## AMUL: *The Cooperative Dairy Development Program*

India is also home to one of the most successful cooperatives in the world, which has changed the country's status from a net importer to an exporter of milk. Operation Flood, a nationwide dairy development program implemented by the National Dairy Development Board (NDDB) over three decades, has transformed the Indian dairy industry. It began small, with the Anand Milk Producers Union Limited (AMUL) cooperative in Anand, Gujarat, created to bypass exploitative middlemen. In 2003–04, the dairy cooperative movement involved nearly 12 million farmers, supplying on average 15 million liters of milk per day with an annual value of US$20 billion to more than 750 towns and cities (NDDB 2005).

## *International Trade Centre (ITC) e-choupals*

The fourth program involves the placing of computers in villages to facilitate agribusiness. In less than five years, the *e-choupal* program has connected more than three million farmers in India to markets, increasing their profits through village-based Internet kiosks. It was initiated in 2000 by an Indian private for profit company, ITC, which has annual revenues of US$2.95 billion (ITC 2005a; Deveshwar 2005). ITC introduced the innovation when its agribusiness division had become unprofitable due to the opening up of the Indian economy. With more international companies entering the agricultural market, ITC's margins were under threat. Its margin-to-risk ratios could not compete with international players that had wider options of risk management and arbitrage. Threatened with closure, *e-choupals* started as an experiment and eventually emerged as a means for the company's agribusiness division to reduce its costs and remain competitive. *E-choupals* provide farmers with free information on the prices of agricultural commodities, without obliging them to sell to the information provider, ITC. After checking prices, the farmers can choose to buy or sell through ITC or go to the local markets (*mandis*). Computers are placed in the home of a middle-class farmer whose commission depends on the number of transactions he completes successfully with local farmers buying or selling products through the *e-choupal*. Efficiency improvements in transactions have led to increased revenues both for the farmer and for ITC.

Today, *e-choupals* generate more than US$100 million in business for ITC, sourcing agricommodities through 5,200 kiosks across 31,000 villages in India, with plans to cover 100,000 villages or one-sixth of rural India in the next five years. By 2010, ITC aims to achieve revenues worth US$2.5 billion in *e-choupal* transactions (ITC 2005b; Deveshwar 2005).

**Key Lessons**

This section highlights six lessons regarding the scaling up of poor people's participation in markets on fairer terms. The conceptual framework on economic empowerment is used to frame these lessons.

*Focus on the Interconnectedness of Assets*

Poor people's assets, and therefore their asset accumulation processes, are intimately interconnected. Hence, they require an integrated approach. A salt worker can go out to work if she has the option of leaving her children at a crèche. Loans to build the financial assets of a poor gum collector can help her if she is assured of a physical claim over the gum she gathers from the forest.

In practice, it is difficult to address every interconnected need simultaneously. Hence the need for sequencing and for addressing priority survival needs first, enabling poor women and men to cross some minimal threshold level, so that they can make a different set of consumption or investment trade-offs. The way in which this is done varies infinitely and is influenced by the experiences, vision, and objectives of the implementers.

SEWA began with a focus on improving the incomes of women workers by fighting unfair government and private sector labor practices, as related to head loaders, street vendors, and home-based workers. SEWA realized very quickly that, to do this, investment would be needed in health protection, medical care, and literacy. Women workers, as mothers with young children, needed childcare; as spouses, they needed the support of their husbands.

The self-help group movement started with forming groups of poor women from low castes. The focus was on addressing problems like alcohol abuse, domestic violence, and caste discrimination that these women faced in their everyday life. The groups were also seen as instruments that could serve women's small credit requirements and help in building infrastructure within communities. However, it was recognized very early in the program that individual survival needs were so severe because of lack of food, frequent drought, and ill-health that they had to be addressed before using the collective agency of the women to build community infrastructure, as in the original design. One of the early successes involved the establishment of new ways to manage and distribute government food aid for the poorest. Group development became the focus; as the groups gained strength both in numbers and experience, they became federations and began to address a range of social and other economic needs. By the fourth year, the project implementers had reconceptualized the program as a livelihoods program with a strong social protection agenda, rather than a community infrastructure agenda.

The entry point for the *e-choupal* program was a better agriprocurement chain both benefiting the middle farmer and making profits for ITC. ITC is now adding new features, including supermarkets and centers for education and health care.

## Invest in Collective Agency for Socially Marginalized Groups

The assumption that individuals can build assets and move out of poverty through their own efforts, by overcoming exogenous constraints, does not take into account the social and cultural norms and constraints imposed by the more powerful social groups and internalized by the very group discriminated against. Entire social categories of poor people have limited social or economic mobility because of institutionalized inequality. Historically, the caste system in India has been held in place because the hierarchy is practiced and internalized across the castes. Thus life chances are overwhelmingly affected by social categories into which individuals are born, rather than through individual effort (Tilly 1999; Loury 2002; Narayan and others 2000a, 2000b; Narayan and others 2002; Rao and Walton 2004; World Bank 2005).

Investment in the collective agency and organizations of marginalized social groups is characterized by market, state, and civil society failure. Yet without representative and accountable organization, which aggregates the power of millions, the economic and societal interests of marginalized groups will not be met.

Three of the four programs discussed in this chapter invest heavily in collective agency by building a new sense of identity focused on dignity, self-respect, equity, and justice, and a sense of solidarity through group formation. Two programs, SHGs in Andhra Pradesh and SEWA, focus specifically on marginalized women. They use rituals, songs, and prayers to help women break through old self-imposed and other imposed barriers to recognizing their own worth and their own sense of self. In Andhra Pradesh, the program focuses on *dalits*, the untouchables. The first request from the women is that collective action break the taboos of untouchability, by actions such as drawing water from a public well previously monopolized by higher castes. At the community level, none of the programs adopt a confrontational approach. Rather, the focus is on changing self through collective strength and letting social and economic change happen over time. In both SEWA and the SHG movement, when women are asked about the most important difference in their lives, they tend to cite loss of fear, as well as rising self-confidence and speaking in public, often before economic change.

The AMUL milk cooperative builds collective agency through a three-tier federation. It focuses only on those who own cattle, primarily marginal and small farmers, but does not exclude the better off. At the village level, dairy cooperative societies are formed wherein decisions are made on the basis of one member one vote. There are more than 110,000 village dairy cooperatives owned by 12 million farmers. Membership is open, to all and even the smallest quantity of milk can be sold to the cooperative by any member. Some 70 percent of the members are small and marginal farmers (Kurien 2007).

The only one of the programs to make no investment in the collective agency of the poor is *e-choupal*. Instead, it uses the computer to aggregate demand. It does not focus exclusively on the poor: so far, 70 percent of the farmers using *e-choupals* are middle income, 20 percent are rich, and only 10 percent poor.[5]

The social categories of the poor mask many other differences, including gender differences. Women from the lowest social strata, who are poor, illiterate, and without assets, are bypassed by most programs because they are the most powerless and so invisible to outsiders. It is to overcome such deep, culturally imposed constraints that SEWA and the SHGs focus only on women. AMUL had to create all-women's dairy cooperatives to reach women. ITC also does not reach women and has recently initiated a partnership with SEWA's members to procure and market agricultural produce such as organic sesame seeds.

### Link Changes in Economic Opportunity Structure to Poor People's Livelihoods

The participation of millions of poor people in economic growth requires changes in the economic opportunity structures linked to *their* livelihoods; otherwise it will become "jobless growth."

Modifying the opportunity structure involves changes in the institutional climate of the state, private sector, or civil society organizations influencing poor people's economic activities. Poor people can access markets on fairer terms if interventions truly level the playing field, so that self-inclusion is possible through individual action. Access to information is essential in enabling poor people to take advantage of opportunities and build assets. Also important are transparency; breaking monopolistic power held by traders, buyers, or officials; accountability; and keeping transaction costs low. Otherwise, pervasive power inequality chokes opportunity for those without social connections, political clout, and assets.

When economic initiatives are not targeted to the poor, the involvement of the middle class creates support and rapid expansion. However, to reach marginalized social groups requires special design features, as well as possibly investment in their organizations and collective agency.

SEWA focuses directly on improving the livelihood security of poor women. The early members of the union included poor salt workers in Gujarat. The salt industry in the state employs over 70,000 people, nearly three-quarters of whom work on farms smaller than 10 acres (Crowell 2003). Salt production is a regulated industry in India. A long-standing government regulation stipulates that salt farmers need to own a minimum of 90 acres of land to be eligible to book a train wagon. This rendered the small, informal salt producers in Gujarat unable to use the cheaper rail service to transport their salt. Since 1989, SEWA has worked on organizing informal salt producers into groups to obtain government services, including inputs necessary for salt production. However, it took nearly 10 years to convince the government to change its regulations on the railway wagon quota.

AMUL has been more successful than *e-choupals* in reaching the poor, primarily because more poor people are involved in rearing cattle than in farming soybeans. A majority of milk producers (accounting for some 70 percent of India's milk production) has one or two cows (Kurien 2005). The AMUL cooperative has aggregated the efforts of these farmers, becoming, in three decades, the largest food company in India. In 2003 it ranked first in milk powder and milk-related products in India, beating other well-known multinational companies (NDDB 2005).

*E-choupals* focused first on soybeans, targeting the median farmer. The computers are accessible to all, free of charge, irrespective of caste or wealth, and have broken the monopoly of information on market prices. They provide an alternative to the traditional *mandis*, in which farmers are required to sell through middlemen even though the entire process is stacked against them: they discover the prices only at auction time, and so price information is not separable from the decision to sell. They also bear the costs of transportation and bagging of grain and watch helplessly as the weighing scales are tipped in favor of the buyer.

By contrast, in the *e-choupal* system, if the farmer decides to sell to ITC on a given day, he is given a written quote of the price that he takes with his produce to the local procurement hub. His produce is weighed using electronic scales, and transport costs are borne by ITC. The response of farmers to the alternative market has changed the institutional climate governing interactions between millions of farmers and traders. Farmers now prefer selling through ITC even when their prices are lower than at the *mandi,* because they get immediate payment and know that they will not be cheated.

While the *e-choupal* system is technically open to all and operates on the principle of self-inclusion, studies indicate that social barriers still keep many small farmers and women away from the network operated by a farmer with median income (Prahalad 2005). However, poor people benefit even when they don't sell to *e-choupals* because, with an increase in the prices received by the middle-class farmers, the prices that other traders have to pay in the area rise. In some of the soy-growing areas where *e-choupals* are active, the proportion of farmers planting soy has increased from 50 to 90 percent.[6]

The achievements of the SHG women almost rival those of *e-choupals* in terms of scale achieved over a short period of time. However, unlike *e-choupals*, the lead time before poor women could engage in these procurement and marketing activities was long, as the federated networks of SHGs had to be created from scratch.

### Aggregate Demand and Manage Demand Responsiveness

Poor people receive less for just about everything. Because they sell in small quantities, they have little bargaining power. Moreover, transaction costs are higher per unit. They are also more vulnerable to depleting their limited asset base when faced with idiosyncratic health shocks such as accidents, illness, or death, or covariate shocks such as droughts.[7]

Aggregation of the poor through collective organizations can help overcome the disadvantages of their being small and powerless as producers. Such organizations, however, may be difficult to rely on in the event of covariate shocks, like droughts, that affect everyone. More direct interventions such as insurance schemes may then be needed to protect the asset base of the poor.

*Aggregating demand.* Two ways have emerged to aggregate demand: through organizations of the poor; and through computers providing public access to information at low cost, thereby increasing value and efficiency in the production, procurement, processing, and marketing chain.

The dairy cooperative movement started with the objective of putting more rupees into the hands of the farmer for every liter of milk sold. It organized farmers into a three-tier network, with each tier serving distinct functions so as to return higher value. Milk production is decentralized, handled by 12 million individual farmers. Procurement of milk is done by the 110,000 village level cooperative societies, composed of these individual farmers. The cooperatives federate into 170 district level unions that serve as centralized milk processing centers. These unions combine into 22 state level marketing federations, whose primary job is to market the milk and milk products (NDDB 2005).

In the SHG movement, the recipient of the help is specifically identified: the poor *dalit* women. However, the overall vision in terms of empowering them and improving their well-being is cast in broad terms. The strategy revolves around social transformation through group formation. It recognizes that interventions to build collective organizations of poor women and to protect their limited asset base, through mechanisms such as food security and insurance programs, are the first step to expanding their asset base. Women are organized into groups of 10 to 15; each group selects two women to form a representative village organization. Women have been organized into 617,472 self-help groups and 27,350 village organizations. These village organizations have been federated into 864 Mahila Mandal Samakhyas (MMSs) at the *mandal* or subdistrict level. Irrespective of the diverse activities undertaken at the group or village level, all groups and village organizations federate upwards into the same MMS. This aggregation, the power of sheer numbers and the ability to leverage this power, eventually shifted the program's strategy to focus on marketing a more limited number of agricultural commodities with the aim of improving the livelihoods of members.

Like SHGs, SEWA started with a broad objective of women's empowerment as producers through self-employment and self-reliance. It first focused on poor urban women and only later extended into rural areas and has won several legal battles to get the rights of informal workers recognized. It invests heavily in organizing women into groups, with more than 70 trades organized into cooperatives and unions. At the state level, while all 700,000 poor women are members of SEWA, the dispersion across occupations limits SEWA's bargaining power for each occupation, both with the state and markets.

Drawing on its experiences, SEWA also believes that livelihood security is not complete without access to health care, childcare, and insurance to protect against shocks. It tries to link its members to government provided services but often ends up providing the services itself.

ITC's *e-choupals* is the only program that does not invest directly in collective organizations of the poor. The computer serves both as an aggregator of farmers' demand for markets and an aggregator for supplies needed.

*Managing demand responsiveness.* Maintaining demand responsiveness over time is easier when objectives are clear and incentives, norms, management structure, and institutional climate are aligned with these objectives. When working with poor people, programs face a special challenge of maintaining focus while remaining responsive to demand, as poor men and women face multiple, interlinked disadvantages. The temptation is to keep adding components addressing additional problems.

The dairy cooperative movement has managed to remain a single commodity program. Its demand responsiveness remained fixed for decades on the *doodhwala* (milkman): how to improve the quality of his product and how to market it to get the best returns. The movement adopted technologies, such as electronic fat content readers to remove any discretion in setting milk prices in the village, and introduced innovations including spot payment based on publicly announced prices, if desired, or a monthly payment in cash, based on entries in a passbook. However, it did not start schools for children or offer insurance schemes for its members to protect against health shocks (Candler and Kumar 1998).

Unlike AMUL, the SHGs started with a wide-ranging set of activities, including savings; credit; provision of insurance covering life, health, crops, and livestock; enrolling children in school; watershed management; provision of food from government fixed price shops; forestry; health campaigns; community infrastructure development; and training for livelihoods. The midterm appraisal of *Velugu* confirms the program's success in increasing the proportion of households in the intervention area able to withstand drought from 4 to 11 percent and those able to withstand health shocks from 5 to 13 percent. Distress sales of assets also declined from 14 to 3.5 percent over the project, along with a drop in those members seeking work as bonded/attached labor (from 2 to 0.7 percent) and opting for formal borrowings (from 9 to 6.2 percent) when faced with shocks (CESS 2005).

Of all four organizations, SEWA is perhaps the most demand responsive to members involved in varied occupations, each with their own set of problems. It believes in addressing all their needs, since these needs are interrelated. In doing so, however, its expertise has become diffuse. For example, SEWA started an innovative insurance scheme to provide its members cover against illness, maternity, property loss, and death. However, evaluations of the scheme have revealed both low frequency of submission of claims and low coverage: the scheme reached only about 18 members for every 1,000 members per year covering about one-quarter of the estimated episodes of hospitalization (Chen, Khurana, and Mirani 2005).

ITC's objective clarity, combined with financial benchmarks from the beginning, helped steer the program. ITC has managed demand for *e-choupals* by starting with soybeans in one state and then extending to other agricultural commodities, while changing features to fit different needs. In response to farmer demand, it has now started providing quality assured inputs like seeds and is experimenting with opening supermarkets (*Choupal Sagar*), as well as extending credit and providing health, education, and insurance services.

### Leverage Collective Agency into Economic Power through Business Orientation

Poor people gain income when their social organizations are leveraged to access or create new economic opportunities linked to their livelihoods. This process of using organizational strength to gain advantage in markets is not automatic for several reasons:

- First, pervasive inequality keeps poor people's organizations on the margin.
- Second, the process of creating large cooperatives, unions, or federated organizations of poor people is time, skill, and finance-intensive. Since returns come many years later, there is collective (state, markets, and civil society) failure in investing in the creation of such organizations, nurturing them so they evolve and gain strength over time while eluding capture by the elite from within or outside the groups.
- Third, many civil society organizations reject or do not have the mindset or experience to create profitable businesses on a large scale.
- Fourth, the efforts of support agencies who want to be responsive to poor people's needs become too scattered to effectively gain a large enough market share to change their bargaining power with government and markets.
- Finally, most civil society groups focus too much on supply and not enough on demand, markets, and the value chain.

The expansion of SHGs in Andhra Pradesh is a good example of successfully leveraging social capital of groups to become important economic players on behalf of group members. While Andhra Pradesh has a history of SHGs, it was only when federations of groups started emerging in the third year that the program realized the full potential of these federations. The program changed its strategy and intervention point, realizing that social transformation through organization and social protection did not by itself change the economic reality of poor women in fundamental ways. It focused instead on improving poor women's economic power by leveraging their social capital in a federated network. The new strategy was informed by a detailed livelihood survey and the advice of business experts. Middlemen were identified as a big part of the problem; it was decided that, instead of losing profits to the middlemen, women's groups would become procurement agents for the state for about 50 agricultural commodities.

Andhra Pradesh is one of the highest producers of *neem* or margosa. In one area, women started buying *neem* fruit from their members and other farmers in the village at higher prices than other traders. They captured 60 percent of the *neem* market in 2004 (7,500 metric tonnes) and will procure 90 percent of the *neem* for the state in 2005.[8] Similarly, women's groups are becoming the favored procurers of maize in the state. SHGs have procured 140,000 metric tonnes of maize worth US$26 million from 260 village procurement centers in 2005, with plans to expand to 1,500 procurement centers and procurement worth US$45 million next year. The prices paid by other maize traders have gone up in these areas, cutting the shares of the middlemen.[9] Private companies are also discovering the power of poor people's organizations. Godrej, the largest cattle food company in India, has contracted with SHGs in Andhra Pradesh to grow maize on 7,000 acres.

AMUL is unique in combining a cooperative with a hardheaded, business-oriented approach. Decisions are made based on how they affect the bottom line and the farmer's share for every rupee worth of milk produced. While the farmers control the cooperative unions, marketing is in the hands of professionals who have the skills and education needed for a highly competitive local and global marketplace. The professionals can be hired and fired by a farmer-controlled board. The managers can recommend closure of a village cooperative if the costs of collection are not profitable. Until recently, SEWA has been less successful in capturing significant market shares for its members. It is steeped in the Gandhian principle of self-reliance. Additionally, because of its union origins, it has often had to engage in long, legal battles on behalf of its members, inching forward with great tenacity over decades in forcing government to "liberalize from below." One case is that of the gum collectors.

In the Banaskantha district of Gujarat, a majority of women are involved in gum [a majority of the women are in gum collection rather than the other way round] collection. However, an arcane regulatory regime permitted sale of forest products only to those with government licenses and permits. This resulted in women selling gum to middlemen for a tenth of market prices. After a decade of struggle, SEWA members were granted permission in 2000 to sell indefinitely on the open market. It now sells about 60,000 kilograms of gum per year at rates varying from US$0.45 cents to US$1.20, while the government continues to procure at 20 cents per kilogram (Chen, Jhabvala, and Nanavati 2003). More recently, SEWA has been experimenting with new partnerships with private companies, including one with ITC to supply 250 tonnes of sesame seeds involving 1,450 of its members. ITC provided training in quality requirements, resulting in women earning an additional 20 cents per kilogram on their produce in 2003 over the previous year.

To organize poor people into social and economic organizations is costly in terms of money and time. The paradox is that, while it requires external funding, the organization has to keep independent of financier control and eventually become self-sustaining. This process is helped by two factors. First, social organizations must generate their own income streams. Second, the program must be driven by a vision of achieving financial viability.

The AMUL pattern cooperatives received high levels of funding for expansion through Operation Flood from the government and a number of donors, including loans from the World Bank and food aid from others. Following heavy initial investments and subsidies, the cooperatives have been financially independent for close to two decades. The SHG movement has been financed by government agencies, donors, and loans from the World Bank. It also received a major boost from the Government of India's policy in 1998, asking all commercial, rural, and cooperative banks to lend to SHGs as a priority sector, without asking for collateral (Reddy 2005). In response to the recent growth of the subdistrict federations (MMS), the program is beginning to define exit strategies and the minimum income stream needed per year by an MMS for self-reliance.

SEWA, too, has received grant funding from innumerable donors, as well as government funding for various schemes.[10] However, it is unclear whether SEWA has achieved financial independence for most of its activities. Its most successful financial venture is SEWA Bank.

ITC is the only program that has no government or donor subsidies in its development. Each *e-choupal* costs US$6,000—to set up and an additional US$100—every year to maintain. Investment is recovered through the saving of 2.5 percent of total transaction cost for ITC, while the farmer saves 2.5 percent in prices—shares that were earlier taken by middlemen (Annamalai and Rao 2007).

### Translate Agency and Organization into Political Clout

Large numbers of poor people organized as economic players almost instantly draw the attention of politicians and political parties, particularly in democracies. As they become important, such organizations become identifiable "vote banks" whose interests matter and who are potential "swing voters" (Acemoglu and Robinson 2005).

The milk cooperatives and the SHG women's movement both have apex organizations that are representative of their members. Both have also walked the fine line between high levels of government support and noninterference in the internal policies, directions, and management of the program.

AMUL, led by Verghese Kurien, used the power of numbers to lobby effectively for policy change and the creation of new autonomous institutions such as the National Dairy Development Board, as well as large flows of financing to "prime the pump," from the government, the European Union (EU), and the World Bank. The dairy development movement was the first to use food aid from the EU to develop the dairy industry and stabilize prices rather than dump free milk into the market and depress local prices. Kurien (2005) developed close relationships with India's successive prime ministers, all of whom gave him policy space to drive the dairy development movement.

The SHG movement has also been supported by successive governments because the power of numbers of organized rural women has not been lost on the politicians. Just before the last election, the chief minister sent a signed postcard to every women's group in the state, putting new burdens on the postmen, who had to read out the card to the mostly illiterate women. (He still lost the election.) The new chief minister has announced a subsidy reducing interest on loans to SHGs to just 3 percent. The program has managed this policy announcement with finesse: group members continue to pay interest rates of 8 percent to 11 percent and the difference goes into a corpus fund for group activities. Managed through an autonomous government-created society, the Society for Elimination of Rural Poverty (SERP), by senior government bureaucrats on deputation, the movement can leverage connections with government while protecting itself from becoming a honeypot to dispense favors.

*Dalit* women at the village level in Andhra Pradesh have also experienced their growing political clout. As leader of one of the self-help groups in a village put it: "Earlier we could never even see the local MLA (Member of the State Legislative Assembly); now when he sees me, he gets up and comes personally to greet me by name."[11] Women are also standing for and winning local *gram panchayat* (village body) elections. Even when they do not seek elected office, women now report that the *panchayat* presidents in most villages not only attend key meetings of the groups but also provide more information on new government projects and activities.

SEWA has managed its relationship with government skillfully, remaining independent although often dependant on government funds. Recognized the world over as the first union of women in the informal economy, it is also respected for its ethical approach. Ela Bhatt and SEWA as an organization have both won innumerable national and international awards. The country's National Policy on Street Vendors, promulgated in 2004, results from SEWA's work (Chen, Khurana, and Mirani 2005). Unlike other programs, however, SEWA has an explicit policy against members' participation in political parties and prohibits its members from standing for local elections except as independents.

ITC's *e-choupals* did not, at first, involve people's organizations or any change in the government regulatory regime. However, its superior responsiveness to farmers has won farmers' support and increased political clout. In the state of Madhya Pradesh, a 15-day strike orchestrated by the *mandi* associations, that had lost some 50 percent of sales to *e-choupals*, had to be called off when 25,000 farmers took to the streets of the state capital. Madhya Pradesh also amended the Agricultural Produce Marketing Committee Act, allowing companies legally to procure directly from farmers. Several other states are doing the same.

## Conclusion

Poor people do not cause poverty. What poor people want is economic opportunity and a fair chance. Given this chance, they demonstrate over and over again that there is indeed "fortune at the bottom of the pyramid" (Prahalad 2005). They want liberalization from below. Poor people gain economic clout in markets when they achieve scale through aggregation, most commonly through federated organizations or when thousands of individual financial transactions are aggregated through computers. Without this aggregation, the bargaining power of poor illiterate women with markets and other providers does not change. This process of aggregation does not happen automatically, but it can be successfully initiated by civil society, the private sector, or the government. The lessons discussed above point to both policy and programmatic actions.

- *First, the investment climate to create new economic opportunities linked to poor people's livelihoods must be improved.* Poor women and men's economic activities are primarily in the informal economy, which is unprotected by laws, and are constrained by an astonishing number of regulations restricting investment, production, processing, procurement, selling, and buying choices. The most basic action is to lift these dysfunctional regulations. Poor people also need financial products such as loans, venture capital, and guarantees, delivered in ways fitting poor people's needs. This requires detailed knowledge about their economic lives as producers, consumers, suppliers, and citizens embedded in particular social and political relationships. Social policy has an important role to play in bringing research-based evidence on the value chain, in which poor people's economic activities are embedded, to the policy discussions on economic growth, investment climate, trade, and poverty reduction. This needs to happen both within the country and at the global level.
- *Second, the domestic investment climate for the private sector must be improved.* Innovations spread quickly when they benefit the middle class. Poor people can gain from overall improvements in investment climate, particularly from infrastructure and free information about prices with low transaction costs. This is even more powerful in combination with real choice on when and to whom to sell. Under most circumstances, however, special design features are needed to help poor people overcome a range of social, cultural, and economic constraints not faced by the middle class or rich.
- *Third, ways must be found to protect the limited assets of the poor as consumers.* Aggregate their supply and demand as producers so as to alter their bargaining power in markets and trigger changes in supply responses from the private sector, the state, and civil society. Poor

people's organizations can play critical roles. The challenge is to manage the demand responsiveness of these organizations and avoid their capture by their own or an external elite. Information technology can be used effectively to aggregate the demand of small producers. Social protection is critical in enabling poor people to accumulate assets, rather than consume savings to survive shocks.

- *Fourth, financial subsidies from different sources must be used to build organizations and corporations of the poor driven by a vision of generating income streams and achieving financial independence over time.*[12] The paradox is that nobody wants to invest in autonomous organizations of the poor without getting something in return. Yet these programs prove that poor men and women are canny entrepreneurs even when they are illiterate and can lift themselves and their families out of poverty within five to seven years.

Finally, given the market failure in investing in poor people and poor women's organizations, one of the most important and enlightened investments by the private sector as part of its corporate social responsibility can be to finance and support the emergence of strong, autonomous federated networks of poor people who can become able business partners over time or corporations of the poor.

## Notes

1. This term was first used several years ago by Ela Bhatt, founder of the Self-Employed Women's Association.
2. For detailed discussion of the framework and its applications, see Narayan 2002 (in particular Section 1 and Section 5 containing experiences around the world in 20 practice notes). Also see chapter 1, Narayan 2005.
3. See also Petesch, Smulovitz, and Walton 2005 and World Bank 2005 for a full discussion.
4. Personal Communication, Vijay Kumar, CEO, SERP, December 9, 2005.
5. Personal communication, S. Sivakumar, CEO, International Business Division, ITC, November 30, 2005.
6. For details, please see http://www.digitaldividend.org/.
7. A midterm assessment of the Velugu project illustrates the high level of risk faced by SHG member households because of frequent droughts in the intervention areas. Nearly 42 percent of households had experienced at least one incident of drought in three years prior to the project, each household losing approximately US$180 in income, which in many cases was higher than the per capita income of the household (CESS 2005).

8. Field notes from a three-day village immersion program in November 2005 in a village in Kurnool district, Andhra Pradesh.
9. Personal Communication, Vijay Kumar, CEP, SERP, November 30, 2005.
10. In orders of magnitude, the levels of external and government funding are probably lower for SEWA than for AMUL or SHGs.
11. Field notes from a three-day village immersion program in November 2005 in a village in Kurnool district, Andhra Pradesh.
12. Ideas that Rehman Sobhan from Bangladesh is simultaneously promoting.

## References

Acemoglu, D., and J. Robinson. 2005. *Economic Origins of Dictatorship and Democracy*. Cambridge, U.K.: Cambridge University Press.

Annamalai, K., and S. Rao. 2007. "E-Choupals and Rural Transformation: Web Based Tools for Indian Farmers." In *Ending Poverty in South Asia: Ideas That Work*, eds. D. Narayan and E. Glinskaya. Washington, DC: World Bank.

Appadurai, A. 2004. "The Capacity to Aspire: Culture and the Terms of Recognition." In *Culture and Public Action*, eds. V. Rao and M. Walton, 59–84. Stanford, CA: Stanford University Press.

Bandura, A. 1998. "Personal and Collective Efficacy in Human Adaptation and Change." In *Advances in Psychological Science*, Vol. 1 of *Social, Personal, and Cultural Aspects*, eds. J. G. Adair, D. Belanger, and K. L. Dion, 51–71. Hove, U.K.: Psychology Press.

Candler, W., and N. Kumar. 1998. *India: The Dairy Revolution*. Washington, DC: World Bank.

CESS (Center for Economic and Social Studies). 2005. *Mid-Term Appraisal of District Poverty Initiatives Project*. Hyderabad: CESS.

Chen, M. A., R. Khurana, and N. Mirani. 2005. *Towards Economic Freedom: The Impact of SEWA*. Bhadra, Ahmedabad: SEWA Academy.

Chen, M., R. Jhabvala, and R. Nanavati. 2003. "*Investment Climate for Female Informal Business: A Case Study from Urban and Rural India*." World Development Report 2005, Background Paper, World Bank, Washington, DC.

Crowell, D. W. 2003. *The SEWA Movement and Rural Development: The Banaskantha and Kutch Experience*. New Delhi: Sage.

Deveshwar, Y. C. 2005. "Inclusive and Sustainable Growth: ITC's Enduring Contribution." *India Today*, October 24.

International Trade Centre (ITC). 2005a. "About ITC." http://www.echoupal.com/home/itcfamily1.asp.

———. 2005b. "ITC e-Choupal." http://www.itcportal.com/sets/echoupal_frameset.htm.

Kurien, V. 2005. *I Too Had a Dream*. New Delhi: Roli Books.

Kurien, V. 2007. "India's Milk Revolution: Investing in Rural Producer Organizations." In *Ending Poverty in South Asia: Ideas That Work,* eds. D. Narayan and E. Glinskaya. Washington, DC: World Bank.

Loury, G. C. 2002. *The Anatomy of Racial Inequality.* Cambridge, Mass.: Harvard University Press.

Narayan, D., ed. 2002. *Empowerment and Poverty Reduction: A Sourcebook.* Washington, DC: World Bank.

Narayan, D., ed. 2005. *Measuring Empowerment: Cross Disciplinary Perspectives.* Washington, DC: World Bank.

Narayan, D., with R. Patel, K. Schafft, A. Rademacher, and S. Koch-Schulte. 2000a. *Voices of the Poor: Can Anyone Hear Us?* New York: Oxford University Press for the World Bank.

Narayan, D., R. Chambers, M. K. Shah, and P. Petesch. 2000b. *Voices of the Poor: Crying out for Change.* New York: Oxford University Press for the World Bank.

Narayan, D., and P. Petesch, eds. 2002. *Voices of the Poor: From Many Lands.* New York: Oxford University Press for the World Bank.

NDDB (National Dairy Development Board). 2005. *Achievements of Dairy Cooperatives: Facts at a Glance.* Anand, India: NDDB.

Petesch, P., C. Smulovitz, and M. Walton. 2005. "Evaluating Empowerment: A Framework with Cases from Latin America." In *Measuring Empowerment,* ed. D. Narayan. Washington, DC: World Bank.

Prahalad, C. K. 2005. *The Fortune at the Bottom of the Pyramid: Eradicating Poverty through Profits.* New Delhi: Pearson Education Inc.

Rao, V., and M. Walton, eds. 2004. *Culture and Pubic Action.* Stanford, CA: Stanford University Press.

Reddy, Y. V. 2005. *RBI Bulletin.*

SEWA (Self-Employed Women's Association). 2003. *SEWA Annual Report.* Ahmedabad, India: SEWA.

Tilly, C. 1999. *Durable Inequality.* Berkeley: University of California Press.

Unni, J. 2002. *Women and Men in the Informal Economy: A Statistical Picture.* International Labour Organization.

World Bank. 2000. *World Development Report 2000/2001: Attacking Poverty.* New York: Oxford University Press.

———. 2005. *World Development Report 2006: Equity and Development.* New York: Oxford University Press.

*Figures, notes, and tables are indicated by f, n, and t respectively.*

civil society organizations, 19–20*t*, 37*n*12,
99–101, 294
*See also* nongovernmental organizations
(NGOs)
Coady International Institute, 62
Coalition on Violence against Women
(Kenya), 224
*Codesarrollo* (Ecuador), 101
Colchester, M., 269
Colombia, voting rights for migrants from,
99
color-coded spatial representation of state
presence, 240–41, 249
commercial sex work, 227
Commission for Social Development
(COSD, UN), 7, 36–37*n*7
community development and return migra-
tion, 116, 123
community-driven development (CD), 101
community exchanges, 180
community forest enterprises (CFEs), 20*t*,
266–68
Community-Led Infrastructure Finance
Facility (India), 185
Community Organizations Development
Institute (CODI, Thailand), 26, 195,
198, 200, 208, 211
community policing, 228
CONAMU (Ecuador), 100
"Concept Note: New Frontiers of Social
Policy" (Dani), 47
conflict and natural resources, 11
conservation. *See* forest rights
Conway, G., 51
coping strategies, 72*n*15
Corruption Perceptions Index (CPI), 219
Côte d'Ivoire, 23, 107–26
background, 108–10
characteristics of return migrants,
113–14
influence of transnational return, 13–14,
15*t*, 114–21
financial capital transfers, 114–17
human capital transfers, 119*t*, 119–21
social capital transfers, 117–19, 124
pro-poor policy alternatives, 121–23
recommendations, 123–25
sources of data, 110–11
sustainability of return, 111–13
courier services, 90, 101–2, 139
*coyoterismo*, 89–90

CPB. *See* Crown Property Bureau (Thailand)
CPI (Corruption Perceptions index), 219
credit unions for cash transfers, 102
crime and violence
*See also* Nicaraguan youth gangs
domestic violence, 223–24
in Kenya, 26–27, 218, 223–29, 232
in Latin America and Caribbean, 218
state effectiveness and, 11
Crown Property Bureau (CPB, Thailand),
205, 206
Cuba and nurse migration, 157
"culture of dependency," 95
customs duties, 146*n*5

**D**

DANCED (Danish Cooperation for Envi-
ronment and Development), 199
Dani, A.A., 3, 47, 48, 66
Danish Cooperation for Environment and
Development (DANCED), 199
de Aghion, B.A., 281
de-agrarianisation, 220
debt swap, 99, 100
deforestation, 266
*See also* forest rights
Delgado Travel, 102, 104*n*5
*Delivering on the Promise of Pro-Poor
Growth* (Besley & Cord), 8
Delphy, C., 152
demand-driven development, 116
demasculation, 222, 232*n*3
Department for Economic and Social Af-
fairs (UN-DESA), 7–8
Department for International Development
(DFID, U.K.), 47, 54–55, 72*n*16, 185
depression in Kenya, 230, 233*n*7
DFID. *See* Department for International
Development (U.K.)
domestic care laborers, 152–54
*See also* care worker migration
domestic violence, 223–24
dual nationality. *See* citizenship
Dunaway, W., 152
Durban Accord, 263

**E**

*e-choupals* (India), 305, 307–17
Economic and Social Council (ECOSOC,
UN), 7–8, 36–37*n*7

Spain
  local development in Ecuador and, 99,
    100–101
  migration and, 86–89, 98–99, 101,
    104$n$10
  remittances and, 90
Spanish Overseas Development Agency,
  100
SPARC (India), 37$n$12, 174, 179, 182, 185
Sri Lanka
  economic development and ethnic
    conflict in, 10
  toilet programs in, 179
state effectiveness, 11–12, 37$n$8
state sovereignty, 245–46
Stern Report, 266
stochastic poverty, 59
Sub-Saharan Africa
  See also specific countries
  informal economy in, 4, 9
  migration and PRSPs in, 121
  remittances in, 115
substance and alcohol abuse, 223, 229–30,
  232–33$n$3, 233$nn$7–8
suicide, 230, 233$n$8
sustainable livelihoods (SL), 43–44
  See also microenterprises
  asset-based social policy and, 48–49
  asset-building frameworks and, 49–63
    asset-based approaches (ABAs),
      59–63
    commonalities in backgrounds,
      49–51, 50$b$
    comparative analysis of SL and AB
      frameworks, 51–63, 52–53$t$, 70$f$
    vulnerability, risks, and assets, 58–59
Sustainable Livelihoods Support Office
  (DFID), 55, 56
sustainable return migration. See Côte
  d'Ivoire; Ghana
Swaziland and nurse migration, 155
Swedish International Development
  Cooperation Authority, 185

## T

Taiwan, Family Development Account
  Program in, 73$n$34
Tanzania, informal economy in, 4, 9
taxation
  asset-building policies and, 60–61

emigrants and, 23
forest rights and, 268–69
Taylor, C., 242
Thailand, 25–26, 27, 195–214
  Baan Mankong Program, 26, 185,
    195–96, 200–204, 213
    achievements in, 13, 18, 210$t$
    central houses for needy community
      members, 211
    conventional upgrading compared,
      203–4
    methodology, 202–3
    techniques to upgrade, 27, 208–9
  community upgrading in, 196–204
    achievements in upgrading process,
      13, 16$t$, 18, 209–10, 210$f$
    Ayutthaya, 209
    Bangkok, 209
    blind land in, 212–13
    lessons learned from, 210–13
    methodology, 202–3
    new government programs for secure
      housing in, 200–201
    quality of people's assets, changes in,
      211–13
    from UCDO to CODI, 26, 198–200
    Uttaradit, 208–9
  decentralized action within cities, 207–8
  national forest associations in, 269
  pilot upgrading programs in, 202–3,
    204–7
    Bon Kai, 205
    Boon Kook, 207
    Charoenchai Nimitmai, 205
    Klong Lumnoon, 206–7
    Klong Toey Block 7-12, 206
    Ramkhamhaeng, 206
Tiemoko, R., 112, 119, 122
Tilly, C., 246, 250
toilet programs, 179, 185
Transfer of Knowledge Through
  Expatriate Nationals (TOKTEN,
  UNDP), 122
transnationalism, 12–13, 24, 112
  See also care worker migration; forest
    rights; Pakistan; Philippines; Thai-
    land; urban poor federations and
    housing development; wealth creation
    for poor
transparency. See accountability and
  transparency

## ECO-AUDIT
## *Environmental Benefits Statement*

The World Bank is committed to preserving endangered forests and natural resources. The Office of the Publisher has chosen to print *Assets, Livelihoods, and Social Policy* on recycled paper with 30 percent postconsumer fiber in accordance with the recommended standards for paper usage set by the Green Press Initiative, a nonprofit program supporting publishers in using fiber that is not sourced from endangered forests. For more information, visit www.greenpressinitiative.org.

Saved:
- 9 trees
- 6 million BTUs of total energy
- 774 lbs. of $CO_2$ equivalents greenhouse gases
- 3,213 gallons of waste water
- 413 lbs. of solid waste

green press
INITIATIVE